"Merkle and Plummer show how to get started with New Testament Greek without getting lost in an ancient language. This book explains Greek in a way that people who are not language nerds can easily understand and eventually progress toward being able to read the New Testament in the original Greek. This book is informed by good knowledge of linguistics and pedagogy, but it doesn't drown readers in acronyms, scholarly jargon, or technical details. Lots of good explanations on things like textual criticism and word-study fallacies that students should learn in their language studies. In short, this is a book that students will enjoy and instructors will appreciate."

—**Michael Bird,** academic dean and lecturer in theology, Ridley College

"*Beginning with New Testament Greek* is exactly what today's teachers and students need. The layout is realistic, the progression through the material makes perfect sense, and the use of NT texts throughout is motivating. Students will benefit from Merkle and Plummer's linguistic expertise, their masterful pedagogy, and their love for God's Word. Students can rest assured they are getting here the very best of scholarship in the service of the church. I recommend *Beginning with New Testament Greek* with enthusiasm—an abundant feast for mind and heart alike."

—**J. Scott Duvall,** professor of New Testament and J. C. and Mae Fuller Chair of Biblical Studies, Ouachita Baptist University

"Incorporating up-to-date research and helpful links to digital resources, here is a comprehensive introductory grammar written by experienced teachers for the serious student of New Testament Greek. Recent developments in the understanding and significance of verbal aspect, middle voice and discourse analysis are discussed and threaded pervasively through the conversational style of this work. Directed throughout at reading for meaning, all translation exercises and illustrations of grammatical features are taken from the New Testament itself. These attributes along with the many supporting materials make this a valuable resource not only for the classroom but also for teachers and scholars wishing to update or further their own understanding of Koine Greek."

—**Sue Kmetko,** adjunct lecturer in New Testament Greek, Stirling Theological College

"Two of the most important elements of a first-year Greek experience aiming for student success are methodical presentation and motivational enrichment. Merkle and Plummer load this textbook with first-quality material of both kinds. Two of the leading motivational factors are extensive direct interaction with the actual New Testament text—both in the lesson exercises and in exegetical discussions showing the value of knowing Greek—and excursus introducing students to broader fields of Greek studies and resources to aid their exegetical pursuits, both in print and online. Measured exposure to 'state-of-the-discussion' questions about the meanings of the verb tenses and the middle voice contribute further value to assure this grammar has a lasting place as a marketplace heavyweight."

—**Randy Leedy,** founder, NTGreekGuy.com, and former professor of New Testament, Bob Jones University

"Do we really need another beginning Greek grammar? Merkle and Plummer show us that the answer is, 'Yes!' The book is written by two veterans of teaching Elementary Greek, by two master teachers, and the clarity of their teaching is evident on every page of their grammar. The book is not only accessible but also practical. They explain with helpful illustrations why the study of Greek makes a difference. Also, they are up-to-date on recent scholarship on Greek grammar. Whether they discuss verbal aspect or deponent verbs, students and teachers can have confidence that Merkle and Plummer know the current state of the question. I recommend this textbook with enthusiasm."

—**Thomas R. Schreiner,** James Buchanan Harrison Professor of New Testament Interpretation, professor of biblical theology, and associate dean, the School of Theology, The Southern Baptist Theological Seminary

"Simple. Practical. Up-to-date. User-friendly. Beginners in Greek will benefit from this introduction to the language of the New Testament. The text carries the student into the complexities of the language with relative ease, always taking the time to make the grammar accessible and understandable. What is good for the learner is also good for effective teaching. This new work by Merkle and Plummer is highly commendable."

—**Mark A. Seifrid,** professor of exegetical theology, Concordia Seminary

"The first great strength of this textbook is that the approach has been field tested in many classes by two gifted pedagogues. The second strength is that the student gets to work quickly on the real Greek of the New Testament in the excellent exercises (from the very first chapter)! The third strength is something unique. Where in any other beginning textbook will the student also be introduced to the critical texts of the Greek NT, the lexical resources, good Greek commentaries, diagramming, and the available digital resources? This textbook makes me want to teach Elementary Greek again!"

—**William C. Varner,** professor of Bible and Greek, The Master's University

"Drs. Merkle and Plummer have given us an excellent volume that serves as a beginning for the study of the Greek New Testament. Though this volume is primarily directed to those beginning the study, it will also serve as an excellent refresher for those of us who have been studying New Testament Greek for many years. I commend this current volume to all who are beginning and who are continuing to study God's inerrant Greek New Testament."

—**Jerry Vines,** pastor emeritus, First Baptist Church, Jacksonville, FL, and two-time president, the Southern Baptist Convention

"Merkle and Plummer have a strong reputation of being clear and effective teachers of New Testament Greek. In their grammar, they combine both their knowledge of Greek and their seasoned pedagogy to provide the beginning students of New Testament Greek with a valuable and clear resource that will help them develop the necessary skills to begin their journey to read and understand the Greek New Testament."

—**Jarvis J. Williams,** associate professor of New Testament interpretation, The Southern Baptist Theological Seminary

BEGINNING
WITH NEW
TESTAMENT GREEK

BEGINNING GREEK

WITH NEW TESTAMENT

An **Introductory** Study of the Grammar
and Syntax of the New Testament

Benjamin L. **Merkle** and Robert L. **Plummer**

ACADEMIC
NASHVILLE, TENNESSEE

At the Classroom Door

Lord, at Thy word opens yon door, inviting
Teacher and taught to feast this hour with Thee;
Opens a Book where God in human writing
Thinks His deep thoughts, and dead tongues live for me.

Too dread the task, too great the duty calling,
Too heavy far the weight is laid on me!
O if mine own thought should on Thy words falling
Mar the great message, and men hear not Thee!

Give me Thy voice to speak, Thine ear to listen,
Give me Thy mind to grasp Thy mystery;
So shall my heart throb, and my glad eyes glisten,
Rapt with the wonders Thou dost show to me.

—J. H. Moulton
Bangalore, India
February 21, 1917

CONTENTS

////////////////

ACKNOWLEDGMENTS

////////////////

The authors of this textbook have been friends for many years. In fact, the early years of our comaraderie were forged in the shared experience of teaching Elementary Greek (class 22400) as we finished our doctoral programs at The Southern Baptist Theological Seminary. In those early years, we both used S. M. Baugh's *New Testament Greek Primer*, which is a model of careful pedagogy and clear writing. We thus credit Dr. Baugh with inspiring our division of practice exercises to focus on specific skill sets. We have also learned much from many other teachers and peers—both in person and through their writings—and we have sought to err on the side of abundant citation when we are able to recall where we first encountered a helpful grammatical explanation or specific way of presenting the material. To all these brothers and sisters—living and deceased—a great cloud of witnesses, we thank you. We also want to thank the friends, students, and proofreaders who corrected many of our mistakes: Southern Seminary students in class 22400A of Fall 2019, Southeastern Seminary students in GRK5110D of Fall 2019, Elijah Hixson, Rod Elledge, Gregory Wolff, Mike Borland, Chris Jones, Kelly Nall, Simon DeAngelo, Philip Owen, and Mike Merritt. We want to give a special thanks to Audrey Greeson for her skilled editorial oversight of this book. It is a much better product for her input and corrections.

Finally, to our beloved families—to our wives (Marian and Chandi) and our children (Brandon, Mariah, Jaden, and Cameron; Sarah Beth, Chloe, and Anabelle)—thank you for supporting us in the work to which God has called us. We love you.

Benjamin L. Merkle
Robert L. Plummer
Pentecost 2020

MORPHOLOGICAL ABBREVIATIONS

//////////////

Tense

present	pres
imperfect	impf
future	fut
aorist	aor
perfect	per
pluperfect	pluper

Voice

active	act
passive	pass
middle	mid

Mood

indicative	ind
participle	ptc
subjunctive	sub
imperative	imp
infinitive	inf
optative	opt

Person

first	1st
second	2nd
third	3rd

Gender

masculine	masc
feminine	fem
neuter	neut

Case

nominative	nom
genitive	gen
dative	dat
accusative	acc
vocative	voc

Number

singular	sg
plural	pl

INTRODUCTION

//////////////

I f you are a student who has been assigned this textbook, it is our prayer that it will help instill in you a passion for reading the Greek New Testament. After all, what is more exciting than reading the very words that God inspired? Our advice to you at this point is to follow carefully your instructor's advice. If you are using this book for self-study, start each chapter by watching its brief overview video via the web links provided. After that, read the chapter, study the material, and test your mastery by doing the practice exercises at the end of the chapter. Answers to the exercises are found at the back of the book. Additional free materials are available for you at beginninggreek.com.

We wish we could also provide you with dozens of inspiring quotes or stories, advice on study habits, and many effective memory techniques. In fact, we do provide such a "personal trainer in paperback" for your Greek journey in our volume, *Greek for Life: Strategies for Learning, Retaining, and Reviving New Testament Greek* (Baker, 2017). We encourage you to read that volume along with this one.

Here we turn to address a broader audience—especially the professors who might adopt this textbook for classroom use. "There is no end to the making of many books" (Eccl 12:12). The biblical sage's observation is especially true of New Testament Greek grammars penned in English. More than 100 introductory Greek grammars have been published in the last century. Why one more?

- Advances in technology now enable the production of a textbook seamlessly integrated with other pedagogical resources, greatly improving student learning. (Note the web links throughout the book whereby students can immediately watch mini-lectures and listen to Greek vocabulary pronounced.) We recommend that you immediately check out beginninggreek. com to see many other free resources prepared for both students (vocabulary flashcards, PDFs of PowerPoint files, links to videos and other resources, etc.) and professors (tests, quizzes, PowerPoint files, syllabi, etc.).

- Beginning Greek students need to be informed accurately and engagingly of the growing consensus among Greek scholars on verbal aspect, discourse functions of tenses, and middle voice/deponency. Recent decades of linguistic analysis have helped Greek scholarship to speak more precisely and objectively about patterns that the best Greek grammarians have observed for centuries. We are hopeful that students who use our textbook will never wander through the wasteland of confusion over these topics.

- Though most beginning grammars do not discuss text criticism, commentaries, critical editions of the Greek New Testament, diagramming, Greek word studies, or digital resources, we have included a brief introductory essay for each one of these topics. A professor may choose to cover all, part, or none of these matters in the classroom, but students will have been provided with accurate, up-to-date information on critical matters—with recommendations of additional resources to explore the topics further.

- The vocabulary lists at the end of each chapter provide working vocabulary for the *following* chapters. This simple and innovative tweak to the traditional method of learning Greek vocabulary enables students to focus on new grammatical concepts without the distraction of learning many new words at the same time.

- Without sacrificing accuracy or essential detail, this textbook streamlines and consolidates essential Greek grammar into 24 chapters—giving professors maximum flexibility in choosing to cover the material in one or two semesters.

Though not original to our grammar, we also think the following features help increase its pedagogical effectiveness:

- Each chapter begins with a "significance" section—looking at specific text from the Greek New Testament that illustrates the meaning payoff of the new grammatical category that is being introduced.

- Chapters contain multiple practice exercises that isolate specific new skills before applying them to translation sentences.

- All translation sentences come directly from the Greek New Testament—a great encouragement to students who are learning Greek in order to read the Bible more faithfully. If you find the exercises at the end of the chapter are taking your students too long, feel free to assign only a percentage of them.

- An answer key is provided in the back of the book, allowing students to check their work immediately.

We love seeing students ablaze with a passion to read, understand, believe, obey, enjoy, and teach the Greek New Testament. It is our prayer and hope that this textbook aids in igniting that fire in many hearts.

CHAPTER 1

//////////////

THE GREEK ALPHABET

1.1 Overview[1]

In this opening chapter, we will introduce you to the Greek alphabet as well as how to pronounce the various letters and letter combinations. We will also explain breathing marks, accent marks, and punctuation marks. Are such terms completely new to you? Don't worry. We are here to guide you. Your joyful journey into reading the Greek New Testament is about to begin!

1.2 Significance

In this chapter, you will learn the letters of the Greek alphabet. Did you know that a single Greek letter can make a difference in interpretation? The Greek text of James 2:14 looks like this:

> Τί τὸ ὄφελος, ἀδελφοί μου, ἐὰν <u>πίστιν</u> λέγῃ τις ἔχειν, ἔργα δὲ μὴ ἔχῃ; μὴ δύναται **ἡ** <u>πίστις</u> σῶσαι αὐτόν;

An English translation (ESV) reads this way:

> What good is it, my brothers, if someone says he has <u>faith</u> but does not have works? Can **that** <u>faith</u> save him?

The bold Greek letter toward the end of the verse is an eta (ἡ). It looks much like the English letter "n." This one-letter word is the Greek article (similar to "the" in English), but it also has other functions. One function is called "the article of previous reference." That is, in some contexts, it can serve to mark a previous reference to the same noun (which usually appears the first time without an article).

---

[1] For an overview video lecture of chapter 1, go to bit.ly/greeklecture1 or beginninggreek.com.

Note above how the first (underlined) instance of faith (πίστιν) does not have an eta in front of it, but the second (also underlined) appearance of the word (πίστις) does. This use of eta allows the writer to say, in effect, "the kind of faith I just mentioned above." Observe the apt translation of the ESV above ("that faith"). Of course, interpretations based on Greek grammatical observations should always be further supported by the surrounding context, as this interpretation is. Not to translate the noun "faith" with an explicit marker for previous reference in English (e.g., "such" or "that") actually introduces significant theological distortion. Note how the Douay-Rheims version (DRA) introduces this error:

> What shall it profit, my brethren, if a man say he hath faith, but hath not works? Shall faith be able to save him?

This translation wrongly gives the impression that faith cannot save. James actually says that a *false* faith characterized by an empty verbal profession ("that faith") is unable to save. One Greek letter can make a significant difference in interpretation.

1.3 Alphabet[2]

LOWER CASE	UPPER CASE	LETTER NAME	ERASMIAN PRONUNCIATION	RECONSTRUCTED KOINE GREEK[3] PRONUNCIATION	MODERN PRONUNCIATION
α	A	Alpha	father		
β	B	Beta	ball	Habana vault	vault
γ	Γ	Gamma	gift	ghoul yes	ghoul yes
δ	Δ	Delta	dog	dh	dh, that
ε	E	Epsilon	echo		
ζ	Z	Zeta	kudzu	zoo	zoo
η	H	Eta	ate	Pedro	eat
θ	Θ	Theta	thin		
ι	I	Iota	sit (short) ski (long)	ski	ski
κ	K	Kappa	key		
λ	Λ	Lambda	lock		
μ	M	Mu	mom		

[2] For instructions on handwriting Greek letters, see bit.ly/greeklecture1. To hear the Greek alphabet song, go to bit.ly/greekalphabetsong or beginninggreek.com.

[3] This is adapted from Randall Buth, "Notes on the Pronunciation System of Koine Greek," https://www.biblicallanguagecenter.com/wp-content/uploads/2012/08/Koine-Pronunciation-2012.pdf.

LOWER CASE	UPPER CASE	LETTER NAME	ERASMIAN PRONUNCIATION	RECONSTRUCTED KOINE GREEK[3] PRONUNCIATION	MODERN PRONUNCIATION
ν	N	Nu	**n**ail		
ξ	Ξ	Xi	fo**x**		
ο	O	Omicron	**o**ften	**o**bey	**o**bey
π	Π	Pi	**p**ond	**sp**ill	**p**ond **b**ond
ρ	P	Rho	**rh**yme		
σ / ς	Σ	Sigma	**s**and		
τ	T	Tau	**t**ap	**st**ill	**t**oe **d**oe
υ	Υ	Upsilon	b**oo**t	German "**ü**"	b**ea**t
φ	Φ	Phi	**ph**one		
χ	X	Chi	**a**che	German "**ch**"	**a**che **h**ue
ψ	Ψ	Psi	oo**ps**		
ω	Ω	Omega	**o**bey		

1.4 Pronunciation

Since you are using a textbook written in English, it's possible you have never thought about other languages in the world, such as Chinese, that use tiny pictures (or ideographs) to convey meaning. To be competent in reading such a language one must learn thousands of characters. English and Greek, on the other hand, employ a limited number of symbols (26 and 24, respectively) to create a phonetic approximation of spoken speech. The famous biblical archaeologist W. F. Albright (1891–1971) once quipped about the Hebrew alphabet: "Since the forms of the letters are very simple, the 22-letter alphabet could be learned in a day or two by a bright student and in a week or two by the dullest."[4] We take alphabets for granted, but their introduction was revolutionary—akin to the introduction of the smartphone in more recent history.

Scholars debate the best way to pronounce Koine Greek, which is Greek used from roughly 300 BC to AD 330 and the language in which the New Testament was penned. We follow a pronunciation system ultimately derived from Desiderius Erasmus (1466–1536). This system is used by most Greek professors and has the benefit of clearly differentiating the various vowel sounds. In contrast, modern

---

[4] Carl H. Kraeling and R. M. Adams, eds., *City Invincible: A Symposium on Urbanization and Cultural Development in the Ancient Near East* (Chicago: University of Chicago Press, 1960), 123.

Greek is pronounced such that eta (η), iota (ι), and upsilon (υ) all have the same sound.

Some scholars advocate pronouncing Koine Greek the same way as modern Greek because we don't know precisely how Koine Greek was pronounced. Others argue for a "reconstructed Koine" pronunciation based on a study of spelling mistakes made by ancient scribes. There are benefits and limitations to any pronunciation scheme. Therefore, we suggest that you use the pronunciation system employed by your instructor.

Note that sigma has two forms. The first form (σ) is used at the beginning (σύν) and middle (πίστιν) of a word. The final sigma (ς) is used if it is the last letter of a word (λόγος).

The Greek alphabet has 24 letters. Perhaps you will find it easier to learn them in six groups of four:

> **DESIDERIUS ERASMUS** (1466–1536) published the first printed Greek New Testament in 1516. He wrote, "It was not for empty fame or childish pleasure that in my youth I grasped at the polite literature of the ancients, and by late hours gained some slight mastery of Greek and Latin. It has been my cherished wish to cleanse the Lord's temple of barbarous ignorance, and to adorn it with treasures brought from afar, such as may kindle in hearts a warm love for the Scriptures." ~Erasmus, *Enchiridion Militis* (1501)

α β γ δ   ν ξ ο π
ε ζ η θ   ρ σ/ς τ υ
ι κ λ μ   φ χ ψ ω[5]

One of the most effective ways to learn a new language's alphabet is with a song. Use the web links in this book to access additional audio and video resources, including a version of the Greek alphabet song.[6]

Five Greek letters are considered **_double consonants_** since they require the use of two letters when transliterated: θ (th), ξ (xs), φ (ph), χ (ch), and ψ (ps). **_Transliteration_** means writing one language phonetically (that is, writing out its sounds) with another language's letters or characters.

The letter *gamma* (γ), by itself, is always pronounced with a hard *g* (as in "goat" but never like "giraffe"). When placed before certain other consonants (γ, κ, ξ, χ), it is pronounced with an "n" sound. For example, ἄγγελος is pronounced an-ge-los (not ag-ge-los).

Pay attention, since some letters are easy to confuse with others:

γ → ν   ζ → ξ   θ → φ   κ → χ   ν → υ   ο → σ   π → τ   φ → ψ

---

[5] Hint: The letter's name includes the sound of the letter. For example, the letter beta makes the "b" sound found in the name of the letter (*beta*).

[6] To hear the Greek alphabet song, go to bit.ly/greekalphabetsong or beginninggreek.com.

Moreover, you will soon notice that Greek fonts differ slightly from each other. The difference seems huge to some beginning students, but in a short time, you will barely notice the slight variations—just as you likely don't consciously think about the differences between the Times New Roman and Courier fonts. Even if you are one of those aesthetically sensitive people who does notice the differences in English fonts, you're neither confused nor troubled by them.

Take care because some Greek letters closely resemble letters in the English alphabet.

η (eta) → "n"	ρ (rho) → "p"	χ (chi) → "x"
ν (nu) → "v"	υ (upsilon) → "u"	ω (omega) → "w"

1.5 Vowels

In using the terms "short vowel" and "long vowel," linguists are classifying sounds based on how long it originally took to say them, relative to other vowels in the same language. This time difference is not something you will be able to distinguish by listening to Greek and is somewhat hypothetical based on where and how the vowels are articulated in the mouth. These labels of "short" and "long," however, will become important later.[7] For now, learn this: there are seven vowels in Greek: α, ε, η, ι, ο, υ, and ω. Some of these vowels are considered short (α, ε, ι, ο, υ) and others are considered long (α, η, ι, υ, ω). Note that the vowels α, ι, and υ can be either long or short. Later, you will learn that vowels can sometimes lengthen (shift from short to long) when changes are made to a word. Here is a chart demonstrating how short vowels lengthen:

Short		Long		Short/Long
ε	→	η	←	α
ο	→	ω		ι
				υ

When the letter iota (ι) follows the long vowels α, η, and ω, it is frequently written underneath that vowel and is not pronounced. This is called an *iota subscript*: καρδίᾳ, ἀγάπῃ, λόγῳ. You will not have to decide whether to subscript the iota. It will just be part of the spelling of the word or form you are memorizing or reading.

1.6 Diphthongs

A *diphthong* (from the Greek word διφθόγγος, meaning "having two sounds") is two vowels together that are pronounced as one sound.

---

[7] The technical term for vowels that change their length (short → long or long → short) is *ablaut*.

LOWER CASE	PRONUNCIATION
αι	a**isle**
αυ	kr**aut**
ει	fr**eigh**t
ευ	f**eu**d
οι	**oi**l
ου	s**ou**p
υι	s**ui**te

When two vowels are together yet *not* a diphthong, a ***diaeresis mark*** (i.e., two raised dots above the vowel: ï, ü) is frequently placed above the second vowel to signal that the two vowels are pronounced separately (cf. the English word naïve).[8] This mark is most commonly found on proper nouns (names and places—especially those imported from Hebrew or Aramaic) and usually occurs above an iota (e.g., Κάϊν = Kah-een, "Cain"; Μωϋσῆς = Mō-oo-seys, "Moses"; Ἑβραϊστί = Heh-bra-ee-stee, "in Hebrew/Aramaic"). Other vowel combinations don't form diphthongs and are also pronounced separately (e.g., ηυ = ay-oo; ιε = ee-eh, and ιη = ee-ay). Because this last vowel combination (ιη) is used to mirror the Hebrew/Aramaic *yod* sound, the vowels are typically pronounced together ("yea"). Thus, the name for "Jesus" is Ἰησοῦς and is pronounced "yea-soos."

1.7 Breathing Marks

Every Greek word that begins with a vowel (including a diphthong) is given a ***breathing mark***. Writing a breathing mark is analogous to dotting the lowercase letter "i" in English. Most of the time, it does not even effect pronunciation; the accepted conventions of writing the language just require it. There are two types of breathing marks: smooth and rough. With a smooth breathing mark ('), the most common type, there is no change in pronunciation. With a rough breathing mark ('), an "h" sound is added to the beginning of the word. If a word begins with a single uppercase (capital) vowel, the breathing mark is written to the left of that letter, at the top of the line (e.g., Ἀβαδδών, "Abaddon" or Ἡρῴδης, "Herod").[9] Also, if a word begins with a diphthong, the breathing mark appears over the second letter (αἷμα, "blood" or Αἴγυπτος, "Egypt"). An initial upsilon (υ) always has a rough

---

[8] *Diaeresis* is pronounced die-AIR-eh-sis. In other languages, two dots above a vowel can have a different function, as the umlaut does in German. Although it is important for us to note them, diaeresis marks are uncommon.

[9] Note that the initial capital Greek letter in the name Ἡρῴδης that looks like an English *H* is actually a capital *eta*—a vowel pronounced like the "ay" in the English word *may*. It is only the rough breathing mark that gives the Greek word Ἡρῴδης an initial "h" sound in pronunciation.

breathing mark. The only consonant to receive a (rough) breathing mark is rho (ῥ). The "h" sound does not affect the pronunciation of rho but is evidenced in English words derived from Greek (e.g., rhetoric → ῥητορική). If you have a Greek lexicon, flip to the list of words that begin with rho and note how few there are. Observe too how all the words that begin with rho have a rough breathing mark. In ancient Greek, the rough breathing mark over the rho was apparently a cue to the reader to trill the "r sound."

ἁμαρτία	→	hah-mar-teé-ah	"sin"
ἑπτά	→	hep-táh	"seven"
ἡμέρα	→	hey-mér-ah	"day"
ὁδός	→	hah-dós	"way/road"
ὕδωρ	→	hoó-dōr	"water"
ὡσαννά	→	hō-san-náh	"hosanna"
ῥῆμα	→	ráy-mah	"word"

1.8 Accent Marks

Most words in a modern Greek New Testament will have **accent marks**. According to tradition, it was the head of the library in Alexandria, Aristophanes of Byzantium (c. 257–180 BC), who first developed a system of accentuation to help non-native speakers pronounce Greek. In the second and third centuries BC, Greek was still a tonal language, with accents guiding speakers on rising and falling pitches. By the first century AD, the time of the composition of the New Testament, Greek likely had lost its tonality; thus, we should understand the accents as communicating stress or emphasis to the reader/speaker. That is, a reader should say the accented syllable a bit louder or longer, stressing or emphasizing it. For example, as we saw above, the word for "sin" is ἁμαρτία, pronounced "hah-mar-teé-ah." The accent mark signifies that the emphasis is given to the third syllable ("teé"). The presence and behavior of accents on words can also help readers know whether a vowel is long or short, which reveals the proper pronunciation. Accents are not found widely in Greek manuscripts until the fifth century AD and are lacking from the oldest manuscripts of the Greek New Testament.

We consistently stress certain syllables when we say English words, but we don't mark those syllables with accents. Can emphasizing a different syllable change meaning? You bet! Pronounce Indianapolis with the "an" stressed (In-diANapolis), and it sounds like you are saying "Indiana police," rather than the city, "IndiaNApolis."

Modern editions of the Greek New Testament have three different accent marks:

Acute   ά   →   ἀγάπη   ah-gáp-ay
Grave[10]   ὰ   →   κεφαλὴ   keh-fal-áy
Circumflex ᾶ   →   σοφῶν   sah-fóne

Accent marks can only be placed on a word's last three syllables. The names of these syllables are the (1) antepenult (before next-to-last syllable), (2) penult (next-to-last syllable), and (3) ultima (last syllable).

antepenult	penult	ultima
ἄν—	θρω—	πος

We will not spend much time on accent marks except when it is significant, especially in distinguishing words (e.g., τίς ["who"] versus τις ["anyone"] or εἰ ["if"] versus εἶ ["you are"]). For now, we simply provide the following guidelines: (1) the acute can be placed on any of the last three syllables; (2) the circumflex can be placed on the last two syllables; and (3) the grave can be placed only on the last syllable. Finally, if the ultima is long (that is, if it contains a long vowel or diphthong with a long value), the accent cannot be placed on the antepenult (ἄνθρωπος → ἀνθρώπων). Also, if the ultima is long, any accent on the penult will be an acute rather than a circumflex (δοῦλος, but δούλου). In addition, the circumflex can only occur over a long syllable (that is, one that contains a long vowel or a diphthong with a long value). Unless your instructor tells you otherwise, we recommend that your main focus on accents at this point would be to let them guide you in stressing the correct syllables when you read Greek aloud.[11]

1.9 Punctuation Marks

Punctuation marks are rarely found in Greek manuscripts written before the eighth century. In the earliest extant (that is, still existing) New Testament manuscripts, the script consists of all capital letters (majuscule script) that lacks spacing between words and that has only rare, erratic punctuation. Over time, copies of the New Testament came to be written with lowercase letters (miniscule script) and spacing between words. Eventually, other editorial elements were added which today include paragraphs, indentations, and breaks between clauses and sentences. Below is an example of John 1:1 in a format likely similar (though neater!) to how the apostle John originally penned it. This majuscule text is followed by the same words as they appear in most modern editions of the Greek New Testament:

ΕΝΑΡΧΗΗΝΟΛΟΓΟΣΚΑΙΟΛΟΓΟΣΗΝΠΡΟΣΤΟΝΘΕΟΝΚΑΙΘΕΟΣ
ΗΝΟΛΟΓΟΣ

---

[10] Pronounced "grauve" like the color "mauve." If you view the grave accent like a small picture, it's like a slide going down into the grave (tomb). This will help you remember its pronunciation.
[11] For an accurate and accessible introduction to Greek accents, we recommend John A. K. Lee's *Basics of Greek Accents: Eight Lessons with Exercises* (Grand Rapids: Zondervan, 2018).

Ἐν ἀρχῇ ἦν ὁ λόγος, καὶ ὁ λόγος ἦν πρὸς τὸν θεόν, καὶ θεὸς ἦν ὁ λόγος.

"In the beginning was the Word, and the Word was with God, and the Word was God."

Modern Greek editions of the New Testament do not capitalize the first word of each sentence. Capitalization usually occurs (1) in the title of New Testament books (with every letter capitalized), and in the first letter of (2) proper names, (3) direct quotations, and (4) words that begin a new paragraph. Here are the punctuation marks commonly used in most modern editions of the Greek New Testament:

Period (.)	.	α.
Comma (,)	,	α,
Semicolon (;)	·	α·
Question Mark (?)	;	α;

1.10 Practice[12]

A. Alphabet: Memorize the Greek alphabet (see section 1.3). The easiest way to do this is to learn to sing it (e.g., to the tune of "Twinkle, Twinkle Little Star"). You'll know you have it when you can write out the lowercase script of the alphabet in the correct order and form ten times from memory.

α β γ δ—ε ζ η θ—ι κ λ μ—ν ξ ο π—ρ σ/ς τ υ—φ χ ψ ω

B. Vowels: Circle the words in Eph 1:3–6 that have a diphthong:

Εὐλογητὸς ὁ θεὸς καὶ πατὴρ τοῦ κυρίου ἡμῶν Ἰησοῦ Χριστοῦ, ὁ εὐλογήσας ἡμᾶς ἐν πάσῃ εὐλογίᾳ πνευματικῇ ἐν τοῖς ἐπουρανίοις ἐν Χριστῷ, καθὼς ἐξελέξατο ἡμᾶς ἐν αὐτῷ πρὸ καταβολῆς κόσμου εἶναι ἡμᾶς ἁγίους καὶ ἀμώμους κατενώπιον αὐτοῦ ἐν ἀγάπῃ, προορίσας ἡμᾶς εἰς υἱοθεσίαν διὰ Ἰησοῦ Χριστοῦ εἰς αὐτόν, κατὰ τὴν εὐδοκίαν τοῦ θελήματος αὐτοῦ, εἰς ἔπαινον δόξης τῆς χάριτος αὐτοῦ ἧς ἐχαρίτωσεν ἡμᾶς ἐν τῷ ἠγαπημένῳ.

C. Accents: Identify the accent marks (A = acute; G = grave; C = circumflex) and the breathing marks (S = smooth; R = rough), if any, in the following words:

Key Word	Accent	Breathing Mark
1. εὐλογητὸς	_____	_____
2. Ἰησοῦ	_____	_____
3. ἡμᾶς	_____	_____

---

[12] Answers to activities are found in the back of this book, but before checking the answers, you should (1) study the material in this chapter and (2) attempt the activities without reference to the print answers or videos.

4. καθὼς   _____   _____
5. αὐτῷ   _____   _____
6. πρὸ   _____   _____
7. εἶναι   _____   _____
8. ἁγίους   _____   _____
9. ἀγάπη   _____   _____
10. ἧς   _____   _____

D. Reading: Read aloud John 3:16–18, paying close attention to accent and breathing marks. (Although you may not yet understand what the words mean, learning to read Greek out loud is vital. It is very difficult to learn, understand, or translate words that you cannot pronounce.)[13]

> Οὕτως γὰρ ἠγάπησεν ὁ θεὸς τὸν κόσμον, ὥστε τὸν υἱὸν τὸν μονογενῆ ἔδωκεν, ἵνα πᾶς ὁ πιστεύων εἰς αὐτὸν μὴ ἀπόληται ἀλλ᾽ ἔχῃ ζωὴν αἰώνιον. οὐ γὰρ ἀπέστειλεν ὁ θεὸς τὸν υἱὸν εἰς τὸν κόσμον ἵνα κρίνῃ τὸν κόσμον, ἀλλ᾽ ἵνα σωθῇ ὁ κόσμος δι᾽ αὐτοῦ. ὁ πιστεύων εἰς αὐτὸν οὐ κρίνεται· ὁ δὲ μὴ πιστεύων ἤδη κέκριται, ὅτι μὴ πεπίστευκεν εἰς τὸ ὄνομα τοῦ μονογενοῦς υἱοῦ τοῦ θεοῦ.

1.11 Vocabulary[14]

In this text, some new vocabulary terms will be presented at the end of a chapter in preparation for the next chapter's teaching. We believe familiarity with new words will aid in assimilating the new grammatical discussion.

The words are listed alphabetically and are often grouped together. For instance, nouns in this lesson are all "first declension nouns"; they are further subdivided into nouns ending in eta (η) and nouns ending in alpha (α). A ***declension*** is a grammatical term for a pattern. Greek nouns follow certain patterns, as discussed in the next chapter. For now, you just need to know that all the nouns below are "first declension" or "pattern 1" nouns.

Also, you will notice that the article (ἡ) follows the noun, indicating the gender of the noun—something we will discuss in more detail in the next chapter. ἡ is the feminine article, so all the nouns below are feminine. In English, we have an indefinite article "a" and definite article "the." Greek only has one article, but it is used similarly to our definite article and is frequently translated "the." Note that below the list of nouns are two conjunctions. ***Conjunctions*** are small words (e.g., "and," "but," "also") that speakers and writers use to stitch together larger groups of words (clauses).

The vocabulary words listed appear in their ***lexical forms*** (i.e., the dictionary forms which are the nominative singular form for nouns). Another term for a

---

[13] To hear John 3:16–18 read, go to bit.ly/greekhw1or beginninggreek.com.
[14] To hear an author of your textbook read through the vocabulary for chapter 1, go to bit.ly/nt-greekvocab1 or beginninggreek.com.

dictionary is a lexicon. Below, each Greek term is given at least one English *gloss* (i.e., a brief English equivalent of the Greek term). Be mindful that an English definition given is merely one of many possible renderings. The more Greek you learn, the more your knowledge of individual vocabulary words will be nuanced.

One of the most helpful ways to learn new Greek vocabulary words is to note English cognates, that is, English words that can ultimately be traced to a Greek ancestor form. English cognates will be given in parentheses and italicized alongside English definitions. If a Greek word does not list any English cognates, or the cognates are not familiar to you, you are advised to create your own memory device.

For example, the word ἁμαρτία means "sin." Those who know the term *hamartiology* from systematic theology should have no trouble remembering the meaning of ἁμαρτία. Most beginning Greek students, however, do not know such a rare, specialized word. So, you may need to make your own memory device based on associations and visual images related to the sound of the vocabulary word. When pronounced, the word ἁμαρτία sounds sort of like "hammer tea-a," so you can imagine sinning against your mother by smashing her favorite tea cup with a hammer. In fact, the more memorable, shocking, and visual an association can be, the better. So, involve all your senses. You can even act out walking to a table, closing your eyes, raising your arm, and seeing yourself smash the tea cup with a hammer. As you do, say ἁμαρτία. Then imagine your poor mother looking at you in amazement, pointing her trembling, outstretched finger at you and yelling, "Sin!" After all, the most effective memory devices are the ones you create!

For further help in creative methods to learn Greek, we recommend another book we penned: *Greek for Life: Strategies for Learning, Retaining, and Reviving New Testament Greek* (Grand Rapids: Baker, 2017). We also suggest this helpful free website that includes a section on learning foreign language vocabulary: www.mullenmemory.com.

ἀγάπη, ἡ	love
γῆ, ἡ	earth, land, ground (*geology*)
ζωή, ἡ	life (*zoo, zoology*)
φωνή, ἡ	voice, sound (*phonetics, phonograph, phone*)
ἀλήθεια, ἡ	truth
ἁμαρτία, ἡ	sin (*hamartiology*—the theological study of sin)
βασιλεία, ἡ	kingdom, reign (*basilica*)
δόξα, ἡ	glory, majesty (*doxology*)
ἐκκλησία, ἡ	congregation, assembly, church (*ecclesiastical*)
ἡμέρα, ἡ	day (*ephemeral*, "for a day")
καρδία, ἡ	heart (*cardiologist*)
δέ	and, but, now
καί	and, even, also
μέν	on the one hand, indeed
ὁ, ἡ, τό	the

//////////////

CHAPTER 2

FIRST DECLENSION NOUNS

2.1 Overview[1]

A *noun* is a word that refers to a person, place, thing, or idea (e.g., Paul, Rome, ship, or peace). Greek nouns are different from English nouns. Most significantly, Greek nouns appear with many different endings. Word order was very fluid in ancient Greek; speakers added "case endings" to nouns to indicate to their listeners how these nouns were functioning in sentences. For example, a specific ending could cue the listener/reader as to whether a noun was the subject, the direct object, or the indirect object. English, by contrast, primarily communicates such noun functions through word order.

In this chapter, we will study the first of three noun ending patterns (case endings). To properly understand Greek nouns, we must also consider the gender (feminine, masculine, or neuter) and number (singular or plural) of nouns. Finally, we will discuss the forms and functions of the Greek article. We will see that the Greek article often functions similarly to the English definite article, "the."

2.2 Significance

In Acts 9:7, we read Luke's report of the apostle Paul's Damascus road conversion: "The men who were traveling with him stood speechless, hearing (ἀκούοντες) the sound (τῆς φωνῆς) but seeing no one." Later, in Acts 22:9, Paul recounts the same event and says, "Now those who were with me saw the light, but they did not hear (ἤκουσαν) the voice (τὴν . . . φωνὴν) of the one who was speaking to me." Both verses use the same verb for hearing (ἀκούω) and the same word for voice/sound

---

[1] For an overview video lecture of chapter 2, go to bit.ly/greeklecture2 or beginninggreek.com.

(φωνή)—a first declension noun that will serve as a key word for this chapter. So, did Paul's traveling companions hear or not hear the Lord speaking to him?

One solution to what seems an apparent discrepancy is to note the different case endings for the word translated "voice/sound." In Acts 9, the noun has a genitive (often showing possession or relationship) ending (–ης), while in Acts 22, the noun has an accusative (often indicating the direct object) ending (–ην). Even if you do not know the genitive and accusative case endings yet, you can clearly see the spelling differences in the words above. It is then suggested by some commentators that the verb ἀκούω followed by a genitive object (τῆς φωνῆς, Acts 9:7) conveys simply the fact of hearing (without implying understanding), while the accusative object (τὴν φωνήν, Acts 22:9) implies both hearing *and* understanding.[2] A careful look at additional biblical and extra-biblical texts from the time period of the New Testament, however, does not support this grammatical pattern. A better solution is to recognize that all words do have a range of meaning (both "hear" and "understand" are frequently used to translate ἀκούω), and the broader context supports a harmonizing view whereby Paul's companions witnessed both a supernatural light and sound but were not privy to the personal appearance and instructions given to Paul. In his commentary on Acts, John Polhill makes a similar observation:

> The most significant difference between Paul's account and the earlier conversion narrative occurs in 22:9, where it is said that Paul's traveling companions saw the light but did not understand the voice speaking to Paul. In 9:7 the companions are said to have heard the sound but not to have seen anyone. Paul's account emphasizes their seeing; the earlier account, their hearing. Both accounts make the same point. The companions were witnesses to the experience and could verify that something objective took place. It was not merely an inner experience of Paul's psyche. On the other hand, the companions were not participants in the experience: they heard a sound but did not receive the message, saw a light but not the risen Lord. The vision itself was solely Paul's experience.[3]

2.3 Number

When we talk about the ***number*** of a noun, we are indicating whether it is singular or plural. In English, plurality is usually communicated by adding an "s" or "es" to the end of a word: boy → boy**s**; box → box**es**.[4] In Greek, number is also usually communicated through the ending.

φωνή ("voice")   →   φωναί ("voices")
καρδία ("heart")   →   καρδίαι ("hearts")

---

[2] E.g., Gleason L. Archer, *Encyclopedia of Bible Difficulties* (Grand Rapids: Zondervan, 1982), 382–83.

[3] John B. Polhill, *Acts*, New American Commentary 26 (Nashville: Broadman, 1992), 459–60.

[4] But, note: man → men. English has many irregularities too!

2.4 Gender

Although English has become, for the most part, a language in which nouns are unmarked for gender, there are still remnants of masculine and feminine noun forms: host → hostess; actor→ actress; prince → princess. Unlike English, every Greek noun has a gender, though it is usually only a grammatical gender and thus does not correspond to any particular gender/sex in the real world. A small number of Greek nouns that refer to gender-specific persons (e.g., ἀδελφή, "sister") correspond in grammatical and natural gender (although the masculine ἀδελφός can be used for both "brothers and sisters"). As you grow in knowledge of Greek, you will begin to note additional patterns with grammatical gender. Abstract nouns, for example, are usually grammatically feminine (ἀγάπη, "love"; ἀλήθεια, "truth"; ἁμαρτία, "sin"; δόξα, "glory"). An abstract noun is "a substantive that signifies a concept, quantity, quality or state (among other things), as in *hatred* and *sportsmanship*. It is the opposite of a concrete noun, which refers to something tangible (wall, ocean, etc.)."[5]

In the Greek language, there are three genders: masculine, feminine, and neuter (i.e., from the Latin, meaning "neither"), though each individual noun has only one gender. The ending of a noun usually indicates its gender. All the first declension nouns in this chapter are feminine and end in –η or –α.

2.5 Case

Greek nouns contain much more information than English nouns. How an English noun functions in a sentence (e.g., as a subject or direct object) is usually communicated by the word order of the sentence. For example, the sentence "The apostle rebuked the demon" means something very different than "The demon rebuked the apostle," even though the same words are used. The word order of the first sentence indicates that the *apostle* is the subject of the verb and the *demon* is the direct object. Word order is important for communicating the function of words in English.

Imagine that we want to change the English language so that we can put the words in any order. We might say, "Rebuked the demon the apostle." But, how would we know which word was the subject and which was the object? We could tweak our language so that we add suffixes (endings) to our English words to let us know what they are doing in a sentence—"SU" for subject, "DO" for direct object, "IO" for indirect object, etc. Thus, we could say and write our new transformed sentence this way: "Rebuked the demonDO the apostleSU." Or, we could say, "The apostleSU the demonDO rebuked." If we all adopted this new system of noun suffixes, we could communicate just as clearly, but be liberated from set word order! This is akin to what Greek nouns do. They have a series of case

---

[5] Matthew S. DeMoss, *Pocket Dictionary for the Study of New Testament Greek* (Downers Grove: Intervarsity, 2001), 13. A **substantive** (subst) is any part of speech that functions as a noun.

endings (suffixes) that inform the hearer or reader how the nouns are functioning in the sentence. A noun listed with all possible case endings for both singular and plural forms is called a "declension" (noun pattern).

The function of Greek nouns depends on the case ending of the noun. For example, the word φωνή communicates that the noun functions as the subject of the sentence whereas φωνήν indicates that the noun functions as the direct object. (There are, in fact, many functions of the different cases, but for now, we are going to oversimplify and focus on the main ones.)

It can be helpful to see that English pronouns have distinct forms to communicate different functions in the sentence—similar to Greek nouns with case endings. You would never say, "This is **me** book" (unless you are Scottish, perhaps). The proper way to communicate possession is with the form "my"—"This is **my** book."

Function	Singular	Plural	Case[6]
Subject	I	we	Nominative
Possession	my	our	Genitive
Indirect Object	to me	to us	Dative
Direct Object	me	us	Accusative

Similar to the distinct spellings of English pronouns, Greek *case* endings likewise indicate the function of nouns in a sentence (not word order). There are five cases in Greek. (Note that we will discuss the fifth in the next chapter). The ***nominative case*** is typically the subject of the verb, answering "who?" ("*The Son* of God gave the gift to the man"). The ***genitive case*** expresses possession or family relationship, which is often indicated by adding "of," answering "whose?" ("The Son *of God* [or *God's* Son] gave the gift to the man").[7] The ***dative case*** often functions as the indirect object of the verb ("The Son of God gave the gift *to the man*").[8] The word "to" or "for" is added to convey this function in English, which answers the question, "to/for whom?" The ***accusative case*** often functions as the direct object of the verb, answering the question "what?" ("The Son of God gave *the gift* to the man").

Case	Function	Singular	Plural
Nominative	Subject	φωνή (voice)	φωναί (voices)
Genitive	Possession	φωνῆς (of a voice)	φωνῶν (of voices)
Dative	Indirect Object	φωνῇ (to/for a voice)	φωναῖς (to/for voices)
Accusative	Direct Object	φωνήν (voice)	φωνάς (voices)

---

[6] S. M. Baugh has a similar chart comparing English pronouns to Greek cases (*A New Testament Greek Primer*, 3rd ed. (Phillipsburg, NJ: P&R, 2012), 9.

[7] The term in the genitive case will almost always follow the noun that it is modifying (which is often called the **head noun**). Note, too, that the genitive has many more functions than indicating possession or relationship (e.g., source, "from").

[8] The dative has many more functions than indicating the indirect object (e.g., instrument, "by/with").

2.6 Paradigms

A *paradigm* is a representative pattern or example chart. The following two paradigms represent the eta (η) and alpha (α) patterns, respectively. Note that the feminine article (the same for both charts) also has distinct spellings depending on the gender, number, and case of the noun it modifies. The feminine article has only eight possible forms, all of which occur in the charts below. You will notice that the spelling of the article frequently matches the noun ending with either a tau (τ) or rough breathing mark added at the beginning. In the English translations below, the Greek article is rendered as "the."[9]

FIRST DECLENSION NOUN—ETA PATTERN[10]						
	SINGULAR			PLURAL		
NOM	ἡ	φωνή	the voice	αἱ	φωναί	the voices
GEN	τῆς	φωνῆς	of the voice	τῶν	φωνῶν	of the voices
DAT	τῇ	φωνῇ	to/for the voice	ταῖς	φωναῖς	to/for the voices
ACC	τὴν	φωνήν	the voice	τὰς	φωνάς	the voices

FIRST DECLENSION NOUN—ALPHA PATTERN						
	SINGULAR			PLURAL		
NOM	ἡ	καρδία	the heart	αἱ	καρδίαι	the hearts
GEN	τῆς	καρδίας	of the heart	τῶν	καρδιῶν	of the hearts
DAT	τῇ	καρδίᾳ	to/for the heart	ταῖς	καρδίαις	to/for the hearts
ACC	τὴν	καρδίαν	the heart	τὰς	καρδίας	the hearts

2.7 Morphology

Morphology refers to the study of the parts of a word, and a *morpheme* is the smallest meaning-unit of a word. Unlike English, Greek is a highly inflected language. An *inflection* refers to a change or addition made to a word that alters its meaning or function in a sentence. The various case endings (i.e., morphemes) in the paradigms above alter its meaning (singular or plural) and function (subject, possession, indirect object, or direct object).

---

[9] Notice that the eta and alpha paradigms overlap. Once you memorize the eta pattern, you will note that the plural endings are identical. Furthermore, the singular endings are similar, with the eta being replaced with an alpha.

[10] To hear a mnemonic song for first and second declension nouns, go to bit.ly/1st2ndnounsong or beginninggreek.com.

Notice that there are two different (but related) paradigms for this lesson: (1) the eta pattern (φωνή) and (2) the alpha pattern (καρδία). Each word in the paradigms above includes the stem and an ending. Thus, for φωνή, the stem is φων– and the ending is –η. Likewise, for καρδία, the stem is καρδι– and the ending is –α. The alpha pattern applies to words with stems ending in rho, iota, or epsilon. This is sometimes called the alpha pie rule (which sounds like "apple pie") because rho (ρ), iota (ι), and epsilon (ε) written together (ριε) look somewhat like the English word "pie." If you memorize the lexical (dictionary) forms in the vocabulary lists, the last letter of the first declension forms will almost always indicate to you which pattern the noun will follow.

Eta Pattern	Alpha Pattern	
ἀγάπη	ἀλήθεια	ἐκκλησία
γῆ	ἁμαρτία	ἡμέρα
ζωή	βασιλεία	καρδία
φωνή		

Observe above in the paradigm chart that for the first declension alpha pattern (καρδία), the genitive singular and accusative plural have the same form (καρδίας). The reader can determine which case an author intended by (1) the use of the article (the genitive singular is τῆς whereas the accusative plural is τάς) or (2) the context.

The noun δόξα is somewhat irregular since it uses a combination of both eta and alpha pattern endings in the singular forms: δόξα, δόξης, δόξῃ, δόξαν. The first declension feminine plural forms are the same for all eta, alpha, and irregular forms. The irregularity of δόξα is caused by the xsi (ξ), a double consonant. Nouns that end in a double sigma (σσ) also follow this pattern (γλῶσσα, "tongue," and θάλασσα, "sea").[11]

We should note that the endings of the nouns in the paradigms above have been simplified. From a historical and morphological perspective, the actual stems of φωνή and καρδία are not φων– and καρδι– but φωνη– and καρδια–. Thus, the case endings for these forms are technically not –η, –ης, –ῃ, –ην, –αι, –ων, –αις, –ας. Rather, the real ending has often contracted with the eta (η) and alpha (α) ending of the stem. Most students learn more easily the simplified explanation of noun stems and case endings presented above, but we present below the actual endings and contractions for the sake of comparison. If you find this morphological nuancing confusing, feel free to ignore it.[12]

---

[11] The feminine form of the adjective πᾶσα ("all") also follows this pattern.

[12] For those interested in learning more precise historical morphology, William D. Mounce provides many helpful charts and explanations in his introductory grammar (*Basics of Biblical Greek: Grammar,* 4th ed. [Grand Rapids: Zondervan, 2019]). A few other introductory grammars also emphasize morphology (e.g., H. Daniel Zacharias, *Biblical Greek Made Simple: All the Basics in One Semester* [Bellingham, WA: Lexham, 2018]).

	Singular		Plural	
Nom	φωνη + -	→ φωνή	φωνη + ι	→ φωναί
Gen	φωνη + ς	→ φωνῆς	φωνη + ων	→ φωνῶν
Dat	φωνη + ι	→ φωνῇ[13]	φωνη + ις	→ φωναῖς
Acc	φωνη + ν	→ φωνήν	φωνη + ς	→ φωνάς

	Singular		Plural	
Nom	καρδια + -	→ καρδία	καρδια + ι	→ καρδίαι
Gen	καρδια + ς	→ καρδίας	καρδια + ων	→ καρδιῶν
Dat	καρδια + ι	→ καρδίᾳ	καρδια + ις	→ καρδίαις
Acc	καρδια + ν	→ καρδίαν	καρδια + ς	→ καρδίας

The accent on first declension nouns tends to remain on the same syllable as in the lexical form. But if the ultima is long, the accent will move to the penult (ἀλήθεια → ἀληθείᾳ). The genitive plural is always accented with a circumflex on the ultima (ἁμαρτιῶν).

2.8 The Article

English has a ***definite article*** ("the") and an ***indefinite article*** ("a/an"). Greek, however, only has one article, which functions similarly to the English definite article and is frequently translated as "the." The Greek article should not be called a "definite article," though, because it also has other functions. There is no indefinite article in Greek (though a few words in the Koine period are beginning to function that way).[14] When a noun in Greek is not preceded by the article, it is often necessary to add "a/an" for an English translation (e.g., ἐκκλησία = "a church" or "church"; ὥρα = "an hour" or "hour"). A Greek noun that has no article is called ***anarthrous***. A Greek word preceded by an article is technically termed as ***arthrous*** or ***articular***.

Whereas the English definite article is always spelled the same way ("the"), the Greek article changes spelling to match the noun it modifies (ὁ, ἡ, τό), one for each gender.

Masculine: ὁ   Feminine: ἡ   Neuter: τό

Note, too, that these three forms of the article are only for the nominative singular forms of the respective genders! In fact, there are specific forms to match each case, number, and gender of a noun (3 genders x 8 forms of each noun = 24 forms of the article!), with some overlap in spelling among them. Know that in this chapter you are introduced to one set of feminine articles that will be the exact same

---

[13] The iota (ι) subscripts (as in all dative singular forms).
[14] For example, εἷς (one) and τις (someone, anyone, any, some).

eight forms for any feminine noun. In the next chapter, you will learn the eight forms of the masculine article and the eight forms of the neuter article.

Because of its frequency (almost 20,000 occurrences in the New Testament) and because it will help you identify the gender and case of nouns, the article must be mastered. It helps to learn the memory paradigms with the articles. When reading English text that has been translated from Greek, you will notice that sometimes the article is included in Greek when it is not needed in English (e.g., ἡ ἀγάπη μακροθυμεῖ, "love is patient"; 1 Cor 13:4) and, conversely, sometimes it is omitted in Greek but needed in English (ἑαυτοὺς ἐν ἀγάπῃ θεοῦ τηρήσατε, "keep yourselves in **the** love of God"; Jude v. 21). Finally, proper names and abstract nouns will often have an article which is usually not needed in English. Here are two rules of thumb for translating: (1) If translating the Greek article into English and "the" sounds weird, drop it. (2) If an article is needed for the sentence to conform to normal English usage, add one. Languages are not like algebraic equations. Don't expect a one-word English equivalent in your translation for every underlying Greek word.[15]

2.9 Conjunctions

Conjunctions are indeclinable[16] words used to link words, phrases, clauses, and larger discourse (communication) units. Thus, conjunctions designate the relationship between various parts of a discourse. The three conjunctions learned for this lesson (δέ, καί, μέν) are all coordinating conjunctions—meaning they communicate a parallel (or equal rank) relationship between the words, phrases, or clauses that they link. In contrast, subordinating conjunctions link words, phrases, or clauses in a dependent (or unequal) relationship with another word, phrase, or clause (e.g., ὅτι, "that"). Additionally, δέ is a *postpositive* conjunction—meaning that it never will occur as the first word in a clause but is usually found as the second word (though when translated into English, it should be put first).[17] Sometimes δέ is also called a postpositive *particle*. In grammatical terminology, "particle" just means a small indeclinable word that communicates grammatical relationships.

2.10 Parsing

Parsing is a crucial skill when learning Greek. It is similar to playing scales when learning a musical instrument. At first, playing scales is difficult and time consuming, but such repetitive work is essential if one is to become proficient with an instrument. Playing scales is not the goal, but such practice enables one to play

---

[15] Even the most "word for word" Bible translations sometimes employ more functionally or dynamically equivalent renderings. See Dave Brunn, *One Bible, Many Versions: Are All Translations Created Equal* (Downers Grove, IL: IVP Academic, 2013).

[16] ***Indeclinable*** means the word does not "decline" or add case endings. Its spelling remains unchanged.

[17] δέ is sometimes written as δ' when the next word begins with a vowel (ὃς δ' ἂν, "and whoever"). δέ rarely occurs as the third or even fourth element in a clause.

beautiful music eventually. Similarly, parsing is not the goal, but it gives one the tools to become proficient in Greek. To practice parsing, we recommend visiting the free website www.mastergreek.com.

To **parse** a word involves describing all the grammatical elements of that word to determine its meaning. Some grammars prefer to retain the term "parse" for verbal forms and instead speak of "locating" or "declining" a noun. Regardless of the terminology adopted, to parse or locate a noun involves identifying its (1) lexical form, (2) gender, (3) case, and (4) number. Once this is done, a proper translation of the noun can be offered. Eventually, you will develop a more intuitive grasp of Greek nouns, but for now, it's good to rigidly hold yourself to demonstrating your knowledge through parsing.

Lexical Form: Dictionary form (nominative singular)
Gender: Feminine [Masculine, Neuter—to be learned in next chapter]
Case: Nominative, Genitive, Dative, Accusative
Number: Singular or Plural

Here are a few examples of how to parse a noun:

Inflected Form	Lexical Form	Gender	Case	Number	Translation
καρδίαν	καρδία	fem	acc	sg	"a heart" or "heart"
φωναῖς	φωνή	fem	dat	pl	"to/for voices"
ζωῆς	ζωή	fem	gen	sg	"of a life"

2.11 Practice

A. Paradigms: Memorize the paradigms for φωνή and καρδία (see section 2.6), and then write out each paradigm ten times from memory. (Include the article and the English meaning.)

B. Eta and Alpha Nouns: Circle the forms that are incorrect.

1. φωνῆς   ἀλήθεια   ζῷα   ἡμέραι
2. ἁμαρτίη   ἐκκλησιῶν   ἀγάπα   βασιλείαν
3. γῆν   καρδίας   δόξῃ   φωνᾳ
4. ἡμέρας   ἐκκλησιῆς   ζωῆς   δόξαν
5. δόξας   βασιλείας   ἁμαρτία   ἀληθείην

C. The Article: Parse the following nouns, circling the examples in which the article does not match the noun (in gender, case, and number), then supply the correct article.

1. τὴν ἀλήθειαν
2. τῆς ζῶης
3. αἱ ἡμέρα
4. τὴν ἁμαρτιῶν
5. ταῖς ἐκκλησίαις

6. τὰς ἀγάπης
7. ἡ γῆ
8. τῇ βασιλείᾳ
9. ταῖς καρδίας
10. τὴν δόξαν

D. Case: Circle the Greek word that best translates the English phrase.

1. to the churches   τῇ ἐκκλησίᾳ   τὰς ἐκκλησίας   ταῖς ἐκκλησίαις
2. of the heart   τὴν καρδίαν   τῆς καρδίας   τὰς καρδίας
3. the days (subject) αἱ ἡμέραι   τὰς ἡμέρας   ἡ ἡμέρα
4. for the truth   τὴν ἀλήθειαν   τῇ ἀληθείᾳ   τῆς ἀληθείας
5. of the love   ἡ ἀγάπη   τὴν ἀγάπην   τῆς ἀγάπης

E. Translation: Underline the first declension nouns learned for this chapter. Then parse and translate each one.

1. ἡ φωνὴ τὴν γῆν ἐσάλευσεν (Heb 12:26).

2. λέγει αὐτῷ [ὁ] Ἰησοῦς, Ἐγώ εἰμι ἡ ὁδὸς καὶ ἡ ἀλήθεια καὶ ἡ ζωή (John 14:6).

3. τὸ δὲ τέλος τῆς παραγγελίας ἐστὶν ἀγάπη ἐκ καθαρᾶς καρδίας καὶ συνειδήσεως ἀγαθῆς καὶ πίστεως ἀνυποκρίτου (1 Tim 1:5).

4. Ἐγένετο δὲ ἐν ἐκείνῃ τῇ ἡμέρᾳ διωγμὸς μέγας ἐπὶ τὴν ἐκκλησίαν τὴν ἐν Ἱεροσολύμοις (Acts 8:1).

2.12 Vocabulary[18]

ἀδελφός, ὁ	brother (and sister) (*Philadelphia*, the city of brotherly love)
ἄνθρωπος, ὁ	man, human being, husband (*anthropology, anthropomorphic*)
θεός, ὁ	God (*theology*)
κόσμος, ὁ	world, universe; adornment (*cosmos, cosmology, cosmetics*)
κύριος, ὁ	Lord, master, sir

---

[18] English cognates are provided in parentheses after definitions. To hear an author of your textbook read through the vocabulary for chapter 2, go to bit.ly/ntgreekvocab2 or beginninggreek.com.

λόγος, ὁ	word, message, account (*logic*, *theology*, *psychology*)
νόμος, ὁ	law, principle (*theonomists*)
οὐρανός, ὁ	heaven, sky (*Uranus*)
υἱός, ὁ	son, descendant
Χριστός, ὁ	Christ, Messiah, Anointed One (*Christ*)
ἔργον, τό	work, deed (*ergonomic*)
εὐαγγέλιον, τό	good news, gospel (*evangelistic*, *evangelical*)
ἱερόν, τό	temple, sanctuary
σημεῖον, τό	sign (*semiotics*)
τέκνον, τό	child, son, descendant

CHAPTER 3

//////////////

SECOND DECLENSION NOUNS

3.1 Overview[1]

This chapter discusses nouns that follow a different set of case endings and are grouped together in a pattern called the second declension. This declension (pattern) includes both masculine and neuter nouns.[2] We will also discuss the vocative case and proper nouns. If this grammatical terminology is causing you anxiety, don't worry. We will explain all these terms below.

3.2 Significance

I (Rob) recently had a pastor ask me how Jesus being circumcised as a Jewish boy was significant for our salvation. The question took me by surprise! It turned out that this pastor was looking at Col 2:11 in the ESV, and he was confused by the phrase, "the circumcision of Christ." The surrounding text of the ESV reads:

> In him also you were circumcised with a circumcision made without hands, by putting off the body of the flesh, **by the circumcision of Christ** (Col 2:11).

The Greek text of the passage is instructive:

> Ἐν ᾧ καὶ περιετμήθητε περιτομῇ ἀχειροποιήτῳ ἐν τῇ ἀπεκδύσει τοῦ σώματος τῆς σαρκός, **ἐν τῇ περιτομῇ τοῦ Χριστοῦ**.

The final word in the verse is an articular (i.e., preceded by the article) genitive form of Christ (a second declension form you will learn in this chapter). It is

---

[1] For an overview video lecture of chapter 3, go to bit.ly/greeklecture3 or beginninggreek.com.
[2] There are a few feminine second declension nouns, e.g., ἡ ὁδός, "way, road, path."

rendered above by the ESV as "of Christ." This is a valid translation, but it also opens up the potential misunderstanding that Paul is writing about the circumcision that Jesus underwent as an eight-day old infant. Nevertheless, "the circumcision of Christ" can also mean the circumcision performed by Christ, as the context here favors. The technical name for this relatively common function of the genitive is the "subjective genitive"—where the genitive functions as the subject of the verbal idea in the head noun. We could rephrase the last few words of the sentence as "Christ circumcises [believers]." To avoid the potential confusion of simply translating the genitive τοῦ Χριστοῦ as "of Christ," several modern English translations go a different route from the ESV. The NET Bible reads:

> In him you also were circumcised—not, however, with a circumcision performed by human hands, but by the removal of the fleshly body, that is, **through the circumcision done by Christ.**

Similarly, the NIV says:

> In him you were also circumcised with a circumcision not performed by human hands. Your whole self ruled by the flesh was put off when **you were circumcised by Christ.**

These latter translations bring out more clearly that it was Christ who (spiritually) circumcised us Christians by regenerating us by his Spirit and setting us apart as his people.

As a beginning student of Greek, you are rightly developing a translational reflex to translate genitive nouns with "of" in front of them, but please remember that much more than possession or family relationship can be communicated by the genitive. You will learn more about the nuances of the genitive in intermediate Greek.

3.3 Number

English differentiates plural nouns from singular nouns with the addition of an "s" or "es" (boys, boxes). But this is not the only way to form a plural noun in English. Sometimes plurality is communicated by changing a vowel (man → men; foot → feet). Likewise, in Greek there are several ways (patterns) to indicate a change in number (or case), which is communicated through a noun's ending.

First Declension (Feminine)

φωνή ("voice")   →   φωναί ("voices")
καρδία ("heart")   →   καρδίαι ("hearts")

Second Declension (Masculine and Neuter)

λόγος ("word") → λόγοι ("words")

τέκνον ("child") → τέκνα ("children")

3.4 Gender

The second declension nouns we will learn in this chapter can be either masculine or neuter (each noun has only one gender). The nouns for this chapter that end in –ος are masculine, and those that end in –ον are neuter. Remember that the gender of a noun refers to the grammatical gender and usually has no correspondence to actual gender/sex.

3.5 Case

The cases of the second declension nouns function in the same manner as first declension nouns. At this point, you will need to learn this simplified list of functions:

Nominative	→	Subject
Genitive	→	Possession or Family Relationship
Dative	→	Indirect Object
Accusative	→	Direct Object

3.6 Paradigms[3]

SECOND DECLENSION NOUN—MASCULINE						
	SINGULAR			PLURAL		
NOM	ὁ	λόγος	the word	οἱ	λόγοι	the words
GEN	τοῦ	λόγου	of the word	τῶν	λόγων	of the words
DAT	τῷ	λόγῳ	to/for the word	τοῖς	λόγοις	to/for the words
ACC	τὸν	λόγον	the word	τοὺς	λόγους	the words

SECOND DECLENSION NOUN—NEUTER						
	SINGULAR			PLURAL		
NOM	τὸ	τέκνον	the child	τὰ	τέκνα	the children
GEN	τοῦ	τέκνου	of the child	τῶν	τέκνων	of the children
DAT	τῷ	τέκνῳ	to/for the child	τοῖς	τέκνοις	to/for the children
ACC	τὸ	τέκνον	the child	τὰ	τέκνα	the children

---

[3] To hear a mnemonic song for first and second declension nouns, go to bit.ly/1st2ndnounsong or beginninggreek.com.

3.7 Morphology

Although there are two paradigms to memorize in this chapter, they are not unrelated patterns.[4] First, note that the genitive and dative endings and articles (for both singular and plural) are identical. Second, the neuter nominative and accusative forms (singular and plural) have the same endings (context will dictate which case is intended). It is also important to note where first declension and second declension endings overlap in spelling and could be confusing—e.g., the need to distinguish καρδία (feminine, nominative, singular) from τέκνα (neuter, nominative/accusative, plural). Furthermore, observe that the masculine and neuter genitive plural form (–ων) is the same as the feminine genitive plural form (φωνῶν, καρδιῶν).[5] Finally, the dative forms always have an iota, though it is subscripted in the singular. This is true for all three genders. It is easiest to memorize the masculine paradigm first and then learn the neuter forms by simply noting how the endings differ.

From the perspective of historical morphology, our discussion of the paradigms above has been simplified. The actual stems of λόγος and τέκνον are not λογ– and τεκν– but λογο– and τεκνο–. Thus, the case endings for λόγος are technically not –ος, –ου, –ῳ, –ον, –οι, –ων, –οις, –ους. Rather, the real ending has often contracted with the omicron (o) ending of the stem. Below are the actual historical endings and contractions for both the masculine and neuter forms. Please note that you will never see the uncontracted forms, so most Greek textbooks do not even delve into this history of the word's formation. Nevertheless, noting the morphology of first and second declension nouns may help you learn third declension nouns more quickly because you will see the underlying similarity that is often veiled in the combined forms. If the morphological discussion below is confusing to you, though, feel free to skip it.[6]

	Singular		Plural	
Nom	λογο + ς	→ λόγος	λογο + ι	→ λόγοι
Gen	λογο + υ	→ λόγου[7]	λογο + ων	→ λόγων
Dat	λογο + ι	→ λόγῳ[8]	λογο + ις	→ λόγοις
Acc	λογο + ν	→ λόγον	λογο + υς	→ λόγους

Because the genitive and dative forms are the same for masculine and neuter second declension nouns, and because the nominative and accusative forms for neuter nouns are identical, we need to offer only the singular and plural forms.

---

[4] These nouns are, after all, classified as belonging to the same (second) declension. Technically, second declension nouns have a stem that ends in omicron (o).

[5] You need to own (ων) this ending, which also conveniently communicates ownership.

[6] For questions of historical morphology about words in the New Testament, there is no better resource than William D. Mounce, *The Morphology of Biblical Greek* (Grand Rapids: Zondervan, 1994). We credit Mounce with helping us rightly understand the morphological patterns presented in this book.

[7] The actual ending is not upsilon (υ) but omicron (o). The omicron, however, contracts with the omicron of the stem to form ου: λογο + ο → λογοο → λογόυ.

[8] There are a few steps in the process: λογο + ι → λογοι → λογωι → λόγῳ.

	Singular		Plural	
N/A	τεκνο + ν → τέκνον		τεκνο + α → τέκνα[9]	

Parsing second declension nouns is similar to parsing first declension nouns.

Inflected Form	Lexical Form	Gender	Case	Number	Translation
λόγοι	λόγος	masc	nom	pl	"words"
τέκνον	τέκνον	neut	n/a	sg	"child"

3.8 Vocative Case

The vocative case is the fifth case in Greek, although it is not included in the paradigms due to its infrequency and overlap with other forms.[10] The *vocative case* is used for direct address. That is, the vocative is used when an author or speaker addresses someone (or a group) directly. For example, the woman at the well addresses Jesus by saying, "Sir (Κύριε), give me this water" (John 4:15). The masculine singular ending (–ε) is the most common form and should be memorized.[11] Other masculine singular nouns include διδάσκαλε ("teacher"), δοῦλε ("slave"), υἱέ ("son"), and ὦ ἄνθρωπε ("O man!"). Outside of the second declension masculine singular, most vocative forms are identical to the nominative forms of the noun in question (τέκνον μου, "my child" [2 Tim 2:1 ESV]; τέκνα μου, "my children" [Gal 4:19]). Because there is no vocative article, when the article is used before a noun that is directly addressing someone, it is an example of the nominative used to communicate direct address—the "nominative of address" (οἱ ἄνδρες, ἀγαπᾶτε τὰς γυναῖκας, "husbands, love your wives"; [Eph 5:25]). In a manner similar to English, vocatives will typically be set off by commas, making them easy to recognize. Furthermore, they also are commonly found at the beginning of a paragraph.

3.9 Proper Nouns

Proper nouns identify a person, place, or thing and are capitalized in Greek (as is the case with proper nouns in English). Many proper nouns are imported from other languages (especially Hebrew and Aramaic) and can often be understood when pronounced. For example, the name Ἀβραάμ is clearly "Abraham." (Remember, the Greek language does not have an "h" sound except for a rough breathing mark, which can only go over the initial letter of a word.) Here are twenty of the most common proper nouns in the New Testament:

---

[9] There is an extra step in the process: τεκνο + α → τεκνοα → τέκνα.

[10] Although there are about 640 uses of the vocative, this comprises less than 1 percent of all nouns in the New Testament.

[11] The masculine singular form of the vocative (–ε) accounts for more than half of the vocative forms in the New Testament.

Ἀβραάμ, ὁ	Abraham
Γαλιλαία, ἡ	Galilee
Δαυίδ, ὁ	David
Ἡρῴδης, ὁ	Herod
Ἰάκωβος, ὁ	James
Ἱεροσόλυμα, τό	Jerusalem
Ἱερουσαλήμ, ἡ	Jerusalem
Ἰησοῦς, ὁ	Jesus
Ἰουδαία, ἡ	Judea
Ἰουδαῖος, ὁ	Jewish; a Jew
Ἰούδας, ὁ	Judah, Judas
Ἰσραήλ, ὁ	Israel
Ἰωάννης, ὁ	John
Ἰωσήφ, ὁ	Joseph
Μωϋσῆς, ὁ	Moses
Παῦλος, ὁ	Paul
Πέτρος, ὁ	Peter
Πιλᾶτος, ὁ	Pilate
Σίμων, ὁ	Simon
Φαρισαῖος, ὁ	Pharisee[12]

Some proper nouns are declinable (as are those appearing in bold font above). But many, especially foreign names, are not (as in the case of those not bolded above). When a noun does not decline, the article will communicate its function in the sentence (τῷ Ἰσραήλ = "to Israel"). When the article is not provided, then the context determines the meaning (Ἐλέησόν με, κύριε υἱὸς **Δαυίδ** = "Have mercy on me, Lord, Son **of David**"; Matt 15:22). Also note that in Greek the article will often be used before a proper name, but there should not be an equivalent English word in your translation (e.g., ὁ Ἰωσήφ = "Joseph," not "the Joseph").

Finally, it will be helpful to highlight the declension of the name "Jesus" (Ἰησοῦς) because of its frequent use. Notice that the genitive and dative forms are the same. Either the distinct articles (τοῦ or τῷ) or the context must clarify whether Ἰησοῦ is genitive or dative.

	SINGULAR		
NOM	ὁ	Ἰησοῦς	Jesus
GEN	τοῦ	Ἰησοῦ	of Jesus
DAT	τῷ	Ἰησοῦ	to/for Jesus
ACC	τὸν	Ἰησοῦν	Jesus

---

[12] This material has been in our teaching notes for years, and we cannot locate its origin.

3.10 Practice

A. Paradigms: Memorize the paradigms for λόγος and τέκνον (see section 3.6). Then write out each paradigm ten times, including the article and the English meaning.

B. Masculine Nouns: Circle the words that are masculine, including articles.

1. ἀδελφοῦ	θεόν	τά	ἡμέραι
2. τούς	τέκνοις	νόμου	υἱῶν
3. καρδίᾳ	ὁ	ἀλήθεια	λόγους
4. ἀνθρώποις	σημεῖα	κόσμῳ	τό
5. ἔργῳ	τοῖς	ἱερόν	Χριστοῦ

C. The Article: Parse the following nouns, circling the examples in which the article does not match the noun (in gender, case, and number). Then supply the correct article.

1. τῷ θεῷ	6. τὴν νόμον
2. τὸν εὐαγγέλιον	7. ὁ υἱός
3. αἱ ἄνθρωποι	8. ταῖς οὐρανοῖς
4. τοῦ κυρίου	9. τῷ Ἰησοῦ
5. τῶν σημείων	10. τὰ ἔργα

D. Case: Circle the Greek word that best translates the English phrase.

1. for the Lord	τοῦ κυρίου	τῷ κυρίῳ	τὸν κύριον
2. of heaven	τοῦ οὐρανοῦ	τῶν οὐρανῶν	τῷ οὐρανῷ
3. to the sons	υἱοῖς	οἱ υἱοί	τοῖς υἱοῖς
4. the brothers (subject)	ὁ ἀδελφός	τοῖς ἀδελφοῖς	οἱ ἀδελφοί
5. of the temple	τῷ ἱερῷ	τοῦ ἱεροῦ	τό ἱερόν

E. Translation: Underline the second declension nouns you have learned. Then parse and translate each one.

1. ὥστε κύριός ἐστιν ὁ υἱὸς τοῦ ἀνθρώπου καὶ τοῦ σαββάτου (Mark 2:28).

2. ἣν προηκούσατε ἐν τῷ λόγῳ τῆς ἀληθείας τοῦ εὐαγγελίου (Col 1:5).

3. Καὶ ἐξελθὼν ὁ Ἰησοῦς ἀπὸ τοῦ ἱεροῦ ἐπορεύετο, καὶ προσῆλθον οἱ μαθηταὶ αὐτοῦ ἐπιδεῖξαι αὐτῷ τὰς οἰκοδομὰς τοῦ ἱεροῦ (Matt 24:1).

4. ἐν τούτῳ φανερά ἐστιν τὰ τέκνα τοῦ θεοῦ καὶ τὰ τέκνα τοῦ διαβόλου· πᾶς ὁ μὴ ποιῶν δικαιοσύνην οὐκ ἔστιν ἐκ τοῦ θεοῦ, καὶ ὁ μὴ ἀγαπῶν τὸν ἀδελφὸν αὐτοῦ (1 John 3:10).

3.11 Vocabulary[13]

You will note that most Greek verbal lexical forms end in –ω. The verbs whose lexical forms end in –ομαι are considered "middle-only" regarding voice. (The next chapter will explain these terms in more detail.) For now, know that middle-only verbs often describe predictable fields of activity—when the subject both performs and is affected by the action. Whenever a middle-only verb is listed in the vocabulary, we will note its field of subject-affectedness. It is our hope that you will gradually absorb a proper understanding of the middle voice through these brief exposures.

εἰμί	I am, exist
ἀκούω	I hear, listen to, obey (*acoustics*)
γινώσκω	I know, understand, acknowledge (*knowledge, Gnostics*)
γράφω	I write (*graphics*)
ἔχω	I have, hold
λέγω	I say, speak (*legend*)
λαμβάνω	I take, receive
λύω	I loose, destroy
πιστεύω	I believe, have faith/trust in
ἀποκρίνομαι	I answer, reply[14]
γίνομαι	I become, come, exist, am born[15]
ἔρχομαι	I come, go[16]
πορεύομαι	I go, travel[17]
ἀλλά[18]	but, yet, nevertheless
ὅτι	that, because

---

[13] To hear an author of your textbook read through the vocabulary for chapter 3, go to bit.ly/nt-greekvocab3 or beginninggreek.com.

[14] A verb of reciprocity. That is, the action cannot happen without two parties involved. Verbs of reciprocity are often middle-only.

[15] Verbs in which the subject is inherently passive and is unable to avoid the action by personal choice are often middle-only.

[16] Greek verbs of movement are often middle-only. The subject is both acting and affected by self-locomotion.

[17] Greek verb of movement, middle-only.

[18] The final vowel of ἀλλά is dropped when the next word begins with a vowel (ἀλλ'). Nevertheless, in many early manuscripts of the Greek New Testament, ἀλλά often appears unelided before words that begin with a vowel. Editors of the Tyndale House Edition of the Greek New Testament (Crossway, 2018) have complained that many modern editions of the Greek New Testament too quickly standardize such features in the text without attention to the actual manuscript evidence. See www.thegreeknewtestament.com.

CHAPTER 4

/////////////////

THE BASICS OF GREEK VERBS

4.1 Overview[1]

This chapter will provide an overview of the Greek verbal system. It will include a discussion of (1) person and number, (2) voice, (3) mood, and (4) tense and aspect. In it, you will also learn the present indicative form of the verb εἰμί ("I am").[2] We will be surveying a lot of information in this chapter, but you are not expected to understand all of it thoroughly. We will be revisiting relevant information from this chapter in future chapters, so you can always turn back here and review basic concepts as you progress in your study of Greek.

In the Greek language, the verb is the foundation of the sentence. A **verb** is a word that conveys an action or state. An **_action verb_** typically requires an act of will to perform the action ("I run"). A **_stative verb_** describes a state or condition ("I am thirsty"). Verbs in English are somewhat limited since they only communicate the action being performed (e.g., "hunting"). More words are needed to be more precise. For example, to say "I am hunting," it requires three words ("I" = pronoun; "am" = helping/auxiliary verb; "hunting" = main verbal idea). In contrast, verbs in Greek are very compact. They communicate a considerable amount of information through a single word. For example, to communicate the idea of "we are loosing" in Greek, only one word (λύομεν) is required since Greek verbs express both person and number through attached endings (in this example, –ομεν communicates that the verb has a first person plural subject = "we"). Furthermore, a separate term is not needed for the word "are" since that information is communicated by the single verbal form itself.

---

[1] For an overview video lecture of chapter 4, go to bit.ly/greeklecture4 or beginninggreek.com.
[2] "Indicative" is a mood that represents something as certain or asserted.

4.2 Significance

In 1 Corinthians 12, Paul rebukes the Corinthians because they are seeking spiritual gifts for the purpose of self-exaltation rather than service. He ends with this censure: "You *only* want the better gifts, but I will show you the best thing to do" (1 Cor 12:31 GW).[3] Following this rebuke, the apostle pens his famous chapter on love, 1 Corinthians 13.

But is that a proper understanding of the flow of the passage?

Most modern English translations actually end chapter 12 with an apostolic concession rather than a correction. The ESV is typical: "But earnestly desire the higher gifts. And I will show you a still more excellent way" (1 Cor 12:31).

So, the ESV (and most other modern English translations) render Paul's statement about "greater/better gifts" as a command rather than a statement: "Eagerly desire" vs. "You *only* want" (GW). As you will soon know, the underlying Greek verb rendered here as "desire" (command) or "want" (observation) is ambiguous in form; the verb could be an imperative or an indicative. Only the context can help you determine which meaning is intended by the author. Most translation committees have judged that it is more likely for Paul to make a positive concession about the "greater" gifts (of teaching and prophecy, for example) at the end of his argument. In other words, such public gifts, when used for building up the body of Christ, are of widespread ecclesiastical benefit. It is right to desire them, as long as one does so with the intent of using them properly.[4]

Without access to the Greek text, something else of significance is obscured in the English translations of 1 Cor 12:31. Paul's command is in the plural—"you *all* eagerly desire." Although there is individualistic application of this desire, it is a yearning that the *community* should have. It is improper to desire public gifts for one's own exaltation, but it is good to want God to raise up persons who are gifted for the edification of the local church. Indeed, to pray for and desire such teachers/preachers is to believe the apostle Paul's teaching in Eph 4:11–12—that the exalted Lord graciously dispenses Spirit-enabled leaders as his gifts to the church.

4.3 Person and Number

As stated above, Greek verb endings communicate information regarding the subject of the verb. That is, they communicate the person and number of the one performing the action (active voice) or the one who is receiving the action (passive

---

[3] Other translations that render the text similar to the GW include Etheridge Translation of the NT Peshitta (1849), Murdock Translation of the NT Peshitta (1851), and MGI NT Peshitta Translation (2006).

[4] The *ESV Study Bible* notes on 1 Cor 12:31 spell out this understanding nicely: "**Earnestly desire** implies that Christians can and should desire additional spiritual gifts (cf. 1 Cor. 14:1, 13; James 1:5). **The higher gifts** means those that do more to build up the church (see 1 Cor. 14:5, 12, 17, 26). 'Higher' here and 'greater' in 14:5 translate the same Greek (*meizōn*, comparative form of *megas*). A still more excellent way than merely seeking the higher gifts is to use the gifts in love (ch. 13) so that others are built up (ch. 14)" (formatting original to *ESV Study Bible*).

voice). Thus, ***person*** refers to the subject of the verbal idea. The options for the person of the verb are these: first person ("I" or "we"), second person ("you" [singular or plural]), or third person ("he/she/it" or "they").

1st person: The subject is speaking.
2nd person: The subject is being spoken to.
3rd person: The subject is being spoken about.

Similarly, ***number*** refers to whether there is only one person related to the action of the verb ("I," "you" sg, or "he/she/it") or more than one person ("we," "you" pl, or "they"). Note, in formal English, the same form ("you") is used for both singular and plural second person communication, but in colloquial English, there are various regional preferences for the second person plural (e.g., "y'all," "you guys," "you'uns").

	SINGULAR	PLURAL
1ST	I	we
2ND	you (sg)	you (pl)
3RD	he, she, it	they

In Greek, each person and number (six in all) has a different ending which identifies the subject of the verb. Typically, the verb will agree with the subject of the sentence in both person and number. This agreement is known as ***concord***. For example, in the sentence "the Lord himself will descend" (1 Thess 4:16), both the verb (καταβήσεται) and the subject (ὁ κύριος) are third person singular. A *he*-subject requires a *he*-verb. Occasionally, however, there is ***discord*** when the subject and the verb do not formally agree in person and number.[5]

In the next chapter, you will begin learning the regular endings of Greek verbs.

---

[5] In the Greek New Testament, there are three common examples of discord where a grammatical or conceptual *plural subject* takes a *singular verb*. These can occur when the subject is (1) Neuter Plural: "test the **spirits** (τὰ πνεύματα, pl) if **they are** (ἐστιν, sg) from God" (1 John 4:1). Neuter plural nouns frequently take third person singular ("he"/"it") verbs in Koine Greek, but they can also appear with third person plural ("they") verbs. The observation that neuter plural subjects frequently take singular verbs is sometimes called "The Animals Run (τὰ ζῷα τρέχει) Rule," because that short sentence (in Greek) illustrates the pattern, with τὰ ζῷα ("the animals") being a neuter plural subject but τρέχει ("it runs") being a third person singular verb. (2) A Compound Subject: "**Jesus** and his **disciples** (2 subjects) **entered** (ἐξῆλθεν, sg) into the villages" (Mark 8:27). Normally, a Greek compound subject takes a plural verb, but not always. A compound subject with a singular verb is sometimes called a "Pindaric construction," after the ancient Greek author Pindar (517–438 BC), who employed it frequently in his poems. (3) A Collective Noun: "And a large **crowd** (ὄχλος, sg) **was following** (ἠκολούθει, sg) him" (John 6:2). Note that here the noun, while referring to a plural concept, is singular. The noun *does*, in fact, agree grammatically with the verb. English behaves the same with collective nouns. Occasionally, a singular Greek collective noun will take a plural verb—an example of a *constructio ad sensum*, "a construction according to sense." English speakers do the same thing, for example, in referring back to a crowd (sg) with a plural verb: "The crowd . . . they were coming up the hill."

4.4 Voice

The *voice* of a verb indicates the way in which the subject relates to the action or state expressed by the verb. There are three voices in Greek:

Active: The subject performs the action.
Middle: The subject both performs and is affected by the action.
Passive: The subject receives the action.

Active Voice

In the *active voice*, the subject performs the action ("I see a tree"). Verbs can be either transitive or intransitive. *Transitive* verbs are those that can take a direct object. If someone states, "I see," the listener will naturally want to know what it is that the person saw. The direct object, then, complements (or completes) the verb (e.g., "I see *a tree*"). *Intransitive* verbs do not take direct objects to complete their meaning (e.g., "I am walking"). Active verbs will often have direct objects, unless they are intransitive (or stative) verbs.

Middle Voice

In the *middle voice*, the subject both performs the action and is in some way affected by the action. Because there is no exact parallel in English, beginning Greek students often struggle with the middle voice. Many learn to translate the middle voice as a *reflexive* idea ("I see myself"), but the reflexive meaning is actually quite rare for the Greek middle voice. More common is *special interest* ("I see for myself"), but often an explicit special interest translation is misleading as well.

Many verbs that have active forms can also have middle forms. For example, "we ask" can be either αἰτῶμεν (active) or αἰτώμεθα (middle). Some verbs, however, have *no* active form. Many older grammars refer to these as *deponent* verbs. The word "deponent" comes from the Latin verb *deponō*, which means "I set aside." Deponency, then, is the idea that all verbs began with an active form, but that some verbs became defective and laid aside their active form. Consequently, it is thought that deponent verbs are middle (or passive) in form but are active in meaning. Recent Greek scholarship favors laying aside the category of deponency itself. The majority of Greek scholars contend that we should understand the middle voice as the ancient Greeks did rather than fitting it into our English language (or Latin language) categories.

So-called deponent verbs are better viewed as *middle-only* verbs. That is, some verbs have no active voice because, to ancient Greeks, the activity these verbs describe was inherently "subject affected" in a way that demanded they be marked by middle voice endings. Passive voice endings (see below) frequently convey a middle voice idea in the Koine period. One way to distinguish middle-only verbs is to note that their lexical forms (i.e., dictionary forms which are typically first person singular forms) end with –ομαι instead of –ω (see, e.g., ἀποκρίνομαι, γίνομαι, ἔρχομαι, or πορεύομαι). The following sampling of categories demonstrates the wide usage of the middle voice.[6]

- **Reciprocity:** A verb of reciprocity is "where two parties are involved and where the removal of one party would render the verb meaningless." Such verbs are commonly middle only (δέχομαι, "I take, receive, welcome"; ἀποκρίνομαι, "I answer, reply").

- **Movement:** Verbs of movement, in which the subject is both acting and immediately affected by the action, are often middle only (ἔρχομαι, "I come, go"; πορεύομαι, "I go, travel").

- **Self-Involvement:** Verbs of thinking (intellectual activities), feeling (emotional states), and deciding (volitional activities) are frequently middle-only (λογίζομαι, "I consider, reckon"; βούλομαι, "I wish, want, desire").

- **Passivity:** Verbs in which the subject is passive in the sense that he or she does not choose or cannot refuse to be the subject of the action (γίνομαι, "I am," "I become"; κοιμάομαι, "I fall asleep," "I die"; μαίνομαι, "I am insane").

Passive Voice

In the *passive voice*, the subject does not perform the action but receives the action ("I was seen [by someone else]"). In this sense, then, the subject is passive and the one performing the action (i.e., the *agent*) is either implied or referenced typically by using a prepositional phrase. For example, when Paul states, "we ourselves are comforted by God" (2 Cor 1:4 ESV), the subject "we" is not performing an action but is passive because something is happening to them (God is comforting them). The one performing the act is God, but grammatically he is not the subject of the sentence since the agent of the action is given in a prepositional phrase ("by God").

Occasionally, the passive voice is used with no agent mentioned. For example, in the Sermon on the Mount, Jesus teaches that "those who mourn" are "blessed" since "they will be comforted" (Matt 5:4). It is understood that those who mourn will be comforted *by God*. When God is the implied agent of a passive verb, it is called a "divine passive." If the sentence were in the active voice, it would state, "God will comfort them."

4.5 Mood

The *mood* of a verb indicates an author's understanding of the verbal action's relation to reality—that is, whether the author views the event as factual, possible, desired, commanded, contingent, etc. There are four moods in Greek:

---

[6] Both the categories and quoted material come from Neva F. Miller, "Appendix 2: A Theory of Deponent Verbs," in *Analytical Lexicon of the Greek New Testament*, ed. Timothy Friberg, Barbara Friberg, and Neva F. Miller (Grand Rapids: Baker, 2000), 427–29.

- The ***indicative mood*** represents something as certain or asserted ("He went fishing" or "Will he go fishing?"). Statements in the indicative mood do not necessarily indicate an objective fact. By using the indicative mood, the author or speaker is choosing to present his speech as factual, at least for consideration. Consequently, it is possible for someone to lie (see Acts 6:13) or be mistaken (see Luke 7:39) while using the indicative mood.

- The ***subjunctive mood*** represents something as probable, contingent, or indefinite ("He might go fishing" or "Whenever he goes fishing").

- The ***optative mood*** represents something as possible or hoped for ("I wish he would go fishing").

- The ***imperative mood*** represents something as requested or commanded ("Go fishing" or "Please, go fishing").

Although participles and infinitives are not technically "moods" since they are dependent on main verbs, for purposes of convenience they will be labeled as such when parsed (i.e., when describing all the grammatical elements of a verb).

4.6 Tense and Aspect

New Testament Greek has six ***tenses***: present, future, imperfect, aorist, perfect, and pluperfect.[7] The following are examples in the active voice and indicative mood.

Present	λύω	"I am loosing" or "I loose"
Imperfect	ἔλυον	"I was loosing"
Future	λύσω	"I will loose"
Aorist	ἔλυσα	"I loosed"
Perfect	λέλυκα	"I have loosed"
Pluperfect	ἐλελύκειν	"I had loosed"

Only in the indicative mood is there any inherent element of time communicated by the verbal form; even then, it is a secondary element of meaning. Beyond the inherent lexical meaning of the verb, the primary element of meaning communicated by both indicative and non-indicative verbal forms is something called verbal aspect.

Verbal Aspect is the subjective perspective or viewpoint from which an author communicates the action of a verb. Because time is relevant only in the indicative mood, in Greek, verbal aspect is the more dominant force of the verb's tense. In English (a time-focused language), the word "tense" is essentially synonymous with time. For that reason, we are tempted to refer to Greek "tense-forms" rather than "tenses"—to remind you that time is a secondary element in the indicative verbal forms and completely contextually determined in non-indicative forms. Yet, conforming to centuries of standard usage, we will usually use the label "tense" by

---

[7] These are sometimes referred to as ***tense-forms*** since tense (or "time") is not always conveyed by the form of the verb.

itself.[8] But, please remember that Greek verbs primarily communicate the author's portrayal of an action. Greek is an "aspect prominent" language, unlike English, which is more "time prominent."

Most scholars agree that there are three aspects in New Testament Greek.

- **Imperfective Aspect** (present and imperfect tenses): the author depicts the action as ongoing or in process, without attention to the action's beginning or ending. Depending on the context, the action might be depicted as incomplete ("was or is happening"), inceptive ("started to happen"), durative ("continues to happen"), or some other kind of process. One scholar has called the imperfective aspect the "progressive perspective" of the author.[9]

- **Perfective Aspect** (aorist tense): the author depicts the action as complete or as a whole. The beginning and ending of the action (and everything in-between) are included in the depiction of the action. The perfective aspect describes a given action simply as occurring or as having occurred without indicating how the action took place ("it happened"). The perfective aspect has been called the "wholistic perspective" of the author. Greek grammarians debate whether the future tense presents action with perfective aspect or is aspectually non-specific. We are inclined to think the future tense should also be understood as conveying perfective aspect.

- **Stative Aspect** (perfect and pluperfect tenses): the author depicts a state of affairs or ongoing relevance resulting from a previous action or state ("it has happened, and it is relevant to the present context"). Depending on the context, there can be more emphasis on the completion of the action or its ongoing relevance. This aspect has also been called the "combinative aspect" because it often combines elements of ongoing (imperfective) relevance with a wholly (perfective) completed past action.

In the indicative mood, tenses include both the time of action *and* the author's perspective on the action (aspect), but the author's perspective (aspect) is primary. In non-indicative mood verbs, however, time drops out with only the aspect remaining. With non-indicative mood verbs, time is communicated by the literary context.

4.7 Morphology

As mentioned in chapter 2, Greek is a highly inflected language that makes changes to words through various morphemes. It is important, therefore, to analyze these morphemes, including a word's stem and various *affixes* (i.e., prefixes, infixes, and

---

[8] In fact, ancient Greek grammarians referred to their tenses as χρόνοι (times!).
[9] Robert E. Picirilli, "The Meaning of the Tenses in New Testament Greek: Where Are We?" *Journal of the Evangelical Theological Society* 48 (September 2005): 533–55.

suffixes). The **stem** is the word's uninflected part to which affixes may be added and carries its basic (lexical) meaning. A **prefix** is a morpheme that is added in front of the stem; an **infix** is placed in between the stem and the suffix; and the **suffix** is placed at the end of the word.

The **connecting vowel** (or variable/theme vowel) is an example of a verbal infix, and the **personal ending** is an example of a suffix.[10] The personal ending identifies the built-in subject of the verb, specifying both the person and number (e.g., –ομεν = "we").

λύετε	λυ + ε + τε
	stem + connecting vowel + personal ending
ἐλάβομεν	ε + λαβ + ο + μεν
	prefix + stem + connecting vowel + personal ending

4.8 The Present Indicative of εἰμί

The verb εἰμί is common, so it will be helpful to learn this verb first.[11] The difficulty with this verb is that it is somewhat irregular, similar to the verb "to be" in English (I am, you are, he is, we are, you are, they are). Learn this paradigm well![12] Please note that the subject information is included within the verb form itself. For example, it is not necessary to explicitly include a "he" (αὐτός) in the sentence. The verb ἐστίν, by itself, is translated "he/she/it is."[13] If an explicit subject is present in Greek, however, the translator should not provide an additional "he/she/it" for the verb. χριστὸς ἐστίν is translated "Christ is," not "Christ, he is."

PRESENT INDICATIVE—εἰμί[14]				
	SINGULAR		PLURAL	
1ST	εἰμί	I am	ἐσμέν	we are
2ND	εἶ	you are	ἐστέ	you are
3RD	ἐστίν	he/she/it is	εἰσίν	they are

Because εἰμί is a **copulative** or **equative verb**, it does not take a direct object (which would typically be in the accusative case); it takes a predicate nominative.[15]

---

[10] The connecting vowel merely helps with pronunciation.

[11] The verb εἰμί occurs 2,462 times in the New Testament. Thirty-six percent (897 occurrences) are the third person singular form (ἐστίν).

[12] Remember, a paradigm is a pattern (chart) that has similar qualities to other words. Also note that verbs conjugate whereas nouns decline. Thus, we can speak of a verb's conjugation but a noun's declension.

[13] Nevertheless, there does seem to be a strong stylistic pattern in Koine Greek to include explicit subject pronouns with the verb εἰμί without any additional emphasis or contrast intended.

[14] To hear a mnemonic song, go to bit.ly/bibletobesong or beginninggreek.com.

[15] The verbs γίνομαι and ὑπάρχω can also function as copulative verbs.

A *predicate nominative* is another nominative form that predicates (asserts/claims) something about the other nominative form (subject nominative) in the sentence. As a result, in a sentence that includes εἰμί, there will often be two nouns in the nominative case: the subject (nominative) and the predicate nominative. For example, in the sentence ὁ θεὸς ἀγάπη ἐστίν ("God is love"; 1 John 4:8), the subject is ὁ θεός, and the predicate nominative is ἀγάπη (both in the nominative case). Sometimes the verb εἰμί is not expressed but is implied: πιστὸς ὁ θεός ("God *is* faithful"; 1 Cor 1:9). Finally, the subject of the verb may be impersonal: οὐκ ἔστιν θέλημα ἔμπροσθεν τοῦ πατρὸς ὑμῶν ("*it is* not the will of your Father"; Matt 18:14).

In Koine Greek literature, the nu (ν) for the third personal singular (ἐστίν) and plural (εἰσίν) endings is sometimes missing. This is known as a *movable nu*. Most of the time, however, the nu is present. This is especially true for the third person forms of εἰμί in the New Testament. For example, the verb εἰμί occurs almost 900 times in the present active indicative third singular (ἐστίν), and the movable nu is only missing once. Additionally, the third person plural form (εἰσίν) occurs more than 150 times; every time it occurs, the movable nu is present.

Because εἰμί expresses a state (and not an action), it technically is a stative verb (referring to a state of existence) rather than having an active, middle, or passive voice. Yet, we can also observe that εἰμί follows active voice *endings* in the present and imperfect tenses, but middle voice *endings* in the future tense.

4.9 Practice

A. Paradigms: Memorize the present active indicative paradigm of εἰμί (see section 4.8). (Learn to sing it if possible.) Write out the paradigm ten times from memory. Include the English meanings.

B. Person and Number: Choose the correct pronoun that would correspond to the description of the person and number.

1. _____ second person plural	A. I
2. _____ first person singular	B. you (sg)
3. _____ third person plural	C. he/she/it
4. _____ first person plural	D. we
5. _____ second person singular	E. you (pl)
6. _____ third person singular	F. they

C. Voice: Identify the highlighted verbs in the following sentences as active (A), middle (M), or passive (P). Middle voice will be nearly impossible to detect in English translation alone, so verbal forms that are middle in Greek have an asterisk (*).

1. _____ "Jesus **took** bread, **blessed** and **broke** it, **gave** it to the disciples" (Matt 26:26).

2. _____ "For he **chose*** us [for himself] in him" (Eph 1:4).

3. _____ "Now the Son of Man **is glorified**, and God **is glorified** in him" (John 13:31).

4. _____ "For they don't **wash*** their hands when they eat" (Matt 15:2).

5. _____ "John came **baptizing** in the wilderness and **proclaiming** a baptism of repentance for the forgiveness of sins" (Mark 1:4).

6. _____ "So then I **ask*** you not to be discouraged" (Eph 3:13).

7. _____ "Long ago God **spoke** to our ancestors by the prophets at different times and in different ways" (Heb 1:1).

8. _____ "Knowing that whatever good each one does . . . he will **receive*** this **back** from the Lord" (Eph 6:8).

9. _____ "In those days Jesus came from Nazareth in Galilee and **was baptized** in the Jordan by John" (Mark 1:9).

D. Aspect: Indicate whether the descriptions below best describe the Imperfective (I), Perfective (P), or Stative (S) aspect.

1. _____ The author depicts the action as complete or as a whole.

2. _____ The author depicts a state of affairs resulting from a previous action or state.

3. _____ The author depicts the action as in process.

4. _____ Is represented by the present or imperfect tense-form.

5. _____ Is represented by the aorist tense-form.

6. _____ Is represented by the perfect or pluperfect tense-form.

E. Translation: Translate the following sentences.

1. εἰμι ὁ ἄρτος (bread) τῆς ζωῆς (John 6:48).

2. βασιλεὺς (king, *nominative*) Ἰσραήλ (*genitive*) ἐστιν (Matt 27:42).

3. ναὸς (temple) θεοῦ ἐσμεν (2 Cor 6:16).

4. υἱὸς τοῦ θεοῦ εἰμι (John 10:36).

5. εἰμι ἡ ὁδὸς (way) καὶ ἡ ἀλήθεια καὶ ἡ ζωη (John 14:6).

6. ὁ θεὸς ἀγάπη ἐστίν (1 John 4:16).

7. εἰμι τὸ ἄλφα καὶ τὸ ὦ (Rev 1:8).

8. υἱὸς ἀνθρώπου ἐστίν (John 5:27).

9. ἐσμὲν τέκνα θεοῦ (Rom 8:16).

10. ἐστιν ὁ Χριστός; (John 7:26). [Remember, what looks like an English semicolon (;) represents a question mark in Greek.]

F. Translation: Translate the following sentences into Greek. Include breathing marks, but not accents.

1. The church is the temple of God.

2. The words of truth are of the Lord.

3. The heart of man is sin.

4. Heaven and earth are the glory of Jesus.

5. The sign of the kingdom of God is the gospel.

4.10 Vocabulary[16]

ἄγω	I lead, bring (*pedagogical*)
βλέπω	I see, look at
διδάσκω	I teach (*didactic*)
ἐγείρω	I raise up
κρίνω	I judge, condemn (*critic*)
μένω	I remain, abide, dwell (*remain*)
ὑπάγω	I go away, depart
δοῦλος, ὁ	slave (*doula*)
θάνατος, ὁ	death ("*Thanatopsis*," poem by William Cullen Bryant)
ψυχή, ἡ	soul, life, living being (*psychology*)
ὥρα, ἡ	hour
εἰ	if, whether
εἴτε	if, whether
καθώς	as, just as, even as
ὡς	as, like

---

[16] To hear an author of your textbook read through the vocabulary for chapter 4, go to bit.ly/greekvocab4 or beginninggreek.com.

Which Printed Greek New Testament Should I Buy?

Introducing Critical Texts of the Greek New Testament

Never has there been less need to purchase a Greek New Testament. There are many excellent, free online options which allow students to read the Greek New Testament from a smartphone, tablet, or computer. However, never has it been easier or cheaper to acquire a printed Greek New Testament. And there are many reasons to buy one—not the least of which is the joy of reading the biblical text without the constant temptation to digital distraction. Also, most people find that their memories of reading a printed Greek New Testament include an added spatial dimension. In other words, it has this added benefit: you may remember where on the physical page you read certain phrases, and as you flip back through your printed Greek New Testament, your memory of the placement of those words on the page helps you relocate a particular passage and further reinforces your memory.

If someone hands you a Greek New Testament, the first question you should ask is, "What text is this?" He or she might respond, "Well, it's the Greek New Testament, of course!" But, in actuality, there are many versions of the Greek New Testament, and you should be aware of the version you are reading. We will think more about text criticism later in this textbook (see pages 89–95), but for now, you need to realize that all the original manuscripts of the New Testament have been lost. We do not have the Gospel of John written in the apostle's handwriting. Instead, we have copies of copies, and copies of copies of copies. We have thousands of ancient handwritten Greek New Testament manuscripts (or portions of manuscripts) stretching from the early second century up until the sixteenth century, when the printing press began to be widely used in Europe.[1]

Evangelical New Testament scholars believe that God has faithfully preserved his Word, but most evangelicals believe he did not do so through specially protecting one

---

[1] There are even a few handwritten New Testament Greek manuscripts from the seventeenth century.

lineage of manuscripts. In other words, priority should not be given to manuscripts coming from a particular locale or tradition (e.g., preference to the Byzantine text tradition, as we find in the King James Only movement). It seems, rather, that God has preserved his Word through a multiplicity of ancient witnesses, traditions, and text families. Though these manuscripts agree in the majority of places, where they disagree, it is incumbent upon us to compare the manuscripts and consider their age, provenance, and the best explanation of the differences where they disagree. That is, we must seek to reconstruct the original apostolic wording through the practice of text criticism.

Depending on one's text-critical presuppositions, a student can reach slightly different conclusions—resulting also in different preferences for which printed Greek New Testament to buy. Below are the main options.

• **Nestle-Aland, 28th edition** (Also known as NA28). The majority of New Testament scholars, whether evangelical or non-evangelical, consider the most recent Nestle-Aland (or United Bible Societies) edition of the Greek New Testament to be the most reliable. The text is overseen by an international committee of scholars from the *Institut für Neutestamentliche Textforschung* (INTF),[2]

based in Münster, Germany. The actual Greek words of the Nestle-Aland edition and the United Bible Societies edition are the same, but they differ in some small ways—such as punctuation, formatting, and most significantly, in the choice and presentation of textual variants (that is, variant spelling or wording present in the ancient manuscripts).

The NA28 employs about a dozen "critical signs" (e.g., small circles, squares, squiggly lines) that are inserted within the Greek text to inform the reader of differences in the manuscript tradition. An apparatus at the bottom of the page gives more details. Significant variants that are contenders for the original wording are always included. But, many noted variants are simply included as a matter of scholarly interest. The quantity and content of ancient manuscripts listed in the apparatus gives indication of whether a variant is significant or not, but the reader must have some familiarity with this material to assess it properly.

At the time of this book's publication, the Nestle-Aland 28th edition (first published in 2012) is the most recent NA edition, though a 29th edition is anticipated in 2021 or 2022. It is expected to have revisions in Acts and Mark, as the detailed work of the *Editio Critica Maior* (see below) is gradually incorporated into the NA and UBS editions. The NA28 can be

---

[2] Also known by English speakers as the Institute for New Testament Textual Research, founded by Kurt Aland in 1959.

viewed free online (www.nestle-al-and.com/en/read-na28-online/), but the online version does not include critical signs within the Greek text, nor the textual apparatus.

• **United Bible Societies, 5th edition**—Like the Nestle-Aland edition (see above), the text of the UBS5 is considered a scholarly standard, based on many decades of international committee work. Hundreds of years of New Testament textual study lie behind the more formal formation and oversight of the *Institut für Neutestamentliche Textforschung* (INTF), based in Münster, Germany. The main difference between the UBS and NA editions is in the presentation of textual variants. The UBS edition focuses on variants that are either (1) more significant contenders for the original wording and/or (2) those that genuinely affect meaning and translation. As a result, far fewer variants are included in the textual apparatus at the bottom of the pages. Perhaps only one or two variants are listed per page, but a great amount of textual evidence is presented for these few variants. Also, variants are graded with a letter grade (i.e., A, B, C, or D) based on the editorial committee's certainty of reconstructing the original wording of the Greek New Testament.

Though it needs to be updated, the *Textual Commentary on the Greek*

New Testament, 2nd ed. by Bruce Metzger (based on the 4th UBS edition), provides an invaluable discussion of the editorial committee's reasoning on every variant listed in the UBS.[3] Any serious student of the Greek New Testament should own either a NA or UBS, perhaps in a reader's edition format (see below).

• **Tyndale House Edition**—The Tyndale House evangelical study center at Cambridge University published an alternate eclectic critical text of the Greek New Testament in 2017.[4] The text is also referred to with the abbreviation THGNT. A helpful introduction to and defense of the edition appeared in 2019 as *An Introduction to the Greek New Testament Produced at Tyndale House, Cambridge*, by Dirk Jongkind (Crossway). The Tyndale House edition seeks to reflect some of the earliest features of extant ancient manuscripts, including unusual spellings, the dominant early order of New Testament books (i.e., placing the General Epistles prior to the Pauline Epistles), and ancient methods of segmenting the text through *ekthesis* (extending the initial line of a paragraph into the margin, rather than indenting). The editors of the Tyndale House edition claim that the discovery of additional primary material (early papyri), improvements in the accuracy with which we can use early versions,

---

[3] See also Philip Comfort's helpful *Commentary on the Manuscripts and Text of the New Testament* (Grand Rapids: Kregel, 2015).
[4] See www.thegreeknewtestament.com.

and recent insights into scribal habits warrant a new critical edition of the Greek New Testament.[5] Every reading in the Tyndale House edition is represented by at least one Greek manuscript from the fifth century or earlier.[6] In an extensive blog post, Dirk Jongkind, the lead editor of this new edition, gives some sense of the differences between the Tyndale House and NA by comparing the book of Acts. He lists sixty-eight places where the texts differ.[7]

The Tyndale Greek New Testament is the *second* Greek New Testament you should buy (after the more widely-accepted standard NA or UBS, perhaps in reader's edition formats). The THGNT, in fact, has a very nice reader's edition aimed at students and pastors. To view a 20-minute video review of the Tyndale House edition by Rob Plummer, see https://vimeo.com/313496503.

• **Society of Biblical Literature (SBL) Greek New Testament**—Because it is freely available in digital format, many students use an SBL Greek New Testament for years without properly understanding its origin. The Society of Biblical Literature is a professional society of biblical scholars (of varied theological commitments), which has overseen the publication of this text (presented mainly in digital form). Michael Holmes, the editor of the SBL Greek New Testament, adjudicated between four previously published eclectic texts[8] to arrive at the wording of his text, which differs from the NA28/UBS5 in about 540 places. At a practical level, the SBL Greek New Testament provides a close approximation to the NA/UBS text that can be legally distributed for free. Thus, for example, if you are viewing the Greek New Testament on the Biblearc app, you are probably viewing the SBL Greek New Testament. A printed edition is available, but we do not recommend it for purchase.

• **Zondervan ("Goodrich and Lukaszewski") Greek New Testament**—If you purchase a reader's edition (see below) of the Greek New Testament published by Zondervan, the Greek text you will find inside is the one that "underlies the New International Version." In other words, the Committee on Bible Translation (CBT), which oversees the New International Version (NIV), made decisions about textual variants in the process of translation. Those cumulative decisions created, in essence, an underlying Greek New Testament, published in edited form by Richard J. Goodrich and Albert L.

---

[5] Wording taken from the Tyndale House edition website: www.thegreeknewtestament.com.
[6] A rule only violated in the Book of Revelation.
[7] See http://evangelicaltextualcriticism.blogspot.com/2018/08/the-text-of-acts-differences-between.html.
[8] Westcott and Hort (WH), Tregelles (Treg), Goodrich and Lukaszewski (NIV), and Robinson and Pierpont (RP).

Lukaszewski. On a practical level, this underlying Greek text is very close to the NA/UBS text—allowing Zondervan to publish it without copyright violations. There are, however, around 230 differences between the NA28/UBS5 and the Zondervan ("Goodrich and Lukaszewski") Greek New Testament.

• **Robinson-Pierpont Greek New Testament:** Republished recently as *The New Testament in the Original Greek: Byzantine Textform 2018*, the Robinson-Pierpont text provides a critical edition of the Byzantine textform. A small minority of scholars believe the Byzantine text tradition provides the most reliable transmission of the Greek New Testament manuscripts, and a defense of that view by Maurice Robinson can be read online.[9] The Byzantine text tradition underlies the King James Version, so a commitment to Byzantine text priority is usually part of the King James Only movement. Nevertheless, not every scholar favoring the Byzantine text tradition is a proponent of King James-onlyism. For a helpful response to KJV-only claims, see James R. White, *The King James Only Controversy: Can You Trust the Modern Translations?* 2nd ed. (Bethany House, 2009).

• *Editio Critica Maior:* The *Editio Critica Maior (ECM)* is a multivolume, in-process, critical scholarly edition of the Greek New Testament. Because of the detail and price of this work, most students will only view it in a library. The *ECM* provides a comprehensive, computer-based analysis of all significant text variations within the first thousand years of the Greek New Testament's transmission and is overseen by the *Institut für Neutestamentliche Textforschung* (INTF), in Münster, Germany.

The INTF is gradually incorporating the published decisions of the *ECM* into new revisions of the NA/UBS. The NA28/UBS5, for example, reflects the *ECM* text of the General Epistles (James–Jude), differing in thirty-four places from the NA27/UBS4. The NA29/UBS6 (forthcoming in 2021 or 2022) is expected to incorporate *ECM*-based revisions in the Book of Acts[10] and Gospel of Mark. The entire *ECM* project is slated to be completed by 2030.

In addition to deciding which Greek text to buy, one must make a decision about formatting preferences. The main choices are (1) regular text, (2) reader's edition, and (3) interlinear. We do not recommend an interlinear version because, in the long run, it will hamper your reading of the actual Greek text by causing you to glance too readily at the English. A reader's edition provides rare vocabulary at the bottom of the page; many students thus find this to be a good choice. After all, it can be discouraging to constantly stop

---

[9] See www.reltech.org/TC/v06/Robinson2001.html.
[10] There are fifty-two differences between the ECM and the NA28 in the Book of Acts.

and look up rare vocabulary. A regular text edition can also be a good option—usually providing more extensive text critical information, supplementary apparatuses, and introductory essays (in comparison with a reader's version). If you buy a regular text version of the Greek New Testament and are struggling with rare vocabulary, you can always use a digital resource (such as Biblearc) for vocabulary assistance. A printed reader's lexicon[11] can help speed you along as well.

Optional Assignment 1: Write a one-paragraph essay explaining which printed edition of the Greek New Testament you would purchase and why. Provide an online link to your preferred edition. Compare and contrast the version you want with other versions of the Greek New Testament.

Optional Assignment 2: In a one-paragraph essay, outline the benefits and risks of reading *only* a digital copy of the Greek New Testament. Then explain why you are not going to buy a printed Greek New Testament at this time.

---

[11] We recommend Michael H. Burer and Jeffrey E. Miller, *A New Reader's Lexicon of the Greek New Testament* (Grand Rapids: Kregel, 2008). This resource provides rare vocabulary of the Greek New Testament, verse by verse, in canonical order. See also Christopher J. Fresch, *A Book-by-Book Guide to New Testament Greek Vocabulary* (Peabody, MA: Hendrickson, 2019).

//////////////////

CHAPTER 5

PRESENT INDICATIVE VERBS

5.1 Overview[1]

In the last chapter, we offered an overview of the Greek verbal system and introduced the present tense paradigm of the verb εἰμί ("I am"). This irregular verb was
prioritized because of its frequent usage in the New Testament. In this chapter,
you will learn the paradigms of the regular verbs for the present active and present
middle/passive indicative verbs.

5.2 Significance

If you read through the Gospels in Greek, you will soon notice that the aorist tense
is the default tense for historical narrative. In Matt 8:3, for example, we read, "And
Jesus stretched out his hand and touched (ἥψατο, aorist tense) [the leper], saying,
'I will; be clean.' And immediately his leprosy was cleansed (ἐκαθαρίσθη, aorist
tense)" (ESV). The aorist tense is the normal way of saying, "This happened . . .
then that happened." But, as you continue reading the Gospels, especially Mark
and John, you will regularly run into present tense verbs in the narrative. If you
look at English Bible translations, these Greek present tense verbs are invariably
rendered with an English past tense verb. (Otherwise, the English translations
would sound too strange!) Why did these ancient authors repeatedly employ the
present tense during the reporting of past events? Are we missing any nuances by
simply labeling these Greek present tense verbs as "historical presents" or "narrative presents" and then translating them with English past tense forms?

   The use of the narrative or historical present is certainly not limited to the New
Testament, and recent scholarship continues to shed more light on its use in the

---

[1] For an overview video lecture of chapter 5, go to bit.ly/greeklecture5 or beginninggreek.com.

Koine period. For example, ancient authors frequently employed the narrative present with verbs of speaking and movement. Also, present tense verbs in narratives often indicate a shift in location or the introduction of a new person into the story. So, to employ more technical linguistic terminology, we see the present tense performing a discourse function within historical narrative. That is, authors employed the present tense in historical narratives to help divide up the text—in much the same way we might use subheadings and indentations to help "chunk" our writing into more manageable units.[2]

Following is the Greek text of Mark 1:37–38, with narrative present tense verbs (in bold font in Greek and English) translated literalistically into English present tense verbs:

> καὶ εὗρον αὐτὸν καὶ **λέγουσιν** αὐτῷ ὅτι πάντες ζητοῦσίν σε. καὶ **λέγει** αὐτοῖς· ἄγωμεν ἀλλαχοῦ εἰς τὰς ἐχομένας κωμοπόλεις, ἵνα καὶ ἐκεῖ κηρύξω· εἰς τοῦτο γὰρ ἐξῆλθον.

> And they found him and **they are saying** to him, "Everyone is seeking you." And **he is saying** to them, "Let us go elsewhere—to the surrounding villages so that also there I may preach. For this [reason] I came forth."

It would be a mistake to translate the Greek text literalistically (as above) because Mark is not using the present tense to indicate that the time frame suddenly switches to the present. Rather, he is conforming to a standard ancient method of segmenting his narrative. Unless you are reading the New Testament in Greek, these subtle authorial indications of narrative structure are inaccessible to you.

5.3 Tense-Form and Meaning

The present tense in the indicative mood communicates both the *time of action* (typically present or non-past time) and *aspect* (the author depicts the action in process, without attention to the beginning or conclusion). *Aspect* is a linguistic term that refers to the way an author or speaker chooses to present an action. Undoubtedly, Koine Greek is a language that prioritizes the communication of aspect, with time having a lesser place—and then only in the indicative mood. The present tense-form alone does not necessarily communicate that the action is actually in progress. One must look at two other factors: (1) the inherent procedural nature of the activity described by the verb. Is the action described by the verb durative (ongoing, e.g., "walking"), punctiliar (completed in a moment, e.g., "fall"), stative (referring to an ongoing state, e.g., "standing"), etc.? and (2) context. Context is the most important factor for determining authorial nuance in the choice of the present tense. Here is a sampling of common ways the present tense is used in the Greek New Testament.

---

[2] Steve Runge regularly speaks of "chunking" the text. See his helpful chapter on the historical present in *Discourse Grammar of the Greek New Testament: A Practical Introduction for Teaching and Exegesis* (Peabody, MA: Hendrickson, 2010), 125–43.

- **Progressive Present:** Expresses an action in progress: "all **are looking** for you," πάντες ζητοῦσίν σε (Mark 1:37).

- **Iterative Present:** Describes an action performed repeatedly or regularly or a state that is ongoing: "Everyone who abides in him **does** not **continue in sin**," πᾶς ὁ ἐν αὐτῷ μένων οὐχ **ἁμαρτάνει** (1 John 3:6).

- **Historical Present** or **Narrative Present:** Used in historical narratives to describe a past event, often with verbs of speaking or motion, and possibly indicating to the reader that there is a change in location or the introduction of new person(s) at this point in the narrative. The present form is translated as a past tense verb in English: "and **they came** to him bringing a paralytic," καὶ **ἔρχονται** φέροντες πρὸς αὐτὸν παραλυτικὸν (Mark 2:3).

5.4 Voice

As discussed in the previous lesson, the Greek verbal system has three voices.

Active: The subject performs the action.
Middle: The subject performs the action and is also affected by the action.
Passive: The subject receives the action.

Verbs with lexical forms ending with –ω can add endings that communicate active, middle, or passive involvement of the verb's subject. If the endings of a verb follow the endings found in the λύω paradigm (–ω, –εις, –ει, –ομεν, –ετε, –ουσιν), then it is active. But if it follows the endings found in the λύομαι paradigm (–ομαι, –η, –εται, –ομεθα, –εσθε, –ονται), it is either middle or passive (and only context can decide). In contrast, verbs with lexical forms that end with –ομαι can be only middle in meaning, though they may follow middle *or* passive endings. Middle and passive endings are the same, however, for present tense verbs.

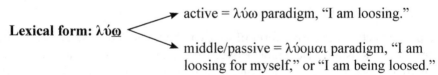

Lexical form: λύω
active = λύω paradigm, "I am loosing."
middle/passive = λύομαι paradigm, "I am loosing for myself," or "I am being loosed."

Lexical form: πορεύομαι   middle meaning only, "I am going."

5.5 Mood

The *mood* of a verb indicates the author's attitude toward an event (i.e., its actuality or potentiality). That is, the author indicates that the action is actually taking place (indicative mood), or that the action might happen (subjunctive), or that he is commanding the action (imperative). The indicative mood is the most common mood used in the New Testament and is the one we will seek to master first. In choosing the indicative mood, the author is asserting something as a factual statement or, depending on context, raising a question.

Indicative Statement: "You are the Christ" (σὺ εἶ ὁ Χριστὸς, Matt 16:16).
Indicative Question: "Are you the [Christ], the Son of the Blessed One?" (σὺ εἶ ὁ Χριστὸς ὁ υἱὸς τοῦ εὐλογητοῦ; Mark 14:61).

5.6 Paradigms

You should memorize the forms given in this section. It is best to memorize forms down the columns (λύω, λύεις, λύει—λύομεν, λύετε, λύουσιν). Be sure to know both the form *and* the meaning of the form.

PRESENT ACTIVE INDICATIVE[3]				
	SINGULAR		PLURAL	
1ST	λύω	I am loosing	λύομεν	we are loosing
2ND	λύεις	you are loosing	λύετε	you are loosing
3RD	λύει	he/she/it is loosing	λύουσι(ν)	they are loosing

PRESENT MIDDLE/PASSIVE INDICATIVE[4]				
	SINGULAR		PLURAL	
1ST	λύομαι	I am being loosed	λυόμεθα	we are being loosed
2ND	λύῃ	you are being loosed	λύεσθε	you are being loosed
3RD	λύεται	he/she/it is being loosed	λύονται	they are being loosed

5.7 Morphology

Present Active Indicative

The present active indicative form of λύω can be translated "I loose" or, perhaps better, "I am loosing." Deciding between these options will usually depend on the particular verb you are translating as well as the context in which the verb is found. Here is a more precise breakdown of the component parts (morphemes) of the various forms.

---

[3] To hear a mnemonic song, go to bit.ly/activeindicative or beginninggreek.com.
[4] Only the passive meaning is included in the paradigm. The middle forms could be translated this way: I loose [for] myself; you (sg) loose [for] yourself; he looses [for] himself; we loose [for] ourselves; you (pl) loose [for] yourselves; and they loose [for] themselves. To hear a mnemonic device, go to bit.ly/greekprespass or beginninggreek.com.

Inflected Form	Stem[5]	Connecting Vowel	Personal Ending		Combined Ending[6]
λύω	λυ	[o]	ω[7]	→	ω
λύεις	λυ	ε	ις[8]	→	εις
λύει	λυ	ε	ι[9]	→	ει
λύομεν	λυ	ο	μεν	→	ομεν
λύετε	λυ	ε	τε	→	ετε
λύουσιν	λυ	ο	νσι[10]	→	ουσι(ν)

For our purposes, it is easiest to memorize the combined endings. Knowing the original connecting vowels and personal endings, however, will prove helpful in learning other forms that will be introduced later. The connecting vowel is omicron (o) before mu (μ) or nu (ν) and epsilon (ε) before other letters. Additionally, because the connecting vowels in the subjunctive mood will lengthen (o→ω, ε→η), it helps to be aware of the dissected components of a verb. For example, in Rom 5:1 Paul affirms, "since we have been justified by faith, *we have* peace with God." Although there is a textual variant here, most English versions opt for the indicative mood (ἔχομεν = "we have"). There are, however, several significant manuscripts that have the subjunctive form (ἔχωμεν = "let us have"). The only difference is the lengthening of the connecting vowel. Very likely, omicron and omega were pronounced the same way in the Koine Greek period, and it would be easy for a scribe to interchange them by an accident of hearing or spelling.

The third person plural form of the present active indicative has a movable nu (ν). That is, sometimes the nu is absent but most of the time it is present. Its absence or presence does not affect meaning. Greeks apparently included it for euphonic reasons. (That is, they thought it sounded good!)

---

[5] The present tense stem is determined by removing the –ω or the –ομαι from the lexical (dictionary) form (e.g., βλέπω → βλέπ and ἔρχομαι → ἔρχ). The actual root of the verb may or may not overlap with the present tense stem. Many times, a verb's true historical root shows up more clearly in the aorist form. Regarding morphological comments made concerning this chart, see William D. Mounce, *Basics of Biblical Greek: Grammar*, 4th ed. (Grand Rapids: Zondervan, 2019), 163.

[6] The combined ending includes the connecting vowel and the personal ending.

[7] Technically, the connecting vowel is omicron (o) which then lengthens to an omega (ω) to compensate for the lack of a personal ending. For simplicity, we will view ω as the personal ending.

[8] The actual personal ending is σι but the two letters switched order (ις).

[9] The actual personal ending is τι but the tau (τ) dropped out (cf. ἐστίν).

[10] The actual personal ending is νσι but the nu (ν) dropped out because of the following sigma (σ) causing the omicron to lengthen to ου to compensate. Also note that the form will usually take the movable nu.

Present Middle/Passive Indicative

Inflected Form	Stem	Connecting Vowel	Personal Ending		Combined Ending
λύομαι	λυ	ο	μαι	→	ομαι
λύῃ	λυ	[ε]	[σαι][11]	→	ῃ
λύεται	λυ	ε	ται	→	εται
λυόμεθα	λυ	ο	μεθα	→	ομεθα
λύεσθε	λυ	ε	σθε	→	εσθε
λύονται	λυ	ο	νται	→	ονται

Again, focus on memorizing the combined endings, though knowing the connecting vowel and personal endings will be helpful later.

The conjugation of other verbs can be obtained by placing the combined endings on their stems. For example, the conjugation of the present active indicative of ἔχω ("I have") is ἔχω, ἔχεις, ἔχει, ἔχομεν, ἔχετε, ἔχουσιν.

5.8 Parsing

Parsing a verb involves describing all the grammatical elements of a verb to determine its meaning. This involves identifying a verb's (1) lexical form, (2) tense, (3) voice, (4) mood, (5) person, and (6) number. Once this is done, an initial translation of the verb can be offered. Of course, a final translation is dependent on reading the verb within the broader context.

Lexical Form:	Dictionary form (1st person singular)
Tense:	Present [Imperfect, Future, Aorist, Perfect, Pluperfect]
Voice:	Active, Middle, Passive
Mood:	Indicative [Subjunctive, Imperative, Optative]
Person:	1st (I, we), 2nd (you [sg, pl]), or 3rd [he/she/it, they])
Number:	Singular or Plural

Here are a few examples of how to parse a verb:

Inflected Form	Lexical Form	Tense	Voice	Mood	Person	Number	Translation
λύουσιν	λύω	pres	act	ind	3rd	pl	"they are loosing"
πορεύῃ	πορεύομαι	pres	mid	ind	2nd	sg	"you are going"
ἔχομεν	ἔχω	pres	act	ind	1st	pl	"we have"

---

[11] Technically, the connecting vowel is epsilon (ε) and the personal ending is σαι. When a sigma is forced between two vowels because of the addition of the connecting vowel, it drops—causing the epsilon and the alpha (α) to lengthen to an eta (η) and the iota (ι) to subscript (ῃ): ε + σαι → εσαι → εαι → ηι → ῃ. See Mounce, *Basics of Biblical Greek*, 184–85.

5.9 Practice

A. Paradigms: Memorize the present active and middle/passive paradigms of λύω (see section 5.6). Then write out each paradigm ten times from memory.

B. Parsing: Parse the following verbs.

1. ἀκούεις

2. πιστεύουσιν

3. ἔρχονται

4. βλέπετε

5. ἐγείρεται

6. λέγει

7. ἀποκρίνῃ

8. μένομεν

9. κρίνομαι

10. ἄγεσθε

C. Translation: Translate the following sentences. Be sure to start with the verb. Then find the subject and then the object—if there is one.

1. βλέπω τοὺς ἀνθρώπους (Mark 8:24).

2. ἄγουσιν τὸν Ἰησοῦν (John 18:28).

3. πορεύομαι εἰς (into) Ἰερουσαλήμ (Acts 20:22).

4. ὁ δὲ Ἰησοῦς ἀποκρίνεται αὐτοῖς (them) (John 12:23).

5. γινώσκετε τὴν χάριν (grace) τοῦ κυρίου ἡμῶν (our) Ἰησοῦ Χριστοῦ (2 Cor 8:9).

6. ἐξουσίαν (authority) ἔχει ὁ υἱὸς τοῦ ἀνθρώπου ἐπὶ (on) τῆς γῆς (Matt 9:6).

7. δόξαν παρὰ (from) ἀνθρώπων οὐ (not) λαμβάνω (John 5:41).

8. ὁ υἱὸς τοῦ ἀνθρώπου ὑπάγει καθὼς γέγραπται (it is written) (Matt 26:24).

9. τί (why?) κρίνεις τὸν ἀδελφόν σου (your); (Rom 14:10).

10. πιστεύεις ὅτι εἷς (one) ἐστιν ὁ θεός (Jas 2:19).

11. ἀλλὰ ἔρχεται ὥρα καὶ νῦν (now) ἐστιν (John 4:23).

12. πῶς (how?) ἡ ἀγάπη τοῦ θεοῦ μένει ἐν (in) αὐτῷ (him); (1 John 3:17).

D. Translation: Translate the following sentences into Greek. Include breathing marks, but not accents.

1. The Lord of the world hears the voice.

2. The law judges the hearts of men.

3. The souls of men know the truth.

4. The slave is led to the Lord.

5. We are teaching the children.

5.10 Vocabulary[12]

βαπτίζω	I baptize, immerse, dip (*baptize*)
θεραπεύω	I heal (*therapeutic*)
κράζω	I cry out
ἄγγελος, ὁ	angel, messenger (*angel*)
μαθητής, ὁ	disciple, follower (*mathematics*)
ὄχλος, ὁ	crowd
προφήτης, ὁ	prophet (*prophet*)
γάρ	for, because
ἐκεῖ	there, in that place
κἀγώ	and I (καί + ἐγώ)[13]
οὖν	then, so, therefore
οὕτως	in this manner, thus, so
τέ	and, but
οὐ, οὐκ, οὐχ	no, not
οὐχί	no! (emphatic)

[12] To hear an author of your textbook read through the vocabulary for chapter 5, go to bit.ly/greekvocab5 or beginninggreek.com.

[13] The is called a *crasis*. That is, the merger of two words into one.

//////////////

CHAPTER 6

IMPERFECT INDICATIVE VERBS

6.1 Overview[1]

In the last chapter, we introduced present tense verbs (including active and middle/passive forms). In this one, we will move to our second tense: the imperfect. The *imperfect tense* describes a past action that was not completed or perfected; thus, in that sense it is imperfect. We will also consider the use of the particle οὐ ("not") in negating verbs.

6.2 Significance

Many years ago, when I (Rob) was a young assistant professor, my wife and I lived in a small house. Since there wasn't room for a study in that home, I always worked in my office at the seminary. The dean's secretary came to know of my regular presence on campus and soon began transferring to me many telephone calls from outsiders who randomly contacted the seminary to ask their theological questions. (I wish I had kept a record of those calls. They would make an interesting book!)

One day, I was chatting with a gentleman who was upset about a change in his favorite Bible translation. An updated version of this translation had come out, and it read differently from the text to which he was accustomed. As I recall, in the original translation, it reported that someone was doing something; in the updated version, it said they were "trying" to do something. The caller was quite upset by this, assuming that a Bible translation committee or publisher was changing the words of Scripture. I explained to him that in the Greek language, the imperfect tense (the tense you are learning in this chapter) can convey both the idea of doing something or trying to do something—depending on the context. So,

---

[1] For an overview video lecture of chapter 6, go to bit.ly/greeklecture6 or beginninggreek.com.

for example, in Gal 1:23, Paul reports that after his Damascus road conversion, the Judean churches heard this: "The man who formerly persecuted us is now preaching the faith he once tried to destroy" (NIV). The verb translated "tried to destroy" (ἐπόρθει) is in the imperfect tense; therefore, in other contexts, it could legitimately be translated "was destroying." The early church (reporting this particular news), however, clearly did not think Paul was successfully destroying the church—though he certainly was trying. The NIV translates this text well.

One reason you are learning Greek is to be able to answer questions about English Bible translations. You are becoming a source of accurate, peaceable, and wise information. There may come a day when you need to take a stand against a translational distortion of the Word of God, but in the meantime, you likely will have many conversations in which you can help others understand the complexity of Bible translation when needed.

6.3 Tense-Form and Meaning

The imperfect tense in the indicative mood communicates both the *time of action* (typically past time) and *imperfective aspect* (that is, the author depicts the action as ongoing or as a process). The action is being reported as unfolding without the beginning or ending of the action in the frame of reference. It is possible that the author intended his readers to understand the action of the verb to be in progress or repeated, but such information is communicated by a combination of the verbal aspect with other factors—the lexical meaning of the verb and the literary context. Here is a sampling of ways the imperfect tense is used in the Greek New Testament:

- **Progressive Imperfect:** Portrays an action or state in the past that is in progress from the perspective of the author: "and many rich **were putting in** much [money]," καὶ πολλοὶ πλούσιοι **ἔβαλλον** πολλα (Mark 12:41).

- **Inceptive Imperfect:** Emphasizes the beginning of an action or state. "Began" or "started" is usually added to the English translation: "he stood and **began to walk**," ἔστη καὶ **περιεπάτει** (Acts 3:8).

- **Iterative Imperfect:** Conveys repeated or customary action in the past. In English, the words "kept on," "repeatedly," or "continually" are often added: "And with many other words he solemnly testified and **kept on exhorting** them," ἑτέροις τε λόγοις πλείοσιν διεμαρτύρατο καὶ **παρεκάλει** αὐτοὺς (Acts 2:40).

As you learned in the previous chapter, Greek tenses can also serve a discourse function—helping segment or "chunk" the text for earlier readers/listeners. The aorist tense, which you have not learned yet, is the default tense of historical narrative—reporting that "This happened . . . then that happened . . . etc." The imperfect tense, on the other hand, is sometimes employed in narrative to step aside from the main flow of the story and give background information, descriptive detail, or "offline" information.[2] For example, in Mark 16:3, the evangelist employs the imperfect tense to inform readers of the conversation of the women as they walk to the tomb: "[The women] were saying (ἔλεγον, imperfect tense) to one another, 'Who will roll away the stone from the entrance to the tomb for us?'" This conversation, presented as an aside, helps us understand their astonishment to find the tomb already open when they arrive.

6.4 Voice

Verbs with lexical forms that end with –ω can be active, middle, or passive. If the ending of the "omega verb" follows the endings found in the ἔλυον paradigm (–ον, –ες, –εν, –ομεν, –ετε, –ον), then it is active. But if it follows the endings found in the ἐλυόμην paradigm (–ομην, –ου, –ετο, –ομεθα, –εσθε, –οντο), then it is either middle or passive. (Only context can decide). In contrast, verbs with lexical forms ending with –ομαι can be only middle in meaning.

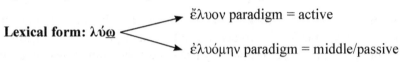

Lexical form: λύω → ἔλυον paradigm = active
→ ἐλυόμην paradigm = middle/passive

Lexical form: πορεύομαι ἐπορευόμην middle only

6.5 Paradigms

IMPERFECT ACTIVE INDICATIVE[3]				
	SINGULAR		PLURAL	
1ST	ἔλυον	I was loosing	ἐλύομεν	we were loosing
2ND	ἔλυες	you were loosing	ἐλύετε	you were loosing
3RD	ἔλυε(ν)	he/she/it was loosing	ἔλυον	they were loosing

IMPERFECT MIDDLE/PASSIVE INDICATIVE[4]				
	SINGULAR		PLURAL	
1ST	ἐλυόμην	I was being loosed	ἐλυόμεθα	we were being loosed
2ND	ἐλύου	you were being loosed	ἐλύεσθε	you were being loosed
3RD	ἐλύετο	he/she/it was being loosed	ἐλύοντο	they were being loosed

---

[2] Michael Todd Graham, Jr., "The Discourse Function of Koine Greek Verb Forms in Narrative: Testing Current Proposals in the Book of Judith" (PhD dissertation, The Southern Baptist Theological Seminary, May 2018), 133.

[3] To hear a mnemonic song, go to bit.ly/activeindicative or beginninggreek.com.

[4] Only the passive meaning is included in the paradigm. The middle forms could be translated like so: I was loosing [for] myself; you (sg) were loosing [for] yourself; he was loosing [for] himself; we were loosing [for] ourselves; you (pl) were loosing [for] yourselves; and they were loosing [for] themselves. For a mnemonic device, go to bit.ly/greekimpfpass.

6.6 Morphology

Augment

The epsilon prefix (ε–) on imperfect forms is called an ***augment***; it indicates that the verb's time of action occurs in the past. The augment is analogous to the "–ed" ending on English past tense verbs (slip → slipped; cook → cooked). When an augment is added to the verb, if the verbal stem begins with a consonant, then the epsilon is simply added with no change.[5] If, however, the first letter of the stem begins with a vowel, then the vowel is lengthened. By "lengthening," we simply mean that the vowel shifts to a related vowel according to the patterns listed below:

α → η	ἀκούω	→	ε + ακουον	→	ἤκουον
ε → η	ἔρχομαι	→	ε + ερχομην	→	ἠρχόμην
ο → ω	ὀφείλω	→	ε + οφειλον	→	ὠφείλον[6]

If the stem of the verb begins with the diphthong αι–, the alpha (α) lengthens to an eta (η), causing the iota (ι) to become subscripted (αἰτοῦμαι → ᾐτοῦμην).[7] Verbs beginning with η, ι, υ, or ω normally leave their beginning vowel unchanged when the augment is added (ἴσχυον, "I was strong," [or, "they were strong"], impf act ind 1st sg [3rd pl] from ἰσχύω, "I am strong, able").

The verb ἔχω does not augment to ἤχον but to εἶχον. This apparent exception is due to the original stem of the verb (which is not found in the present tense-form). The root form of ἔχω is σεχ–. When the epsilon augment is added to the form (εσεχον), it causes the ***intervocalic sigma*** to drop out (εεχον).[8] The two epsilons then contract to form a diphthong (εἶχον). This discussion is an introductory foray into historical morphology. Such study is fascinating, but if we went back in a time machine and asked Paul why he began the imperfect form of ἔχω with an εἶ– rather than an ἤ– (Rom 6:21), he would likely stare at us confusedly and say, "Because that's the correct way to spell it. I learned it that way growing up in Tarsus!" Regardless of the time period or language, most people are not conscious of the morphological history of the words they use.

Stem		Augment		Dropped Sigma		Contraction
σεχ	→	εσεχον	→	εεχον	→	εἶχον

Hint: If a verb begins with an eta (η), assume it is an augmented form since few verbs begin with an eta in their lexical form.

---

[5] This epsilon prefix always has a smooth breathing mark (ἐ).

[6] ὀφείλω = "I owe." Most imperfects lengthen from α– or ε–, not ο–.

[7] αἰτέω = "I ask."

[8] An intervocalic sigma is a sigma (σ) that is in between two vowels due to the addition of the connecting vowel, usually causing the sigma to drop and the vowels to contract.

Imperfect Active Indicative

The imperfect active indicative form ἔλυον is translated "I was loosing." Here is a more precise breakdown of the component parts (morphemes) of the various forms:

Inflected Form	Augment	Stem	Connecting Vowel	Personal Ending		Combined Ending
ἔλυον	ε	λυ	ο	ν	→	ον
ἔλυες	ε	λυ	ε	ς	→	ες
ἔλυεν	ε	λυ	ε	(ν)[9]	→	εν
ἐλύομεν	ε	λυ	ο	μεν	→	ομεν
ἐλύετε	ε	λυ	ε	τε	→	ετε
ἐλύον	ε	λυ	ο	ν	→	ον

Note that the first person singular and third person plural forms are the same (ἔλυον). Although it is true that only context can decide, the third person plural forms occur almost nineteen times more frequently than the first person singular (485 to 26). Also, the first person plural (–ομεν) and second person plural (–ετε) endings are the same as the present active tense-form endings. The difference, however, is found in the addition of the augment with the imperfect forms (λύ**ομεν** → ἐλύ**ομεν**).

Imperfect Middle/Passive Indicative

Inflected Form	Augment	Stem	Connecting Vowel	Personal Ending		Combined Ending
ἐλυόμην	ε	λυ	ο	μην	→	ομην
ἐλύου	ε	λυ	[ε]	[σο][10]	→	ου
ἐλύετο	ε	λυ	ε	το	→	ετο
ἐλυόμεθα	ε	λυ	ο	μεθα	→	ομεθα
ἐλύεσθε	ε	λυ	ε	σθε	→	εσθε
ἐλύοντο	ε	λυ	ο	ντο	→	οντο

Again, notice that the first person plural (–ομεθα) and second person plural (–εσθε) endings are the same as the present middle/passive tense-form endings. The difference is found in the addition of the augment with the imperfect forms (λύ**εσθε** → ἐλύ**εσθε**).

---

[9] There is no personal ending, only a movable nu. Note: the other forms that end with nu are part of the ending (–ον, –ομεν, –ομην).

[10] The intervocalic sigma drops, causing the vowels to contract: ἐλυεσο → ἐλυεο → ἐλύου. See William D. Mounce, *Basics of Biblical Greek: Grammar*, 4th ed. (Grand Rapids: Zondervan, 2019), 228.

6.7 The Use of Οὐ

The particle οὐ is used to negate an indicative verb (οὐ λύει = "he is *not* loosing").[11] If the verb begins with a vowel having a smooth breathing mark, then the form οὐκ is used (οὐκ ἔλυεν = "he was not loosing"). The addition of the kappa (κ) allows a consonant to break the ending vowel of the word οὐ and the beginning vowel of the verb. (This is similar to adding "n" in "a̲n apple"). If the word begins with a vowel with a rough breathing mark, then the form οὐχ is used (οὐχ ὑπάγω, "I am not departing"). The form οὐχί, which appears fifty-four times in the Greek New Testament, is used for emphasis (no!).

Another particle, μή, is used to negate non-indicative forms (i.e., participles, infinitives, subjunctives, imperatives, and optatives).

The words οὐ and μή can also serve a discourse function, allowing the author to indicate whether his rhetorical question expects a positive or negative answer. Similarly, we alter the way we ask questions in English to indicate similar information. Compare, for example, "You will clean your room, won't you?" and "You didn't clean your room, did you?" The first question expects a positive answer whereas the second expects a negative one. In Greek, when the author expects a positive answer to a question, οὐ is used. For example, when the disbelieving people ask, οὐχ οὗτός ἐστιν ὁ τέκτων; (literally, "Is this not the carpenter?" Mark 6:3), this question functions rhetorically as an assertion: "This is [only] the carpenter!"

In contrast, when the author expects a negative answer, μή is used. For example, when Paul asks μὴ πάντες γλώσσαις λαλοῦσιν; (1 Cor 12:30), he is really stating, "Not all speak in tongues, do they?" The implied answer is "Of course not!"[12]

6.8 Irregular Masculine Nouns

Some nouns like μαθητής ("disciple") and προφήτης ("prophet") are first declension nouns that are masculine in gender but have feminine forms (except for the nominative and genitive singular forms). Because their grammatical gender is masculine, they are modified by masculine articles and masculine adjectives (τὸν ἀγαθὸν μαθητήν, "the good disciple").

	SINGULAR			PLURAL		
NOM	ὁ	μαθητής	the disciple	οἱ	μαθηταί	the disciples
GEN	τοῦ	μαθητοῦ	of the disciple	τῶν	μαθητῶν	of the disciples
DAT	τῷ	μαθητῇ	to/for the disciple	τοῖς	μαθηταῖς	to/for the disciples
ACC	τὸν	μαθητήν	the disciple	τοὺς	μαθητάς	the disciples

---

[11] Remember: a "particle" is a small indeclinable word that communicates relationships among words or groups of words.

[12] Student Mike Borland suggests this mnemonic device he learned from another professor: μή rhymes with "nay," which is the response one expects when a rhetorical question begins with μή.

Notice that the genitive singular form follows the second declension ending (μαθητοῦ; cf. λόγου) and the true gender of this form is masculine, as signified by the article. We recommend memorizing the nominative forms of these nouns with the article as a reminder of their gender and cue to their irregularity. In other words, if we were to ask you the Greek word for "disciple," we would want you to be able to say, "ὁ μαθητής."

6.9 Practice

A. Paradigms: Memorize the imperfect active and middle/passive paradigms of λύω (see section 6.5). Then write out each paradigm ten times from memory.

B. Parsing: Parse the following verbs.

1. ἐθεραπεύοντο

2. ἔβλεπον

3. ἐκρινόμεθα

4. ἐπορευόμην

5. ἤγεσθε

6. ἤρχου

7. ἐγίνετο

8. ἐπιστεύετε

9. ἤκουεν

10. εἶχες

C. Translation: Translate the following sentences.

1. Ἰησοῦς αὐτὸς (himself) οὐκ ἐβάπτιζεν (John 4:2).

2. ἔκραζον λέγοντες (saying) ὅτι Σὺ (you) εἶ ὁ υἱὸς τοῦ θεοῦ (Mark 3:11).

3. ἄνθρωπος εἶχεν τέκνα δύο (two) (Matt 21:28).

4. καὶ ἐδίδασκεν καὶ ἔλεγεν αὐτοῖς (to them) (Mark 11:17).

5. πολλοὶ (many) . . . ὑπῆγον τῶν Ἰουδαίων καὶ ἐπίστευον εἰς (in) τὸν Ἰησοῦν (John 12:11).

6. ὁ δὲ Ἰησοῦς ἐπορεύετο σὺν (with) αὐτοῖς (them) (Luke 7:6).

7. ἔγραφεν εἰς (on) τὴν γῆν (John 8:8).

8. καὶ ἐλάμβανον πνεῦμα (Spirit) ἅγιον (holy) (Acts 8:17).

9. καὶ ἐβαπτίζοντο ἐν (in) τῷ Ἰορδάνῃ (Matt 3:6).

10. οὐδὲ (not even) γὰρ οἱ ἀδελφοὶ αὐτοῦ (his) ἐπίστευον εἰς (in) αὐτόν (him) (John 7:5).

11. οὐκ εἶχες ἐξουσίαν (authority) (John 19:11).

12. ὁ ὄχλος ἤρχετο πρὸς (to) αὐτόν (him), καὶ ἐδίδασκεν αὐτούς (them) (Mark 2:13).

D. Translation: Translate the English sentences into Greek.

1. We were taught the law.

2. The crowd was crying out to the prophet.

3. I don't know the day and the hour.

4. The disciple of the Lord was being healed.

5. The angel of glory raises the child.

6.10 Vocabulary[13]

ἀγαπάω	I love
γεννάω	I give birth to, bear, beget (*genealogy*)
ἐπερωτάω	I ask
ἐρωτάω	I ask, question, request
αἰτέω	I ask, demand
ἀκολουθέω	I follow (*acolyte*)
ζητέω	I seek, look for
καλέω	I call, invite, name (*call*)
λαλέω	I speak, say (*glossolalia*)
μαρτυρέω	I testify, bear witness (*martyr*)
παρακαλέω	I call, urge, comfort
περιπατέω	I walk, live (*peripatetic*)
ποιέω	I do, make (*poet*)
φοβέομαι	I am afraid, fear, respect (*phobia*)[14]
πληρόω	I fill, fulfill, complete

---

[13] To hear an author of your textbook read through the vocabulary for chapter 6, go to bit.ly/greekvocab6 or beginninggreek.com.

[14] Greek verbs of emotion are often middle-only. Emotions are actions that inhere within the emoting actor. Thus, emotions are verbs with a high level of subject affectedness.

/////////////////

CHAPTER 7

CONTRACT VERBS

7.1 Overview[1]

A *contract verb* is one whose stem ends with the short vowels alpha (α), epsilon (ε), or omicron (o)—for example, γεννάω ("I begat"), ποιέω ("I do"), and πληρόω ("I fulfill"). (Observe the short vowels in **bold** in these examples.) In this chapter, we will discuss the challenges of conjugating contract verbs. We will also learn the imperfect indicative paradigm of εἰμί.

7.2 Significance

In John 21:15–17, when Jesus reinstates Peter, the contract verbs ἀγαπάω ("love") and φιλέω ("love") are central to the conversation. Many sermons have been preached claiming that properly understanding this passage turns on the nuanced difference between these two verbs—with Jesus asking if Peter loves him with a pure, divine love (ἀγαπάω), while Peter can only affirm a "friend-type" love (φιλέω). According to this understanding of the flow of the passage, Jesus ends with a piercing, "Peter, do you even love me like a friend (φιλέω)?" Jesus's conversation here certainly is piercing. (How would you like the Lord Jesus to ask you *three times* in succession, "Do you love me?"—especially after you denied him *three times*?). But the assertion that the verb φιλέω means here "just a friend-type love" is likely wrong. We should probably see no difference in meaning here between ἀγαπάω and φιλέω. Modern English translations are correct to translate both words as "love." What are some arguments in favor of this view?

---

[1] For an overview video lecture of chapter 7, go to bit.ly/greeklecture7 or beginninggreek.com.

- In John 21:17, Peter was grieved because Jesus asked him "the third time" (note the explicit wording) as to whether he loved him. It is Jesus's repetition of the question, which implies some doubt about Peter's previous responses, that grieved the apostle.

- All writers and speakers have certain stylistic tendencies. The apostle John, for example, loves using nearly synonymous words with no intended different nuances of meaning. (See John 6:53–59, where John uses both the verbs ἐσθίω and τρώγω for eating.) In fact, John uses both verbs ἀγαπάω and φιλέω for the Father's love of the Son (e.g., John 3:35; 5:20). John's idiolect (i.e., his personal stylistic patterns) argues against seeing any intended semantic difference between the two verbs for "love" in John 21:15–17.

- During the Koine Greek period, the word φιλέω was used to mean both "love" (John 21:17) and "kiss" (Mark 14:44). It's understandable how a word with this range of meaning could cause confusion.[2] Does this potential confusion perhaps explain early Christians' statistically-verifiable preference for the verb ἀγαπάω?

- It is sometimes wrongly asserted that ἀγαπάω can only refer to divine, self-giving love. God's love certainly is unique and self-giving, but we know that truth from the many descriptions of God's love in Scripture— not from the inherent semantic range (that is, the range of possible meanings) of the word ἀγαπάω. In the ancient Greek translation (LXX, or Septuagint) of 2 Sam 13:15, for example, the verb ἀγαπάω is used to describe Amnon's incestuous lust for his half-sister, Tamar.

7.3 Morphology

So, why do we have a separate chapter for verbs whose stems end with an alpha (α), epsilon (ε), or omicron (ο)? And why are they called contract verbs? In English, when we speak about a "contraction," we expect letters to drop out or combine. For example, "Don't" is a contraction of "Do not." In Greek, contract verbs will frequently have letters drop out or combine when the various personal endings are added to the stem.[3] There is a visible contraction that takes place between the verb stem and these personal endings—resulting in students' difficulties in recognizing the combined forms. Thus, we need a chapter to talk about these tweaks to contract verbs' spellings.

---

[2] Moisés Silva, *Biblical Words and Their Meaning: An Introduction to Lexical Semantics*, rev. ed. (Grand Rapids: Zondervan, 1994), 96.

[3] By "personal endings," we mean the verb endings you have already learned, like –ω, –εις, –ει, –ομεν, –ετε, and –ουσιν, which really include a connecting vowel and personal ending in combined form.

Please note: we are not introducing new tenses or endings in this chapter! We are only discussing how the endings you have already learned for the present and imperfect tenses will "crash" into the stem vowels of contract verbs and cause changes in spelling.[4] Contract verbs are mainly affected in the present and imperfect tenses because other tenses (which we have not covered yet) have a consonant inserted before verbs' personal endings, preventing a "crash" or contraction of the verb stem and personal ending. To say it differently: for the future, aorist, and perfect tenses (covered in future chapters), the inserted consonant acts as a buffer which prevents the vowel at the end of the verb stem and the connecting vowel from colliding (καλεσ + εις → καλέσεις, future: "you will call").

What does a contract verb conjugation actually look like? Below is the present active indicative paradigm for ποιέω ("I do"):

PRESENT ACTIVE INDICATIVE (EPSILON STEM)			
	SINGULAR		PLURAL
1ST	ποιῶ	I do	ποιοῦμεν	we do
2ND	ποιεῖς	you do	ποιεῖτε	you do
3RD	ποιεῖ	he/she/it does	ποιοῦσι(ν)	they do

You may have noticed several things. For starters, you likely could have guessed the parsings of these forms. In fact, four of the six contracted endings appear the same as the present active indicative endings of λύω, except for accents. Only the first person plural form (ποιοῦμεν) and second person plural form (ποιεῖτε) have endings that differ from the λύω paradigm; even then, the differences are slight. Note how a circumflex stands over each place where the vowels have contracted.[5] This accentuation pattern (accents standing over combined vowels) is consistent for present tense verbs, but it does not hold true for the imperfect tense. Also, observe how the lexical form (ποιέω) is different from the actual form as it will appear conjugated in a written text (ποιῶ).

How do we arrive at the lexical form? It is as if we pried apart the contracted form and stuck a piece of glass between the vowels to keep them from combining. We then place that artificial form on the page of a lexicon for safe keeping. You will never actually see the form ποιέω in any Greek text. Nevertheless, by memorizing the word in this artificial un-contracted form, you will be reminded that it belongs to a special class of verbs ("Oh, yeah, this is one of those contract verbs!"). You also will be able to predict or recognize the various combined ("contracted") forms, if you know the artificial (lexical) forms well.

---

[4] The (long) vowels iota (ι) and upsilon (υ) do not contract (ἀκούω).

[5] You can think of the circumflex as two hands shaking, the formalization of a "contract."

Truth be told, starting with ποιέω is a bit misleading because of the various contract verb paradigms; it has the least changes from the λύω paradigm. Sometimes contract forms can be challenging to parse.

At this point, we recommend that you focus mainly on recognizing (rather than memorizing) the contract verb paradigms. Perhaps create flash cards of the various possible forms from the charts below and see if you can recognize them when you encounter them in random order.

There are various methods that introductory Greek grammars have used to teach students all the ways contract vowels can combine with personal endings. One such method is to list all possible vowel combinations under the alpha, epsilon, and omicron headings.

Alpha Contract Verbs

−α + ε, η	→ α
−α + ει, η	→ α
−α + ο, ου, ω	→ ω

Epsilon Contract Verbs

−ε + ε, ει	→ ει
−ε + η	→ η
−ε + ῃ	→ ῃ
−ε + ο, ου	→ ου
−ε + ω	→ ω

Omicron Contract Verbs

−ο + ε, ο, ου	→ ου
−ο + ει, η	→ οι
−ο + ῃ, ω	→ ω

Another way of conveying this same information is through a chart that summarizes all possible vowel combinations, such as this:

SUMMARY CHART[6]							
	ε	ει	η	ῃ	ο	ου	ω
−α	α	ᾳ	α	ᾳ	ω	ω	ω
−ε	ει	ει	η	ῃ	ου	ου	ω
−ο	ου	οι	ω	οι	ου	ου	ω

Perhaps the most student-accessible method condenses this tempestuous sea of combinations into a summary list. Bill Mounce, in his *Basics of Biblical Greek*, wins the pedagogy prize for giving us an accessible summary of seven possible combinations. We gratefully acknowledge these rules as coming directly from him.[7] Note below how the seven guidelines are further divided into five rules for a contract vowel combining with a singular vowel at the beginning of a verb's personal ending and two rules for a contract vowel combining with a diphthong at the beginning of a verb's personal ending.

---

[6] Rodney J. Decker includes a similar chart in his chapter on contract verbs. *Reading Koine Greek: An Introduction and Integrated Workbook* (Grand Rapids: Baker, 2014), 344.

[7] See William D. Mounce, *Basics of Biblical Greek: Grammar*, 4th ed. (Grand Rapids: Zondervan, 2019), 173–75.

Contract Vowel + Singular Vowel at Beginning of Verb's Personal Ending (5 rules)

1. ε + o, o + ε, o + o = ου

2. ε + ε = ει

3. ω is formed from almost any vowel combined with o or ω, except for cases covered by the first bullet point above.

4. α + ε = α

5. o + ει = οι

Contract Vowel + Diphthong at Beginning of Verb's Personal Ending (2 rules)

1. If the contract vowel and the first vowel of the diphthong are the same, they simplify (i.e., one of the double letters drops out).

   ε + ει = ει
   o + ου = ου

2. If the contract vowel and the first vowel of the diphthong are different, they contract. If the second vowel of the diphthong is an iota, it subscripts if possible; if it is an upsilon, it drops off.

   ε + ου = ου
   α + ει = ᾳ

7.4 Summary of Contract Verb Forms

Below is a summary of both present and imperfect contract verb forms. We recommend you go through each chart, using Mounce's seven rules, and see how every verb contraction is explained by the rules. A video for this chapter applies this very method.[8]

	PRESENT ACTIVE INDICATIVE			
	–ω	**–εω**	**–αω**	**–οω**
1S	λύω	ποιῶ	ἀγαπῶ	πληρῶ
2S	λύεις	ποιεῖς	ἀγαπᾷς	πληροῖς
3S	λύει	ποιεῖ	ἀγαπᾷ	πληροῖ
1P	λύομεν	ποιοῦμεν	ἀγαπῶμεν	πληροῦμεν
2P	λύετε	ποιεῖτε	ἀγαπᾶτε	πληροῦτε
3P	λύουσι(ν)	ποιοῦσι(ν)	ἀγαπῶσι(ν)	πληροῦσι(ν)

---

[8] See the overview video lecture for this chapter.

PRESENT MIDDLE/PASSIVE INDICATIVE			
–ω	**–εω**	**–αω**	**–οω**
1S λύομαι	ποιοῦμαι	ἀγαπῶμαι	πληροῦμαι
2S λύῃ	ποιῇ	ἀγαπᾷ	πληροῖ
3S λύεται	ποιεῖται	ἀγαπᾶται	πληροῦται
1P λυόμεθα	ποιούμεθα	ἀγαπώμεθα	πληρούμεθα
2P λύεσθε	ποιεῖσθε	ἀγαπᾶσθε	πληροῦσθε
3P λύονται	ποιοῦνται	ἀγαπῶνται	πληροῦνται

IMPERFECT ACTIVE INDICATIVE			
–ω	**–εω**	**–αω**	**–οω**
1S ἔλυον	ἐποίουν	ἠγάπων	ἐπλήρουν
2S ἔλυες	ἐποίεις	ἠγάπας	ἐπλήρους
3S ἔλυε(ν)	ἐποίει	ἠγάπα	ἐπλήρου
1P ἐλύομεν	ἐποιοῦμεν	ἠγαπῶμεν	ἐπληροῦμεν
2P ἐλύετε	ἐποιεῖτε	ἠγαπᾶτε	ἐπληροῦτε
3P ἔλυον	ἐποίουν	ἠγάπων	ἐπλήρουν

IMPERFECT MIDDLE/PASSIVE INDICATIVE			
–ω	**–εω**	**–αω**	**–οω**
1S ἐλυόμην	ἐποιούμην	ἠγαπώμην	ἐπληρούμην
2S ἐλύου	ἐποιοῦ	ἠγαπῶ	ἐπληροῦ
3S ἐλύετο	ἐποιεῖτο	ἠγαπᾶτο	ἐπληροῦτο
1P ἐλυόμεθα	ἐποιούμεθα	ἠγαπώμεθα	ἐπληρούμεθα
2P ἐλύεσθε	ἐποιεῖσθε	ἠγαπᾶσθε	ἐπληροῦσθε
3P ἐλύοντο	ἐποιοῦντο	ἠγαπῶντο	ἐπληροῦντο

7.5 The Imperfect Indicative of εἰμί

The imperfect form of εἰμί must be mastered (i.e., memorized) since it occurs almost 450 times in the New Testament.

IMPERFECT INDICATIVE—εἰμί[9]			
	SINGULAR		PLURAL
1ST	ἤμην	I was	ἦμεν	we were
2ND	ἦς	you were	ἦτε	you were
3RD	ἦν	he/she/it was	ἦσαν	they were

These forms all begin with an eta (η) since the epsilon of εἰμί lengthens to an eta when augmented. The first person singular form (ἤμην) is closer to the middle/passive form (cf. ἐλυόμην). The third person plural form (ἦσαν) uses an alternate form that is closer to one you will learn later (the aorist active tense-form: ἔλυσαν). The third singular form (ἦν) represents about half of the occurrences (226x). Finally, there are rare alternate forms for the second person singular (ἦσθα, 2x) and first person plural (ἤμεθα, 5x) forms.

7.6 Alternate Direct Object Cases

Although the direct object is typically found in the accusative case, some verbs can take their direct objects in the genitive or dative case. When this occurs, "of" (gen case) or "to/for" (dat case) is *not* added. Verbs that have direct objects in the genitive case include: ἀκούω, ἄρχω (chapter 10), κρατέω (chapter 17), and πληρόω. For example, ἀκούουσιν **τῆς φωνῆς** ("they hear **the voice**") or ἐπληροῦντο **χαρᾶς** ("they were filled with **joy**"). Verbs that have direct objects in the dative case include: ἀκολουθέω, ἀποκρίνομαι, πιστεύω, and προσκυνέω (chapter 10), For example, ἀκολουθοῦσιν **αὐτῷ** ("they are following **him**") or οὐ πιστεύετέ **μοι** ("you do not believe **me**").

7.7 Practice

A. Paradigms: Memorize the imperfect paradigm of εἰμί (see section 7.5). Then write out the paradigm ten times from memory.

B. Parsing: Parse the following verbs.

1. γεννῶσιν

2. ἦμεν

3. ἠρώτων

4. ἠκολούθουν

5. ἐζήτει

---

[9] To hear a mnemonic song, go to https://bit.ly/imptobesong or beginninggreek.com.

6. φοβούμεθα

7. ἐμαρτυρεῖτο

8. παρακαλοῦμεν

9. ἐποιοῦντο

10. φοβῇ

C. Translation: Translate the following sentences.

1. τὰ ἔργα τοῦ Ἀβραὰμ ἐποιεῖτε (John 8:39).

2. ἐφοβοῦντο γὰρ τὸν λαόν (people) (Luke 22:2).

3. καὶ περιεπάτει ὁ Ἰησοῦς ἐν (in) τῷ ἱερῷ (John 10:23).

4. γινώσκομεν ὅτι ἀγαπῶμεν τὰ τέκνα τοῦ θεοῦ (1 John 5:2).

5. αἰτεῖτε καὶ οὐ λαμβάνετε (Jas 4:3).

6. ἀλλὰ λαλοῦμεν θεοῦ σοφίαν (wisdom) (1 Cor 2:7).

7. ἦτε δοῦλοι τῆς ἁμαρτίας (Rom 6:17).

8. ἀδελφοί, ἐρωτῶμεν ὑμᾶς (you, pl) καὶ παρακαλοῦμεν ἐν (in) κυρίῳ Ἰησοῦ (1 Thess 4:1).

9. ᾐτοῦντο εἰρήνην (peace) (Acts 12:20).

10. καὶ ἀκολουθοῦσιν αὐτῷ (him) οἱ μαθηταὶ αὐτοῦ (his) (Mark 6:1).

11. καὶ ζητοῦσιν τὴν ψυχήν μου (my) (Rom 11:3).

12. ἡ πέτρα (rock) δὲ ἦν ὁ Χριστός (1 Cor 10:4).

13. οἵ τε μαθηταὶ ἐπληροῦντο χαρᾶς (joy) (Acts 13:52).

14. Τί (Why) δέ με (me) καλεῖτε, Κύριε, κύριε καὶ οὐ ποιεῖτε ἃ (what) λέγω; (Luke 6:46).

D. Translation: Translate the following sentences into Greek.

1. You (pl) were calling the sons of men.

2. Do you (sg) seek the Lord?

3. They were speaking the words of truth.

4. The slave loves the church.

5. The prophet is walking to the disciples.

7.8 Vocabulary[10]

Note: Some Greek prepositions have different meanings depending on the case of the objects that follow them. So, for example, see below how κατά means "down" or "against" when followed by a genitive object, but the preposition is best translated as "according to" when followed by an accusative object. The accompanying video of the vocabulary will help explain this concept.

ἀπό	from, away from (gen)
διά	through (gen); because of (acc) (*diameter*)
εἰς	into, among, for (acc) (*eisegesis*)
ἐκ	from, out of (gen) (*exhale, exegesis*)
ἐν	in, on, at, by, with (dat)
ἐπί	on, upon, over (gen); on, upon, at, in (dat); on, upon, to, for (acc) (*epigraph*)
κατά	down, against (gen); according to (acc) (*cataphoric*)
μετά	with, among (gen); after (acc)
παρά	from (gen); with (dat); beside, on, at (acc) (*parable, paramedic*)
περί	about, concerning (gen); around (acc) (*perimeter*)
πρός	to, toward (acc) (*prosthesis*)
σύν	with (dat) (*syntax*)
ὑπέρ	for, on behalf of (gen); above, beyond (acc) (*hypercritical, hyperactive*)
ὑπό	by (gen); under, below (acc) (*hypotaxis, hypothesis*)
ἐνώπιον	before, in the presence of (gen)

---

[10] To hear an author of your textbook read through the vocabulary for chapter 7, go to bit.ly/greekvocab7 or beginninggreek.com.

CHAPTER 8

//////////////

PREPOSITIONS

8.1 Overview[1]

Prepositions are extremely common in the New Testament. The fifteen presented in this lesson occur more than 10,000 times in the Greek New Testament. In this chapter, we will learn the English definitions of Greek prepositions and how they function in a sentence.

8.2 Significance

Greek prepositions are similar in function to English prepositions, but they also have some differences. As you will soon discover, Greek prepositions require their objects to be in certain cases. For example, the preposition ἀπό is always followed by a noun or pronoun in the genitive case. There are hundreds of examples of this construction in the New Testament. Yet, in reading Rev 1:4, we encounter a strange deviation from this grammatical pattern:

> John to the seven churches that are in Asia: Grace to you and peace from him who is and who was and who is to come (ἀπὸ ὁ ὢν καὶ ὁ ἦν καὶ ὁ ἐρχόμενος), and from the seven spirits (ἀπὸ τῶν ἑπτὰ πνευμάτων) who are before his throne. (ESV)

There are two instances of the preposition ἀπό in this verse. The second one, as expected, is followed by a genitive object (τῶν ἑπτὰ πνευμάτων). The first instance of ἀπό, however, is followed by three nominative forms (ὁ ὢν καὶ ὁ ἦν καὶ ὁ ἐρχόμενος). Even though you don't yet know all the constructions in this compound object, you can see the repeated nominative article (ὁ . . . ὁ . . . ὁ); ἀπό

---

[1] For an overview video lecture of chapter 8, go to bit.ly/greeklecture8 or beginninggreek.com.

79

followed by the nominative. Why does John do this? A number of explanations have been given:

1. Perhaps within the broad colloquial usage of Koine Greek, John's deviations from dominant grammatical patterns would not have been that unusual—just as spellings varied greatly in early American history, even among educated authors.

2. John frequently does vary from standard grammatical usage, and some New Testament scholars think he does so to aid his readers in hearing echoes of Old Testament text. In Rev 1:4, the apostle John is clearly intending his readers to hear an echo of God's self-revelation in Exod 3:14, where the voice from the burning bush identifies himself to Moses as ἐγώ εἰμι **ὁ ὤν** ("I Am Who I Am") [ESV]. Note how the two bold words in the Greek text of Exod 3:14 are repeated exactly in Rev 1:4—aiding readers in hearing this allusion.

3. From a theological standpoint, is it significant that God's majestic revelation of himself appears unchanged after the preposition? Could John's breaking a grammatical pattern be a subtle way of asserting the unchangeability of God—the One who is and was and is to come . . . the eternal, immutable One?

8.3 Meaning

A *preposition* is a word used with a noun or pronoun to clarify that noun's or pronoun's relationship to another word or words in a sentence.[2] This relationship is often spatial, but it can also be temporal or even logical. For example, if someone states, "The apple is *on the desk*," the preposition "on" expresses a spatial relationship of the apple to the desk. The term "desk" is the object of the preposition, and the entire construction ("on the desk") is considered a prepositional phrase. Other prepositional phrases may express a temporal idea ("*on* the third day") or a logical relationship ("*for* honor").

Unlike English, in Greek, the meaning of a preposition can sometimes change depending on the case of its object. For example, διὰ τοῦ ἱεροῦ means "through the temple" because τοῦ ἱεροῦ is in the genitive case. If the phrase was in the accusative case (διὰ τὸ ἱερόν), it would mean "because of the temple." Thus, it is important to pay attention to the case of the preposition's object.

---

[2] Frank X. Braun, *English Grammar for Language Students: Basic Grammatical Terminology Defined and Alphabetically Arranged* (Ann Arbor, MI: Ulrich's Books, 1947), 16. Matthew S. DeMoss defines a preposition as "an indeclinable word that governs a prepositional phrase, indicating a relationship between a substantive and another word—a verb, adjective, or another substantive." *Pocket Dictionary for the Study of New Testament Greek* (Downers Grove: InterVarsity, 2001), 101.

Not all prepositions take their objects in multiple cases. Some prepositions will require their objects to always be in the same case, whereas others can be used with two cases and still others with three.

1-CASE PREPOSITIONS		
PREPOSITION	CASE	GLOSS
ἀπό	Genitive	"from"
ἐκ		"out of"
ἐν	Dative	"in"
σύν		"with"
εἰς	Accusative	"into"
πρός		"toward"

2-CASE PREPOSITIONS		
PREPOSITION	CASE	GLOSS
διά	Genitive	"through"
	Accusative	"because of"
κατά	Genitive	"against"
	Accusative	"according to"
μετά	Genitive	"with"
	Accusative	"after"
περί	Genitive	"concerning"
	Accusative	"around"
ὑπέρ	Genitive	"on behalf of"
	Accusative	"above"
ὑπό	Genitive	"by"
	Accusative	"under"

3-CASE PREPOSITIONS		
PREPOSITION	CASE	GLOSS
ἐπί	Genitive	"on"
	Dative	"upon"
	Accusative	"to"
παρά	Genitive	"from"
	Dative	"with"
	Accusative	"beside"

Note that a two-case preposition always occurs with the genitive and accusative cases (and not the genitive and dative or dative and accusative). Furthermore, the nominative case is never used as the object of a preposition (except in Rev 1:4 as noted above).

When translating prepositional phrases, it is not necessary to add "of" for genitive nouns or "to/for" for dative nouns since the preposition takes the place of such terms. For example, the phrase ἀπὸ τῆς οἰκίας (Luke 7:6) is translated "from the house" and not "from of the house."

It should also be noted that prepositions often have a broad range of meaning and cannot be limited to one or two glosses. In fact, some Greek prepositions could accurately be rendered in various contexts with more than a dozen different English terms. Thus, it is often important to use a reliable lexicon and realize that the glosses learned in the vocabulary lists are just a starting place. Context is the determining factor for accurately translating prepositions.

8.4 Form Variations

Sometimes the form of the preposition will alter depending on the beginning letter of the word that immediately follows. For example, the preposition ἐκ has a kappa when followed by a word that begins with a consonant, but becomes ἐξ when the following word begins with a vowel.

ἐκ νόμου	→	"from [the] law"
ἐξ ἀνθρώπων	→	"from men"

Additionally, most prepositions that end with a vowel drop their final vowel when the following word begins with a vowel.[3]

δι' ἐπαγγελίας	→	"through [the] promise"
παρ' ἀγγέλους	→	"beside [the] angels"

Note that the place where the letter dropped out is marked with an apostrophe. This is called ***elision***. Also note that these prepositions lose their accent and are pronounced with the following word. If an elided preposition's final letter is pi (π) or tau (τ) *and* the following word's vowel has a rough breathing mark, the consonant of the elided preposition is changed to its aspirated form: φ or θ.

π → φ	ἀφ' ἡμερῶν	"from [the] days"
τ → θ	μεθ' ἡμέρας ἕξ	"after six days"

Here is a summary of the variations that can occur with the prepositions in this chapter:

ἀπό	→	ἀπ' or ἀφ'

---

[3] Exception: the prepositions περί and πρό (+ genitive = "before") do not drop their final vowels when they occur immediately prior to words beginning with vowels.

διά	→	δι’
ἐκ	→	ἐξ
ἐπί	→	ἐπ’ or ἐφ’
κατά	→	κατ’ or καθ’
μετά	→	μετ’ or μεθ’
παρά	→	παρ’
ὑπό	→	ὑπ’ or ὑφ’

When prepositions are prefixed to verbs (see below), their spellings are sometimes slightly altered for ease of pronunciation (i.e., **euphony**). For example, σύν can be spelled συμ–, συλ–, or συγ–, and ἐν can be spelled ἐμ–.[4]

8.5 Compound Verbs

Some prepositions can be found prefixed to verbs, known as **compound verbs**. For example, the verb ἐκβάλλω is made up of the preposition ἐκ plus the verb βάλλω. All of the prepositions in this chapter (except ἐνώπιον, "before, in the presence of") can be prefixed to verbs. Such prepositions are called **proper prepositions**. An **improper preposition**, on the other hand, is the technical term for one that is never prefixed to a verb.

When a preposition is added to a verb, it can have one of four possible effects: (1) the meaning of both the verb and the preposition are preserved; (2) the meaning of the verb is intensified; (3) the verb experiences no additional change in meaning; or (4) the meaning of the verb is changed but is not noticeably related to the preposition's meaning.

1. Additional Meaning: ἐκβάλλω = I throw out (ἐκ + βάλλω)

2. Intensive Meaning: καταλύω = I destroy (κατά + λύω)

3. No Change in Meaning: ἐπερωτάω = I ask (cf. ἐρωτάω)

4. Unrelated Meaning: ἀναγινώσκω = I read (ἀνά + γινώσκω)[5]

We must also note that compound verbs are augmented after the prepositional prefix (ἐπερωτάω → ἐπηρώτων). This rule impacts the following verbs learned thus far: ἀποκρίνομαι, ἐπερωτάω, παρακαλέω, περιπατέω, and ὑπάγω. With two of these, the prepositional prefix has dropped its final vowel because the stem of the verb begins with a vowel: ἐπερωτάω (ἐπί + ἐρωτάω) and ὑπάγω (ὑπό + ἄγω). When the preposition ends with a vowel (and the stem of the verb begins with a consonant), that vowel is usually replaced by the augment (παρακαλέω →

---

[4] As helpfully noted by Decker, *Reading Koine Greek*, 160.
[5] ἀνά (+ accusative) = "up" or "again." In some sense, when you read something, you know it "again," but it's questionable whether this transparent etymology was conscious in the minds of those who employed the verb to refer to reading.

παρεκάλει). Finally, when the preposition ends with an iota (ι), that ending vowel is retained when the augment is added (περιπατέω → περιεπάτει).[6]

8.6 Usage

Prepositional phrases have two main uses: (1) adverbial and (2) adjectival. Most prepositional phrases are adverbial; as such, they modify the verbal idea by answering a question (where? when? how? or why?). For example, "[he] went out *of the temple* (ἐκ τοῦ ἱεροῦ)" (John 8:59). The prepositional phrase ("out of the temple") describes *where* the verbal idea ("[he] went") occurs.

Adjectival prepositional phrases are much less common than adverbial ones and modify a noun (or other substantive) by answering the question "which?" or "what kind of?" For example, in the expression "the glory that comes from the only God" (τὴν δόξαν τὴν παρὰ τοῦ μόνου θεοῦ; John 5:44), the prepositional phrase (παρὰ τοῦ μόνου θεοῦ) modifies the noun "glory" (δόξαν). The repetition of the article before the prepositional phrase grammatically links the prepositional phrase, causing it to function as a giant adjective. Simply put, the Greek phrase essentially reads this way: "the which-is-from-the-only-God glory." In English, we need to smooth this out by using a relative clause ("the glory *that comes from the only God*").

It is also possible for the prepositional phrase to function as a noun (substantival use). In this construction, the phrase follows the article but there is no noun in the immediate context that it is modifying. Oftentimes the article will be a neuter plural form (τά). For example, in 1 John 2:15 we read, "Do not love the world or *the things in the world* (τὰ ἐν τῷ κόσμῳ)." In the phrase τὰ ἐν τῷ κόσμῳ, the article (τά) governs the prepositional phrase, making it a virtual noun. Again, this could woodenly be translated, "the in-the-world things." The word "things" is added because the article is neuter and plural.

Prepositions that are prefixed to verbs are often repeated afterwards as a matter of common stylistic convention—not for emphasis. For example, πῦρ **ἐκ**πορεύεται **ἐκ** τοῦ στόματος αὐτῶν ("fire comes from their mouths"; Rev 11:5). Also, nouns and adjectives that follow prepositions are often considered definite—even if they do not have an article. For example, ἀπὸ κυρίου is translated "from the Lord" (Col 3:24). In other words, definite objects of prepositions frequently lack the article. How do you know, then, whether the object of a preposition is definite ("the Lord") or indefinite ("a lord")? Context will usually clarify.

Finally, prepositions were on the rise during the Koine period. Although it is possible to communicate relationship via case-endings alone, a preposition makes the relationship more explicit. For example, to communicate "on the third day," a dative case-ending could be used (τῇ τρίτῃ ἡμέρᾳ). It is arguably less ambiguous, however, to use a preposition (ἐν τῇ τρίτῃ ἡμέρᾳ).

---

[6] Some verbal forms have two prepositional prefixes (e.g., ἐπισυνάγω = ἐπί + σύν + ἄγω).

8.7 Practice

A. Cases and Meaning: Identify the case(s) that can be used in construction with the following prepositions. Then provide a possible gloss for the preposition for each case.

1. ὑπέρ
2. ὑπό
3. ἐκ
4. περί
5. σύν
6. κατά
7. ἐν
8. ἀπό
9. πρός
10. εἰς
11. διά
12. ἐπί
13. μετά
14. παρά

B. Form Variations: Identify the lexical form of the following.

1. ἐφ᾽
2. παρ᾽
3. καθ᾽
4. ἐξ
5. ὑφ᾽
6. μετ᾽
7. δι᾽
8. ἀφ᾽

9. κατ᾽

10. ἐπ᾽

C. Translation: Translate the following sentences.

1. καὶ ἔρχεται εἰς οἶκον (a house) (Mark 3:20).

2. καὶ ἦν παρὰ τὴν θάλασσαν (lake) (Mark 5:21).

3. οὐ περὶ τοῦ κόσμου ἐρωτῶ (John 17:9).

4. μετὰ τρεῖς (three) ἡμέρας ἐγείρομαι (Matt 27:63).

5. ἐζήτουν κατὰ τοῦ Ἰησοῦ μαρτυρίαν (testimony) (Mark 14:55).

6. σὺ πιστεύεις εἰς τὸν υἱὸν τοῦ ἀνθρώπου; (John 9:35).

7. καὶ ἐβαπτίζοντο ὑπ᾽ αὐτοῦ (him) ἐν τῷ Ἰορδάνῃ ποταμῷ (river) (Mark 1:5).

8. εἰρήνην ἔχομεν πρὸς τὸν θεὸν διὰ τοῦ κυρίου ἡμῶν (our) Ἰησοῦ Χριστοῦ (Rom 5:1).

9. οὐκ ἔστιν μαθητὴς ὑπὲρ τὸν διδάσκαλον (teacher) οὐδὲ (nor) δοῦλος ὑπὲρ τὸν κύριον αὐτοῦ (his) (Matt 10:24).

10. Ἰησοῦς ἐξῆλθεν (went out) σὺν τοῖς μαθηταῖς αὐτοῦ (his) (John 18:1).

11. τοῖς ὑπὸ νόμον [I became] ὡς ὑπὸ νόμον (1 Cor 9:20).

12. δόξα ἐν ὑψίστοις (highest) θεῷ καὶ ἐπὶ γῆς εἰρήνη ἐν ἀνθρώποις (Luke 2:14).

13. χάρις (grace) ὑμῖν (to you) καὶ εἰρήνη ἀπὸ θεοῦ πατρὸς (father) ἡμῶν (our) καὶ κυρίου Ἰησοῦ Χριστοῦ (Rom 1:7).

14. οὐκ ἔστιν ἡ ἀγάπη τοῦ πατρὸς (father) ἐν αὐτῷ (him) (1 John 2:15).

D. Translation: Translate the following sentences into Greek.

1. They know the gospel according to the disciples.

2. We are received by God because of Christ.

3. The children are coming toward the crowd.

4. The angel was speaking upon the earth.

5. The men of peace[7] believe in the truth from the heart.

8.8 Vocabulary[8]

αὐτός, –ή, –ό	he, she, it; self, same (*autopilot*)
ἐγώ, ἡμεῖς	I; we (*ego, egomaniac*)
ὅς, ἥ, ὅ	who, which, that
σύ, ὑμεῖς	you (sg); you (pl)
ἄρτος, ὁ	bread, food
δικαιοσύνη, ἡ	righteousness, justice
εἰρήνη, ἡ	peace (*irenic, Irene*)
ἐξουσία, ἡ	authority, right, power
θάλασσα, ἡ	lake, sea (*thalassic*)
λαός, ὁ	people, crowd (*laity*)
ὁδός, ἡ	way, road (*exodus*)
οἰκία, ἡ	home, dwelling, family (*economy*)
οἶκος, ὁ	house, household, family
ὀφθαλμός, ὁ	eye (*ophthalmology*)
τόπος, ὁ	place (*topography*)

---

[7] See the vocabulary list below for the Greek word "peace."
[8] To hear an author of your textbook read through the vocabulary for chapter 8, go to bit.ly/greekvocab8 or beginninggreek.com.

Can I Be Confident That I Am Reading the Words of the Apostles?

Introducing Textual Criticism

Every curious Christian must at some point ask, "How can I be confident that the Bible I am reading has been faithfully preserved from the days of the prophets and apostles?" Some popular movies, books, and radio-show pundits raise this question with intense skepticism.

Since the book in your hands is on the subject of New Testament Greek, we are going to narrow that original question a bit more: "How can you be confident that the words in your modern, critical Greek New Testament (whether in printed or digital format) are a faithful transmission of the apostles' originally penned words?" This is a legitimate question, and it is the question answered by **textual criticism**, a field of study which seeks to determine the original wording of an ancient manuscript when there are variants in the ancient manuscripts.

A detailed introduction to textual criticism is beyond the scope of this book. Nevertheless, in the next few pages, we hope to overview the topic and point you in the direction of resources that offer more extensive discussion.[1]

We do not have the original autographs of the New Testament documents. Yet, even within the New Testament itself, we have evidence that the individual New Testament documents were copied by hand and that these copies circulated among the churches. In Col 4:16, for instance, Paul writes, "After this letter has been read at your gathering, have it read also in the church of the Laodiceans; and see that you also read the letter from Laodicea."[2] Over time, the early church grouped selections of inspired writings and copied them together. By the mid-second century, the four canonical Gospels and Paul's Letters were apparently grouped and

---

[1] Several of the paragraphs below are adapted from Andreas J. Köstenberger, Benjamin L. Merkle, and Robert L. Plummer, *Going Deeper with New Testament Greek: An Intermediate Study of the Grammar and Syntax of the New Testament*, rev. ed. (Nashville: B&H Academic, 2020), 24–32.

[2] Some scholars have suggested that this "letter from Laodicea" may be Paul's canonical letter to the Ephesians, as the words ἐν Ἐφέσῳ ("in Ephesus," Eph 1:1) are lacking in significant ancient manuscripts.

copied as units. Not much later, the entire New Testament was grouped and copied as a recognized body of inspired writings. The earliest extant canonical list we have of the New Testament (the Muratorian Canon) has been dated to AD 190.[3]

As early Christians hand-copied, recopied, and copied copies, small variations were inevitably introduced into the manuscripts. And, although church fathers sometimes speculated about copyist errors or the original reading of manuscripts,[4] it was virtually impossible to codify such discussion accurately until one could reproduce a text without any variation. Thus, after the printing press was introduced to Europe in 1454, possibilities for comparing manuscripts with an unchanging standard arose. At roughly the same time, Europe experienced a revival of interest in classical learning (including the Greek language) and the arrival

of the Protestant Reformation (where focus on the meaning of the inspired Scripture necessitated careful argumentation from the text of Scripture in the original languages). The printing press, a revived knowledge of Greek, and a growing interest in the gospel combined to result in the first published printed edition of the Greek New Testament by Erasmus in 1516.[5] In producing this text, Erasmus relied on only seven manuscripts, most of poor quality.[6] Today, we have more than 5,000 ancient manuscripts (or partial manuscripts) of the Greek New Testament, with the number increasing yearly.[7]

Subsequent generations continued to build on the foundational work of Erasmus in producing "standard" printed versions of the Greek New Testament derived from the various ancient manuscripts available to them. Until the mid-nineteenth century, the Byzantine text tradition was

---

[3] This canon is dated by some scholars as late as the fourth century. For a brief presentation of the views, see Edmon L. Gallagher and John D. Meade, *The Biblical Canon Lists from Early Christianity* (Oxford: Oxford University Press, 2017), 174–83. Certainly, however, Christians distinguished canonical from non-canonical writings prior to the earliest extant canonical lists, as is evidenced within both the New Testament (e.g., 2 Thess 2:2; 3:17) and the writings of the apostolic fathers.

[4] For example, Jerome, Augustine, and Origen (see Bruce M. Metzger and Bart D. Ehrman, *The Text of the New Testament: Its Transmission, Corruption, and Restoration*, 4th ed. [New York: Oxford University Press, 2005], 200–3).

[5] The Complutensian Polyglot, a printed Greek New Testament produced under the direction of Cardinal Ximenes, was apparently completed in 1514 but not formally published until after Erasmus's text.

[6] See Edwin M. Yamauchi, "Erasmus' Contributions to New Testament Scholarship," *Fides et Historia* 19.3 (1987): 10–11. Yamauchi writes, "Although Erasmus claimed that he used 'the oldest and most correct copies of the New Testament,' the press of the publisher's deadline forced him to rely on but seven rather late and inferior manuscripts available at Basle" (10).

[7] Daniel Wallace, director of the Center for the Study of New Testament Manuscripts (CSNTM), regularly reports the discovery of new and significant ancient manuscripts at www.csntm.org.

assumed as the standard.[8] It was sometimes called the *Textus Receptus* (received text), so labeled in the preface to a Greek New Testament published by the Elzevir brothers in 1633. Over time, principles for adjudicating disputed readings were developed and accepted by the majority of scholars.[9] The Byzantine text came to be viewed by many as a later conflation of text traditions and lost its primacy to "eclectic" scholarly editions produced by text critics. Principles that dethroned the Byzantine text and codified the modern discipline of textual criticism can be traced to the seminal work of Brian Walton (1600–1661), Johann Bengel (1687–1752), Karl Lachmann (1793–1851), Constantine von Tischendorf (1815–1874), B. F. Westcott (1825–1901), F. J. A. Hort (1828–1892), and others.

It should be noted that a small minority of scholars insist that only one "family" of ancient manuscripts (the Byzantine family) preserves the most reliable text of the New Testament.

Yet, even within this Byzantine family of manuscripts, there are numerous minor variations. Modern English-speaking persons who insist on the priority of the Byzantine text family are often aligned in some way with the King James Only movement.[10] They argue that the King James Version (the New Testament of which is translated from a Byzantine version of the Greek text) is the most reliable because it is based on the best-preserved manuscript tradition. The majority of evangelical Christian scholars, however, believe the evidence points to God preserving his Word through the multiplicity of manuscripts in a variety of text families. God has left us so many manuscripts of such high quality that, even in the places where there are variants in the manuscripts, we can reach a high level of certainty as to what the original text said.[11] God has not seen fit to preserve the autographs (apostolically-penned originals) of the New Testament, but he has preserved *all the words of the autographs* in the

---

[8] Scholars also speak of "the Majority text," which means the reading found in the majority of extant New Testament manuscripts. As the majority of extant New Testament manuscripts are Byzantine, there is an overlap in the terms. Most Byzantine text readings are considered, by pure mathematical reckoning, as "the Majority text." Of course, because nearly all New Testament text traditions overlap at roughly 90 percent, any New Testament text will be representative of "the Majority text" at most points.

[9] See Eldon Jay Epp's critique of these traditional text-critical principles in "Traditional 'Canons' of New Testament Textual Criticism: Their Value, Validity, and Viability—or Lack Thereof," in *The Textual History of the Greek New Testament: Changing Views in Contemporary Research*, Text Critical Studies 8, ed. Klaus Wachtel and Michael W. Holmes (Atlanta: SBL, 2011), 79–127.

[10] For an irenic and cogent refutation of the King James Only position, see James R. White, *The King James Only Controversy: Can You Trust the Modern Translations?*, 2nd ed. (Minneapolis: Bethany House, 2009).

[11] For an essay defending the reliability of the Greek New Testament, see Daniel B. Wallace, "Has the New Testament Text Been Hopelessly Corrupted?," in *In Defense of the Bible: A Comprehensive Apologetic for the Authority of Scripture*, ed. Steven B. Cowan and Terry L. Wilder (Nashville: B&H, 2013), 139–63.

many manuscripts that have come down to us.

Traditionally, the discipline of text criticism has sought to determine the original wording of an ancient text for which the autograph has disappeared, and for which disputed witnesses exist today. The criteria for determining the original reading of the text can be divided into external and internal criteria. *External criteria* concern the age, quantity, and provenance (or geographical origin) of the manuscripts consulted. *Internal criteria* consider how a disputed variant fits within the context of the document (the author's style or the context of his argument). Some prominent modern text critics are known for strongly favoring external or internal criteria, but a reasoned use of all available criteria seems judicious. As scholars consider manuscript variants, they are like detectives—using their knowledge of the manuscript they are studying along with their understanding of common scribal mistakes or tendencies to reconstruct both the original text and to explain variant readings.

The Greek New Testament that results from deciding among disputed readings is called an *eclectic text*. The word "eclectic" means "drawn from a variety of sources." In labeling our final product as an eclectic text, we are recognizing that there is no ancient manuscript that parallels it word-for-word. While our eclectic Greek New Testament overlaps overwhelmingly with the vast majority of all ancient Greek New Testament manuscripts, it is, in the end, drawn from a multiplicity of sources and does not agree at every point with any of them.

Changes by ancient scribes to the wording of the manuscripts they were copying (i.e., to the exemplars) can be loosely classified as unintentional errors and intentional changes. We will briefly look at examples of both:

Unintentional Errors[12]

1. *Errors of Sight.* Scribes sometimes copied texts by looking back and forth to a manuscript. By this method, they inevitably made a number of errors of sight. For example, they confused letters that looked similar in appearance, divided words wrongly (the oldest Greek manuscripts of the Bible have no spaces between words), repeated words or sections (i.e., copied the same thing twice), accidentally skipped letters, words, or sections, or changed the order of letters in a word or words in a sentence. In Codex Vaticanus, for example, at Gal 1:11, a scribe accidentally wrote τὸ εὐαγγέλιον ("the gospel") three times in succession.

---

[12] The material below is from Robert L. Plummer, *40 Questions About Interpreting the Bible* (Grand Rapids: Kregel, 2010), originally derived from Arthur G. Patzia, *The Making of the New Testament: Origin, Collection, Text & Canon* (Downers Grove, IL: InterVarsity, 1995), 138–46.

2. *Errors of Hearing.* When scribes copied manuscripts through dictation (i.e., scribes wrote as a manuscript was being read), errors of hearing were made. For example, vowels, diphthongs, or other sounds were misheard—as in Matt 2:6 in Codex Sinaiticus, where ἐκ σοῦ ("from you") has been wrongly heard and written as ἐξ οὗ ("from whom"). We make similar mistakes in English, for instance, writing "night" when someone says, "knight."

3. *Errors of Writing.* Sometimes scribes introduced errors into texts simply by writing the wrong thing. For example, a scribe might accidentally add an additional letter to the end of a word—resulting in a different meaning. In Codex Alexandrinus, at John 13:37, a scribe accidentally wrote δύνασαί μοι rather than δύναμαί σοι. Thus, rather than saying to Jesus, "why can't I follow you now," Peter queries, "why can't you follow me now?"[13]

4. *Errors of Judgment.* Sometimes scribes exercised poor judgment by incorporating marginal glosses (ancient footnotes) into the body of the text or by incorporating similar unintentional corrupting influences. In the fourteenth-century Codex 109, for example, an incompetent scribe has apparently copied continuous lines of text from a manuscript that listed the genealogy of Jesus (Luke 3:23–38) in two columns. The resulting genealogy has all the family relations scrambled, even listing God as the son of Aram.[14]

Intentional Errors

A minority of textual variants resulted from intentional activity on the part of scribes. Such changes included the following:

1. *Revising Grammar and Spelling.* In an attempt to standardize grammar or spelling, scribes sometimes corrected what they perceived as orthographic or grammatical errors in the text they were copying. For example, though John originally put the nominative case after the preposition ἀπό in Rev 1:4, later scribes have inserted a genitive form.[15]

2. *Harmonizing Similar Passages.* Scribes had a tendency to harmonize parallel passages and introduce uniformity to stylized expressions. For example, details from the same incident in multiple Gospels might be included when copying any one

---

[13] This variant is also possibly an "error of sight" (i.e., the scribe's eyes jumped to the parallel expression in John 13:36). We are indebted to Elijah Hixson for pointing out this variant, as well as some others mentioned in this section.
[14] Metzger and Ehrman, *Text of the New Testament,* 259.
[15] Metzger and Ehrman, 262.

Gospel. We have seen students sometimes unintentionally insert "Lord" or "Christ" when translating a passage with the name "Jesus." Normally, such students are not intending to promote a "higher Christology"; they are simply conforming their speech to a stylized reference to the Savior. Ancient scribes behaved in a similar way.

3. *Eliminating Apparent Discrepancies and Difficulties.* Scribes sometimes attempted to fix what they perceived as a problem in the text. Metzger and Ehrman report that because Origen perceived a geographical difficulty at John 1:28, he changed Βηθανίᾳ ("Bethany") to Βηθαραβᾷ.[16]

4. *Conflating the Text.* Sometimes when a scribe knew of variant readings in the manuscript base from which he was copying, he would simply include both variants within his copy, conflating them. For example, in Acts 20:28, some early manuscripts read τὴν ἐκκλησίαν τοῦ θεοῦ ("the church of God"), while others read τὴν ἐκκλησίαν τοῦ κυρίου ("church of the Lord"). Later manuscripts conflate the readings as τὴν ἐκκλησίαν τοῦ κυρίου καὶ [τοῦ] θεοῦ ("the church of the Lord and God").[17]

5. *Adapting Different Liturgical Traditions.* In a few isolated places, it is possible that church liturgy (i.e., stylized prayers or praises) influenced some textual additions or wording changes (e.g., Matt 6:13, "For yours is the kingdom and the power and the glory forever. Amen").

6. *Making Theological or Doctrinal Changes.* Sometimes scribes made theological or doctrinal changes—either omitting something they saw as wrong or making clarifying additions. For example, in Matt 24:36, some manuscripts omit the reference to the Son's ignorance of the day of his return—a passage that is obviously difficult to understand.[18]

In recent decades, the field of New Testament textual criticism has experienced a revival of interest. The digitization of most significant ancient Greek New Testament manuscripts has democratized access to primary materials. (View, for example, the entire Codex Sinaiticus in stunning clarity at www.codexsinaiticus.org). Computers have also changed the traditional and overly simplistic

---

[16] Metzger and Ehrman, *Text of the New Testament,* 264.
[17] Metzger and Ehrman, 265.
[18] In this text, as in a few others (e.g., John 4:6), Scripture seems to speak of Jesus from the perspective of his human nature, not intending to deny the omniscience or omnipotence of his divine nature. Others have explained this passage by claiming that prior to his exaltation, Jesus emptied himself of certain divine prerogatives (i.e., the Kenotic theory).

categorization of manuscripts into broad text families; algorithms are helping sort out complex genealogical relationships between ancient manuscripts and are at the heart of the ongoing revision of the standard critical editions of the Greek New Testament (i.e., the *Editio Critica Maior*, the Nestle-Aland, and the United Bible Societies editions). Also, there has been a flowering of interest in scribal tendencies and what they reveal about the theological predilections of ancient scribes and the communities they represent. There has never been a more exciting time to explore the field of text criticism.

Resources for Further Study:

• Elijah Hixson and Peter J. Gurry, eds. *Myths and Mistakes in New Testament Textual Criticism*. Downers Grove: IVP Academic, 2019. This is a recent and engaging book edited by two young text critical scholars.

• https://evangelicaltextualcriticism.blogspot.com/. This blog provides an evangelical window into current text critical discussions.

• "The Basics of New Testament Textual Criticism" Apple podcast, by the Center for the Study of New Testament Manuscripts. Via this free podcast, you can view fifteen foundational lectures on New Testament text criticism by evangelical text critic Dan Wallace.

• www.credocourses.com/product/textual-criticism/. This text criticism class, also by Dan Wallace, is more extensive than the free podcast videos mentioned above. The class and accompanying resources are available for purchase from the apologetics ministry Credo House.

• www.csntm.org. The Center for the Study of New Testament Manuscripts (CSNTM) is a non-profit ministry led by Dan Wallace that focuses on digitizing manuscripts of the Greek New Testament.

• http://www.ntgateway.com/textual-criticism/resource-pages/. The "Text Criticism Resource Pages" at ntgateway.com (overseen by Mark Goodacre of Duke University) provide many interesting and helpful links.

• https://newtestamentgreekportal.blogspot.com/p/textual-criticism.html. Southeastern Seminary's David Alan Black's "text criticism" section of his New Testament Greek Portal provides summaries of text critical resources and helpful links.

Optional Assignment: Spend twenty minutes exploring the online resources above. Then read an entire blog entry at https://evangelicaltextualcriticism.blogspot.com/. After that, write one paragraph summarizing what you learned in your foray into the world of New Testament textual criticism.

Does this topic interest you enough to study further on your own? If so, make a plan of specific next steps.

//////////////

CHAPTER 9

PERSONAL AND RELATIVE PRONOUNS

9.1 Overview[1]

A *pronoun* is a word that takes the place of a noun or other substantive.[2] The noun that is replaced by the pronoun is called the *antecedent*. In the sentence, "you are to name him **Jesus**, because **he** will save his people from their sins" (Matt 1:21), "Jesus" is the antecedent for the pronoun "he."

In this chapter, we will discuss two types of pronouns: (1) personal pronouns and (2) relative pronouns. Personal pronouns can further be distinguished as first person ("I," "we"), second person ("you," sg or pl), and third person ("he," "she," "they").

9.2 Significance

The New Living Translation (NLT) of 1 John 1:1, reads like this:

> We proclaim to you the one who existed from the beginning, whom we have heard and seen. We saw him with our own eyes and touched him with our own hands. He is the Word of life.

Compare this rendering to the New American Standard (NASB) version:

> What was from the beginning, what we have heard, what we have seen with our eyes, what we have looked at and touched with our hands, concerning the Word of Life.

---

[1] For an overview video lecture of chapter 9, go to bit.ly/greeklecture9 or beginninggreek.com.

[2] A "substantive" is any part of speech that functions as a noun.

Both translations are accurate, but the NASB is closer to the structure of the original Greek text:

Ὃ ἦν ἀπ᾽ ἀρχῆς, ὃ ἀκηκόαμεν, ὃ ἑωράκαμεν τοῖς ὀφθαλμοῖς ἡμῶν, ὃ ἐθεασάμεθα καὶ αἱ χεῖρες ἡμῶν ἐψηλάφησαν περὶ τοῦ λόγου τῆς ζωῆς

The bold Greek word (ὅ) is a relative pronoun, translated as "what" or "that which" in most modern English translations. This string of relative clauses (i.e., "what was . . . what we have . . . what we have . . . what we have") serves as the object of the verb ἀπαγγέλλομεν "we proclaim" (1 John 1:3). The author's delay in identifying the subject and verb is significant. About this structure, Howard Marshall remarks, "The result—which is important—is that the opening emphasis falls on the nature of the object which is proclaimed rather than on the activity of proclaiming it. The writer's purpose is to remind his readers of the character of the Christian message rather than to draw attention to the actual act of preaching it."[3]

You are becoming a reader of the Greek New Testament. As such, you will sometimes see nuances conveyed by the structure of the original language that are difficult to render in an English translation.

9.3 Personal Pronouns

Because there are three "persons" (first, second, third) in Greek grammar, it follows that there are also three different types of **personal pronouns**.

	Singular	Plural
First Person:	ἐγώ ("I")	ἡμεῖς ("we")
Second Person:	σύ ("you")	ὑμεῖς ("you" or "you all")
Third Person:	αὐτός, –ή, –ό ("he/she/it")	αὐτοί, –αί, –ά ("they")

As in English, a pronoun must agree with its antecedent in gender and number but not necessarily in case. The reason the pronoun does not need to agree with its antecedent in case is because it can have a different grammatical function in its clause. In Matt 1:21 ("you are to name him **Jesus**, because **he** will save his people from their sins"), the antecedent "Jesus" (Ἰησοῦν) is in the accusative case because it is functioning as the object complement of the verb "call." The pronoun "he" (αὐτός) is in the nominative case because it is functioning as the subject of the verb "save." Yet, both the antecedent and the pronoun are masculine and singular.

If the pronoun also agreed with the antecedent in case, the sentence would read this way: "you are to name him Jesus, because **him** will save his people from their sins." Obviously, such a rendering would be grammatically incorrect. Similarly, if the gender did not match, the sentence would read, "you are to name him Jesus, because **she** will save his people from their sins." Finally, if the number did not

---

[3] I. Howard Marshall, *The Epistles of John*, NICNT (Grand Rapids: Eerdmans, 1978), 100.

match, it would read, "you are to name him Jesus, because **they** will save his people from their sins."

9.4 Paradigms

FIRST PERSON PERSONAL PRONOUNS[4]				
	SINGULAR		PLURAL	
NOM	ἐγώ	I	ἡμεῖς	we
GEN	μου	of me, my	ἡμῶν	of us, our
DAT	μοι	to/for me	ἡμῖν	to/for us
ACC	με	me	ἡμᾶς	us

SECOND PERSON PERSONAL PRONOUNS				
	SINGULAR		PLURAL	
NOM	σύ	you	ὑμεῖς	you
GEN	σου	of you, your	ὑμῶν	of you, your
DAT	σοι	to/for you	ὑμῖν	to/for you
ACC	σε	you	ὑμᾶς	you

THIRD PERSON PERSONAL PRONOUNS					
	SINGULAR			PLURAL		
	MASC	FEM	NEUT	MASC	FEM	NEUT
NOM	αὐτός	αὐτή	αὐτό	αὐτοί	αὐταί	αὐτά
GEN	αὐτοῦ	αὐτῆς	αὐτοῦ	αὐτῶν	αὐτῶν	αὐτῶν
DAT	αὐτῷ	αὐτῇ	αὐτῷ	αὐτοῖς	αὐταῖς	αὐτοῖς
ACC	αὐτόν	αὐτήν	αὐτό	αὐτούς	αὐτάς	αὐτά

9.5 Personal Pronoun Morphology

The paradigms for the first and second person personal pronouns must be memorized. Notice that the genitive forms (sg: μου, σου; pl: ἡμῶν, ὑμῶν) have endings similar to second declension nouns (sg: λόγου; pl: λόγων). In addition, the dative forms have the predictable iota (sg: μοι, σοι; pl: ἡμῖν, ὑμῖν; cf. λόγῳ, λόγοις). Finally, note that the first and second person forms differ only by the first letter (except in the nominative singular):[5]

---

[4] To hear a mnemonic song, go to bit.ly/Pronounssong or beginninggreek.com.
[5] There is no gender for first and second person personal pronouns.

	Singular			Plural		
Nom	ἐγώ	→	σύ	ἡμεῖς	→	ὑμεῖς[6]
Gen	μου	→	σου	ἡμῶν	→	ὑμῶν
Dat	μοι	→	σοι	ἡμῖν	→	ὑμῖν
Acc	με	→	σε	ἡμᾶς	→	ὑμᾶς

The third person forms do not need to be memorized since the endings are identical to first and second declension nouns and/or articles (αὐτός → λόγος, αὐτή → φωνή, αὐτό → τέκνον).[7]

Several alternate forms of the first and second person personal pronouns have an additional epsilon (ε) at the beginning of the word or have an accent mark. Such forms are used more commonly for objects of prepositions and to communicate stress, emphasis, or contrast.

μου	→	ἐμοῦ	σου	→	σοῦ
μοι	→	ἐμοί	σοι	→	σοί
με	→	ἐμέ	σε	→	σέ

The singular unemphatic forms have no accent and are pronounced with the preceding word (ὁ πατήρ μου → ὁ πατήρμου).[8] In some circumstances, the preceding word adds an accent (τὸ **ὄνομά** μου).

9.6 Personal Pronoun Use

Personal pronouns are often not needed in a sentence since the information of person and number is communicated through the verb's personal ending. For example, in the sentence "He has a demon" (δαιμόνιον ἔχει; Matt 11:18), the ending of the verb (ἔχει) communicates that the subject is "he" (i.e., third person singular). Thus, because Greek verbs include subject information, pronouns in the nominative case are not required.

Emphatic Use

When a pronoun is supplied but not required, it may be employed for the sake of clarity or stylistic variation—or the explicit pronoun may make the subject more emphatic. For example, Luke records Paul pleading with the Ephesian elders with the very words of Jesus: "he **himself** said, 'It is more blessed to give than to receive'" (**αὐτὸς** εἶπεν, Μακάριόν ἐστιν μᾶλλον διδόναι ἢ λαμβάνειν; Acts 20:35). The addition of αὐτός presses the authority of what Paul is claiming

---

[6] These forms are easy to confuse. One simple way to keep them straight is by remembering that the upsilon of ὑμεῖς corresponds to the "u" which sounds like "you."

[7] The neuter nominative and accusative singular forms have dropped the nu (ν), but see the article τό which also lacks the nu.

[8] A word that lacks an accent and is pronounced with the previous word is said to be *enclitic*. In contrast, if the word has no accent (such as some articles or prepositions) and is linked with the following word, it is *proclitic*.

since he is quoting Christ personally. In other words, when the personal pronoun is included but not necessary, it often adds emphasis (or contrast).[9] Context must indicate what is being emphasized or contrasted.

Another example is Mark 1:8: "**I** baptize you with water, but **he** will baptize you with the Holy Spirit" (ἐγὼ ἐβάπτισα ὑμᾶς ὕδατι, **αὐτὸς** δὲ βαπτίσει ὑμᾶς ἐν πνεύματι ἁγίῳ). Notice that both uses of the pronouns (ἐγώ, αὐτός) are unnecessary since "I" and "he" are communicated by the verbs (ἐβάπτισα [first singular], βαπτίσει [third singular]). The emphatic use of the pronouns can be communicated in the English translation by adding a reflexive pronoun ("myself," "himself"). The emphatic use of subject pronouns in Mark 1:8 draws a grammatical line in the sand between two different orders of ministry—the preparatory work of John the Baptist and the new covenant-fulfilling ministry of Jesus.

Intensive Use (αὐτός)

The third person personal pronoun is sometimes employed to intensify an explicit noun or pronoun in the sentence. In such cases, it matches the intensified substantive in gender, case, and number and is always anarthrous (lacking an article), while the intensified noun is usually articular (having the article). For example, Paul writes, "the Lord **himself** will descend" (**αὐτὸς** ὁ κύριος . . . καταβήσεται; 1 Thess 4:16). This usage differs from the emphatic use (see above) because there is an explicit subject in the sentence to intensify (ὁ κύριος). As we can see from the English translation, αὐτός intensifies the subject that is already explicitly present in the original sentence ("the Lord *himself*").

Less commonly, a form of αὐτός will be used to intensify an explicitly present or implied first or second person personal pronoun in the nominative case. This usage can be confusing for beginning students. So, let's consider an example from Paul's letter to the Philippians. Paul mentions that he hopes to send Timothy to them. He later adds, "I am confident in the Lord that I **myself** will also come soon" (πέποιθα δὲ ἐν κυρίῳ ὅτι καὶ **αὐτὸς** ταχέως ἐλεύσομαι; Phil 2:24). The verb is first person singular (ἐλεύσομαι), so the implied subject is ἐγώ (nom, sg, and [based on the context] masc). This ἐγώ is singular and nominative; with Paul as the writer, it should also be understood, in context, as masculine. What form of αὐτός is needed to intensify this implied ἐγώ? One that matches its gender, case, and number—a masculine, nominative, singular form: αὐτός.

Beginning Greek students tend to think wrongly of αὐτός as always meaning "he." Remember that various forms of αὐτός can also be used to intensify an explicit noun or pronoun (or implied pronoun); moreover, the form of αὐτός will match its intensified substantive in gender, case, and number and is never preceded by an article.

---

[9] Emphasis is usually not intended with the use of the pronoun and the verb εἰμί or with other copulative verbs. See, e.g., S. M. Baugh, *A First John Reader: Intermediate Greek Reading Notes and Grammar* (Phillipsburg, NJ: P&R, 1999), 93.

Identical Use (αὐτός)

Finally, the third person personal pronoun can, in certain contexts, be rendered with the adjective "same" in English. That is, αὐτός also has an identical function. Here is a helpful rule: when the article directly precedes a form of the pronoun αὐτός, it should be translated "same." This identical use occurs several times in 1 Cor 12:4–6: "Now there are different gifts, but **the same** Spirit (**τὸ αὐτὸ** πνεῦμα). There are different ministries, but **the same** Lord (**ὁ αὐτὸς** κύριος). And there are different activities, but **the same** God (**ὁ δὲ αὐτὸς** θεός) works all of them in each." In each of these instances, the article directly precedes the pronoun. This use can occur in other cases as well. James states, "Blessing and cursing come out of **the same** mouth" (**ἐκ τοῦ αὐτοῦ** στόματος ἐξέρχεται εὐλογία καὶ κατάρα; Jas 3:10). Note that in the identical usage (that is, where a form of αὐτός means "same"), αὐτός matches the gender, case, and number of the noun it modifies. αὐτός can also function alone as a substantive (ὁ αὐτός, "the same man"; αἱ αὐταί, "the same women"; τὸ αὐτό, "the same thing").

9.7 Relative Pronouns

English relative pronouns include "who," "which," "that," "whose," or "whom." We are not speaking of question words here, but words that usually relate back (thus called *relative* pronouns) to an explicit antecedent in the sentence and that thus allow the author to say more about it. For example, "**Bill** is the man **who** lives next to me." In this English example, "Bill" is the antecedent, "who" is the relative pronoun, and "who lives next to me" is the entire relative clause. Think of a relative clause as a large adjectival phrase attached to the noun it is modifying with a relative pronoun. Luke 5:18 provides us an example from the New Testament: "Some men came, carrying on a stretcher **a man** (ἄνθρωπον) **who** (ὅς) was paralyzed." The relative pronoun "who" (ὅς) introduces a dependent clause which further expands on the noun "man" (ἄνθρωπον). Specifically, we learn that the man was a paralytic. Again, the (relative) pronoun will agree with the antecedent in gender and number but not necessarily in case. Case is determined by how the relative pronoun is functioning in the sentence.

9.8 Relative Pronoun Morphology

	SINGULAR			PLURAL		
	MASC	FEM	NEUT	MASC	FEM	NEUT
NOM	ὅς	ἥ	ὅ	οἵ	αἵ	ἅ
GEN	οὗ	ἧς	οὗ	ὧν	ὧν	ὧν
DAT	ᾧ	ᾗ	ᾧ	οἷς	αἷς	οἷς
ACC	ὅν	ἥν	ὅ	οὕς	ἅς	ἅ

Notice that the relative pronoun forms are similar to the first and second declension endings. In fact, they are simply personal endings with a rough breathing mark and an accent. Compare, for example, the masculine declension of λόγος with the masculine relative pronoun:

Singular		Translation	Plural		Translation
λόγος	→ ὅς	who	λόγοι	→ οἵ	who
λόγου	→ οὗ	whose	λόγων	→ ὧν	whose
λόγῳ	→ ᾧ	to/for whom	λόγοις	→ οἷς	to/for whom
λόγον	→ ὅν	whom	λόγους	→ οὕς	whom

The masculine and feminine nominative (sg and pl) relative pronouns have alternate forms. These forms are a combination of the relative pronoun and the indefinite pronoun (ὅς + τις, "anyone, someone") and can be called ***indefinite relative pronouns***. Although these forms carried an indefinite meaning during an earlier stage of the Greek language (i.e., ὅστις = "who*ever*"), in New Testament times these forms typically functioned synonymously with the regular relative pronoun (ὅς).[10] Occasionally, however, the alternate forms do seem to maintain a qualitative sense (Phil 2:20, "who [is of such a sort that]").

Singular			Plural	
ὅς	→ ὅστις	οἵ	→ οἵτινες	
ἥ	→ ἥτις	αἵ	→ αἵτινες	

9.9 Relative Pronoun Use

Interestingly, relative pronouns in Greek and English are similar! Just like in Greek, English relative pronouns are inflected, having different forms based on their function in the sentence: subject = "who"; possession = "whose"; indirect object = "to/for whom"; and direct object = "whom, which."

Nom "Are you greater than our father Abraham **who** died?" (μὴ σὺ μείζων εἶ τοῦ πατρὸς ἡμῶν Ἀβραάμ, **ὅστις** ἀπέθανεν; John 8:53).

Gen "There was a certain official **whose** son was ill" (ἦν τις βασιλικὸς **οὗ** ὁ υἱὸς ἠσθένει; John 4:46).

Dat "To the only wise God, through Jesus Christ, **to [whom]** be glory forever" (μόνῳ σοφῷ θεῷ, διὰ Ἰησοῦ Χριστοῦ, **ᾧ** ἡ δόξα εἰς τοὺς αἰῶνας; Rom 16:27).

---

[10] These alternate forms are quite common: ὅστις (26x), οἵτινες (60x), ἥτις (38x), and αἵτινες (10x).

Acc   "They believed the Scripture and the statement [**which**] Jesus had made" (ἐπίστευσαν τῇ γραφῇ καὶ τῷ λόγῳ ὃν εἶπεν ὁ Ἰησοῦς; John 2:22).

It is also possible for a relative pronoun to have no antecedent: "for **whoever** has, more will be given to him" (ὃς γὰρ ἔχει, δοθήσεται αὐτῷ; Mark 4:25). A clause like this, where the relative pronoun has no explicit antecedent, is called a *headless relative clause*.[11] Various rhetorical or stylistic considerations can cause an author or speaker to employ headless relative clauses. As we saw in the "Significance" section at the beginning of this chapter, the string of headless relative clauses in 1 John 1:1–3 places a striking emphasis on the object of the apostolic proclamation—"the historical manifestation of the eternal."[12]

Occasionally a relative pronoun will be attracted to (and thus take on) the case of its antecedent (especially the genitive case). Handily, grammarians refer to this morphing of the relative pronoun to match the case of its antecedent as *attraction*. John 15:20 provides us with an example from the New Testament: "Remember the word [**which**] I spoke to you" (μνημονεύετε τοῦ λόγου οὗ ἐγὼ εἶπον ὑμῖν). The relative pronoun (οὗ) should be in the accusative case based on its function (as object of the verb of speaking), but it is attracted to the genitive case of its antecedent (τοῦ λόγου).

Finally, it is easy to confuse relative pronouns with other parts of speech—especially the article and the verb εἰμί. Below is a comparison of forms. If you remember that a relative pronoun *always* has both a rough breathing mark and an accent, that will save you much confusion.

Relative Pronouns	Article	εἰμί
ὅ	ὁ	
ἥ, ᾗ	ἡ	
ἧς		ἧς
ἥν		ἥν

9.10 Practice

A. Paradigms: Memorize the paradigms for ἐγώ and σύ (see section 9.4). Then write out each paradigm ten times from memory.

B. Personal Pronouns: Match the correct personal pronouns.

1. _____ 1st person dative plural   A. αὐτά

[11] This is one of those scary grammatical terms, but don't be afraid—the clause is not actually decapitated!

[12] John R. W. Stott, *The Letters of John*, rev. ed., TNTC 19 (Grand Rapids: Eerdmans; Leicester: InterVarsity Press, 1988), 63.

2. _____ 3rd person feminine accusative singular   B. σύ

3. _____ 2nd person genitive plural   C. ἡμῖν

4. _____ 3rd person neuter nominative plural   D. αὐταῖς

5. _____ 1st person accusative singular   E. ὑμῶν

6. _____ 2nd person dative singular   F. σοι

7. _____ 3rd person masculine accusative plural   G. με

8. _____ 2nd person nominative singular   H. αὐτήν

9. _____ 3rd person feminine dative plural   I. μου

10. _____ 1st person genitive singular   J. αὐτούς

C. Relative Pronouns: Circle the relative pronouns.

1. ᾗ   ἡ   οὕς   τούς

2. ᾧ   αἱ   ὁ   ὅ

3. ὅστις   τῶν   ἥ   ὅς

4. ὧν   αἵ   εἶ   ἥτις

5. τῆς   ἧς   ἧς   ἅς

D. Translation: Translate the following sentences.

1. ὁ ἀδελφός σου ἔχει τι (something) κατὰ σου (Matt 5:23).

2. καὶ ἐπίστευσαν (they believed) τῇ γραφῇ (Scripture) καὶ τῷ λόγῳ ὃν εἶπεν (said) ὁ Ἰησοῦς (John 2:22).

3. τὰ γὰρ αὐτὰ πράσσεις (you are doing) (Rom 2:1).

4. αὐτὸς δὲ Ἰησοῦς οὐκ ἐπίστευεν[13] αὐτὸν αὐτοῖς (John 2:24).

5. ὃ ἐγὼ ποιῶ σὺ οὐκ οἶδας (know) (John 13:7).

6. καὶ ἐγὼ αὐτὸς ἄνθρωπός εἰμι (Acts 10:26).

7. καὶ ὃς οὐ λαμβάνει τὸν σταυρὸν (cross) αὐτοῦ καὶ ἀκολουθεῖ ὀπίσω (after) μου, οὐκ ἔστιν μου ἄξιος (worthy) (Matt 10:38).

---

[13] πιστεύω is best translated here "entrust."

8. Πᾶς (everyone) οὖν ὅστις ἀκούει μου τοὺς λόγους . . . καὶ ποιεῖ αὐτούς (Matt 7:26).

9. τὰ ἔργα ἃ ἐγὼ ποιῶ ἐν τῷ ὀνόματι (name) τοῦ πατρός (father) μου . . . μαρτυρεῖ περὶ ἐμοῦ (John 10:25).

10. ἀναβαίνω (I am going up) πρὸς τὸν πατέρα (father) μου καὶ πατέρα ὑμῶν καὶ θεόν μου καὶ θεὸν ὑμῶν (John 20:17).

11. ἔλεγεν δὲ καὶ πρὸς τοὺς μαθητάς, Ἄνθρωπός τις (certain) ἦν πλούσιος (rich) ὃς εἶχεν οἰκονόμον (a manager/steward) (Luke 16:1).

12. Χριστὸς δὲ ὡς υἱὸς ἐπὶ τὸν οἶκον (house) αὐτοῦ· οὗ οἶκός ἐσμεν ἡμεῖς (Heb 3:6).

E. Translation: Translate the following sentences into Greek.

1. My house is your house.

2. He speaks peace to her.

3. . . . the man, who hears your voice.

4. The child himself walks beside their lake.

5. The people have bread which comes from heaven.

9.11 Vocabulary[14]

διώκω	I pursue, persecute
δοξάζω	I glorify, praise (*doxology*)
πέμπω	I send
πράσσω	I do, practice (*practical, pragmatic*)
σώζω	I save, rescue, heal (*soteriology*)
τηρέω	I keep, guard, obey
ἀπόστολος, ὁ	apostle, messenger (*apostle*)
ἐντολή, ἡ	command
καιρός, ὁ	time, season
κεφαλή, ἡ	head (*encephalitis*)
πρόσωπον, τό	face, appearance
σάββατον, τό	Sabbath, week (*Sabbath*)
ἔτι	still, yet, more
μᾶλλον	more, rather
οὐκέτι	no longer

---

[14] To hear an author of your textbook read through the vocabulary for chapter 9, go to bit.ly/greekvocab9 or beginninggreek.com.

CHAPTER 10

//////////////

FUTURE INDICATIVE VERBS

10.1 Overview[1]

In this chapter, we will discuss the future tense, which represents the third tense studied in this book. (We have already overviewed the present and imperfect tenses.) One different element of the future tense is that it has distinct middle and passive forms (in contrast to having one paradigm whose forms function to convey both middle or passive ideas, depending on the context).

10.2 Significance

A mother says, "You will clean your room after you come home from school today" as she surveys the chaos of her teen daughter's bedroom. In employing the English future tense, is this mother claiming prophetic powers? (Does she really mean,"I have seen a vision, and I can predict that after you get home, you are going to do this"?) Obviously not. This mother is employing a future tense verb as an imperative—not an especially common English usage, but one that's readily understood and adds a sense of solemnity or emphasis to the command.

Within the Greek New Testament, the future tense regularly appears with its predictive sense (εὑρήσετε πῶλον δεδεμένον ἐφ᾽ ὃν οὐδεὶς οὔπω ἀνθρώπων ἐκάθισεν, "**you will find** a colt tied there, on which no one has ever sat," Mark 11:2), but the future tense also can function as an imperative. For example, in Matt 22:37–39, we read (from a literal English translation which formats Old Testament quotations in small caps):

---

[1] For an overview video lecture of chapter 10, go to bit.ly/greeklecture10 or beginninggreek.com.

107

And [Jesus] said to him, "'YOU SHALL LOVE (ἀγαπήσεις, future tense) THE LORD YOUR GOD WITH ALL YOUR HEART, AND WITH ALL YOUR SOUL, AND WITH ALL YOUR MIND.' This is the great and foremost commandment. The second is like it, 'YOU SHALL LOVE (ἀγαπήσεις, future tense) YOUR NEIGHBOR AS YOURSELF.'" (NASB)

In pronouncing the double-love command, Jesus quotes from Deut 6:5 and Lev 19:18. In both of those Old Testament texts, an imperatival future appears in the Hebrew text, which is brought over quite literally as an imperatival future in the Septuagint (or, LXX, an early Greek translation of the Old Testament)—a rendering that Matthew mirrors here.

Mark Strauss has noted that many of the imperatival futures in the New Testament are quotations of Old Testament texts and frequently carry with them an increased sense of formality or emphasis, in contrast to a simple imperatival form—a function similar to modern English usage of the future tense to convey a command.[2]

10.3 Tense-Form and Meaning

The future tense communicates an expectation of something that will take place, usually communicated in English with the word "will" or "shall." There are, however, a variety of ways the future tense can be used in the Greek New Testament.

- **Predictive Future:** Predicts a future event or at least indicates the expectation that something will take place from the author's perspective. For example, the angel of God appears to Joseph and declares, "**She will bear** a Son; and you shall call his name Jesus, for he **will save** his people from their sins," τέξεται δὲ υἱόν, καὶ καλέσεις τὸ ὄνομα αὐτοῦ Ἰησοῦν· αὐτὸς γὰρ **σώσει** τὸν λαὸν αὐτοῦ ἀπὸ τῶν ἁμαρτιῶν αὐτῶν (Matt 1:21 NASB).

- **Imperatival Future:** Following Old Testament usage, the future is often used to express an imperative or command. In the example given just above (Matt 1:21 NASB), the middle use of the future reveals a command to Joseph: "**you shall call** his name Jesus," **καλέσεις** τὸ ὄνομα αὐτοῦ Ἰησοῦν. When translating, it is perhaps better to use "shall" than "will" since the former communicates the imperatival quality. This use is mostly found when the New Testament writers quote the Old Testament (especially the Ten Commandments): "YOU SHALL WORSHIP THE LORD YOUR GOD," Κύριον τὸν θεόν σου **προσκυνήσεις** (Matt 4:10; quoting Deut 6:13 NASB); "YOU SHALL NOT COMMIT MURDER," Οὐ **φονεύσεις** (Matt 5:21; quoting Exod 20:13 NASB).

---

[2] Mark L. Strauss, *The Biblical Greek Companion for Bible Software Users: Grammatical Terms Explained for Exegesis* (Grand Rapids: Zondervan, 2016), 33.

- **Deliberative Future:** Involves a real or rhetorical question that implies some amount of uncertainty as to the response. When Jesus asks the Twelve if they also want to leave him, Peter responds, "Lord, to whom **shall we go**? You have words of eternal life," Κύριε, πρὸς τίνα **ἀπελευσόμεθα**; ῥήματα ζωῆς αἰωνίου ἔχεις (John 6:68 NASB). Peter's rhetorical question is not looking for an answer but functions more like an affirmation (i.e., "Lord, there is no other person like you! You alone have the words of eternal life!").

10.4 Voice

Verbs with lexical forms that end with –ω can be active, middle, or passive. If the endings of a verb follow those found in the λύσω Future Active paradigm (–σω, –σεις, –σει, –σομεν, –σετε, –σουσιν), then the verb is active. If it follows the endings found in the λύσομαι paradigm (–σομαι, –ση, –σεται, –σόμεθα, –σεσθε, –σονται), then it is middle. And if the verb follows endings found in the λυθήσομαι paradigm (–θήσομαι, –θήση, –θήσεται, –θησόμεθα, –θήσεσθε, –θήσονται), then it is passive in form. Frankly, during the Koine Greek period, passive endings are employed to convey a middle idea, so context is most important in determining meaning. Some grammarians advocate passive endings as "MP" (medio-passive)—as a reminder that they can convey both a middle or passive idea.

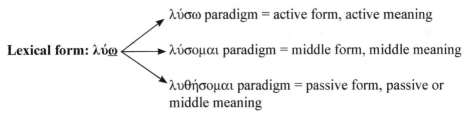

Lexical form: λύ**ω**

λύσω paradigm = active form, active meaning

λύσομαι paradigm = middle form, middle meaning

λυθήσομαι paradigm = passive form, passive or middle meaning

Verbs with lexical forms that end with –ομαι can follow either middle or passive endings, but they will always convey a middle idea, regardless of whether middle or passive endings are employed.

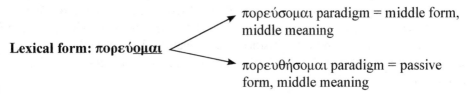

Lexical form: πορεύ**ομαι**

πορεύσομαι paradigm = middle form, middle meaning

πορευθήσομαι paradigm = passive form, middle meaning

10.5 Paradigms

FUTURE ACTIVE INDICATIVE[3]			
	SINGULAR		**PLURAL**
1ST	λύσω	I will loose	λύσομεν	we will loose
2ND	λύσεις	you will loose	λύσετε	you will loose
3RD	λύσει	he/she/it will loose	λύσουσι(ν)	they will loose

FUTURE MIDDLE INDICATIVE			
	SINGULAR		**PLURAL**
1ST	λύσομαι	I will loose (for) myself	λυσόμεθα	we will loose (for) ourselves
2ND	λύσῃ	you will loose (for) yourself	λύσεσθε	you will loose (for) yourselves
3RD	λύσεται	he/she/it will loose (for) him/her/itself	λύσονται	they will loose (for) themselves

FUTURE PASSIVE INDICATIVE			
	SINGULAR		**PLURAL**
1ST	λυθήσομαι	I will be loosed	λυθησόμεθα	we will be loosed
2ND	λυθήσῃ	you will be loosed	λυθήσεσθε	you will be loosed
3RD	λυθήσεται	he/she/it will be loosed	λυθήσονται	they will be loosed

10.6 Morphology

The active and middle forms of the future are not difficult to learn if you know the present tense paradigms. The only difference is the addition of a sigma (σ) to the stem (λύω → λύ**σ**ω; λύομαι → λύ**σ**ομαι), which is known as a ***tense formative***. Otherwise, both the connecting vowels and the personal endings remain the same. The charts below reflect a historical approach to the morphology of these paradigms. If this extra background information confuses you, feel free to ignore these charts.

---

[3] To hear a mnemonic song, go to bit.ly/activeindicative or beginninggreek.com.

FUTURE ACTIVE INDICATIVE

Inflected Form	Stem	Connecting Vowel	Personal Ending		Combined Ending
λύσω	λυσ	[o]	ω[4]	→	ω
λύσεις	λυσ	ε	ις[5]	→	εις
λύσει	λυσ	ε	ι[6]	→	ει
λύσομεν	λυσ	o	μεν	→	ομεν
λύσετε	λυσ	ε	τε	→	ετε
λύσουσιν	λυσ	o	υσι[7]	→	ουσι(ν)

FUTURE MIDDLE INDICATIVE

Inflected Form	Stem	Connecting Vowel	Personal Ending		Combined Ending
λύσομαι	λυσ	o	μαι	→	ομαι
λύση	λυσ	[ε]	[σαι][8]	→	η
λύσεται	λυσ	ε	ται	→	εται
λυσόμεθα	λυσ	o	μεθα	→	ομεθα
λύσεσθε	λυσ	ε	σθε	→	εσθε
λύσονται	λυσ	o	νται	→	ονται

Unlike the present and imperfect tenses, the future has distinct middle and passive paradigms. The key in identifying the passive form is the addition of a –θη– to the stem (before the additional sigma). Thus, the passive form has a –θησ– added prior to the same set of connecting vowels and endings employed in the future middle paradigm.

FUTURE PASSIVE INDICATIVE

Inflected Form	Stem	Connecting Vowel	Personal Ending		Combined Ending
λυθήσομαι	λυθησ	o	μαι	→	ομαι
λυθήση	λυθησ	[ε]	[σαι][9]	→	η

---

[4] Technically, the connecting vowel is omicron (o), which then lengthens to an omega (ω) to compensate for the lack of a personal ending. For our purposes, we will view this as the personal ending.

[5] The actual personal ending is σι but for some reason the two letters switched order (ις).

[6] The actual personal ending is τι but the tau (τ) dropped out (cf. ἐστίν).

[7] The actual personal ending is νσι but the nu (ν) dropped out because of the following sigma (σ) causing the omicron to lengthen to ου in order to compensate. Also note that the form will usually take the movable nu.

[8] Technically, the connecting vowel is epsilon (ε) and the personal ending is σαι. Because the sigma occurs between two vowels, it drops. This causes the epsilon and the alpha (α) to lengthen to an eta (η) and the iota (ι) to subscript (ῃ): ε + σαι → εσαι → εαι → ηι → ῃ.

[9] See note 8.

λυθήσεται	λυθησ	ε	ται	→	εται
λυθησόμεθα	λυθησ	ο	μεθα	→	ομεθα
λυθήσεσθε	λυθησ	ε	σθε	→	εσθε
λυθήσονται	λυθησ	ο	νται	→	ονται

10.7 Stem Variations

When the sigma (σ) tense formative is added to the stem of the verb, it causes certain consonant combinations that either (1) make it difficult to pronounce (σῳζω + σ = σῳζσω → σωσω) or (2) form a sound that can be conveyed through one Greek letter instead of two (πεμπω + σ = πεμπσω → πεμψω). Such changes occur often and in accordance with regular patterns.

One of the most effective ways to recognize these changes is to understand that closely related Greek consonants will behave in the same way when a sigma is combined with them. For example, the consonants τ, δ, and θ are all *dentals*. Pronounce each one of them now and pay attention to the way your tongue hits the back of your teeth (your "dental" functionaries) when you say each consonant. These consonants are differentiated by how much your voice box vibrates in your throat and whether air is still escaping from your mouth as you say the consonant. It takes quite a bit of linguistic maneuvering to shift from a dental to the "s" sound of a sigma, so Greek speakers simply dropped dental consonants before sigmas.

Palatals or *Velars* are consonants made by touching the back of the roof of your mouth (your soft palate) with the top, back part of your tongue (κ, γ, and χ). Say them in succession and you will notice that your tongue is behaving in a similar way. As with dentals, the main difference in your personal linguistic maneuvering is how much your voice box (in your throat) is vibrating as you say the consonant and whether air is still escaping from your mouth (as it does with aspirant letters, such as θ and χ). Any palatal combined with sigma will result in ξ. This combination is easy to predict with κ + σ = ξ. It is less obvious to students that γ + σ and χ + σ also result in ξ, but if you remember that κ, γ, and χ are closely related consonants, the combinations make more sense.

Labials (π, β, and φ) are made when the lips meet together (again, with a difference mainly in how much the voice box vibrates and whether air is escaping from the mouth throughout the articulation of the consonant). Say the consonants in succession and note how your lips are meeting in similar ways with each one. Students easily discern that π + σ = ψ, and when you understand that β and φ are cousin consonants, it's not surprising that β + σ and φ + σ also result in ψ. Consequently, if you see a ξ or a ψ on the end of a stem, it is usually because a σ has been added (future or aorist).

Here is a chart summarizing such changes:[10]

---

[10] Mounce has a similar chart in his textbook, which he calls the "Square of Stops." Though this consonantal pattern is observed elsewhere, Mounce should be given credit for popularizing its usage.

	UNVOICED	VOICED	ASPIRATED	AFTER COMBINING WITH SIGMA:
DENTALS	τ	δ	θ	σ
PALATALS	κ	γ	χ	ξ
LABIALS	π	β	φ	ψ

This information can also be represented a little differently:[11]

Dentals	δ, ζ, θ, τ	+ σ	→ σ	(δοξάζω → δοξάσω)[12]
Palatals	γ, κ, σκ, σσ, χ	+ σ	→ ξ	(διώκω → διώξω)[13]
Labials	π, β, πτ, φ	+ σ	→ ψ	(βλέπω → βλέψω)[14]

Contract verbs do not contract because the added sigma separates the contract vowel (α, ε, or ο) and the connecting vowel/personal ending (ἀγαπήσω). Note, however, that the contract vowel lengthens and that the accent is placed above the lengthened vowel. By the contract vowel "lengthening," we mean that ο shifts to ω, ε shifts to η, and α shifts to η.

10.8 The Future Indicative of εἰμί

The future indicative of εἰμί is irregular as it follows the middle form. Notice that the only letter of the stem is the initial epsilon (ε–).[15] Because these endings are identical to the middle forms of λύω (see λύσομαι), there is no reason to memorize this paradigm as a separate form.

Later, we will see that several Greek verbs take middle endings for their future forms.

	SINGULAR		PLURAL	
1ST	ἔσομαι	I will be	ἐσόμεθα	we will be
2ND	ἔσῃ	you will be	ἔσεσθε	you will be
3RD	ἔσται[16]	he/she/it will be	ἔσονται	they will be

---

[11] S. M. Baugh teaches consonantal combinations with a similar chart (*A New Testament Greek Primer*, 3rd ed. [Phillipsburg, NJ: P&R, 2012], 30).

[12] See also βαπτίζω → βαπτίσω; σῴζω → σῴσω. Technically, the stems of these verbs are βαπτιδ– and σωδ–, respectively. Also, the stem of δοξάζω is δοξαδ–. Note that κράζω does not become κράσω but instead becomes κράξω. This is because its root ends with a gamma (κραγ–).

[13] See also διδάσκω → διδάξω; πράσσω → πράξω; ἔχω → ἕξω. Technically, the root of διδάσκω is διδακ– and the root of πράσσω is πραχ–. Note that ἕξω has a rough breathing mark. Also, remember that the stem of ἔχω is σεχ–. The tense formative sigma (σ) combines with the chi (χ) to form a xsi (ξ), and the initial sigma drops and is compensated with a rough breathing mark: σεχσω → ἔχσω → ἕξω. In addition, the stem of γινώσκω is γνω–, so the future is γνώσομαι (middle only).

[14] See also γράφω → γράψω; πέμπω → πέμψω.

[15] The root of εἰμί is εσ–.

[16] Note that the connecting vowel (ε) has dropped (see λύσεται).

10.9 Practice

A. Paradigms: Memorize the future active, middle, and passive paradigms of λύσω (see section 10.5). Then write out each paradigm ten times from memory.

B. Parsing: Parse the following verbs.

1. βαπτίσει

2. κράξουσιν

3. σωθήσομαι

4. διωχθήσονται

5. τηρήσω

6. ἔσῃ

7. πράξετε

8. ἕξουσιν

9. βλέψετε

10. φοβηθήσομαι

C. Translation: Translate the following sentences.

1. πέμψω τὸν υἱόν μου (Luke 20:13).

2. ἕξει τὸ φῶς (light) τῆς ζωῆς (John 8:12).

3. ἐρωτήσω τὸν πατέρα (father) (John 14:16).

4. καὶ περιπατήσουσιν μετ᾽ ἐμοῦ (Rev 3:4).

5. αὐτοὶ υἱοὶ θεοῦ κληθήσονται (Matt 5:9). (lexical form of verb: καλέω)

6. ἐγὼ ὑπάγω καὶ ζητήσετέ με (John 8:21).

7. σώσει ψυχὴν αὐτοῦ ἐκ θανάτου (Jas 5:20).

8. ὁ δὲ θεός μου πληρώσει πᾶσαν (every) χρείαν (need) ὑμῶν (Phil 4:19).

9. ἀγαπήσεις κύριον τὸν θεόν σου ἐν ὅλῃ (all) τῇ καρδίᾳ σου (Matt 22:37).

10. καὶ ὁ θεὸς δοξάσει αὐτὸν ἐν αὐτῷ, καὶ εὐθὺς (immediately) δοξάσει αὐτόν (John 13:32).

11. πίστευσον (Believe!, *imperative*) ἐπὶ τὸν κύριον Ἰησοῦν καὶ σωθήσῃ σὺ καὶ ὁ οἶκός σου (Acts 16:31).

12. καὶ αὐτοὶ λαοὶ αὐτοῦ ἔσονται, καὶ αὐτὸς ὁ θεὸς μετ᾿ αὐτῶν ἔσται (Rev 21:3).

13. ῥύσεταί (will deliver/rescue, *middle-only verb*) με ὁ κύριος ἀπὸ παντὸς (every) ἔργου πονηροῦ (evil) καὶ σώσει εἰς τὴν βασιλείαν αὐτοῦ (2 Tim 4:18).

14. καὶ γνώσεσθε τὴν ἀλήθειαν, καὶ ἡ ἀλήθεια ἐλευθερώσει (will liberate) ὑμᾶς (John 8:32).

D. Translation: Translate the following sentences from English to Greek.

1. The apostle will glorify the Lord of truth.

2. We will not persecute the children.

3. God will save the men who follow him.

4. They will keep and practice the commands of God.

5. You (pl) shall baptize the head of the house.

10.10 Vocabulary[17]

ἀνοίγω	I open
ἀπολύω	I set free, dismiss, divorce
ἄρχω	I rule, begin (mid) (*oligarch*)
προσεύχομαι	I pray[18]
προσκυνέω	I worship
συνάγω	I gather, bring together (*synagogue*)
ἀρχή, ἡ	beginning (*archaic*)
δαιμόνιον, τό	demon (*demon*)
διδάσκαλος, ὁ	teacher (*didactic*)
θρόνος, ὁ	throne (*throne*)
ἱμάτιον, τό	clothing, garment
καρπός, ὁ	fruit, crop
πλοῖον, τό	ship, boat
συναγωγή, ἡ	synagogue, assembly (*synagogue*)
χαρά, ἡ	joy (*charity*)

---

[17] To hear an author of your textbook read through the vocabulary for chapter 10, go to bit.ly/greekvocab10 or beginninggreek.com.

[18] "Pray" is a verb of reciprocity—verbs that are often middle-only. Praying involves two parties; if one party were removed, the action could not happen.

CHAPTER 11

/////////////////

FIRST AORIST INDICATIVE VERBS

11.1 Overview[1]

In this chapter, we will consider the aorist tense.[2] Because there are two patterns for aorist verbs, this chapter will cover the more regular pattern (first aorist) whereas the next one will discuss the pattern of more irregular verbs (second aorist). English also has verbs that follow a regular pattern for their past tense (walk→walked; cook→cooked) and verbs that follow irregular patterns (run→ran, is→was). This English regular/irregular pattern corresponds roughly to the Greek first aorist/second aorist distinction. There is no difference between the first and second aorist in terms of meaning—both patterns convey a wholistic/simple/unmarked presentation of past action. Generally, a verb will either form its aorist in the regular way (first aorist) or irregular way (second aorist), though there are a few unusual verbs that have both first and second aorist forms. Like the future, the aorist has distinct middle and passive paradigms.

11.2 Significance

The prologue of 1 John has many perfect tense verbs (a tense we have yet to learn). Nevertheless, in the midst of these perfect tenses, we find two aorist verbs—and both appear with less common vocabulary words.

> That which was from the beginning, that which we have heard, that which we have seen with our eyes, that which we **did behold** (ἐθεασάμεθα, aorist), and

---

[1] For an overview video lecture of chapter 11, go to bit.ly/greeklecture11 or beginninggreek.com.
[2] The word "aorist" is from Greek (ἀόριστος), meaning "without boundaries," "undefined," or "indefinite." Pronounced: āərəst.

our hands **did handle** (ἐψηλάφησαν, aorist), concerning the Word of the Life. (1 John 1:1 YLT)

The verb translated "did behold" often has the sense of seeing something with amazement or surprise. The verb translated "did handle," which only occurs four times in the New Testament, does not convey the idea of a quick touch, but more of a handling.

By shifting both to rarer, more intensive vocabulary words and to the aorist tense, the author of 1 John cues his readers to hear this recollection as distinct from the broader eyewitness reflections of the prologue. To look upon the incarnate deity with wonder and to touch his physical body in sensory confirmation—is this not an unmistakable allusion to Jesus's resurrection (e.g., Luke 24:37–39)?

11.3 Tense-Form and Meaning

The *aorist tense* in the indicative mood communicates both the *time of action* (typically in the past) and *perfective aspect* (that is, the author depicts the action as complete or as a whole). With the aorist tense, the author generally depicts the entire action in such a way that it encompasses the beginning, ending, and everything in-between. Of course, depending on the inherent procedural nature of the verb and the surrounding context, the aorist can convey a variety of nuanced meanings. Here is a sampling of the ways the aorist tense is employed in the Greek New Testament.

- **Constative Aorist:** Presents the action as a whole without regard to its beginning or end, or the length of time it took to accomplish the action. The aorist does not necessarily communicate a punctiliar or once-for-all action. Such nuances are communicated by the context and the inherent procedural nature of the verb's action. In Rom 5:14 Paul writes, "death **reigned** from Adam to Moses," ἐβασίλευσεν ὁ θάνατος ἀπὸ Ἀδὰμ μέχρι Μωϋσέως. Notice that the action of the verb is not a once-for-all action since it describes a span of centuries.

- **Inceptive Aorist:** Emphasizes the beginning of a state or action. The inceptive idea is usually expressed by the term "began" in English: "Jesus **began to weep**," ἐδάκρυσεν ὁ Ἰησοῦς (John 11:35 NRSV).

- **Epistolary Aorist:** Used in letters where the author writes from the perspective of the readers. Although the author is currently writing something or is sending someone to the readers, by the time the recipients receive the letter, it will already have been written or the person will have already been sent. Thus, it is translated as an English present tense verb: "**I am sending** [Tychicus] to you," [Τύχικον] ἔπεμψα πρὸς ὑμᾶς (Eph 6:22).

At this point, use the simple past in English unless the context demands otherwise.

11.4 Voice

Verbs with lexical forms that end with –ω can be active, middle, or passive. If the ending of the verb follows the endings (+ tense formative) found in the ἔλυσα paradigm (–σα, –σας, –σεν, –σαμεν, –σατε, –σαν), then it is active. If it follows the endings found in the ἐλυσάμην paradigm (–σαμην, –σω, –σατο, –σαμεθα, –σασθε, –σαντο), then it is middle. And if it follows the endings found in the ἐλύθην paradigm (–θην, –θης, –θη, –θημεν, –θητε, –θησαν), then it is passive in form, but can convey either a middle or passive sense depending on context. Some grammarians call such passive forms "medio-passives" as a reminder that they can convey either middle or passive meanings.

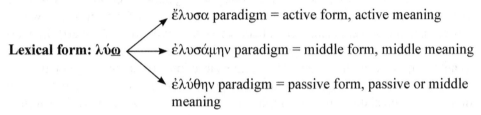

Lexical form: λύω
- ἔλυσα paradigm = active form, active meaning
- ἐλυσάμην paradigm = middle form, middle meaning
- ἐλύθην paradigm = passive form, passive or middle meaning

Verbs with lexical forms ending with –ομαι can follow either middle or passive paradigms, but they always convey a middle sense.

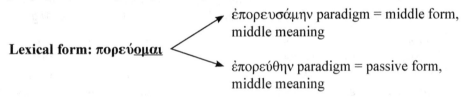

Lexical form: πορεύομαι
- ἐπορευσάμην paradigm = middle form, middle meaning
- ἐπορεύθην paradigm = passive form, middle meaning

11.5 Paradigms

AORIST ACTIVE INDICATIVE[3]			
	SINGULAR		PLURAL
1ST	ἔλυσα	I loosed	ἐλύσαμεν	we loosed
2ND	ἔλυσας	you loosed	ἐλύσατε	you loosed
3RD	ἔλυσε(ν)	he/she/it loosed	ἔλυσαν	they loosed

AORIST MIDDLE INDICATIVE			
	SINGULAR		PLURAL
1ST	ἐλυσάμην	I loosed (for) myself	ἐλυσάμεθα	we loosed (for) ourselves
2ND	ἐλύσω	you loosed (for) yourself	ἐλύσασθε	you loosed (for) yourselves
3RD	ἐλύσατο	he/she/it loosed (for) himself	ἐλύσαντο	they loosed (for) themselves

---

[3] To hear a mnemonic song, go to bit.ly/activeindicative or beginninggreek.com.

AORIST PASSIVE INDICATIVE				
	SINGULAR		PLURAL	
1ST	ἐλύθην	I was loosed	ἐλύθημεν	we were loosed
2ND	ἐλύθης	you were loosed	ἐλύθητε	you were loosed
3RD	ἐλύθη	he/she/it was loosed	ἐλύθησαν	they were loosed

11.6 Morphology

Like the imperfect tense, the aorist also has an augment which indicates that the verb's time of action occurs in the past.[4] If the first letter of the stem begins with a vowel, then the vowel is lengthened (ἀκούω → ε + ακουσα → ἤκουσα). In addition, if the stem of the verb begins with the diphthong αι–, the alpha (α) lengthens to an eta (η), causing the iota (ι) to become subscripted (αἰτεῖτε → ᾐτήσατε).[5] As with the imperfect, the augment comes after the prefix in a compound verb. Here is a more precise breakdown of the component parts (morphemes) of the various forms.

AORIST ACTIVE INDICATIVE

Inflected Form	Augment	Stem	Connecting Vowel[6]	Personal Ending		Combined Ending[7]
ἔλυσα	ε	λυσα	-	-	→	σα
ἔλυσας	ε	λυσα	-	ς	→	σας
ἔλυσε(ν)	ε	λυσε[8]	-	- (ν)[9]	→	σε(ν)
ἐλύσαμεν	ε	λυσα	-	μεν	→	σαμεν
ἐλύσατε	ε	λυσα	-	τε	→	σατε
ἔλυσαν	ε	λυσα	-	ν	→	σαν

Aorist active forms have similar endings to the imperfect (except for the first person singular), with the addition of a sigma/alpha (–σα) tense formative.

---

[4] Although there are exceptions, aorist indicative verbs convey the past about 85 percent of the time.

[5] ἀνοίγω is a rare form that can receive a double and even triple augment. That is, it can be augmented before and after the prepositional prefix, as well as the lengthening of the omicron: aor act 3rd sg: ἀνέῳξεν or ἠνέῳξέν; aor pass 3rd pl: ἀνεῴχθησαν or ἠνοίγησαν.

[6] There is no connecting vowel because the tense formative (–σα) ends with a vowel, causing it to be unnecessary. Some grammars take the tense formative to be sigma and the connecting vowel to be alpha.

[7] Although the –σα tense formative is technically part of the stem, it is helpful to learn it as part of the ending to distinguish it from the present tense-form (λύ-ομεν → ἐλύ-σαμεν).

[8] Note that the alpha (α) has changed to an epsilon (ε). This is probably done to differentiate the third person singular form (ἔλυσε) from the first person singular form (ἔλυσα), which lacks the moveable nu (ν).

[9] There is no personal ending, only a movable nu. Note that the other forms that end with nu are part of the ending (–αμεν, –αν).

AORIST MIDDLE INDICATIVE

Inflected Form	Augment	Stem	Connecting Vowel	Personal Ending		Combined Ending
ἐλυσάμην	ε	λυσα	-	μην	→	σαμην
ἐλύσω	ε	λυσα	-	[σο][10]	→	σω
ἐλύσατο	ε	λυσα	-	το	→	σατο
ἐλυσάμεθα	ε	λυσα	-	μεθα	→	σαμεθα
ἐλύσασθε	ε	λυσα	-	σθε	→	σασθε
ἐλύσαντο	ε	λυσα	-	ντο	→	σαντο

Note that the second person singular form has no alpha in its ending.

AORIST PASSIVE INDICATIVE

Inflected Form	Augment	Stem	Connecting Vowel	Personal Ending		Combined Ending
ἐλύθην	ε	λυθη	-	ν	→	θην
ἐλύθης	ε	λυθη	-	ς	→	θης
ἐλύθη	ε	λυθη	-	-	→	θη
ἐλύθημεν	ε	λυθη	-	μεν	→	θημεν
ἐλύθητε	ε	λυθη	-	τε	→	θητε
ἐλύθησαν	ε	λυθη	-	σαν	→	θησαν

11.7 Stem Variations

The aorist forms experience the same issues as the future forms when the sigma (σ) tense formative is added to the stem of the verb. These changes occur often and in accordance with regular patterns, as was seen in the previous chapter.

Dentals	δ, ζ, θ, τ	+ σ	→ σ	(δοξάζω → ἐδόξασα)[11]
Palatals[12]	γ, κ, σκ, σσ, χ	+ σ	→ ξ	(διώκω → ἐδίωξα)[13]
Labials	π, β, πτ, φ	+ σ	→ ψ	(βλέπω → ἔβλεψα)[14]

Like future forms, aorist contract verbs do not contract because the added sigma separates the contract vowel and the connecting vowel (ἠγάπησα). The contract vowel typically lengthens (ο→ω, ε→η, and α→η) but, unlike the future forms, the accent is not necessarily placed above the lengthened vowel.[15]

---

[10] The intervocalic sigma drops, causing the vowels to contract: ἐλυσασο → ἐλυσαο → ἐλύσω. See William D. Mounce, *Basics of Biblical Greek: Grammar*, 4th ed. (Grand Rapids: Zondervan, 2019), 256.

[11] See also βαπτίζω → ἐβάπτισα; σῴζω → ἔσωσα (cf. κράζω → ἔκραξα).

[12] Or "Velars."

[13] See also διδάσκω → ἐδίδαξα; πράσσω → ἔπραξα.

[14] See also γράφω → ἔγραψα; πέμπω → ἔπεμψα.

[15] Note that ἐκάλεσα is the exception since its contract vowel does not lengthen.

For future and aorist passive forms, the addition of the –θη tense formative also causes slight adjustments to the normal paradigm. Students can usually recognize the forms below without being able to explain or predict these orthographic variations.

Dentals	δ, θ	+ θ	→ σθ	(βαπτίζω → βαπτισθήσομαι, ἐβαπτίσθην)
Palatals	γ, κ	+ θ	→ χθ	(ἄγω → ἀχθήσομαι, ἤχθην)
Labials	π, β	+ θ	→ φθ	(βλέπω → βλεφθήσομαι, ἐβλέφθην)

11.8 Practice

A. Paradigms: Memorize the aorist active, middle, and passive paradigms of λύω (see section 11.5). Then write out each paradigm ten times from memory.

B. Parsing: Parse the following verbs.

1. ἐπέμψατε

2. ἐπράξαμεν

3. ἐδίωξα

4. ἐπιστεύσατε

5. προσεκύνησεν

6. ἐτήρησας

7. ἀπελύθησαν

8. προσηύξατο

9. ἤνοιξεν

10. ἐσώθη

C. Translation: Translate the following sentences:

1. ἔγραψα ὑμῖν ἐν τῇ ἐπιστολῇ (epistle/letter) (1 Cor 5:9).

2. ἔκραξεν οὖν ἐν τῷ ἱερῷ . . . ὁ Ἰησοῦς (John 7:28).

3. Ἰωάννης ἐδίδαξεν τοὺς μαθητὰς αὐτοῦ (Luke 11:1).

4. οὕτως γὰρ ἠγάπησεν ὁ θεὸς τὸν κόσμον (John 3:16).

5. καὶ ἐβαπτίσθη εἰς τὸν Ἰορδάνην (Jordan) ὑπὸ Ἰωάννου (John) (Mark 1:9).

6. καὶ ἐδόξασαν τὸν θεὸν Ἰσραήλ (Israel, *genitive*) (Matt 15:31).

7. προσευχόμεθα πάντοτε (always) περὶ ὑμῶν (2 Thess 1:11).

8. ὁ κύριος τοῦ δούλου . . . ἀπέλυσεν αὐτὸν (Matt 18:27).

9. ἤρξατο διδάσκειν (to teach) παρὰ τὴν θάλασσαν (Mark 4:1).

10. ἐπλήρωσεν ὁ Σατανᾶς (Satan) τὴν καρδίαν σου (Acts 5:3).

11. καὶ ᾐτήσατο τὸ σῶμα (body) τοῦ Ἰησοῦ (Mark 15:43).

12. καὶ ἠνεῴχθησαν αὐτῶν οἱ ὀφθαλμοί (Matt 9:30).

D. Translation: Translate the following sentences into Greek.

1. He prayed in the synagogue.

2. The teacher was gathering the disciples and taught them.

3. The angel glorified God before his throne.

4. We did not believe the demon.

5. The joy of the Lord guarded us in the boat.

11.9 Vocabulary[16]

ἀναβαίνω	I go up, ascend (*Anabasis*)[17]
ἀπέρχομαι	I go away, depart[18]
ἀποθνήσκω	I die (*euthanasia*, "*Thanatopsis*")
βάλλω	I throw, cast out (*ball*, *ballistic*)
εἰσέρχομαι	I go in, enter
ἐκβάλλω	I drive/send out
ἐσθίω	I eat
ἐξέρχομαι	I go out, depart, leave
εὑρίσκω	I find, discover (*heuristic*, *Eureka!*)
καταβαίνω	I go down, descend
πίνω	I drink
πίπτω	I fall
προσέρχομαι	I go to, approach
φέρω	I bear, carry (*metaphor*)
ἐπαγγελία, ἡ	promise

[16] To hear an author of your textbook read through the vocabulary for chapter 11, go to bit.ly/greekvocab11 or beginninggreek.com.

[17] *Anabasis* or *The March Up Country* is a famous book by the ancient Greek writer Xenophon (430–354 BC).

[18] Verbs of movement are frequently middle-only. There is a high level of subject affectedness in self-locomotion. So also εἰσέρχομαι, ἐξέρχομαι, and προσέρχομαι.

CHAPTER 12

/////////////////

SECOND AORIST INDICATIVE VERBS

12.1 Overview[1]

In the previous chapter, we discussed the form and function of first aorist verbs. In this chapter, we will consider a second pattern used with some verbs which have a different form but the same function. The personal endings these verbs use are identical to the imperfect tense-forms. The way to distinguish between the two forms is that second aorist verbs undergo a spelling change to the stem. The change can be very slight (just a single letter!), so students are advised to pay careful attention.

12.2 Significance

If the verb λέγω followed a regular pattern, we would expect its third person singular aorist form to be ἐλέξεν. Yet, like quite a few common Greek verbs, λέγω is not regular. Just as the past tense of the English verb "to go" is unpredictable and irregular (i.e., "he went," not "he go'ed"), so the third person singular past tense of λέγω is εἶπεν. This particular form occurs 613 times in the Greek New Testament! (Think about it—how many times does Jesus or another individual say something to someone in the Gospels or Acts?)

As you read through the Gospels and Acts, you will note that both λέγει (historical present) and εἶπεν (second aorist) are regularly used to introduce direct quotations, with a report of the specific content of what was said. For example,

> And he sent them to Bethlehem and said (εἶπεν), "Go and search carefully for the Child; and when you have found *Him*, report to me, so that I too may come and worship Him." (Matt 2:8 NASB)

---

[1] For an overview video lecture of chapter 12, go to bit.ly/greeklecture12 or beginninggreek.com.

[The devil] said (λέγει) to him, "If you are the Son of God, throw yourself down, for it is written, 'He will command his angels concerning you,' and 'On their hands they will bear you up, lest you strike your foot against a stone.'" (Matt 4:6 ESV)

The verb λαλέω, on the other hand, typically reports the activity of speech without emphasis on the specific content of the speech. See, for example,

After the demon was cast out, the man who had been mute spoke [ἐλάλησεν]. The crowds were amazed and said, "Never has anything like this been seen in Israel!" (Matt 9:33 NET)

Reading the New Testament in Greek allows you to pick up on slight nuances of vocabulary that are inaccessible to English readers.

12.3 Tense-Form and Meaning

For the *second aorist*, both the tense and meaning are the same as for the first aorist. The only difference is the spelling of the verb (form), not the meaning of the tense (function). Thus, second aorist indicative verbs communicate both the *time of action* (typically in the past) and *perfective aspect* (that is, the author depicts the action as complete or as a whole). Thus, it describes a given action simply as occurring or as having occurred without indicating how the action took place. Whereas imperfect verbs are typically translated as a progressive action in the past ("I was eating"), the aorist is typically translated as a simple past action ("I ate"). Verbs will usually be either first or second aorist, not both.

12.4 Paradigms

SECOND AORIST ACTIVE INDICATIVE—λαμβάνω				
	SINGULAR		PLURAL	
1ST	ἔλαβον	I took	ἐλάβομεν	we took
2ND	ἔλαβες	you took	ἐλάβετε	you took
3RD	ἔλαβεν	he/she/it took	ἔλαβον	they took

SECOND AORIST MIDDLE INDICATIVE—γίνομαι				
	SINGULAR		PLURAL	
1ST	ἐγενόμην	I became	ἐγενόμεθα	we became
2ND	ἐγένου	you became	ἐγένεσθε	you became
3RD	ἐγένετο	he/she/it became	ἐγένοντο	they became

12.5 Morphology

The paradigms above do not need to be memorized—because you should already know them! The endings of second aorist verbs are identical to those of the imperfect. The only difference between the two forms is that the imperfect uses the stem of the present tense-form (e.g., λαμβαν–, γιν–) while the second aorist uses the stem of the aorist tense-form (e.g., λαβ–, γεν–).

Although all second aorist verbs undergo stem spelling change, some verbs use an altogether different stem to form the second aorist. This is similar to the English verb "go," where the past tense is "went" (which comes from the obsolete present tense "to wend"). Here are a few verbs that have a completely different root for their second aorist forms. *Memorize* the initial (first person singular) second aorist forms of these verbs.

βλέπω	→	εἶδον[2]
ἔρχομαι	→	ἦλθον
ἐσθίω	→	ἔφαγον
λέγω	→	εἶπον
φέρω	→	ἤνεγκον[3]

About 40 percent of all occurrences of aorist verbs in the New Testament are second aorist verbs. So, although they are outnumbered by first aorist verbs, many of these verbs are extremely common (e.g., ἔρχομαι occurs in the aorist more than 350 times).[4]

Because the second aorist builds on an altered stem, it is extremely useful to learn the stem of each verb. Below are the stems for the verbs learned for this chapter, followed by the verbs learned in previous lessons. You will find it helpful to memorize the **bold** second aorist forms below.

Lexical Form	Imperfect	Second Aorist	Aorist Root
ἀναβαίνω	ἀνέβαινον	**ἀνέβην**	ἀνά + βα–
ἀπέρχομαι	[ἀπηρχόμην][5]	ἀπῆλθον	ἀπ + ἐλθ–
ἀποθνῄσκω	ἀπέθνῃσκον	**ἀπέθανον**	ἀποθαν–
βάλλω	ἔβαλλον	**ἔβαλον**	βαλ–
εἰσέρχομαι	[εἰσηρχόμην]	εἰσῆλθον	εἰς + ἐλθ–[6]
ἐκβάλλω	ἐξέβαλλον	ἐξέβαλον	ἐξ + βαλ–
ἐσθίω	ἤσθιον	**ἔφαγον**	φαγ–
ἐξέρχομαι	ἐξηρχόμην	ἐξῆλθον	ἐξ + ἐλθ–

---

[2] The first aorist of βλέπω does occur once (ἔβλεψα, Rev 22:8).
[3] The first person singular form found in the Septuagint and New Testament is always ἤνεγκα.
[4] This statistic includes all moods.
[5] The forms in brackets indicate that the term does not occur in the imperfect tense-form in the New Testament.
[6] The actual stem is ελευθ– but the vowels (ευ) drop out (ablaut). This is true for all forms of the aorist of ἔρχομαι.

εὑρίσκω	ηὕρισκον[7]	**εὗρον**	εὑρ–
καταβαίνω	κατέβαινον	**κατέβην**	κατα + βα–
πίνω	ἔπινον	**ἔπιον**	πι–
πίπτω	ἔπιπτον	**ἔπεσον**	πετ–[8]
προσέρχομαι	προηρχόμην	προσῆλθον	προς + ἐλθ–
φέρω	ἔφερον	**ἤνεγκον**[9]	ἐνεκ–
ἄγω	ἦγον	**ἤγαγον**	ἀγ–
βλέπω	ἔβλεπον	**εἶδον**	ϝιδ–[10]
γίνομαι	ἐγινόμην	**ἐγενόμην**	γεν–
γινώσκω	ἐγίνωσκον	**ἔγνων**	γνω–
ἔρχομαι	ἠρχόμην	**ἦλθον**	ἐλθ–
ἔχω	εἶχον	**ἔσχον**	σεχ–
λαμβάνω	ἐλάμβανον	**ἔλαβον**	λαβ–
λέγω	ἔλεγον	**εἶπον**	ϝεπ –[11]
συνάγω	[σύνηγον]	**συνήγαγον**	συν + ἀγ–

Here is a more precise breakdown of the component parts (morphemes) of the various forms.

SECOND AORIST ACTIVE INDICATIVE

Inflected Form	Augment	Stem	Connecting Vowel	Personal Ending		Combined Ending
ἔλαβον	ε	λαβ	ο	ν	→	ον
ἔλαβες	ε	λαβ	ε	ς	→	ες
ἔλαβεν	ε	λαβ	ε	(ν)	→	εν
ἐλάβομεν	ε	λαβ	ο	μεν	→	ομεν
ἐλάβετε	ε	λαβ	ε	τε	→	ετε
ἔλαβον	ε	λαβ	ο	ν	→	ον

Like the imperfect, the first singular and third plural forms are spelled the same. Although context will usually make this clear, it is also helpful to know that the third plural form is much more common. Some verbs go from middle in the present or imperfect forms to active in the aorist form (e.g., ἔρχομαι → ἦλθον).

---

[7] The imperfect of εὑρίσκω sometimes does not lengthen the initial vowel (εὑρίσκον instead of ηὕρισκον; see Luke 19:48).

[8] When the sigma (σ) is added to this root to form the aorist form of πίπτω, the tau (τ) drops off.

[9] The first person singular form found in the LXX and NT is always ἤνεγκα.

[10] The letter "ϝ" is called *digamma*. Although it was obsolete in Koine Greek, the memory of it still affects the way words were spelled.

[11] See previous note.

SECOND AORIST MIDDLE INDICATIVE

Inflected Form	Augment	Stem	Connecting Vowel	Personal Ending		Combined Ending
ἐγενόμην	ε	γεν	ο	μην	→	ομην
ἐγένου	ε	γεν	[ε]	[σο][12]	→	ου
ἐγένετο	ε	γεν	ε	το	→	ετο
ἐγενόμεθα	ε	γεν	ο	μεθα	→	ομεθα
ἐγένεσθε	ε	γεν	ε	σθε	→	εσθε
ἐγένοντο	ε	γεν	ο	ντο	→	οντο

12.6 Second Aorist Passive

Most of the second aorist verbs learned thus far do not have a passive form since many of them are intransitive verbs. Below are the passive forms of the second aorist verbs learned to this point. Be able to *recognize* these forms.

Lexical Form		Aorist Passive[13]	
ἄγω	"I lead"	ἤχθην (2x)	"I was led"
βάλλω	"I throw"	ἐβλήθην (12x)	"I was thrown"
γινώσκω	"I know"	ἐγνώσθην (2x)	"I was known"
ἐκβάλλω	"I throw out"	ἐξεβλήθην (1x)	"I was thrown out"
εὑρίσκω	"I find"	εὑρέθην (17x)	"I was found"
λέγω	"I speak"	ἐρρέθην (11x)	"I was spoken"
συνάγω	"I gather"	συνήχθην (11x)	"I was gathered"
φέρω	"I carry"	ἠνέχθην (2x)	"I was carried"

12.7 Second Aorist Active of γινώσκω

Because the aorist stem of γινώσκω is γνω–, the stem vowel (ω) combines with the connecting vowel, causing the connecting vowel to drop (ablaut). Thus, the forms are similar to the second aorist, with the omega in the place of the connecting vowel. The only other differences are (1) the third person singular form does not use the movable nu and (2) the third plural form is not the same as the first singular but follows a first aorist ending (cf. ἔλυσαν).[14]

	Singular		Plural	
1st	ἔγνων	"I knew"	ἔγνωμεν	"We knew"
2nd	ἔγνως	"You knew"	ἔγνωτε	"You (pl) knew"

---

[12] The intervocalic sigma drops, causing the vowels to contract: ἐγενεσο → ἐγενεο → ἐγένου. See William D. Mounce, *Basics of Biblical Greek: Grammar*, 4th ed. (Grand Rapids: Zondervan, 2019), 244.

[13] First person singular forms of the aorist passive are given for illustrative purposes. The frequency statistics apply to all aorist passive forms, regardless of person or number.

[14] These forms should be recognized but do not need to be memorized.

| **3rd** | ἔγνω | "He knew" | ἔγνωσαν | "They knew" |

12.8 Alternate Second Aorist Spelling

Instead of keeping the normal spelling which follows the imperfect endings, some verbs assimilate to the first aorist spelling. Thus, the connecting vowel is switched to an alpha (α). Here are a few examples:

ἦλθον	ἦλθαν	"They came" (also: ἤλθαμεν, ἤλθατε)
ἔβαλον	ἔβαλαν	"They threw"
εἴδομεν	εἴδαμεν	"We saw"
εἶπον	εἶπαν	"They said"

12.9 Practice

A. Second Aorist Stem: Match the lexical form of the verb with its second aorist form.

1.	_____ καταβαίνω	A.	ἐγενόμην
2.	_____ λαμβάνω	B.	εἶδον
3.	_____ ἀποθνήσκω	C.	ἔσχον
4.	_____ βλέπω	D.	ἦλθον
5.	_____ ἐσθίω	E.	κατέβην
6.	_____ γινώσκω	F.	εἶπον
7.	_____ εὑρίσκω	G.	ἔλαβον
8.	_____ ἔρχομαι	H.	ἀπέθανον
9.	_____ ἄγω	I.	ἔβαλον
10.	_____ πίπτω	J.	ἤνεγκον
11.	_____ γίνομαι	K.	ἤγαγον
12.	_____ λέγω	L.	ἔπιον
13.	_____ φέρω	M.	ἔπεσον
14.	_____ ἔχω	N.	ἔγνων
15.	_____ βάλλω	O.	εὗρον
16.	_____ πίνω	P.	ἔφαγον

B. Parsing: Parse the following verbs.

1. ἀπέθανον
2. ἐφάγομεν
3. ἀνέβην
4. εὑρέθημεν
5. κατέβησαν
6. ἠνέχθη
7. ἠγάγετε
8. ἐγένετο
9. ἔσχες
10. συνήχθησαν

C. Translation: Translate the following sentences.

1. ἐντολὴν ἐλάβομεν παρὰ τοῦ πατρός (father) (2 John 4).

2. ἐγὼ γὰρ διὰ νόμου νόμῳ ἀπέθανον (Gal 2:19).

3. ἤνεγκα τὸν υἱόν μου πρὸς σέ (Mark 9:17).

4. ἀνέβη Ἰησοῦς εἰς τὸ ἱερὸν καὶ ἐδίδασκεν (John 7:14).

5. καὶ ἀπῆλθον ἐν τῷ πλοίῳ εἰς ἔρημον (deserted) τόπον (Mark 6:32).

6. Χριστὸς ἀπέθανεν ὑπὲρ τῶν ἁμαρτιῶν ἡμῶν κατὰ τὰς γραφὰς (Scriptures) (1 Cor 15:3).

7. ἡ ἁμαρτία εἰς τὸν κόσμον εἰσῆλθεν καὶ διὰ τῆς ἁμαρτίας ὁ θάνατος (Rom 5:12).

8. ἄγγελος ἐξῆλθεν ἐκ τοῦ ναοῦ (temple) τοῦ ἐν τῷ οὐρανῷ (Rev 14:17).

9. κατέβησαν οἱ μαθηταὶ αὐτοῦ ἐπὶ τὴν θάλασσαν (John 6:16).

10. ἔπεσα πρὸς τοὺς πόδας (feet) αὐτοῦ ὡς νεκρός (dead) (Rev 1:17).

11. ἐν ἐκείνῃ τῇ (that) ὥρᾳ προσῆλθον οἱ μαθηταὶ τῷ Ἰησοῦ (Matt 18:1).

12. εἶδεν τὴν δόξαν αὐτοῦ, καὶ ἐλάλησεν περὶ αὐτοῦ (John 12:41).

13. ἔγνωσαν γὰρ ὅτι πρὸς αὐτοὺς εἶπεν τὴν παραβολήν (parable) (Luke 20:19).

14. ἐν τῷ κόσμῳ ἦν, καὶ ὁ κόσμος δι' αὐτοῦ ἐγένετο, καὶ ὁ κόσμος αὐτὸν οὐκ ἔγνω (John 1:10).

15. εἰσῆλθεν εἰς τὸν οἶκον τοῦ θεοῦ καὶ τοὺς ἄρτους τῆς προθέσεως (presence) ἔφαγον (Matt 12:4).

D. Translation: Translate the following sentences into Greek.

1. The child fell on the road.

2. You (pl) found the Lord of life.

3. He went down to the synagogue.

4. We entered into the house of God and heard the Word.

5. They spoke the promise to the crowd.

12.10 Vocabulary[15]

αἴρω	I take up/away
ἀπαγγέλλω	I announce, report (*angel*)
ἀποκτείνω	I kill, put to death
ἀποστέλλω	I send out (*apostle*)
σπείρω	I sow, plant (*sperm, spore*)
γλῶσσα, ἡ	language, tongue (*glossolalia*)
γραφή, ἡ	writing, Scripture (*graphics*)
λίθος, ὁ	stone (*lithograph*)
ναός, ὁ	temple, sanctuary
παραβολή, ἡ	parable (*parable*)
σοφία, ἡ	wisdom (*sophistry, sophomore*)
σωτηρία, ἡ	salvation, deliverance
χρόνος, ὁ	time (*chronograph, chronology*)
διό	therefore, for this reason
εὐθύς	immediately, straightaway

---

[15] To hear an author of your textbook read through the vocabulary for chapter 12, go to bit.ly/greekvocab12 or beginninggreek.com.

How Can I Be Sure What Greek Words Mean?

Introducing Vocabulary-Building Resources, Lexicons, and Other Word Study Tools

Sometimes a student will raise weary eyes toward the front of the classroom and ask, "How do we know what these Greek words actually mean?" While at times that question may be more of a lament than a genuine inquiry, it does give voice to a foundational concern. At one level, the answer is straightforward—we have many early translations of documents both into Greek (from Hebrew, for example, in the Septuagint) and into other languages from Greek (early New Testament translations into Latin, Syriac, Coptic, etc.). These early translations are, in a real sense, lexicons—just not ones presenting entries in alphabetical order.

The good news for you as a student is that you can benefit from two millennia of prior translational and lexicographical work. We have the best Greek lexicons and Greek word resources that have ever been available in the history of the world! (What an exciting time in which to live!) Below, we will divide our discussion of Greek words into three parts: building vocabulary, lexicons, and word study tools and principles.

Building Vocabulary

To read the New Testament in the language in which it was first penned, you must continue to build your knowledge of Greek words. By the time you complete this book, you will know about 345 words. There are, however, 5,436 distinct words in the Greek New Testament. That number can sound overwhelming and discouraging. But if you learn all the Greek words that occur 10 times or more in the New Testament (there are around 1,100), you will be able to read most passages in the Greek New Testament. Moreover, you will be able to guess the few words you don't know in a passage from context—or perhaps you will recognize roots from related Greek words that you already know.

At this point in your study (i.e., in the middle of learning elementary Greek), the vocabulary lists you are required to memorize are probably all the Greek you want to handle. But, after you finish this class, you will have time to build your Greek vocabulary further on your own. We have three recommendations regarding that endeavor. (1) Greek vocabulary is best learned by reading New Testament passages written in that language. After all, there is far more joy to be found in reading the Greek New Testament than in sorting through vocabulary cards. (2) At the same time, reviewing vocabulary cards can be helpful at an early stage of language learning. So, we recommend going radical on that step. Delete all distracting apps on your smartphone, and install a good Greek vocabulary app (such as Bible Vocab or FlashGreek). Then, anytime you find yourself waiting in line, you will no longer be tempted to waste your time skimming through other people's mindless social media posts. Instead, you will be prepared to redeem the time toward the eternal joy of knowing how to read the New Testament in the original Greek! (3) Be wise in the way you learn vocabulary. As you commit a new Greek word to memory, note English words that are derived from that word, also reviewing related words in Greek. So, for example, let's imagine you are learning the word ἡγέομαι, which means, "I lead, guide, think." To recall that confidently, it's very helpful to know the English word *hegemony*,[1] which is ultimately derived from that new Greek vocabulary word. The meaning of the English word (i.e., dominant *leadership* or *guidance*) is very close to the Greek word's semantic range. Moreover, while learning ἡγέομαι, which occurs 28 times in the New Testament, it is efficient to learn ἡγεμών ("governor, procurator"), διηγέομαι ("I tell, relate"), and ἐξηγέομαι ("I explain, interpret") as well (see exegesis). These three related Greek forms occur 34 times within the New Testament, making for 62 occurrences in the New Testament for this word family (i.e., 28 + 34 = 62). Where can you obtain a vocabulary-building resource that groups Greek words by family and lists helpful English cognates? We recommend Robert E. Van Voorst's *Building Your New Testament Greek Vocabulary*, 3rd ed. (Society of Biblical Literature, 1999). The information provided about ἡγέομαι comes from this book.

Lexicons

Lexicon is just another word for dictionary. Every serious student of the Greek New Testament will need a Greek-English lexicon, whether it's in print or digital format. At first, you are likely to use the small free lexicon at the back of your printed Greek New Testament, or the one you found at a yard sale for five dollars. Perhaps you also will access Thayer's classic lexicon free at the internet archive.[2] There comes a point, however, at which every serious Greek scholar will rightly desire the best New Testament Greek lexicon available.

---

[1] Meaning "preponderant influence or authority over others, domination" (https://www.merriam-webster.com/dictionary/hegemony).

[2] https://archive.org/details/greekenglishlexi00grimuoft/page/n6.

Information on that resource is thus provided here:

• **Danker, Frederick William, rev. and ed.** *A Greek-English Lexicon of the New Testament and Other Early Christian Literature*, **3rd ed. Chicago: University of Chicago Press, 2000.** This Greek lexicon is known as "BDAG." Danker's changes to the third edition have made this text much more user-friendly. The second edition of this text (1979) was known as BAGD because of key scholars who had contributed to it (Walter Bauer, William F. Arndt, F. Wilbur Gingrich, and Frederick W. Danker). In the shorthand title for the third edition of this text (BDAG), Danker's name is now listed second to Bauer's. The latter compiled the German lexicon upon which later editions were based. Though BDAG is expensive, you likely will want a copy—either in digital or print format—eventually.[3]

There are other lexicons that specialize in Greek vocabulary within the Septuagint, in the apostolic fathers, or stretching back into the classical period.[4] But, for now, being aware of BDAG and considering at what point you might wish to acquire your own personal copy of it is a fitting lexical mission.

Additional Word Study Tools and Principles

As students gain facility in Greek, they have a growing desire to go deeper in their understanding of particular words and their theological significance. There are many Greek word study tools that will help you in this endeavor. You can think of these additional resources as theologically-driven lexicons, with expanded discussions written with a pastor in mind. In this introductory grammar, however, we choose to recommend only one Greek word study tool. It's the "best of the best":

• **Silva, Moisés, ed.** *New International Dictionary of New Testament Theology and Exegesis.* **5 vols. Grand Rapids: Zondervan, 2014.** Silva's extensive revision of *The New International Dictionary of New Testament Theology*, ed. Colin Brown (Grand Rapids: Zondervan, 1975–78), has made a valuable linguistic resource even better. For a pastor looking for a scholarly, reliable Greek resource that has an eye to theological application in the church, *NIDNTTE* is unsurpassed.[5]

---

[3] See Rod Decker's extensive review of BDAG, as well as online resources regarding how to use the lexicon, at http://ntresources.com/blog/?page_id=2526.
[4] For more detail on these other lexicons, see chap. 14 of Andreas J. Köstenberger, Benjamin L. Merkle, and Robert L. Plummer, *Going Deeper with New Testament Greek: An Intermediate Study of the Grammar and Syntax of the New Testament*, rev. ed. (Nashville: B&H Academic, 2020).
[5] A free 45-page primer on the *New International Dictionary of New Testament Theology and Exegesis (NIDNTTE)* may be downloaded here: https://zondervanacademic.com/blog/

Below are some key principles to keep in mind as you engage in Greek word studies.[6]

1. Don't Make Any Word Mean More Than the Author Intends

Linguist Martin Joobs has summarized this linguistic principle with the influential phrase, "The least meaning is the best meaning."[7] All words carry a variety of potential meanings, but the best reader-discerned meaning for any word is the one that least disturbs the broader literary context. The surrounding words and phrases prepare the reader to understand any particular word. No word is defined in isolation.

The opposite of the linguistic principle "The least meaning is the best meaning" is the linguistic fallacy called illegitimate totality transfer.[8] When a reader engages in this fallacy, he wrongly ascribes to a word the totality of what the word could mean in each individual instance of that word's usage. We have all heard preachers do this—when, for example, the pastor says, "The Greek word here is

κόσμος. This word means 'adornment,' 'order,' 'the world,' 'the universe,' 'the sum total of all beings above the level of animals,' 'planet earth,' 'humanity,' 'the system of human existence in its many aspects,' and 'totality.'"[9] Of course, words do not mean the totality of what they could mean in any context; rather, each word only means what the author cues his readers to understand in that particular literary setting. We see the foolishness of illegitimate totality transfer when we apply it to English. Imagine a preacher saying, "The man answered his cell phone. What does 'cell' mean? It means (a) a small chamber of incarceration, (b) a blob of protoplasm, (c) a mobile communications network, and (d) a square in a spreadsheet. How rich in meaning was this man's phone!"

2. Prioritize Synchrony Over Diachrony[10]

When we study a word synchronously, we compare usages from the same time period (σύν [with] + χρόνος [time]). When we study a word diachronously, we consider usages from

---

free-resources-collection.
[6] Several of the paragraphs below are adapted from Köstenberger, Merkle, and Plummer, *Going Deeper with New Testament Greek*, 486–88.
[7] This linguistic principle is also called "the rule of maximal redundancy." Cited in Moisés Silva, *Biblical Words and Their Meaning: An Introduction to Lexical Semantics*, rev. ed. (Grand Rapids: Zondervan, 1994), 153–54.
[8] See D. A. Carson's discussion of this linguistic fallacy in *Exegetical Fallacies*, 2nd ed. (Grand Rapids: Baker, 1984), 53; Grant R. Osborne, *The Hermeneutical Spiral: A Comprehensive Introduction to Biblical Interpretation*, rev. and exp. (Downers Grove: InterVarsity, 2006), 84, 105; Andreas J. Köstenberger and Richard D. Patterson, *Invitation to Biblical Interpretation: Exploring the Hermeneutical Triad of History, Literature, and Theology* (Grand Rapids: Kregel, 2011), 645–47.
[9] Various definitions taken from BDAG, 561–63.
[10] See Silva's helpful discussion in *Biblical Words and Their Meaning*, 35–38.

various time periods (διά [through] + χρόνος [time]). Valuing synchrony over diachrony means that we have a much greater chance of rightly understanding a word's meaning if we rely on parallel uses from the same time period. All languages evolve over time, and part of that evolution is the change in meaning of individual words.

For instance, the translators of the King James Version rendered Jas 2:3 this way: "Ye have respect to him that weareth the gay clothing, and say unto him, Sit thou here in a good place." In the early seventeenth century, the word "gay" meant "fine" or "luxurious." The word "gay" has experienced a dramatic "semantic shift" (change in meaning) over the last 400 years; its primary meaning now is "homosexual." One must always remember that the words in the New Testament are merely a snapshot of language in the process of change. For this reason, we should not cite Homer (c. 8th century, BC) as the most authoritative source for the meaning of a New Testament Greek word; rather, we should seek more contemporaneous sources to inform us. The best Greek lexicographers understand this principle, and it informs their work.

The priority of synchrony in defining New Testament Greek words also has an obverse fallacy—the etymological fallacy.[11] This fallacy is the false claim that knowing the etymology (historical origins) of a word gives us deeper insights into its meaning. Many congregations are accustomed to being fed the etymological fallacy as part of their regular homiletical diet. Such supposed insights are introduced by the pastor with phrases such as, "The Greek word here *really* means . . . ." Congregations tolerate absurdities that would be laughable in their own language. For example, the English word "lasagna" comes from a Greek word *lasonon*, a small pot used as a portable bedroom toilet. How many of us have considered this etymology while enjoying a dish of baked pasta? The word "dandelion" comes from the French "dent de lion" (tooth of a lion). When you spray weed killer on the dandelions in your yard, do you imagine yourself as a lion tamer? Similarly, when the apostle Paul wrote a word, he was almost certainly not thinking about the origin of that word. He was unconsciously assuming the contemporary semantic range and then narrowing that range further through cues in the surrounding literary context.

In recent years, some biblical scholars have argued that the emphasis on synchrony in word study has failed to account for biblical authors' reflections on the etymology of some words. This criticism is valid insofar as it points us to an ancient author's *consciously intended*

---

[11] For a discussion of the etymological fallacy, see Carson, *Exegetical Fallacies*, 28–33; Osborne, *Hermeneutical Spiral*, 84–89; Köstenberger and Patterson, *Invitation to Biblical Interpretation*, 631–35.

allusion to a word's prior history. One must always ask, How has the author led the reader to consider the origins or historical echoes in this word? For example, in Matt 1:21, the Gospel author reports that an angel tells Joseph, "[Mary] will give birth to a son, and you are to name him Jesus, because he will save his people from their sins." Matthew clearly intends his audience to understand the etymological origin of Jesus's Hebrew name ("YHWH saves") as significant. In the Scriptures, the etymological meaning of proper names is often viewed as important by biblical authors. We know that because of the inspired authors' *explicit indications* in the text (e.g., Gen 25:26; 27:36; John 9:7–11).[12]

3. Do Not Confuse Words and Concepts

Students sometimes search every instance of a particular word in an effort to understand a theological concept. For example, a student will write a paper on prayer that examines every instance of προσεύχομαι ("I pray") in the New Testament. Such a student fails to consider, however, that the idea of prayer is mentioned in many places where the actual word προσεύχομαι is not used. In fact, the biblical authors employ many Greek words for prayer (e.g., δέησις, εὐχή, εὔχομαι), and the concept is sometimes present even when no explicit "prayer words" are used (John 11:41–42).

4. Do Not View Word Study Tools as Inerrant

The number of excellent Greek word study tools available is intoxicating. Nevertheless, we must remember that these resources are created by fallible human beings who sometimes show their mental frailty or theological biases. Louw and Nida's *Greek-English Lexicon of the New Testament Based on Semantic Domains* is an excellent resource; but like all such resources, it is imperfect. For example, under the word λόγος, Louw and Nida rightly list "gospel" as one of the potential meanings of the word.[13] Under the word ῥῆμα, however, "gospel" is not listed as a possible meaning,[14] even though ῥῆμα carries those connotations in multiple contexts (e.g., Rom 10:8, 17–18; Eph 5:26; 6:17).

Theological bias can also show up in lexicons. In the entry for ἱλασμός, Louw and Nida argue against the English rendering "propitiation" (wrath-appeasing) because "in the NT God is never the object of propitiation since he is already on the side of his people."[15] While the idea

---

[12] Etymological studies are usually a last resort, often most helpful with rare words and proper names.
[13] Johannes P. Louw and Eugene A. Nida, *Greek-English Lexicon of the New Testament Based on Semantic Domains* (New York: United Bible Societies, 1988), 2:153.
[14] Louw and Nida, 2:217.
[15] Louw and Nida, 1:504 (§40.12).

that God is not wrathful toward sinners may be popular in certain theological circles, it directly contradicts New Testament teaching and is not based on linguistic evidence.[16]

Optional Assignment: Assuming you have access to a theological library, choose a theologically significant Greek word you have learned and look it up in BDAG and *NIDNTTE*. Then write two paragraphs answering these questions: (1) What does the word mean? and (2) How do BDAG and *NIDNTTE* differ in their content and presentation of information?

---

[16] E.g., John 3:36, "The one who believes in the Son has eternal life, but the one who rejects the Son will not see life; instead, the wrath of God remains on him" (see also Rom 1:18).

CHAPTER 13

//////////////

LIQUID VERBS

13.1 Overview[1]

After studying the present and imperfect tense-forms, we discussed contract verbs (in chap. 7). As you will recall, the stem of a contract verb ends with the short vowel α, ε, or o. When that vowel comes into contact with the connecting vowel at the head of the personal ending, a contraction occurs (ποιε + ομεν → ποιοῦμεν). Thus, the problem we encountered was too many vowels. The tenses affected were the present and imperfect.

With liquid verbs, we have just the opposite problem—too many consonants. *Liquid verbs* are those whose stems end in lambda (λ), mu (μ), nu (ν), or rho (ρ).[2] Recall that in both the future and (first) aorist tense-forms a sigma (σ) is added to the stem. When a *liquid consonant* (λ, μ, ν, or ρ) comes into contact with the added sigma, something is forced to drop or change, usually because of difficulty in pronunciation. This chapter focuses on the changes that occur when the tense formative (σ) of the future and aorist tenses is added to liquid verbs.

13.2 Significance

Paul writes to the Philippians from prison (Phil 1:13). Imminent death is a real possibility for him. With this in mind, the apostle affirms that to die and be with Christ "is far better" (1:23). He says, "To live is Christ and to die is gain" (1:21).

---

[1] For an overview video lecture of chapter 13, go to bit.ly/greeklecture13 or beginninggreek.com.
[2] This can be remembered with this phrase: **L**earn **m**ore **n**onsense **r**ules (Baugh). Or you might remember these letters as the consonant sounds in "**Mineral**." Note that when you open a bottle of carbonated mineral water, you can hear the "ssss" sound—the sigma is trying to get away from the liquid consonants.

At the same time, Paul observes that the fledgling churches need his ongoing care and instruction. So, he concludes,

> Convinced of this [i.e., that you and other believers need my presence and instruction], I know that **I will remain** and continue with you all for your progress and joy in the faith. (Phil 1:25 NASB)

The Greek word translated "I will remain" here is μενῶ. Why is μενῶ translated with an English future tense? Isn't μενῶ just the present active indicative first person singular, "I remain"? No, it is not. That would be written this way: μένω. The future is μενῶ. Look very carefully. Do you notice the slight difference between the two? The present tense has an acute accent over ε, while the future has a circumflex over ω. The reason that μένω is not conforming to the future paradigm you know is that its stem ends in a liquid consonant (ν). μένω is a liquid verb. Let's learn more about these tricky liquid verbs.

13.3 Liquid Futures

The future active and future middle forms of liquid verbs differ from the typical future forms because of adjustments that must be made when the sigma tense formative (σ) comes in contact with a liquid consonant—lambda (λ), mu (μ), nu (ν), or rho (ρ). Because the stem of a liquid verb ends with a *liquid consonant*—a consonant that does not react well to the added sigma—the sigma is rejected in the future active and future middle forms. The process, however, is slightly more complicated than a mere rejection of the sigma. Actually, from a more precise morphological explanation, what happens is that the tense formative is changed from a sigma (σ) to an "epsilon + sigma" (εσ). When the connecting vowel of the personal ending is placed beside the sigma, however, it is then found between two vowels due to the addition of the epsilon (intervocalic sigma), which then drops out of the word. The two vowels that were separated by a sigma are then found together and after the sigma is gone, they contract (in a manner similar to contract verbs).

$$\mu εν + εσ + ομεν \rightarrow \mu ενεσομεν \rightarrow \mu ενεομεν \rightarrow \mu ενοῦμεν$$

For simplicity's sake, when dealing with liquid futures, you can think of the sigma as being replaced by an epsilon, followed by a contraction with the connecting vowel (or first vowel of the personal ending unit). Below is the paradigm for the future active indicative. This paradigm does not need to be memorized.

	SINGULAR		PLURAL	
1ST	μενῶ	I will remain	μενοῦμεν	we will remain
2ND	μενεῖς	you will remain	μενεῖτε	you will remain
3RD	μενεῖ	he/she/it will remain	μενοῦσι(ν)	they will remain

As you will note, future liquid verbs conjugate the same as present tense epsilon contract verbs (see 7.3). The difference, however, is that liquid verbs following these endings are future; contract verbs following these paradigm endings are present. Also, in four of six possible forms, the only difference between the present and the future conjugation of liquid verbs is the circumflex accent marking where the contraction has occurred. The first and second person plural forms have minor spelling differences where vowel contractions have occurred.

Present Active (Liquid)[3]	Future Active (Liquid)[4]	Present Active (Contract)[5]
μένω	μενῶ	ποιῶ
μένεις	μενεῖς	ποιεῖς
μένει	μενεῖ	ποιεῖ
μένομεν	μενοῦμεν	ποιοῦμεν
μένετε	μενεῖτε	ποιεῖτε
μένουσιν	μενοῦσιν	ποιοῦσιν

In addition to the changes described above, some liquid futures also employ verbal stems that are slightly different from their present tense stems. Sometimes an iota (ι) will drop from the stem (αἴρω → ἀρῶ; ἐγείρω → ἐγερῶ).[6] With other verbs, a lambda will drop from the stem (ἀπαγγέλλω → ἀπαγγελῶ; ἀποστέλλω → ἀποστελῶ; βάλλω → βαλῶ).[7] Because you will be reading Greek texts, not composing them, these slight spelling changes should be welcomed! They are little friends reminding you that you are no longer looking at a present tense verb.

13.4 Liquid Aorists

The aorist forms for liquid verbs do not follow the same pattern as the future forms. Instead of replacing the sigma with an epsilon, the sigma is dropped and the main vowel in the verb stem lengthens to compensate for its loss (***compensatory lengthening:*** μένω → ἔμεινα). In other words, ε→ει, α→η, o→ω, and short ι→long ι (looking the same but being pronounced differently). At the same time, if a verb has a double lambda (λλ) in the present tense, it changes to a single lambda (λ) in the aorist: ἀπαγγέλλω → ἀπήγγειλα; ἀποστέλλω → ἀπέστειλα. Finally, sometimes an iota is dropped from the stem: αἴρω → ἦρα. Such changes help distinguish the aorist from the imperfect (e.g., ἔμεινεν, "he remained"; ἔμενεν, "he was remaining"). Here are the aorist forms of the liquid verb μένω:

---

[3] μένω, "I remain"; μένεις, "you remain"; μένει, "he remains"; μένομεν, "we remain"; μένετε, "you (pl) remain"; μένουσιν, "they remain."

[4] μενῶ, "I will remain"; μενεῖς, "you will remain"; μενεῖ, "he will remain"; μενοῦμεν, "we will remain"; μενεῖτε, "you (pl) will remain"; μενοῦσιν, "they will remain."

[5] ποιῶ, "I do"; ποιεῖς, "you do"; ποιεῖ, "he does"; ποιοῦμεν, "we do"; ποιεῖτε, "you (pl) do"; ποιοῦσιν, "they do."

[6] More precisely, the iota (ι) is added to the stem of the verb in the present tense.

[7] More precisely, the lambda (λ) is added to the stem of the verb in the present tense.

	SINGULAR		PLURAL	
1ST	ἔμεινα	I remained	ἐμείναμεν	we remained
2ND	ἔμεινας	you remained	ἐμείνατε	you remained
3RD	ἔμεινεν	he/she/it remained	ἔμειναν	they remained

For the aorist form of a liquid verb, you will have (1) an augment and (2) an ending with alpha, but you will not have the sigma tense formative because the sigma will have dropped out because it appeared next to the liquid consonant at the end of the verb stem. The main vowel in the verb stem will likely have lengthened to compensate for the loss of the sigma (i.e., ε→ει, α→η, ο→ω).

13.5 Summary of Liquid Verb Forms

Liquid Verb	Future	Aorist
αἴρω	ἀρῶ	ἦρα
ἀπαγγέλλω	ἀπαγγελῶ	ἀπήγγειλα
ἀποκρίνομαι	——	ἀπεκρινάμην
ἀποκτείνω	ἀποκτενῶ	ἀπέκτεινα
ἀποστέλλω	ἀποστελῶ	ἀπέστειλα
ἐγείρω	ἐγερῶ	ἤγειρα
κρίνω	κρινῶ	ἔκρινα
μένω	μενῶ	ἔμεινα
σπείρω	σπερῶ	ἔσπειρα

13.6 Practice

A. Stem Recognition: Indicate whether the form is Present (P), Future (F), or Aorist (A).

1. _____ ἐγείρομαι

2. _____ ἤρατε

3. _____ ἀπαγγελεῖ

4. _____ ἐμείναμεν

5. _____ σπείρεται

6. _____ ἀποκριθήσονται

7. _____ ἀποκτενοῦσιν

8. _____ ἀποστέλλει

9. _____ ἐκρίθησαν

10. _____ ἀποκρίνῃ

B. Parsing: Parse the following verbs.

1. ἀροῦσιν

2. ἀπήγγειλαν

3. ἀποκριθήσονται

4. ἀπεκτείνατε

5. ἀποστελῶ

6. ἠγέρθη

7. ἔκρινας

8. μενεῖ

9. ἐσπείραμεν

10. κρινοῦμεν

C. Translation: Translate the following sentences.

1. ἀπαγγελῶ τὸ ὄνομά (name) σου τοῖς ἀδελφοῖς μου (Heb 2:12).

2. ὁ δοῦλος ἀπήγγειλεν τῷ κυρίῳ αὐτοῦ ταῦτα (these things) (Luke 14:21).

3. λέγω ὑμῖν ὅτι ἀρθήσεται ἀφ᾽ ὑμῶν ἡ βασιλεία τοῦ θεοῦ (Matt 21:43).

4. οἱ μαθηταὶ αὐτοῦ ἦραν τὸ πτῶμα (corpse) (Matt 14:12).

5. ἀπεκρίθη Ἰησοῦς καὶ εἶπεν αὐτῷ, Ἀμὴν (truly) ἀμὴν λέγω σοι (John 3:3).

6. καὶ ἀποκτενοῦσιν αὐτόν, καὶ τῇ τρίτῃ (third) ἡμέρᾳ ἐγερθήσεται (Matt 17:23).

7. Κύριε, τοὺς προφήτας σου ἀπέκτειναν (Rom 11:3).

8. ἀποστελεῖ ὁ υἱὸς τοῦ ἀνθρώπου τοὺς ἀγγέλους αὐτοῦ (Matt 13:41).

9. καθὼς ἐμὲ ἀπέστειλας εἰς τὸν κόσμον, κἀγὼ ἀπέστειλα αὐτοὺς εἰς τὸν κόσμον (John 17:18).

10. ὁ θεὸς τῶν πατέρων (fathers) ἡμῶν ἤγειρεν Ἰησοῦν (Acts 5:30).

11. κρινεῖ κύριος τὸν λαὸν αὐτοῦ (Heb 10:30).

12. καὶ ἐκρίθησαν ἕκαστος (each) κατὰ τὰ ἔργα αὐτῶν (Rev 20:13).

13. καὶ ὑμεῖς ἐν τῷ υἱῷ καὶ ἐν τῷ πατρὶ μενεῖτε (1 John 2:24).

14. μετὰ τοῦτο (this, *accusative*) κατέβη εἰς Καφαρναοὺμ αὐτὸς καὶ ἡ μήτηρ (mother) αὐτοῦ καὶ οἱ ἀδελφοὶ [αὐτοῦ] καὶ οἱ μαθηταὶ αὐτοῦ καὶ ἐκεῖ ἔμειναν οὐ πολλὰς (many) ἡμέρας (John 2:12).

15. ἄνθρωπος ἔσπειρεν ἐν τῷ ἀγρῷ (field) αὐτου (Matt 13:31).

D. Translation: Translate the following sentences into Greek.

1. The stone was taken away.

2. They will announce the wisdom of the Scriptures.

3. Therefore, I will remain in the temple.

4. The man judged the time of salvation.

5. The Lord will send out the good news to the teacher.

13.7 Vocabulary[8]

αἰών, –ῶνος, ὁ	eternity, age, world (*eon*)
ἀνήρ, ἀνδρός, ὁ	man, husband (*androgynous, android*)
ἀρχιερεύς, –έως, ὁ	high priest (*archenemy, arch*)
βασιλεύς, –έως, ὁ	king (*basilica*)
πατήρ, πατρός, ὁ	father, ancestor (*patristics, patriarch*)
γυνή, γυναικός, ἡ	woman, wife (*gynecology*)
μήτηρ, –τρός, ἡ	mother (*matriarch*)
πίστις, –εως, ἡ	faith, trust
πόλις, –εως, ἡ	city, town (*metropolitan*)
σάρξ, σαρκός, ἡ	flesh, body, mortal nature (*sarcoma, sarcophagus*)
χάρις, –ιτος, ἡ	grace, thanks (*charity, Charis*—a woman's name)
ἔθνος, –ους, τό	nation, people; Gentiles (pl) (*ethnic*)
ὄνομα, –ατος, τό	name (*pseudonym*)
πνεῦμα, –ατος, τό	Spirit, spirit, wind (*pneumatology*)
σῶμα, –ατος, τό	body (*psychosomatic*)

---

[8] To hear an author of your textbook read through the vocabulary for chapter 13, go to bit.ly/greekvocab13 or beginninggreek.com.

//////////////

CHAPTER 14

THIRD DECLENSION NOUNS

14.1 Overview[1]

In this chapter, we return to nouns, this time considering the third declension. (Remember that "declension" is just a term for a grammatical pattern.) Just as with first and second declension nouns, we will see how endings added to the stems of third declension nouns communicate how those nouns are functioning in the sentence, i.e., whether the nouns are nominative, genitive, dative, accusative, or vocative. Because this declension has a wide variety of stems, it also has a wide variety of patterns compared to first and second declension nouns.

14.2 Significance

It is not uncommon for one particular anti-Trinitarian cult to claim that the Holy Spirit should not be understood as a Person because the gender of the noun πνεῦμα ("Spirit," a third declension noun) is neuter. Hopefully, even by this early stage in your Greek studies, you know enough not to base your theological reflections on the gender of nouns. Indeed, should we conclude that a human child (τέκνον, a neuter noun) is not really a person? (Granted, some parents of young children could be tempted to conclude that on particularly challenging nights!)

Yes, the noun πνεῦμα is neuter, but we know who the Spirit is not by the gender of the noun, but by the description of him in the Scriptures. He is God (Acts 5:3–4; 1 Cor 3:16–17), yet he is distinguished from the Father and the Son (Matt 28:19; 2 Cor 13:13). He is not a force, but personal and communicative (Acts 13:2).

With the faithful Christian church of all ages, let us agree with the words of the First Council of Constantinople (AD 381): "I believe in the Holy Spirit, the Lord

---

[1] For an overview video lecture of chapter 14, go to bit.ly/greeklecture14 or beginninggreek.com.

and Giver of life, who proceeds from the Father, who with the Father and the Son together is worshiped and glorified, who spoke by the prophets."

14.3 Gender and Case

Whereas most first declension nouns are feminine and most second declension nouns are masculine or neuter, third declension nouns are regularly found in all three genders. Because it is difficult to know the gender of a third declension noun, pay attention to the article (if one is present) since it is consistent and does not change based on the declension of the noun. In fact, we strongly recommend that you memorize the article along with the lexical forms of third declension nouns.

ὁ πατήρ	Masculine
ἡ γυνή	Feminine
τὸ πνεῦμα	Neuter

The cases of third declension nouns function identically as first and second declension nouns. That is, the nominative is frequently the subject, genitive expresses possession, dative functions as the indirect object, and accusative is the direct object.

14.4 Paradigms

THIRD DECLENSION NOUN—FEMININE[2]						
	SINGULAR			PLURAL		
NOM	ἡ	σάρξ	the flesh	αἱ	σάρκες	the flesh(es)[3]
GEN	τῆς	σαρκός	of the flesh	τῶν	σαρκῶν	of the flesh(es)
DAT	τῇ	σαρκί	to/for the flesh	ταῖς	σαρξί(ν)	to/for the flesh(es)
ACC	τὴν	σάρκα	the flesh	τάς	σάρκας	the flesh(es)

THIRD DECLENSION NOUN—NEUTER						
	SINGULAR			PLURAL		
NOM	τό	πνεῦμα	the spirit	τά	πνεύματα	the spirits
GEN	τοῦ	πνεύματος	of the spirit	τῶν	πνευμάτων	of the spirits
DAT	τῷ	πνεύματι	to/for the spirit	τοῖς	πνεύμασι(ν)	to/for the spirits
ACC	τό	πνεῦμα	the spirit	τά	πνεύματα	the spirits

[2] To hear a mnemonic song by Danny Zacharias, go to bit.ly/3rddeclensionsong.
[3] In English, the plural of the noun "flesh" is also "flesh," but we have constructed this artificial form to remind you that the Greek words being translated are, in fact, plural.

14.5 Morphology

From a historical morphological standpoint, the stem of first declension nouns ends in an alpha (α) or eta (η) while the stem of second declension nouns ends in an omicron (o). The stem of third declension nouns, however, ends in a consonant. Thus, nouns whose stems end in a consonant follow the third declension pattern.

Below is the basic pattern followed by third declension nouns. Note that they are two slightly different patterns—a masculine/feminine set of endings and a neuter set of endings. The masculine and feminine forms follow the same pattern. The slashes (/) below separate alternate endings, though any Greek word will only follow one of those two endings.

Masculine/Feminine		Neuter	
–ς/–	–ες	–ς/–	–α
–ος	–ων	–ος	–ων
–ι	–σι(ν)	–ι	–σι(ν)
–α	–ας	–ς/–	–α

The basic stem for the third declension is not found in the nominative singular form because it has experienced a spelling change. Often, part of the original noun stem has dropped off or combined in the nominative form. The genitive singular form, however, usually contains the unaltered noun stem along with the case ending. Consequently, it is crucial to memorize both the lexical (nominative) form and the genitive singular form of third declension nouns. So, with third declension nouns, we are recommending that you memorize (1) the nominative form with the article, and (2) the genitive form. For the purposes of parallelism, it is advisable to recite the article with the genitive form also. Thus, when we say the word "spirit," we advise that you be able to recite from memory: τὸ πνεῦμα, τοῦ πνεύματος.

When third declension endings are added to the stem, changes occur.

	Singular		Plural	
Nom	σαρκ + ς	→ σάρξ[4]	σαρκ + ες	→ σάρκες
Gen	σαρκ + ος	→ σαρκός	σαρκ + ων	→ σαρκῶν
Dat	σαρκ + ι	→ σαρκί	σαρκ + σιν	→ σαρξί(ν)[5]
Acc	σαρκ + α	→ σάρκα	σαρκ + ας	→ σάρκας

	Singular		Plural	
Nom	πνευματ + -	→ πνεῦμα[6]	πνευματ + α	→ πνεύματα
Gen	πνευματ + ος	→ πνεύματος	πνευματ + ων	→ πνευμάτων
Dat	πνευματ + ι	→ πνεύματι	πνευματ + σιν	→ πνεύμασι(ν)[7]
Acc	πνευματ + -	→ πνεῦμα	πνευματ + α	→ πνεύματα

---

[4] The kappa (κ) combines with the sigma (σ) to form a xsi (ξ).
[5] The kappa (κ) combines with the sigma (σ) to form a xsi (ξ). The nu (ν) is movable.
[6] There is no ending and the tau (τ) drops because it cannot be the last letter of a word.
[7] The tau (τ) drops because it is followed by a sigma (σ).

Notice several items based on the third declension pattern:

1. The dative forms have the usual iota (ι), though the singular form is not subscripted as with the first and second declension (φωνῇ, λόγῳ). The dative plural forms have a "movable nu," which is usually present but may drop out in certain situations. The changes to the stem that occur in the nominative singular also happen in the dative plural.

    Nom sg   σαρκ + σ → σάρξ

    Dat pl   σαρκ + σιν → σαρξίν

2. The genitive plural forms are the same as the first and second declension forms (–ων). You need to own (–ων) these endings. (Note that the genitive often communicates possession—owning.)

3. The neuter nominative and accusative forms have the same forms (consistent with all neuter nouns).

4. Liquid nouns (i.e., nouns ending with λ, μ, ν, or ρ), which are also classified as third declension nouns since they end in a consonant, drop the sigma off the endings and sometimes drop or lengthen the previous vowel (πατερ + σ → πατήρ).

5. Some third declension noun stems originally ended with a ***digamma*** (ϝ) or a ***consonantal iota*** (ι̯), archaic letters (or pronunciations) that mostly dropped out of use in Koine Greek. Although these letters are no longer used, their former presence continues to affect the word. In fact, as you continue in your study of Greek, you will see that a word's odd spelling changes can often be explained by a morphological history that includes the dropping out of archaic letters. As you learn more third declension nouns, you will also notice that all nouns whose stems originally ended in a consonantal iota are feminine (e.g., πίστις, πόλις).

6. Nouns ending in –μα are always neuter (ὄνομα, πνεῦμα, σῶμα). Neuter nouns represent the largest group of third declension nouns.

7. Be careful of endings that look the same but are actually different forms. Pay attention to the article if it is provided since it is the easiest way to identify the gender, case, and number of the noun.

ὁ λόγος	masc, nom, sg
τῆς σαρκός	fem, gen, sg
τὸ ἔθνος	neut, nom/acc, sg

14.6 The Square of Stops

In chapter 10, you were introduced to the idea of consonant families (labials, palatals/velars, dentals) and how related consonants combined in similar ways when a sigma was added after them. These same rules apply to third declension noun endings that begin with a sigma and combine with a consonant on the end of the third declension stems.

The related consonants that you learned previously can loosely be labeled "consonantal stops." Mounce calls the square chart that speaks of their possible combinations "the square of stops." A "stop" is a consonant whose sound is made by stopping the air flow through the mouth. As we saw previously, these consonants can be further divided into three types: labials (formed by using the lips), palatals/velars (formed by using the palate or roof of the mouth), and dentals (formed by using the teeth).

LABIALS	π[8]	β	ϕ	+ σ	= ψ
PALATALS	κ	γ	χ	+ σ	= ξ
DENTALS	τ	δ	θ	+ σ	= σ

Reviewing this chart will prove helpful in understanding how the added sigma will alter the spellings of certain words.

14.7 Third Declension Noun Variations

Third declension nouns have more variation than other declensions. Below is a chart with six different third declension representative nouns. Although there are some differences, many of the endings are the same or similar. After memorizing both third declension memory paradigms in this chapter, focus on *recognizing* the forms in the other paradigms.

$-\kappa$ stem	$-\mu\alpha\tau$ stem	$-\delta/\tau$ stem	$-\iota$ stem	$-\varepsilon\varsigma$ stem	$-\varepsilon\digamma$ stem
σάρξ	πνεῦμα	χάρις[9]	πίστις[10]	ἔθνος[11]	βασιλεύς
σαρκός	πνεύματος	χάριτος	πίστεως[12]	ἔθνους	βασιλέως
σαρκί	πνεύματι	χάριτι	πίστει	ἔθνει	βασιλεῖ

---

[8] The first column (π, κ, τ) represents unvoiced sounds, the second column (β, γ, δ) represents voiced sounds, and the third column (φ, χ, θ) represents aspirated sounds.

[9] As expected, the tau (τ) drops out when followed by a sigma (ς): χάριτς → χάρις.

[10] The stem originally ended with a consonantal iota (ι) which is changed to an epsilon (ε) in all forms but the nominative and accusative singular (πίστις, πίστιν).

[11] The stem ends with –ες. But when the ending is added, the intervocalic sigma drops out. In the nominative and accusative singular, the epsilon (ε) changes to an omicron (o). Here are the changes that take place when the endings are added to this noun: ἔθνες → ἔθνος; ἔθνες + ος = ἔθνεσος = ἔθνεος → ἔθνους; ἔθνες + ι = ἔθνεσι → ἔθνει; ἔθνες + α = ἔθνεσα = ἔθνεα → ἔθνη; ἔθνες + ῶν = ἔθνεσῶν = ἔθνεῶν → ἐθνῶν; ἔθνες + σιν = ἔθνεσσιν → ἔθνεσιν.

[12] Note the similarities between the endings –ος and –ως, the latter having the longer vowel.

σάρκα	πνεῦμα	χάριν[13]	πίστιν	ἔθνος	βασιλέα
σάρκες	πνεύματα	χάριτες	πίστεις[14]	ἔθνη	βασιλεῖς
σαρκῶν	πνευμάτων	χαρίτων	πίστεων	ἐθνῶν	βασιλέων
σαρξί(ν)	πνεύμασι(ν)	χάρισι(ν)	πίστεσι(ν)	ἔθνεσι(ν)	βασιλεῦσι(ν)
σάρκας	πνεύματα	χάριτας	πίστεις	ἔθνη	βασιλεῖς

14.8 Practice

A. Paradigms: Memorize the paradigms for σάρξ and πνεῦμά (see section 14.4). Then write out each paradigm ten times from memory (including the article).

B. Declensions: Circle the third declension nouns and then parse them.

1. ἔργων	ἀρχιερεῦσιν	σάρξ	ψυχή
2. αἰῶνι	κυρίου	δόξης	πατέρα
3. γυναιξίν	κεφαλή	πόλεως	ἔθνη
4. θεῷ	ἀνθρώποις	μητρί	βασιλεῖ
5. πίστει	ἄνδρες	καρδίᾳ	ἀπόστολοι
6. οἶκον	χάριν	λόγους	ὀνομάτων
7. πνεύματα	μαθηταῖς	σωμάτων	υἱοῖς

C. Translation: Translate the following sentences.

1. τῷ δὲ θεῷ καὶ πατρὶ ἡμῶν ἡ δόξα εἰς τοὺς αἰῶνας τῶν αἰώνων, ἀμήν (Phil 4:20).

2. ἀπεκρίθη ἡ γυνὴ καὶ εἶπεν αὐτῷ, Οὐκ ἔχω ἄνδρα (John 4:17).

3. ἔχομεν ἀρχιερέα, ὃς ἐκάθισεν (sat) ἐν δεξιᾷ (right hand) τοῦ θρόνου τῆς μεγαλωσύνης (most high) ἐν τοῖς οὐρανοῖς (Heb 8:1).

4. σὺ εἶ ὁ βασιλεὺς τῶν Ἰουδαίων; (Mark 15:2).

5. οὐ γάρ ἐστιν ἀνὴρ ἐκ γυναικὸς ἀλλὰ γυνὴ ἐξ ἀνδρός (1 Cor 11:8).

6. τίμα (honor, *verb, imp*) τὸν πατέρα σου καὶ τὴν μητέρα, ἥτις ἐστὶν ἐντολὴ πρώτη (first) ἐν ἐπαγγελίᾳ (Eph 6:2).

7. ὃ οὐκ ἐκ πίστεως ἁμαρτία ἐστίν (Rom 14:23).

8. ἡ γυνὴ . . . ἀπῆλθεν εἰς τὴν πόλιν καὶ λέγει τοῖς ἀνθρώποις (John 4:28).

9. ὑμεῖς δὲ οὐκ ἐστὲ ἐν σαρκὶ ἀλλὰ ἐν πνεύματι, εἴπερ (if) πνεῦμα θεοῦ οἰκεῖ (dwells/lives) ἐν ὑμῖν (Rom 8:9).

---

[13] In two instances, the expected alpha (α) ending is used (χάριτα). See Acts 24:27 and Jude v. 4.
[14] Actually, the ending is –ες but it has contracted with the epsilon (ε) of the stem (πιστε + ες → πίστεις). Note that the accusative plural has the same form as the nominative plural (similar to neuter nouns).

10. εἰ δὲ χάριτι, οὐκέτι ἐξ ἔργων, ἐπεὶ (since) ἡ χάρις οὐκέτι γίνεται χάρις (Rom 11:6).

11. κρίσιν (judgment) τοῖς ἔθνεσιν ἀπαγγελεῖ (Matt 12:18).

12. ἐπίστευσαν τῷ Φιλίππῳ . . . περὶ τῆς βασιλείας τοῦ θεοῦ καὶ τοῦ ὀνόματος Ἰησοῦ Χριστοῦ, ἐβαπτίζοντο ἄνδρες τε καὶ γυναῖκες (Acts 8:12).

13. ἡμεῖς δὲ οὐ τὸ πνεῦμα τοῦ κόσμου ἐλάβομεν ἀλλὰ τὸ πνεῦμα τὸ ἐκ τοῦ θεοῦ (1 Cor 2:12).

14. καὶ αὐτός ἐστιν ἡ κεφαλὴ τοῦ σώματος τῆς ἐκκλησίας· (Col 1:18).

D. Translation: Translate the following sentences into Greek.

1. The mother of the high priest believed in the name of the Lord.

2. The man of faith knows the Spirit of God.

3. The king of the city will judge the nations.

4. The woman came to the father and prayed over the body of the child.

5. The grace of Christ will kill the flesh into the ages of ages.

14.9 Vocabulary[15]

ἐγγίζω	I approach, draw near
ζάω	I live (*zoo*)
οἶδα	I know, understand
ὁράω	I see, perceive (*panorama*)
πείθω	I persuade, convince (*faith*)
αἷμα, αἵματος, τό	blood (*hematology, hemoglobin*)
γραμματεύς, γραμματέως, ὁ	scribe (*grammar*)
δύναμις, δυνάμεως, ἡ	power, miracle (*dynamic*)
πούς, ποδός, ὁ	foot (*podiatrist*)
πῦρ, πυρός, τό	fire (*pyre, pyromaniac*)
ῥῆμα, ῥήματος, τό	word, saying (*Rhema* Bible Training College)
στόμα, στόματος, τό	mouth (*stomach*)
ὕδωρ, ὕδατος, τό	water (*hydraulics, hydrogen*)
φῶς, φωτός, τό	light (*photon, photograph*)
χείρ, χειρός, ἡ	hand (χείρ + πρακτικός, "effective")

[15] To hear an author of your textbook read through the vocabulary for chapter 14, go to bit.ly/greekvocab14 or beginninggreek.com.

////////////////

CHAPTER 15

PERFECT AND PLUPERFECT INDICATIVE VERBS

15.1 Overview[1]

The perfect and pluperfect tenses are the final tenses to learn. They occur more rarely than the others, so in light of grammarian Steve Runge's dictum "choice implies meaning," we must ask what meaning a biblical author intended to convey in choosing the perfect or pluperfect tenses.

15.2 Significance

In Rev 18, a mighty angel declares the imminent destruction of "Babylon the Great"—a female prostitute who represents the demonic control of economic and political power in active rebellion against God. The angel says,

> [A]ll the nations have drunk (πέπωκαν) the maddening wine of [Babylon's] adul-teries. The kings of the earth committed adultery with her, and the merchants of the earth grew rich from her excessive luxuries. (Rev 18:3 NIV)

Using language of sexual unfaithfulness (mirroring Old Testament metaphorical language of Israel's unfaithfulness to God), the angelic messenger tells the apostle John that nations "have drunk the maddening wine of her adulteries." You will note in the verse printed above that the English translation "have drunk" is a render-ing of πέπωκαν, the Greek perfect of πίνω. The dominant meaning of the Greek perfect is to report a past event (the nations drank wine) that issues in a resulting

---

[1] For an overview video lecture of chapter 15, go to bit.ly/greeklecture15 or beginninggreek.com.

155

state (the nations are now drunk). In other words, a demonically-inspired rebellion against God has been ingested by the nations and is now found enmeshed in their political and economic systems. They are in a state of demonically-empowered inebriation (wicked rebellion) against the Creator and Sovereign of the universe.

When you watch or read the news, do you ever struggle to understand the animosity and illogicality of governmental persecution of Christians—whether in America or elsewhere around the world? Revelation pulls back the veil on this mystery. Indeed, Revelation administers a spiritual breathalyzer test on the nations and finds them demonically drunk on rebellion.

15.3 Meaning of the Perfect Tense

We will consider three nuances of the perfect tense in the indicative mood, beginning with the most common meaning.

- **Past Action with Resulting State:** Within the New Testament, the perfect tense usually communicates a completed past action with a resulting state of affairs in the present (from the perspective of the author, not the reader). The action itself is done and is no longer being performed, although the consequences of the action have continuing results. Thus, the verb's aspect is *stative* because it describes the resulting state or condition of a past action. In a recent technical study, a Greek grammarian calculated that 54 percent of perfects in the New Testament convey a stative idea (completed action, continuing result).[2] For such stative meaning, sometimes the focus of the perfect tense verb is on the past action; other times, the focus is on the resulting state. When the latter is in view, it is usually best to translate the perfect with an English present (e.g., γέγραπται = "it is/stands written" and not "it has been written," Matt 4:4, 7, 10).

- **Past Action with Ongoing Relevance:** The perfect tense can also be used to describe a past action that has ongoing relevance for the writer's discussion. In other words, depending on the literary context, the author may choose the perfect tense not because he is emphasizing an ongoing state that results from past action but because the completed past action has ongoing relevance for his discourse. A Greek grammarian recently calculated that 35 percent of the perfects in the New Testament are rightly understood as conveying continuing relevance.[3]

  One example of such use is found in 1 John 1:1–3, where the author uses several perfect verbs to describe the apostles' experiences of seeing and hearing Jesus (ἑωράκαμεν, "we have seen"; ἀκηκόαμεν, "we have heard"). These past events have immediate relevance for John's discussion,

---

[2] Statistics on perfect tense usage are from the dissertation research of Hanbyul Kang, a doctoral student at The Southern Baptist Theological Seminary (personal correspondence, January 2020).

[3] Kang, dissertation research.

in which John declares for the unified apostolic witness, "We testify and declare to you the eternal life that was with the Father and was revealed to us" (1 John 1:2). The past actions of apostolic seeing and hearing have direct continuing relevance (and logically undergird) the current apostolic actions of testifying and announcing.

Another example of the perfect of continuing relevance is found in Mark 7:36–37. Here, following the healing of the deaf man with a speech impediment, Jesus addresses the eyewitnesses of the miracle. Mark reports: "And Jesus charged them to tell no one. But the more he charged them, the more zealously they proclaimed it. And they were astonished beyond measure, saying, 'He has done (πεποίηκεν, perfect tense) all things well. He even makes the deaf hear and the mute speak'" (ESV). The traditional understanding of the perfect (a completed event with continuing results) does not fit well here. More likely, it is the ongoing relevance of Jesus's amazing works that Mark wants to highlight for his discussion. Indeed, it is because of these amazing works that Jesus has done in the past, that the crowds are astonished in the present. These works done by Jesus (perfect tense) have continuing relevance for understanding the crowds' assessment of Jesus.

- **Past Action from a Wholistic Perspective:** Finally, in the Koine period, we find a third, relatively rare function of the perfect tense (accounting for only 11 percent of perfects in the New Testament). At this point in the development of the Greek language, the perfect tense is beginning to overlap with the aorist, so it is occasionally employed to report a prior past action from a wholistic perspective with seemingly no comment on the resulting state or ongoing relevance of the activity. That is, in such cases, the perfect is essentially synonymous with the aorist. Such usage, while relatively rare, is more common in later New Testament writings. For example, in Rev 8:15, we read, "Then the angel took (εἴληφεν, perfect) the censer, filled it with fire from the altar, and threw it on the earth, and there were crashes of thunder, roaring, flashes of lightning, and an earthquake" (NET). Despite various creative efforts of commentators to explain the perfect tense in some other way, εἴληφεν seems to be functioning the same way that the aorist form (ἔλαβεν) would—simply to report an event in past narrative from a wholistic perspective (perfective aspect). If we trace the usage of the perfect tense into the Byzantine (post-Koine) period, we find that the perfect eventually overlaps completely in meaning with the aorist and thus, redundant, disappears from the language.[4]

---

[4] Our understanding of the meaning of the perfect tense has been significantly assisted by Rutger J. Allan, "Tense and Aspect in Classical Greek: Two Historical Developments; Augment and Perfect," in *The Greek Verb Revisited: A Fresh Approach for Biblical Exegesis*, ed. Steven E. Runge and Christopher J. Fresch (Bellingham, WA: Lexham, 2016), 81–121.

15.4 Paradigms

PERFECT ACTIVE INDICATIVE[5]				
	SINGULAR		PLURAL	
1ST	λέλυκα	I have loosed	λελύκαμεν	we have loosed
2ND	λέλυκας	you have loosed	λελύκατε	you have loosed
3RD	λέλυκε(ν)	he/she/it has loosed	λελύκασι(ν) λελύκαν	they have loosed

PERFECT MIDDLE/PASSIVE INDICATIVE[6]				
	SINGULAR		PLURAL	
1ST	λέλυμαι	I have been loosed	λελύμεθα	we have been loosed
2ND	λέλυσαι	you have been loosed	λέλυσθε	you have been loosed
3RD	λέλυται	he/she/it has been loosed	λέλυνται	they have been loosed

15.5 Morphology

Perfect verbs are typically easy to recognize because of the reduplication of the first letter of the stem with an added epsilon (ε). Reduplication indicates the completion of the action (compare the augment which indicates that the time of the action was in the past). The active forms also have a –κα tense formative affixed to the end of the stem whereas the perfect middle/passive forms lack the tense formative (with no connecting vowel).

Perfect Active

Reduplication: Again, one of the signature features of the perfect tense-form is the reduplication of the initial letter of the stem. That is, the first letter of the stem is added to the beginning of the verb with an epsilon (ε) in between the two consonants to aid in pronunciation.

λε + λυ = λελυ–

---

[5] To hear a mnemonic song, go to bit.ly/activeindicative or beginninggreek.com.

[6] The English translation only includes the passive voice. The middle voice would be translated as follows: I have loosed (for) myself, you have loosed (for) yourself, he/she/it has loosed (for) himself, we have loosed (for) ourselves, you have loosed (for) yourselves, they have loosed (for) themselves. Sometimes, however, the best colloquial English translation of the Greek middle voice will sound just like the translation of the Greek active voice.

Tense Formative: A kappa + alpha (–κα) is added to the end of the stem (similar to the –σα for the aorist tense-form).

λελυ + κα = λέλυ**κα**

Here is a more precise breakdown of the component parts (morphemes) of the active form:

PERFECT ACTIVE INDICATIVE

Inflected Form	Redup.	Stem	Connecting Vowel[7]	Personal Ending		Combined Ending[8]
λέλυκα	λε	λυκα	-	-	→	κα
λέλυκας	λε	λυκα	-	ς	→	κας
λέλυκε(ν)	λε	λυκε[9]	-	- (ν)[10]	→	κε(ν)
λελύκαμεν	λε	λυκα	-	μεν	→	καμεν
λελύκατε	λε	λυκα	-	τε	→	κατε
λελύκασι(ν)	λε	λυκα	-	σι(ν)	→	κασι(ν)

The perfect active endings are exactly the same as those of the first aorist active, except for the variation in the third person plural form. (Therefore, it is important to pay attention to the reduplication and the added kappa.)

First Aorist Active	Perfect Active
ἔλυσα	λέλυκα
ἔλυσας	λέλυκας
ἔλυσε(ν)	λέλυκε(ν)
ἐλύσαμεν	λελύκαμεν
ἐλύσατε	λελύκατε
ἔλυσαν	λελύκασι(ν) / λελύκαν

The alternate third person plural form (λελύκαν) is sometimes used in place of λελύκασιν. (It appears in nine of the thirty-two occurrences in the New Testament).

Perfect Middle/Passive

Reduplication: The same reduplication as found in the active voice also occurs in the middle or passive voice.

---

[7] There is no connecting vowel because the tense formative (–κα) ends with a vowel, causing it to be unnecessary. Some grammars take the tense formative to be kappa and the connecting vowel to be alpha.

[8] Although the –κα tense formative is technically part of the stem, it is helpful to learn it as part of the ending to distinguish it from the aorist tense-form (ἐλύ-σαμεν → λελύ-καμεν).

[9] Note that the alpha (α) has changed to an epsilon (ε). This is probably done to differentiate the third person singular form (λέλυκε) from the first person singular form (λέλυκα).

[10] There is no personal ending, only a movable nu (ν).

λε + λυ = **λελυ**–

No Tense Formative: The middle/passive forms, however, lack the kappa + alpha (–κα) tense formative found with the active forms.

λελυ + μαι = λέλυ**μαι**

PERFECT MIDDLE/PASSIVE INDICATIVE

Inflected Form	Redup.	Stem	Connecting Vowel	Personal Ending		Combined Ending
λέλυμαι	λε	λυ	-	μαι	→	μαι
λέλυσαι	λε	λυ	-	σαι[11]	→	σαι
λέλυται	λε	λυ	-	ται	→	ται
λελύμεθα	λε	λυ	-	μεθα	→	μεθα
λέλυσθε	λε	λυ	-	σθε	→	σθε
λέλυνται	λε	λυ	-	νται	→	νται

15.6 Reduplication Variations

Vocalic Reduplication

For verbs whose stem begins with a vowel, reduplication does not occur. Instead, the initial vowel is lengthened. (This looks similar to an augment for imperfect and aorist verbs.)

Lexical Form	Imperfect	Aorist	Perfect
ἀγαπάω	ἠγάπων	ἠγάπησα	**ἠγάπηκα**

The example above is a contract verb (ἀγαπάω). In such verbs, the contract vowel (in this case an alpha) is lengthened to an eta (α→η; **ἠγάπηκα**); this is similar to future and first aorist contract verbs.

With verbs that begin with a diphthong, the first vowel will typically lengthen. This causes the second vowel to subscript if it is an iota (ι).[12]

αἰτέω   →   **ᾔτηκα**

Some verbs that begin with a vowel reduplicate the first two letters (Attic Reduplication).

---

[11] The true ending is clearly seen here. Usually, the sigma (σ) drops out. This causes the vowels to contract. See William D. Mounce, *Basics of Biblical Greek: Grammar*, 4th ed. (Grand Rapids: Zondervan, 2019), 279.

[12] Some verbs beginning with a diphthong do not reduplicate at all, such as the perfect form of εὑρίσκω → εὕρηκα.

ἀκούω → ἀκήκοα[13]
ἔρχομαι → ἐλήλυθα (from the stem ἐλθ–)

Verbs that begin with two consonants (or a double consonant like ψ, ζ, or ξ) sometimes do not fully reduplicate but add an epsilon (which should not be confused with an augment).

γινώσκω → ἔγνωκα (from the stem γνο–)[14]

Aspirant Reduplication

An **aspirant** is a Greek letter that contains an "h" sound when pronounced. Verbs beginning with an aspirant letter (θ, φ, χ) reduplicate with the non-aspirant counterparts (τ, π, κ): θ → τ, φ → π, χ → κ.[15]

φανερόω → πεφανέρωμαι
χαρίζομαι → κεχάρισμαι
θεραπεύω → τεθεράπευμαι

Compound Verb Reduplication

For verbs that begin with a prepositional prefix, reduplication occurs after the preposition (directly in front of the stem).

ἀπολύω → ἀπολέλυσαι
καταβαίνω → κατα**β**έβηκα

15.7 Irregular Forms

Some verbs have an irregular perfect form. The "second" perfect forms (similar to a second aorist form) have dropped the kappa (κ) and only have an alpha (α) tense formative.

γίνομαι → γέγονα
γράφω → γέγραφα

---

[13] The second vowel becomes lengthened (ἀκήκοα, ἐλήλυθα). Also note that the kappa (κ) that is normally added to perfect active forms is missing. The two kappas in the word (ἀκήκοα) are from the reduplication and from the stem. This is an example of "Attic Reduplication," a term employed by ancient Greek grammarians. Herbert Smyth describes the phenomenon: "Some verbs whose themes begin with α, ε, or ο, followed by a single consonant, reduplicate by repeating the initial vowel and the consonant and by lengthening α and ε to η, ο to ω." Herbert Weir Smyth, *Greek Grammar* (Cambridge, MA: Harvard University Press, 1956), §446.

[14] But compare γράφω, which does reduplicate to γέγραφα. (The most common form is γέγραπται ["it is written"], which occurs sixty-seven times in the New Testament). Such reduplication of a double consonant will usually take place if the second consonant is a lambda (λ) or rho (ρ).

[15] Memory Help: "th" → "t"; "ph" → "p"; "ch" → "c." View the square of stops in 14.6 to see how the aspirated form reduplicates the corresponding non-aspirated (or voiceless) form.

ἔρχομαι	→	ἐλήλυθα
λαμβάνω	→	εἴληφα
πείθω	→	πέποιθα

Other verbs have irregular forms caused by irregular stems, stems beginning with a diphthong, or stems borrowed from other verb forms.

ἀναβαίνω	→	ἀναβέβηκα
εὑρίσκω	→	εὕρηκα
λέγω	→	εἴρηκα

Verb stems ending in τ, δ, θ, or ζ will drop these letters before adding the kappa tense formative.[16] This is similar to dropping τ, δ, or θ when adding a sigma (σ) in the future or aorist tense-forms.

ἐγγίζω	→	ἤγγικα (from the stem ἐγγιδ–)

The verb οἶδα is also irregular since the lexical form is often parsed as a perfect tense-form but the meaning is present.[17] Similarly, the pluperfect form (ᾔδειν) is used like an aorist. With this verb, there is no reduplication since it begins with a diphthong. Additionally, the kappa (κ) tense formative has dropped out, leaving only the alpha (α). This verb is significant since it occurs 212 times as a perfect indicative and 33 times as a pluperfect indicative.

Here are the perfect and pluperfect active forms. It is not necessary to memorize these paradigms, but you should be able to recognize and parse the forms below.

Perfect Active		Pluperfect Active	
οἶδα	"I know"	ᾔδειν	"I knew"
οἶδας	"you [sg] know"	ᾔδεις	"you [sg] knew"
οἶδεν	"he knows"	ᾔδει	"he knew"
οἴδαμεν	"we know"	ᾔδειμεν	"we knew"
οἴδατε	"you [pl] know"	ᾔδειτε	"you [pl] knew"
οἴδασιν	"they know"	ᾔδεισαν	"they knew"

15.8 Meaning and Form of the Pluperfect Tense

We should think of the *pluperfect tense* as primarily conveying a meaning that is comparable to the first function of the perfect described above (completed action, continuing result). Yet, unlike the perfect, the pluperfect tense describes a past state that was brought about by an action even further in the past. This tense is uncommon, occurring only eighty-six times in the New Testament.

---

[16] Verbs whose lexical form ends with –ιζω or –αζω actually have a stem that ends with delta (δ).
[17] Another option is that the perfect is used with an emphasis on the current state with no previous action.

- **Intensive Pluperfect:** Emphasizes the *results* brought about by a past action: "they committed them to the Lord in whom **they had believed**," παρέθεντο αὐτοὺς τῷ κυρίῳ εἰς ὃν **πεπιστεύκεισαν** (Acts 14:23).

- **Consummative Pluperfect:** Emphasizes the *completion of a past action* that brought about the resulting state in the past: "his disciples **had gone** into town," οἱ μαθηταὶ αὐτοῦ **ἀπεληλύθεισαν** εἰς τὴν πόλιν (John 4:8).

Because the perfect and pluperfect tenses are not as common as the other tenses (present, imperfect, future, and aorist), they are often significant for interpretation when they occur.

The form includes (1) an augment (on some but not all forms), (2) reduplication, (3) tense formative (–κ), and (4) connecting vowels (–ει): **ἐλελύκειν**. Here is the full paradigm (which does not need to be memorized) of the pluperfect active indicative:

	SINGULAR		PLURAL	
1ST	(ἐ)λελύκειν	I had loosed	(ἐ)λελύκειμεν	we had loosed
2ND	(ἐ)λελύκεις	you had loosed	(ἐ)λελύκειτε	you had loosed
3RD	(ἐ)λελύκει(ν)	he/she/it had loosed	(ἐ)λελύκεισαν	they had loosed

Again, there are only eighty-six uses of the pluperfect in the New Testament (using twenty-two different verbs), and seventy-nine are found in the active voice.

15.9 Practice

A. Paradigms: Memorize the perfect active and middle/passive paradigms of λύω (see section 15.4). Then write out each paradigm ten times from memory.

B. Tenses: Identify the tense of the following verbs as Present (P), Imperfect (I), Future (F), Aorist (A), or Perfect (Pf).

1. _____ ἔζησεν

2. _____ οἶδεν

3. _____ ἐδίδασκεν

4. _____ κέκρικα

5. _____ μενεῖτε

6. _____ ἐβαπτίσθητε

7. _____ γίνεται

8. _____ κέκραγεν

9. _____ γεγέννηκα

10. _____ ἐρωτήσετε

11. _____ ἠκολούθουν

12. _____ κέκληται

13. _____ περιεπατήσαμεν

14. _____ ποιεῖς

15. _____ σέσωται

16. _____ πράξετε

17. _____ ἔσπειρας

18. _____ ἀπολέλυσαι

19. _____ ἐδίωκον

20. _____ δεδόξασμαι

C. Parsing: Parse the following words.

1. τετήρηκας

2. ᾐτήκαμεν

3. βέβληται

4. πέποιθα

5. ἠγαπήκαμεν

6. ἀκηκόατε

7. γεγόνασιν

8. εἴληφας

9. εὕρηκα

10. εἰρήκατε

D. Translation: Translate the following sentences.

1. πεπλήρωται ὁ καιρὸς καὶ ἤγγικεν ἡ βασιλεία τοῦ θεοῦ (Mark 1:15).

2. γέγραπται, Οὐκ ἐπ᾽ ἄρτῳ μόνῳ (alone) ζήσεται ὁ ἄνθρωπος (Matt 4:4).

3. Ῥαββί (Rabbi), οἴδαμεν ὅτι ἀπὸ θεοῦ ἐλήλυθας διδάσκαλος (John 3:2).

4. ὑμεῖς προσκυνεῖτε ὃ οὐκ οἴδατε· ἡμεῖς προσκυνοῦμεν ὃ οἴδαμεν, ὅτι ἡ σωτηρία (salvation) ἐκ τῶν Ἰουδαίων ἐστίν (John 4:22).

5. οἶδα πόθεν (from where) ἦλθον καὶ ποῦ (where) ὑπάγω· ὑμεῖς δὲ οὐκ οἴδατε πόθεν ἔρχομαι ἢ ποῦ ὑπάγω (John 8:14).

6. κἀγὼ ἑώρακα καὶ μεμαρτύρηκα ὅτι οὗτός (this one) ἐστιν ὁ υἱὸς τοῦ θεοῦ (John 1:34).

7. ἀλλ᾽ εἶπον ὑμῖν ὅτι καὶ ἑωράκατέ με καὶ οὐ πιστεύετε (John 6:36).

8. πεποίθαμεν δὲ ἐν κυρίῳ ἐφ᾽ ὑμᾶς (2 Thess 3:4).

9. ἐγὼ ἐλήλυθα ἐν τῷ ὀνόματι τοῦ πατρός μου, καὶ οὐ λαμβάνετέ με (John 5:43).

10. οὔπω (not yet) γὰρ ἀναβέβηκα πρὸς τὸν πατέρα (John 20:17).

11. καὶ ἡμεῖς ἐγνώκαμεν καὶ πεπιστεύκαμεν τὴν ἀγάπην ἣν ἔχει ὁ θεὸς ἐν ἡμῖν (1 John 4:16).

12. ὁ (he) δὲ εἶπεν αὐτῇ, Θυγάτηρ (Daughter), ἡ πίστις σου σέσωκέν σε (Mark 5:34).

13. καὶ ἡμεῖς πεπιστεύκαμεν καὶ ἐγνώκαμεν ὅτι σὺ εἶ ὁ ἅγιος (holy one) τοῦ θεοῦ (John 6:69).

14. καὶ ἔστιν αὕτη (this) ἡ ἀγγελία (message) ἣν ἀκηκόαμεν ἀπ᾽ αὐτοῦ καὶ ἀναγγέλλομεν (proclaim) ὑμῖν, ὅτι ὁ θεὸς φῶς ἐστιν (1 John 1:5).

E. Translation: Translate the following sentences into Greek.

1. The scribes have approached the fire.

2. I am persuaded/confident in the power of God.

3. They have seen the blood on his hands and feet.

4. The woman knows the word of light.

5. We live at the mouth of the water.

15.10 Vocabulary[18]

ἀγαθός, –ή, –όν	good (*Agatha*)
ἅγιος, –α, –ον	holy; saints (pl subst) (*hagiography*)
ἄλλος, –η, –ο	other, another, different (*allomorph*)
δίκαιος, –α, –ον	righteous, just
ἕτερος, –α, –ον	other, another, different (*heterosexual*)
καλός, –ή, –όν	good, beautiful (*calligraphy*)
μέγας, μεγάλη, μέγα	large, great (*mega-market*, *megalomaniac*)
νεκρός, –ά, –όν	dead (*necromancy*, *necropolis*)
πᾶς, πᾶσα, πᾶν	every, all (*pantheism*, *pan-Hellenic*, *pan-American*)
πιστός, –ή, –όν	faithful, believing
πολύς, πολλή, πολύ	much, many, large, great (*polygon*)
πονηρός, –ά, –όν	evil, wicked
νῦν	now, at present
πάλιν	again
ἤ	or, than

---

[18] To hear an author of your textbook read through the vocabulary for chapter 15, go to bit.ly/greekvocab15 or beginninggreek.com.

///////////////

CHAPTER 16

ADJECTIVES AND ADVERBS

16.1 Overview[1]

This chapter will cover adjectives and will also briefly discuss adverbs. An ***adjective*** describes or qualifies a noun (e.g., the *tall* man; the *kind* woman). That is, it distinguishes a noun (or pronoun) from other nouns by providing more information about it. In contrast, an ***adverb*** modifies a verb (e.g., the tall man *quickly* ate his meal; the kind woman *graciously* helped her friend).

16.2 Significance

God gives to his people in many ways: generously, kindly, lovingly, mercifully. These words that end in –ly are all adverbs—words that further nuance some verbal action. The most common ending for an adverb in English is –ly. The most common ending for an adverb in Greek is –ως.

James 1:5 is a well-known text that employs an adverb to qualify further the activity further of God's giving:

> But if any of you lacks wisdom, let him ask of God, who gives to all generously (ἁπλῶς) and without reproach, and it will be given to him. (NASB)

Here God is described as the One "who gives to all generously and without reproach." The Greek word translated "generously" is ἁπλῶς. Though generosity is within the broad semantic range of ἁπλῶς, it more commonly means "unwavering-ly" or "without hesitation." In weighing both the linguistic evidence and literary context, most scholarly commentaries on James recognize that "unwaveringly"

---

[1] For an overview video lecture of chapter 16, go to bit.ly/greeklecture16 or beginninggreek.com.

is a better translation of ἁπλῶς here.[2] Nevertheless, most modern English Bible translations continue to follow the KJV tradition (i.e., "liberally" or "generously"). If we read the verse in context, we see James is contrasting God with the fickle human of verses 6–8. The doubting man is double-minded, unstable, and erratic as a choppy wave in the storm-tossed sea. God, on the other hand, acts with unwavering intent. He does not offer a gift, only to pull it back a moment later. With this in mind, read meditatively through Jas 1:5–8. Ponder the joy and stability of knowing that we have a God who gives without hesitation, without wavering, without fickleness.[3]

16.3 Paradigms

FIRST AND SECOND DECLENSION ADJECTIVES					
	SINGULAR			PLURAL		
	MASC	*FEM*	*NEUT*	*MASC*	*FEM*	*NEUT*
NOM	ἀγαθός	ἀγαθή	ἀγαθόν	ἀγαθοί	ἀγαθαί	ἀγαθά
GEN	ἀγαθοῦ	ἀγαθῆς	ἀγαθοῦ	ἀγαθῶν	ἀγαθῶν	ἀγαθῶν
DAT	ἀγαθῷ	ἀγαθῇ	ἀγαθῷ	ἀγαθοῖς	ἀγαθαῖς	ἀγαθοῖς
ACC	ἀγαθόν	ἀγαθήν	ἀγαθόν	ἀγαθούς	ἀγαθάς	ἀγαθά

THIRD DECLENSION ADJECTIVES					
	SINGULAR			PLURAL		
	MASC	*FEM*	*NEUT*	*MASC*	*FEM*	*NEUT*
NOM	πᾶς	πᾶσα	πᾶν	πάντες	πᾶσαι	πάντα
GEN	παντός	πάσης	παντός	πάντων	πασῶν	πάντων
DAT	παντί	πάσῃ	παντί	πᾶσι(ν)	πάσαις	πᾶσι(ν)
ACC	πάντα	πᾶσαν	πᾶν	πάντας	πάσας	πάντα

---

[2] Moo writes, "Taken together, then, the evidence suggests that James is not so much highlighting God's generosity in giving as his single, undivided intent to give us those gifts we need to please him." Douglas J. Moo, *The Letter of James*, PNTC (Grand Rapids: Eerdmans; Leicester: Apollos, 2000), 59.

[3] A portion of this paragraph was adapted from Robert L. Plummer, "James" in *ESV Expository Commentary: Hebrews–Revelation*, vol. 12 (Wheaton: Crossway, 2018), 229–30.

16.4 Morphology

First and Second Declension Adjectives

Because an adjective is grammatically linked to the noun it modifies, it must agree with the gender, case, and number of that noun. In fact, the adjective does not have any gender of its own but takes the gender of the noun it describes; thus, all three genders are given in the vocabulary lists.

ὁ ἀγαθὸς ἄνθρωπος	The good man
ἡ ἀγαθὴ ἐντολή	The good command

The first and second declension adjective paradigm above does not need to be memorized for the simple reason that these forms should already be known. That is, the masculine endings are identical to the second declension masculine noun endings; the feminine endings are identical to the first declension (eta pattern) feminine noun endings; and the neuter endings are identical to the second declension neuter noun endings (see chaps. 2 and 3).

If the stem of the adjective ends with an epsilon (ε), iota (ι), or rho (ρ), the adjective will follow the alpha (α) pattern:[4]

ἁγία	νεκρά
ἁγίας	νεκρᾶς
ἁγίᾳ	νεκρᾷ
ἁγίαν	νεκράν

The plural forms are not provided since they are identical to the eta (η) pattern. The spelling of the adjective itself determines whether it will use the alpha or eta pattern. Thus, the adjective may have a different pattern than the noun it modifies (ἡ ἁγία ἐντολή, "the holy command").

Some adjectives differ slightly from the paradigm of ἀγαθός. Here are the masculine singular forms for μέγας and πολύς:

μέγας	πολύς
μεγάλου	πολλοῦ
μεγάλῳ	πολλῷ
μέγαν	πολύν

Notice that the forms are similar except that the final vowel differs. The plural forms are not given since their endings are identical to ἀγαθός.

Third Declension Adjectives

The paradigm for the adjective πᾶς also does not need to be memorized since it is regular in most of its forms except in two instances: (1) the feminine singular

---

[4] From a historical morphological approach, it is the next to the last letter of the stem since the stem ends with alpha (α).

alternates between the alpha (α) and eta (η) patterns: πᾶσα, πάσης, πάσῃ, πᾶσαν and (2) the neuter nominative/accusative singular form is πᾶν (compare πνεῦμα).[5]

Notice that the masculine and neuter genitive forms contain the full stem (παντ–). When the sigma (ς) is added to the masculine nominative singular form, the –ντ drop out (παντ + ς = παντς → πᾶς). Also, the neuter nominative (and accusative) form has no ending added. Consequently, the tau (τ) drops out because it cannot stand as the last letter of a word (παντ + - = παντ → πᾶν). Such morphological rules need not be memorized. Instead, focus on recognition, especially paying attention to context as a key assistant in identifying the form of a word and then translating it properly.

16.5 Adjective Uses

Adjectives are used in a variety of ways: (1) attributively, (2) substantivally, or (3) predicatively.

Attributive	"The *good* word was preached."
Substantival	"The *good* [man] preached."
Predicative	"The man is *good*."

Attributive Use

When the adjective functions adjectivally, it is in the ***attributive position***. That means that the article (when present) occurs *directly in front of* the adjective. The modified noun may or may not have the article. The adjective adds information about a noun, specifying an attribute or characteristic of the noun. The adjective thus modifies an expressed noun and agrees with it in gender, case, and number.

ὁ ἀγαθός [ὁ] λόγος
ὁ λόγος ὁ ἀγαθός   "the good word"

Notice there are two ways to communicate the same idea in English. The first example above is the same as the typical English word order (article-adjective-noun). The article immediately prior to λόγος in the example is in brackets because it may or may not be present. The second example, very common in Greek, follows a different order (article-noun-article-adjective). In both examples, the article directly precedes the adjective.

If an attributive adjective is modifying an indefinite, anarthrous noun, neither noun nor adjective will have the article in Greek:

ἀγαθός λόγος
λόγος ἀγαθός   "a good word"

---

[5] Some third declension adjectives follow alternate paradigms because of their stems. For example, the adjective ἀληθής ("true") is irregular and follows a paradigm similar to ἔθνος. Here are the masculine/feminine forms: ἀληθής, ἀληθοῦς, ἀληθεί, ἀληθῆ, ἀληθεῖς, ἀληθῶν, ἀληθέσι(ν), and ἀληθεῖς. The neuter nominative and accusative forms are ἀληθές (sg) and ἀληθῆ (pl).

Substantival Use

When the adjective functions substantivally, there is no expressed noun that it modifies. The adjective itself functions like a noun. To render it understandably in English, a translator must often supply an implied word like "man," "woman," or "things," depending on the gender, case, and number of the adjectives. The article (when present) occurs *directly in front of* the adjective.

ὁ ἀγαθός	"the good [man]"
ἡ ἀγαθή	"the good [woman]"
τὰ ἀγαθά	"the good [things]"

The *case* of the substantive adjective is determined by its function in the sentence, and the *gender* of the substantive adjective is determined by the person or item referenced. If it refers to a male or to something grammatically masculine, then it will be masculine. Likewise, if it refers to a female or to something grammatically feminine, then it will be feminine. And if it refers to something grammatically neuter, it will be neuter.

Predicate Use

When an adjective asserts something about a nominative subject with a "to be" verb present or implied between the subject and adjective, that adjective is called a predicate adjective. A predicate adjective "predicates" (asserts or claims) something about the subject. The predicate adjective is said to be in the *predicate position*, which means that there is no article *directly in front of* the adjective. There is usually an article in front of the nominative subject.

| ὁ λόγος ἀγαθός. | |
| ἀγαθός ὁ λόγος. | "The word [is] good." |

Notice that the verb "is" was supplied in the English translation. Although sometimes a form of the verb εἰμί is present, often it is simply implied. In such cases, it is necessary to supply the verb in translation. In the examples above, the periods let you know that they are complete sentences and that the "to be" verb must be provided in an English translation.

If there is no article before the noun or adjective, context will determine whether the adjective is functioning adjectivally or if it is used as a predicate adjective. For example, ἀγαθός λόγος and λόγος ἀγαθός can mean either "a good word" or "a word [is] good." Context will clarify whether a form of "to be" is implied (predicate use) or not (attributive use). For example,

| ἀγαθός λόγος. | "A word is good." (predicate use) |
| ἀγαθός λόγος ἐστιν ἀπό τοῦ κυρίου. | "A good word is from the Lord." (attributive use) |

The presence of a period (as in the first example) or a few additional words (as in the second) clarify whether ἀγαθός is functioning predicatively or attributively. If the adjective is functioning predicatively, you will need to provide some form of the verb "to be" in translation (e.g., "is," "was," "were," etc.). Only the context will clarify the person, number, and time of the implied verb.

Uses of πᾶς

Depending on its position in relation to the noun it modifies, πᾶς can be used in slightly different ways. Although the following represent patterns of usage, this is only a general guideline and should not be followed literalistically.[6]

Predicate Position: "all"

πάντες οἱ ἄνθρωποι	"all the men"
πᾶσα ἡ πόλις	"all the city"
πᾶν τὸ σῶμα	"all the body"

Attributive Position: "whole"

ὁ πᾶς ἄνθρωπος	"the whole man"
ἡ πᾶσα πόλις	"the whole city"
τὸ πᾶν σῶμα	"the whole body"

Anarthrous (no article): "every"

πᾶς ἄνθρωπος	"every man"
πᾶσα πόλις	"every city"
πᾶν σῶμα	"every body"

Substantive (no expressed noun): "all"

οἱ πάντες	"all men" or "all people"
αἱ πᾶσαι	"all women"
τὰ πάντα	"all things"

16.6 Degrees

Adjectives have various *degrees*: positive ("strong"), comparative ("stronger"), and superlative ("strongest"). The ***positive adjective*** is used when an author is merely stating something and is not comparing two or more things ("The *strong* lion has no fear"). The ***comparative adjective*** is used when an author wants to compare two things ("The lion is *stronger* than the zebra"). Finally, the ***superlative***

---

[6] For twenty years, we have been using a handout with the Greek examples shown here. We have been unable to recall or track down its origin.

adjective is used when an author wants to compare three or more things ("Between the lion, the zebra, and the giraffe, the lion is the *strongest*"). Here are some other examples in English:

Positive	Comparative	Superlative
small	small**er**	small**est**
young	young**er**	young**est**
good	be**tter**	**best**

Note that in English, the comparative is formed by adding –er and the superlative by adding –est.

Comparative Degree

There are two ways of forming the comparative degree. Depending on the adjective employed for comparison, it will decline in one of two ways. The first method of forming a comparative adjective employs third declension endings. For example, μείζων ("greater") is the comparative form of the adjective μέγας ("great"). Here is the full paradigm:

THIRD DECLENSION COMPARATIVE ADJECTIVE			
SINGULAR		PLURAL	
MASC/FEM	NEUT	MASC/FEM	NEUT
NOM μείζων	μεῖζον	μείζονες	μείζονα
GEN μείζονος	μείζονος	μειζόνων	μειζόνων
DAT μείζονι	μείζονι	μείζοσι(ν)	μείζοσι(ν)
ACC μείζονα	μεῖζον	μείζονας	μείζονα

The adjectives μείζων and πλείων ("more"; the comparative of πολύς, "much") account for nearly half of the comparative adjectives in the New Testament. Two other forms are χείρων ("worse"; the comparative of κακός, "bad") and κρεῖσσον or κρείττων ("better"; the comparative of ἀγαθός/καλός, "good").

The second method of forming a comparative adjective is by adding –τερος, –τερα, or –τερον to the positive adjective. Except for the few common –ων comparatives discussed above, you should expect most other adjectives to form their comparative forms with –τερος, –τερα, or –τερον. Note that these endings contain an "er" sound (–τ**ερ**ος), which will help you remember that they convey a comparative meaning (e.g., smart**er**).

ἄλυπος	"unconcerned"	→	ἀλυπότερος	"more unconcerned"
ἰσχυρός	"strong"	→	ἰσχυρότερος	"stronger"
μικρός	"small"	→	μικρότερος	"smaller"
νέος	"new"	→	νεώτερος	"newer"

πονηρός	"wicked"	→	πονηρότερος	"more wicked"
πρέσβυς	"old"	→	πρεσβύτερος	"older, elder"
σοφός	"wise"	→	σοφώτερος	"wiser"

Not only are there two ways to form a comparative adjective, but there are also two ways of signaling a comparison in Greek. That is, there are two ways to communicate the word "than." The first is the use of the term ἤ ("than"). For example, μείζων ἐστὶν ὁ ἐν ὑμῖν ἢ ὁ ἐν τῷ κόσμῳ, "the one who is in you is greater **than** the one who is in the world" (1 John 4:4). The other is the more common method and involves the use of the genitive case (known as a "genitive of comparison"). For example, ὁ πατὴρ μείζων **μού** ἐστιν "the Father is greater **than I**" (John 14:28). In this instance, the genitive case conveys the sense of "than" (not the typical "of").

Superlative Degree

A Greek adjective will form its superlative in one of two ways. First, for some adjectives, –ιστος is added to the end of a positive adjective. Note that this ending contains almost the same sound as the English superlative ending (cf. –**ιστος**, smart**est**).

μέγας	"great"	→	μέγιστος	"greatest"
πολύς	"much"	→	πλεῖστος	"most"
μικρός	"small"	→	ἐλάχιστος[7]	"smallest"
ὕψος	"high"	→	ὕψιστος	"highest"

Secondly, some adjectives will form their superlatives by adding –τατος, –τατη, or –τατον to the positive adjective.

ἅγιος	"holy"	→	ἁγιώτατος	"holiest"
τίμιος	"valuable"	→	τιμιώτατος	"most valuable"
ἀκριβής	"strict"	→	ἀκριβέστατος	"strictest"

Comparative and positive forms are sometimes used in place of superlative forms (which were dying out in the Koine period). For example, in 1 Cor 13:13, Paul states, "So now faith, hope, and love abide, these three; but the **greatest** (μείζων) of these is love" (ESV). Although three concepts are being compared, calling for a superlative, the comparative adjective μείζων is used.

Elative

The ***elative adjective*** is where a superlative (or sometimes a comparative) adjective is used to convey the idea of "very" or "exceedingly" instead of "most." For example, in Mark 4:1 we read, "a **very large** (πλεῖστος) crowd gathered around him." Although the superlative form is used (πλεῖστος, "largest"), in context it is clear that

---

[7] Observe also the stem change with this form.

the author is not intending a superlative nuance (the *largest* crowd in comparison to others); rather, he is expressing the elative sense (a *very large* crowd). Context clarifies whether a comparative, superlative, or elative sense is intended.

16.7 Adverbs

Whereas adjectives modify nouns, adverbs modify verbs (or other parts of speech). And unlike adjectives, adverbs do not decline. As we noted at the outset of this chapter, the most common ending found on Greek adverbs is –ως. Many adverbs are formed by taking the genitive plural form (e.g., καλῶν from καλός) and substituting a sigma (ς) in place of the nu (ν) → καλῶς. This ending is similar to the –ly ending in English (e.g., quick → quick*ly*).

Occasionally an accusative adjective will function adverbially; this is known as an "adverbial accusative." For example, in 1 Cor 16:19, Paul writes, "Aquila and Priscilla greet you **warmly** (πολλά) in the Lord" (NIV). Here the accusative adjective πολλά (from πολύς, "much") is used adverbially, modifying the verb "greet."

16.8 Practice

A. Adjective Case: Circle the words of the designated cases.

1.	**Nominative**	σοφοί	μεγάλην	μείζονες	πιστοῖς
2.	**Genitive**	πονηρᾶς	νεκρῶν	καλόν	παντός
3.	**Dative**	παντί	δικαίου	ἁγίοις	πᾶν
4.	**Accusative**	ἑτέρῳ	πολύς	ἄλλους	ἀγαθά

B. Adjective Use: Indicate whether the following adjectives are used Attributively (A), Substantivally (S), or Predicatively (P).

1. _____ ὁ θεὸς φῶς ἐστιν

2. _____ φωνῇ μεγάλῃ

3. _____ τὸ ἀγαθόν

4. _____ ἅγιον τὸ ὄνομα αὐτοῦ

5. _____ οἱ ἅγιοι τὸν κόσμον κρινοῦσιν

6. _____ καρποὺς καλούς

7. _____ πᾶν ἔθνος

8. _____ πιστὸς ὁ θεός

9. _____ ἐγείρει τοὺς νεκρούς

10. _____ ὁ υἱός μου νεκρὸς ἦν

C. Adjective Degrees: Circle the words of the designated degrees.

1. **Positive**   νεώτερος   ἀγαθός   ὕψιστος   ἄλλος

2. **Comparative** πλεῖστος   μείζων   πονηρότερος   ἕτερος

3. **Superlative** μέγιστος   τιμιώτατος ἀσθενέστερος   ἅγιος

D. Translation: Translate the following sentences.

1. ὁ ἀγαθὸς ἄνθρωπος ἐκ τοῦ ἀγαθοῦ θησαυροῦ (treasure) ἐκβάλλει ἀγαθά, καὶ ὁ πονηρὸς ἄνθρωπος ἐκ τοῦ πονηροῦ θησαυροῦ ἐκβάλλει πονηρά (Matt 12:35).

2. τὸ πνεῦμα τὸ ἅγιον, ὃ πέμψει ὁ πατὴρ ἐν τῷ ὀνόματί μου, ἐκεῖνος (that one) ὑμᾶς διδάξει πάντα (John 14:26).

3. ὁ γὰρ ναὸς τοῦ θεοῦ ἅγιός ἐστιν, οἵτινές ἐστε ὑμεῖς (1 Cor 3:17).

4. ἠκολούθει δὲ τῷ Ἰησοῦ Σίμων Πέτρος καὶ ἄλλος μαθητής (John 18:15).

5. ἢ πνεῦμα ἕτερον λαμβάνετε ὃ οὐκ ἐλάβετε, ἢ εὐαγγέλιον ἕτερον ὃ οὐκ ἐδέξασθε (δέχομαι, I receive) (2 Cor 11:4).

6. καλὸς ἔσῃ διάκονος (servant) Χριστοῦ Ἰησοῦ (1 Tim 4:6).

7. ἔσται μέγας καὶ υἱὸς ὑψίστου (most high) κληθήσεται (Luke 1:32).

8. ἀμὴν (truly) ἀμὴν λέγω ὑμῖν ὅτι ἔρχεται ὥρα καὶ νῦν ἐστιν ὅτε (when) οἱ νεκροὶ ἀκούσουσιν τῆς φωνῆς τοῦ υἱοῦ τοῦ θεοῦ (John 5:25).

9. εἰ γὰρ νεκροὶ οὐκ ἐγείρονται, οὐδὲ (neither) Χριστὸς ἐγήγερται (1 Cor 15:16).

10. καὶ εἶδον, καὶ ἤκουσα φωνὴν ἀγγέλων πολλῶν (Rev 5:11).

11. νόμος ἅγιος καὶ ἡ ἐντολὴ ἁγία καὶ δικαία καὶ ἀγαθή (Rom 7:12).

12. ἀμὴν ἀμὴν λέγω ὑμῖν, οὐκ ἔστιν δοῦλος μείζων τοῦ κυρίου αὐτοῦ (John 13:16).

13. τὸ μωρὸν (foolishness) τοῦ θεοῦ σοφώτερον (σόφος, wise) τῶν ἀνθρώπων ἐστὶν καὶ τὸ ἀσθενὲς (weakness) τοῦ θεοῦ ἰσχυρότερον (ἰσχυρός, strong) τῶν ἀνθρώπων (1 Cor 1:25).

14. ὁ δὲ μικρότερος (μικρός, small, less) ἐν τῇ βασιλείᾳ τῶν οὐρανῶν μείζων αὐτοῦ ἐστιν (Matt 11:11).

15. ἐγὼ γάρ εἰμι ὁ ἐλάχιστος (superlative of μικρός) τῶν ἀποστόλων (1 Cor 15:9).

E. Translation: Translate the following sentences into Greek.

1. Again I say, the Lord is holy, just, and good.

2. The wicked one is not greater than the faithful One.

3. A very large crowd heard every word. (Hint: Look within the chapter for a superlative form that has the elative sense, "very large.")

4. Now the dead in Christ will be raised.

5. Another slave will announce a different place.

16.9 Vocabulary[8]

εὐαγγελίζω	I announce good news, preach (*evangelist*)
θεωρέω	I gaze, behold, look at
κάθημαι	I sit (*cathedral*—where the "seat" of the bishop is)[9]
κηρύσσω	I herald, proclaim, preach (*kerygma*)
ὑπάρχω	I exist, am
αἰώνιος, –α, -ον	eternal (*aeon*)
ἕκαστος, –η, –ον	each
οὐδείς, οὐδεμία, οὐδέν	no one, nothing (subst)
πρεσβύτερος, –α, –ον	elder, older (*Presbyterian*)
ἀμήν	amen, truly, so be it (*Amen*)
ἔξω	outside (*exoskeleton*)
ἕως	until, while
οὐδέ	and not, neither, nor
οὔτε	and not, neither, nor
τότε	then

[8] To hear an author of your textbook read through the vocabulary for chapter 16, go to bit.ly/greekvocab16 or beginninggreek.com.

[9] This is a middle-only verb, and one can certainly see the high level of subject-affectedness in sitting—as a person both executes and is affected by the action. Also, κάθημαι is a stative verb (referring to an ongoing state), and stative verbs are often middle-only. For example, see κεῖμαι, "lie down," or δύναμαι, "be able."

Who Can Help Me Understand and Apply Biblical Texts?

Introduction to Commentaries

A knowledge of Greek enables one to draw close to the actual words of the apostles, to understand grammatical issues in the Greek New Testament, and to weigh the debated evidence personally. Nevertheless, as you study the Greek New Testament, many interpretive questions will remain. Who can help you navigate these hermeneutical conundrums? Wouldn't it be fantastic if your favorite scholar joined you for your daily reading of the Bible and dialogued with you about personal applications or how to teach or preach the text? Through the writings of others, you have countless trusted mentors. God has gifted people in his church to be teachers of the Word (Eph 4:11–16). How impoverished you will be if you do not avail yourself of the published insights of gifted teachers!

If you have not taken a hermeneutics class or read a book on interpreting the Bible yet, we recommend you pause and consider your goal when interpreting Scripture. In studying any text within it, you should be seeking to understand the inspired biblical author's consciously-intended meaning while also submitting to the implications of that meaning. Of course, God inspired all the biblical authors, so there is also great benefit in tracing the themes that unite the redemptive story of Scripture and find their fulfillment in Christ. So, for a simple and practical guide to interpreting and applying the Bible appropriately, see Robert L. Plummer's *40 Questions About Interpreting the Bible* (Grand Rapids: Kregel, 2010).

Once you have a solid hermeneutical foundation in place, you are ready to find aid in understanding particular passages. We recommend two excellent series that will help you navigate—phrase by phrase—puzzling portions of the Greek New Testament. These are The Exegetical Guide to the Greek New Testament series (B&H Academic) and the *Handbook on the Greek Text* series (Baylor University Press). As of 2019, both include a significant number of published volumes, with the goal of having the entire New Testament covered when the series are complete.

Second, when you need a bit more help with the meaning, background, literary context, or theological implications of a text, a traditional New Testament commentary can prove to be a wonderful asset. Think of a commentary as a dialogue partner and mentor. New Testament professor Andy Naselli insightfully comments on their worth: "Commentaries save us time by providing the historical, linguistic, cultural, canonical and literary insights that we simply do not have time to mine for ourselves week in and week out. For $35.00 we can benefit from ten years of a scholar's life!"[1] In choosing to employ a commentary, you are recognizing the commentary author's divine gifting to teach, while remembering that even the best author is prone to make mistakes and cannot know everything. You, therefore, must live as a "Berean" (Acts 17:10–11), searching the Scriptures to see if what the commentary author has said is indeed the most faithful and convincing interpretation of the biblical text in question. In fact, if you are going to be teaching through a particular book of the Bible, it is worth studying four or five of the best commentaries on that book. One or more of these should be technical resources that engage with the original language. Non-technical or pastoral commentaries can also be helpful as you seek to understand and apply the text.

So, which commentaries should you purchase? Here are two resources we return to when weighing that question for ourselves:

• D. A. Carson. *New Testament Commentary Survey.* 7th ed. (Baker, 2013). We especially like Carson's brief annotations in which he lists strengths,

weaknesses, target audiences, theological biases, etc. of various commentaries. Baker publishes an update of Carson's survey every few years.

• www.BestCommentaries.com: This website, developed by John Dyer (Th.M., Dallas Theological Seminary), provides the following explanation of its approach:

Some professors give students their own lists [of best commentaries] and some have even published their lists (notably D. A. Carson, Temper Longman, III, John Glynn, and Jim Rosscup), but these are not available in one place. BestCommentaries.com has collected these scholarly reviews and averaged them along with reviews from other ministries like John Piper's Desiring God Ministries, R. C. Sproul's Ligonier Ministries, and Denver Seminary Journal, as well as users of the site. The individual reviews are still extremely valuable, but together they can help Bible students at all levels to make good, informed decisions about which commentaries they should purchase.

Optional Assignment: Go to www.bestcommentaries.com and find the top five recommended commentaries for your favorite book of the New Testament. Consider buying one and reading it as you study that Bible book closely. Also, think about purchasing D. A. Carson's *New Testament Commentary Survey* (Baker).

---

[1] http://andynaselli.com/languages.

/////////////////

CHAPTER 17

PRESENT PARTICIPLES

17.1 Overview[1]

A *participle* could be described as a grammatical hybrid since it is part verb and part adjective (i.e., a verbal adjective). It is a word that is built on a verb stem but is declined like an adjective. It can be employed in a variety of ways. Depending on context, participles may function as verbs, adjectives, or substantive adjectives (nouns). Because of the complexity of participles, we will devote three chapters to them. This one will discuss present participles; the next two chapters will discuss aorist and perfect participles, respectively.

17.2 Significance

John, the son of Zechariah and Elizabeth (see Luke 1:5–24), the prophetic forerunner of Jesus, is referred to with the titular noun, ὁ βαπτιστής, "the Baptist" or "the Baptizer."[2] For example, see Matt 3:1:

> In those days John the Baptist (Ἰωάννης ὁ βαπτιστής) came, preaching in the wilderness of Judea. (NIV)

John is also called ὁ βαπτίζων in Mark 6:12–14:

> So [Jesus's disciples] went out and preached that people should repent. They drove out many demons, anointed many sick people with oil and healed them. King Herod heard about it, because Jesus's name had become well known. Some

---

[1] For an overview video lecture of chapter 17, go to bit.ly/greeklecture17 or beginninggreek.com.
[2] The noun βαπτιστής appears in these verses: Matt 3:1; 11:11–12; 14:2, 8; 16:14; 17:13; Mark 6:25; 8:28; Luke 7:20, 33; and 9:19.

said, "John the Baptist (Ἰωάννης ὁ βαπτίζων) has been raised from the dead, and that's why miraculous powers are at work in him." (CSB)

βαπτίζων is a present participle, but it is clearly not describing activity ("baptizing") that is happening in the narrative. (After all, John is dead, so he can't be baptizing!) One of the functions of a present participle is to describe characteristic or habitual activity, with the time-frame of the activity dictated by the broader context. By referring to John as ὁ βαπτίζων in Mark 6:14, his contemporaries show that he was so identified with the regular activity of baptizing that he is known as "that Baptizing Guy." The Scriptures tell us that John's baptizing activity was intended to call people to repentance in preparation for the greater Baptizer who would come after him—the One who would baptize with the Holy Spirit (Matt 3:11; Mark 1:8). What an amazing testimony to John's faithful fulfillment of his ministry that even after his death, he is identified by a title which reflects his prophetic call to repentance from sin and faith in the coming Messiah.

17.3 Definition and Description

A participle can be defined as a verbal adjective. For example, the word "run" is normally used as a verb: "the girl *runs* down the path." In English, if we add "ing" (or "ed") to the verb stem, it can function as an adjective: "The *running* girl fell on the path." Now, the word "running" is describing the girl (not the "sweet" girl or the "fast" girl, but the "running" girl). Also, the indicative verb of the revised sentence is "fell," not "run."

In Greek, participles can function in a similar manner.[3] Since a participle is a verbal adjective, Greek participles have components of both a verb and an adjective. As verbs, they have tense, voice, and mood. As adjectives, they have gender, case, and number. Thus, in the paradigms below you will notice that there are not six forms to memorize (as is the case with verbs); rather, there are eight forms (as is the case with nouns and adjectives). So, instead of the grammatical category of person, participles have gender and case. On the next page, we first look at charts of the masculine present active and middle/passive participles, followed by large charts giving all possible present participle endings. Participles can be translated as adjectives, nouns, or verbs, depending on the context. In the two initial charts, we have provided a provisional translation of the participles as substantives (nouns), though you should note that such a translation decision cannot be made apart from context (more on this below). Also, even if we are sure of the function of a participle (e.g., a substantive), the time frame of any participle is determined by contextual factors. A final translation is impossible apart from referencing the context of a larger discourse unit.

---

[3] English has both participles and gerunds. A verb that has an –ing (or –ed) and functions adjectivally is a participle. If it functions as a noun, it is a gerund. In Greek, participles overlap in function with both the English gerund and participle.

17.4 Paradigms

PRESENT ACTIVE PARTICIPLE—MASCULINE					
(possible substantial translation provided)					
	SINGULAR			PLURAL	
NOM	ὁ	λύων	the one loosing	οἱ	λύοντες	the ones loosing
GEN	τοῦ	λύοντος	of the one loosing	τῶν	λυόντων	of the ones loosing
DAT	τῷ	λύοντι	to/for the one loosing	τοῖς	λύουσι(ν)	to/for the ones loosing
ACC	τὸν	λύοντα	the one loosing	τοὺς	λύοντας	the ones loosing

PRESENT MIDDLE/PASSIVE PARTICIPLE—MASCULINE					
(possible passive substantial translation provided)					
	SINGULAR			PLURAL	
NOM	ὁ	λυόμενος	the one being loosed	οἱ	λυόμενοι	the ones being loosed
GEN	τοῦ	λυομένου	of the one being loosed	τῶν	λυομένων	of the ones being loosed
DAT	τῷ	λυομένῳ	to/for the one being loosed	τοῖς	λυομένοις	to/for the ones being loosed
ACC	τὸν	λυόμενον	the one being loosed	τοὺς	λυομένους	the ones being loosed

Comprehensive charts of all regular forms of the present participle are provided:

PRESENT ACTIVE PARTICIPLE					
SINGULAR			PLURAL		
MASC	FEM	NEUT	MASC	FEM	NEUT
NOM	λύων[4]	λύουσα	λῦον[5]	λύοντες	λύουσαι	λύοντα
GEN	λύοντος	λυούσης	λύοντος	λυόντων	λυουσῶν	λυόντων
DAT	λύοντι	λυούσῃ	λύοντι	λύουσι(ν)[6]	λυούσαις	λύουσι(ν)
ACC	λύοντα	λύουσαν	λῦον	λύοντας	λυούσας	λύοντα

---

[4] Because there is no case ending used here, the tau (τ) drops off; it cannot be the last letter of the word. To compensate for the lost tau, the omicron (ο) lengthens to an omega (ω): λυ + οντ = λυοντ → λυον → λύων. Regarding morphological comments made concerning this chart, see William D. Mounce, *Basics of Biblical Greek: Grammar*, 4th ed. (Grand Rapids: Zondervan, 2019), 243.

[5] Like the masculine nominative form, there is no case ending used. Consequently, the tau (τ) drops off since it cannot be the last letter of the word. This time there is no lengthening of the connecting vowel: λυ + οντ = λυοντ → λυον.

[6] Because of the sigma (σ), the ντ drops off, causing the omicron (ο) to lengthen to ου in order to compensate: λυ + οντσι = λυοσι → λύουσι. Notice that this form is identical to the indicative form

PRESENT MIDDLE/PASSIVE PARTICIPLE					
SINGULAR			PLURAL		
MASC	FEM	NEUT	MASC	FEM	NEUT
NOM λυόμενος	λυομένη	λυόμενον	λυόμενοι	λυόμεναι	λυόμενα
GEN λυομένου	λυομένης	λυομένου	λυομένων	λυομένων	λυομένων
DAT λυομένῳ	λυομένη	λυομένῳ	λυομένοις	λυομέναις	λυομένοις
ACC λυόμενον	λυομένην	λυόμενον	λυομένους	λυομένας	λυόμενα

17.5 Morphology

Participles are important to master since about one in every twenty words in the Greek New Testament is a participle. That equates to almost one participle for every verse! Pay particular attention to the masculine nominative singular form as it is by far the most common form (representing almost 2,500 of the 6,600+ participles). In fact, participles comprise nearly one quarter of all verbal forms in the New Testament. Also note that there are no imperfect participles and only thirteen future participles in the New Testament.

Present Active Participles

Let's take a closer look at the paradigms above, starting with the present active participle. First, the masculine and neuter forms follow the third declension endings.

Masculine		*Neuter*	
–ς/–	–ες	–ς/–	–α
–ος	–ων	–ος	–ων
–ι	–σι(ν)	–ι	–σι(ν)
–α	–ας	–ς/–	–α

The feminine forms, however, follow a mixed form of the first declension endings, similar to the adjective πᾶς, using both the alpha (α) and eta (η) patterns (λύουσα, λύουσης, λύουσῃ, λύουσαν; cf. πᾶσα, πάσης, πάσῃ, πᾶσαν).

Masculine and neuter active participles have a distinctive –ντ– infix (λύοντος). This morpheme communicates that the participle is in the active voice. In addition, these forms contain an omicron (o) connecting vowel (λύοντος). The feminine infix is –ουσ– (λύουσης), also communicating the active voice.[7]

(pres act ind 3rd pl). Only context can determine which form is being used. This is also true for the neuter dative plural form.

[7] Technically, the feminine active morpheme is –ουσα–.

Present Middle/Passive Participles

The endings of present middle/passive participles are regular for all genders. In other words, the endings of the participle are the same as the first and second declension noun endings.

Masculine	λυόμενος	(cf. λόγος)
Feminine	λυομένη	(cf. φωνή)
Neuter	λυόμενον	(cf. τέκνον)

The –μεν– infix communicates that the voice is middle or passive (λυό**μεν**ος), with the addition of the omicron (o) connecting vowel to make pronunciation easier (λυ**ο**μένη).[8]

Contract verbs of participles will react in the same way as the vowel combinations you have already seen.

γεννάω	→	γεννα	+	ομενον	→	γεννώμενον
καλέω	→	καλε	+	ομενον	→	καλούμενον
πληρόω	→	πληρο	+	ομενον	→	πληρούμενον

Remember that the place of the contraction will often be indicated by a circumflex, particularly in the active voice (ἀγαπῶντι, καλοῦντος).

Present Participle of εἰμί

The present participle of εἰμί occurs more than 150 times in the New Testament and so deserves attention.

PRESENT PARTICIPLE—εἰμί[9]					
SINGULAR			**PLURAL**		
MASC	*FEM*	*NEUT*	*MASC*	*FEM*	*NEUT*
NOM ὤν	οὖσα	ὄν	ὄντες	οὖσαι	ὄντα
GEN ὄντος	οὔσης	ὄντος	ὄντων	οὐσῶν	ὄντων
DAT ὄντι	οὔσῃ	ὄντι	οὖσι(ν)	οὔσαις	οὖσι(ν)
ACC ὄντα	οὖσαν	ὄν	ὄντας	οὔσας	ὄντα

Because this form is identical to the combined endings (connecting vowels, infixes, and case endings) of regular forms, this paradigm does not need to be memorized. Once you know the present active participle paradigm of λύω, then you will know the paradigm for εἰμί. For example, the present masculine nominative

---

[8] Technically, the middle/passive morpheme is –μενο/η–.

[9] εἰμί is a stative verb (referring to ongoing existence) and is technically not parsed as "active," though the paradigm does follow the active endings.

singular participle of λύω is λύων. And the present masculine singular participle of εἰμί is ὤν. So, if you see what looks to be an ending all by itself (with its own smooth breathing mark and accent), it is most likely a participial form of εἰμί. As a present participle, εἰμί is usually translated "being." Finally, εἰμί only has an active form and never a middle or passive form.

Parsing

Below are some examples of how participles are parsed. Notice (1) that these forms are parsed as half verbs (tense, voice, and mood) and half adjectives (gender, case, and number); (2) they are not translated since it is not possible to translate them without knowing how they are used; and (3) the mood of the verb is now listed as a participle (a "ptc") instead of indicative.[10]

Inflected Form	Lexical Form	Tense	Voice	Mood	Gender	Case	Number
λύων	λύω	pres	act	ptc	masc	nom	sg
λυομέναις	λύω	pres	m/p	ptc	fem	dat	pl
ὄντος	εἰμί	pres	act	ptc	m/n	gen	sg

17.6 Participle Usage

What makes participles difficult is two-fold. (1) The number of forms to know (3 genders x 4 cases x 2 numbers [singular and plural] = 24 forms for every tense and voice). (2) The variety of uses can be daunting, too. Because a participle is a verbal *adjective*, it can be placed into one of the three adjectival positions: attributive, substantive, or predicate. Each of these uses requires a different method of translation.

Attributive Use

With the attributive use, the article (when present) occurs *directly in front of* the participle which modifies an expressed noun or pronoun. It is often best to translate an attributive participle with an English relative clause ("who" or "which/that").

ὁ πατήρ ὁ βλέπων	"the father who sees"
ὁ προφήτης ὁ ἐρχόμενος	"the prophet who comes"
ὁ ἄρτος ὁ καταβαίνων	"the bread which comes down"
ὁ ἄρτος ὁ ζῶν	"the living bread"
ὕδωρ ζῶν	"living water"

---

[10] Technically, a participle is not a mood since it is not functioning as a verb but a verbal *adjective*. (This is also true for infinitives which are verbal *nouns*). For convenience, however, we list it in the "mood" category.

In the above cases, the participle agrees with the noun it modifies in gender, case, and number. Participles can also take direct objects or can be modified by other parts of speech (e.g., adverbs, prepositional phrases, or negative particles). For example, ὁ ἔχων τὰς ἐντολάς μου, "the one who has my commands." The accusative phrase τὰς ἐντολάς is the direct object of the verbal idea "the one who has."

Substantival Use

A substantive is an adjective (or another part of speech) that functions as a noun. The article (when present) occurs *directly in front of* the participle which modifies an unexpressed noun or pronoun. Thus, a substantival participle is really an attributive participle whose modified noun is unexpressed. Sometimes this type of participle loses its verbal force and becomes a mere noun, especially if the verb describes an occupation or characteristic activity (e.g., ὁ ἄρχων, "the one who rules" = "the ruler"). It is usually best to translate a substantival participle as "the one who" + verbal meaning, but it could also be "he who" or "she who" if the gender of the person is known.

ὁ βλέπων	"the one who sees"
ὁ ἐρχόμενος	"the one who comes"
ὁ ζῶν	"the one who lives"
ὁ ποιῶν	"the one who does"
ὁ βαπτίζων	"the one who baptizes"

The case depends on the participle's function in the sentence, and the gender depends on the referent to which the participle applies.

Adverbial Use

With the adverbial use, the participle is in the predicate position (meaning that the article is *not* directly in front of the participle). Although the most common use involves a *temporal* focus, there are several uses of the adverbial participle (such as causal, purpose, etc.). With a present tense-form temporal participle, the action of the participle often occurs *at the same time* (contemporaneous with) the action of the main verb—whether the main verb is past, present, or future. Ultimately, the broader literary context must determine the temporal relationship. Most adverbial participles are in the nominative case.

The following categories are common enough to mention here. What we are determining is the relationship of the participles to the main verb. (This is why it is an *adverbial* participle.) These categories depend on the context and are not communicated by the participle. It is often necessary to add words in English to communicate the relationship.

- **Temporal:** communicates the time in which the action was performed in relation to the main verb (add "while," "as," or "when").

ταῦτα εἶπεν ἐν συναγωγῇ **διδάσκων** ἐν Καφαρναούμ, "He said these things **while teaching** in the synagogue in Capernaum" (John 6:59).

βλέπων δὲ τὸν ἄνεμον ἐφοβήθη, "But **when he saw** the wind, he was afraid" (Matt 14:30).

- *Causal:* communicates the reason why the verbal idea is performed (add "because" or "since")

    Εὐχαριστῶ τῷ θεῷ μου πάντοτε . . . **ἀκούων** σου τὴν ἀγάπην καὶ τὴν πίστιν, "I always thank my God . . . **because I hear** of your love . . . and faith" (Phlm v. 4–5).

- *Means:* communicates the means by which the verbal idea is accomplished (add "by" or "by means of")

    κοπιῶμεν **ἐργαζόμενοι** ταῖς ἰδίαις χερσίν, "we labor **by working** with our own hands" (1 Cor 4:12).

- *Purpose:* communicates the purpose or motive for the verbal idea performed (add "in order to" or "in order that").

    τοῦτο δὲ ἔλεγεν **πειράζων** αὐτόν, "he was saying this **in order to test** him" (John 6:6).

    ἦν ἐν τῇ ἐρήμῳ τεσσεράκοντα ἡμέρας **πειραζόμενος** ὑπὸ τοῦ Σατανᾶ, "He was in the desert forty days **in order to be tempted** by Satan" (Mark 1:13).

17.7 Participle Voice

Because participles are *verbal* adjectives, they can be in one of three voices: active, middle, or passive.

Active: πιστὸς ὁ **καλῶν** ὑμᾶς, "[the one] **who calls** you is faithful" (1 Thess 5:24).

Middle: σὺν πᾶσιν τοῖς **ἐπικαλουμένοις** τὸ ὄνομα τοῦ κυρίου ἡμῶν,[11] "with all [the ones] who . . . **call** upon the name of our Lord" (1 Cor 1:2 ESV).

Passive: **καλούμενος** ὑπὸ τοῦ θεοῦ, "**when [he is] called** by God" (Heb 5:2–4 ESV).

---

[11] ἐπικαλουμένοις is from the verb ἐπικαλέω (ἐπί + καλέω).

The distinguishing trait of the masculine and neuter active form is the infix –οντ– to which third declension endings are added. The distinguishing characteristic for the feminine is –ουσ– to which first declension endings are added.

Masculine	λύοντος
Feminine	λυούσης
Neuter	λύοντος

The distinguishing trait of the middle or passive form is the infix –μεν– to which the regular adjectival endings are attached.

Masculine	λυόμενος
Feminine	λυομένη
Neuter	λυόμενον

17.8 Participles and Aspect

It is a bit dangerous to talk about "tenses" when it comes to participles since that term involves time. In Greek, participles don't convey the time of the action—that is controlled by the main (usually indicative) verb. Instead, the Greek tense-form communicates the author's perspective on the action.

In the indicative mood, there are six tense-forms: present, imperfect, future, aorist, perfect, and pluperfect. These verbs communicate both time of action (tense) and the author's perspective on the action (aspect). But since participles (like all non-indicative verbs) don't communicate time, the tense-form used only communicates aspect. Because there are only three aspects, the number of tense-forms used with participles is essentially one for each aspect.[12]

1. **Imperfective** (action presented in progress): Present tense-form (no imperfect)

2. **Perfective** (action viewed as a whole): Aorist tense-form (almost no future)

3. **Stative** (action complete with resulting state or relevance): Perfect tense-form (no pluperfect)

Again, the time of the action is *not* determined by the participle, but by the broader context. Indicative verbs nearby provide some of the most significant context, and as an initial attempt at contextual translation, you should translate a present tense-form participle in the same time frame as indicative verbs that are close at hand. To clarify, a present participle does *not* necessarily communicate that the participle's action is contemporaneous with the writer's time of writing; rather, the action is likely in progress when the action of the main verb in the sentence occurs (past, present, or future).

---

[12] The exception is that the future tense-form is used thirteen times in the New Testament (see chap. 19).

- If the action of the main verb is past, then the action of the present participle is likely a continuous past (ἦλθεν ὁ Ἰησοῦς εἰς τὴν Γαλιλαίαν **κηρύσσων**, "Jesus came into Galilee **while he was preaching**," Mark 1:14).

- If the action of the main verb is present, then the action of the participle is likely a continuous present (βλέπει τὸν Ἰησοῦν **ἐρχόμενον** πρὸς αὐτόν, "he sees Jesus **while he is coming** to him," John 1:29).

- And if the action of the main verb is future, then the action of the participle is likely a continuous future (πολλοὶ γὰρ ἐλεύσονται ἐπὶ τῷ ὀνόματί μου **λέγοντες**, "For many will come in my name, **saying**" Matt 24:5 ESV).

This cannot be over-reiterated: the literary context provides the final and definitive guidance regarding into what time frame to translate a participle.[13] The translation guidelines in this chapter are simplified for beginning students.

17.9 Practice

A. Paradigms: Memorize the present active and middle/passive paradigms of λύω (masc only) (see section 17.4). Then write out each paradigm ten times from memory.

B. Parsing: Parse the following words.

1. θεωροῦντας

2. καθημένῳ

3. μένουσαν

4. λαμβάνοντες

5. κρίνοντα

6. ὑπάρχοντος

7. γραφόμενα

8. ἔχοντι

9. καλούμενον

10. οὔσῃ

---

[13] In an undated, unpublished ETS (Evangelical Theological Society) regional conference paper, Robert E. Picirilli observes, "I have recently completed an analytical study of the 562 participles in the Gospel of Mark . . ., and am satisfied that neither tense nor position in the sentence is intended to indicate time, leaving temporal reference to be determined entirely from context" ("The Meaning of the Tenses in Biblical Greek: Where Are We?").

C. Participle Usage: Indicate whether the following participles are used Attributively (A), Substantivally (S), or Adverbially (Adv).

1. _____ τὴν ἀλήθειαν τὴν μένουσαν ἐν ἡμῖν

2. _____ ὁ μένων ἐν τῇ διδαχῇ

3. _____ πορευόμενοι δὲ κηρύσσετε λέγοντες ὅτι ἤγγικεν ἡ βασιλεία τῶν οὐρανῶν

4. _____ ὁ πατήρ σου ὁ βλέπων

5. _____ ἔστιν ὁ ζητῶν καὶ κρίνων

6. _____ ὁ ἄρτος ὁ ἐκ τοῦ οὐρανοῦ καταβαίνων

7. _____ βλέπει τὸν Ἰησοῦν ἐρχόμενον πρὸς αὐτὸν

8. _____ ὁ καταβαίνων ἐκ τοῦ οὐρανοῦ

9. _____ τῷ θεῷ τῷ ἐγείροντι τοὺς νεκρούς

10. _____ ἦλθεν ὁ υἱὸς τοῦ ἀνθρώπου ἐσθίων καὶ πίνων

D. Translation: Translate the following sentences.

1. ὁ πιστεύων εἰς τὸν υἱὸν ἔχει ζωὴν αἰώνιον (John 3:36).

2. βλέπει τὸν Ἰησοῦν ἐρχόμενον πρὸς αὐτὸν καὶ λέγει, Ἴδε (Behold) ὁ ἀμνὸς (lamb) τοῦ θεοῦ ὁ αἴρων τὴν ἁμαρτίαν τοῦ κόσμου (John 1:29).

3. καὶ ἦλθεν κηρύσσων εἰς τὰς συναγωγὰς αὐτῶν εἰς ὅλην (all, whole) τὴν Γαλιλαίαν καὶ τὰ δαιμόνια ἐκβάλλων (Mark 1:39).

4. ὁ δεχόμενος (δέχομαι, I receive) ὑμᾶς ἐμὲ δέχεται, καὶ ὁ ἐμὲ δεχόμενος δέχεται τὸν ἀποστείλαντά (the one who sent) με (Matt 10:40).

5. δικαιοσύνη θεοῦ πεφανέρωται (φανερόω, I reveal) μαρτυρουμένη ὑπὸ τοῦ νόμου καὶ τῶν προφητῶν (Rom 3:21).

6. ἔρχεται πρὸς αὐτοὺς περιπατῶν ἐπὶ τῆς θαλάσσης (Mark 6:48).

7. Καὶ ἐξῆλθον οἱ Φαρισαῖοι . . . ζητοῦντες παρ᾽ αὐτοῦ σημεῖον ἀπὸ τοῦ οὐρανοῦ, πειράζοντες (πειράζω, I test) αὐτόν (Mark 8:11).

8. Σίμων Πέτρος εἶπεν, Σὺ εἶ ὁ Χριστὸς ὁ υἱὸς τοῦ θεοῦ τοῦ ζῶντος (Matt 16:16).

9. καὶ εὐθὺς, ἀναβαίνων ἐκ τοῦ ὕδατος, εἶδεν . . . τὸ πνεῦμα ὡς περιστερὰν (dove) καταβαῖνον εἰς αὐτόν (Mark 1:10).

10. καὶ εἶδον ἄλλον ἄγγελον ἰσχυρὸν (ἰσχυρός, strong) καταβαίνοντα ἐκ τοῦ οὐρανοῦ (Rev 10:1).

11. ὁ λαὸς ὁ καθήμενος ἐν σκότει (τὸ σκότος, darkness) φῶς εἶδεν μέγα (Matt 4:16).

12. ὅτε δὲ ἐπίστευσαν τῷ Φιλίππῳ εὐαγγελιζομένῳ περὶ τῆς βασιλείας τοῦ θεοῦ καὶ τοῦ ὀνόματος Ἰησοῦ Χριστοῦ (Acts 8:12).

13. ὁ δὲ ὀπίσω (after) μου ἐρχόμενος ἰσχυρότερός (ἰσχυρός, strong) μού ἐστιν (Matt 3:11).

14. Καὶ ὑμᾶς ὄντας νεκροὺς τοῖς παραπτώμασιν (trespasses) καὶ ταῖς ἁμαρτίαις ὑμῶν (Eph 2:1).

15. καὶ αὐτὸς ἐδίδασκεν ἐν ταῖς συναγωγαῖς αὐτῶν δοξαζόμενος ὑπὸ πάντων (Luke 4:15).

E. Translation: Translate the following sentences into Greek.

1. He went outside to them, proclaiming the eternal Word.

2. Truly, truly I say to you, they know neither the day nor the hour.

3. The elders brought each child as he beheld the signs.

4. Then Jesus said, "I am the One who sits on the throne."

5. No one saw the one announcing the good news.

17.10 Vocabulary[14]

φανερόω	I reveal, make known, manifest (*phantom, epiphany*)
κρατέω	I grasp, seize, arrest (*democracy*—people [δῆμος] seize/exercise the power)
εἷς, μία, ἕν	one (*hendiadys*—one concept expressed through two words, ἓν διὰ δυοῖν)
δύο	two (*duet*)
τρεῖς	three (*triad*)
τέσσαρες	four (*tesseract*)
πέντε	five (*Pentagon*)

---

[14] To hear an author of your textbook read through the vocabulary for chapter 17, go to bit.ly/greekvocab17 or beginninggreek.com.

ἑπτά	seven (*heptagon*)
δέκα	ten (*decimeter*)
δώδεκα	twelve (*dodecagon*)
πρῶτος, –η, –ον	first (*prototype*)
δεύτερος, –α, –ον	second (*Deuteronomy*, second account of the giving of the law)
τρίτος, –η, –ον	third (*tricycle*)
τέταρτος, –η, –ον	fourth (*tetrarch*—governor over one of four specified territories)
μή	no, not (employed with non-indicative verbs)

//////////////

CHAPTER 18

AORIST PARTICIPLES

18.1 Overview[1]

In the previous chapter, we introduced participles, focusing our attention on the present tense form (imperfective aspect). In this one, we will consider aorist participles and, in the next chapter, perfect participles. This chapter will also explain how participles are negated. Finally, we will cover ordinal and cardinal numbers.

A participle is a verbal adjective. As such, it has some verbal qualities (tense, voice, and mood) and some adjectival qualities (gender, case, and number). Like all participles, aorist participles don't communicate time since the timing of the action is dependent on the main verb. Aorist participles present an action as a whole, which often (but not always) overlaps with the participle being past time from the perspective of the writer/speaker/narrative. Thus, aorist participles are often translated into English with "–ed" added to the verb stem (e.g., the *fixed* camera).

18.2 Significance

You have likely heard the Great Commission (Matt 28:18–20) quoted countless times. Did you know that these three verses include *five* participles? (Note the participles in parentheses below.)

> Jesus came up (προσελθών) and spoke to them, saying (λέγων), "All authority has been given to Me in heaven and on earth. Go (πορευθέντες) therefore and make disciples of all the nations, baptizing (βαπτίζοντες) them in the name of the Father and the Son and the Holy Spirit, teaching (διδάσκοντες) them to observe all that I commanded you; and lo, I am with you always, even to the end of the age." (NASB)

---

[1] For an overview video lecture of chapter 18, go to bit.ly/greeklecture18 or beginninggreek.com.

Let's focus on the aorist participle translated "go" above. Although some maintain that πορευθέντες should be viewed as a temporal (adverbial) participle and should therefore be translated "as you go,"[2] the best evidence supports taking it as a participle of attendant circumstance (see 18.6). A participle of attendant circumstances takes on the mood of the main verb, which in this case is an imperative (μαθητεύσατε, "make disciples"). Thus, the participle πορευθέντες should also be translated as an imperative. This use of the participle is confirmed by looking at similar constructions in both the Septuagint (an early Greek translation of the Old Testament) and the New Testament, especially in the Gospel of Matthew.

First, there are several key texts in the Septuagint that demonstrate that the aorist participle of πορεύομαι paired with an explicit imperative of another verb often functions imperatively.[3]

- Rebekah tells her son Jacob, "Let your curse be on me, my son; only obey my voice, and go (πορευθείς), bring (ἔνεγκέ) them to me" (Gen 27:13). Interestingly, in the Hebrew text, both of these verbs are imperatives. Also, it would not make sense to translate the participle temporally ("as you go, bring") since it clearly bears an imperatival force ("go, bring").

- Jacob instructs his son Joseph, "Go (πορευθείς) now, see (ἰδέ) if it is well with your brothers and with the flock, and bring me word" (Gen 37:14). As with the previous example, the Hebrew has an imperative that the Septuagint translators rendered as a participle.

- Pharaoh commands the people of Israel, "Go (πορευθέντες) now and work (ἐργάζεσθε). No straw will be given you, but you must still deliver the same number of bricks" (Exod 5:18).

- The sons of the prophets say to Elisha concerning Elijah, "Please let them go (πορευθέντες) and seek (ζητησάτωσαν) your master" (2 Kgs 2:16).

These texts confirm that the aorist participle of πορεύομαι often took on the imperatival flavor of an explicit imperative of another verb with which it was paired.

Other uses in Matthew's Gospel also confirm the attendant circumstance use of the participle. Not only does Matthew use this construction often, but he uses the construction with the same verb (πορεύομαι) as an aorist participle, followed by an aorist imperative.

- King Herod urgently commands the wise men, "Go (πορευθέντες) and search (ἐξετάσατε) diligently for the child" (2:8).

---

[2] See, e.g., the International Standard Version (ISV): "Therefore, as you go, disciple people in all nations, baptizing them in the name of the Father, and the Son, and the Holy Spirit."

[3] See Cleon Rogers, "The Great Commission," *BSac* 130 (1973): 260. The remainder of this Significance section is derived directly from Benjamin L. Merkle, *Exegetical Gems from Biblical Greek: A Refreshing Guide to Grammar and Interpretation* (Grand Rapids: Baker, 2019), 97–101.

- Jesus states, "Go (πορευθέντες) and learn (μάθετε) what this means" (9:13).

- Jesus told John's disciples, "Go (πορευθέντες) and tell (ἀπαγγείλατε) John what you hear and see" (11:4).

- Jesus instructs Peter, "Go (πορευθείς) to the sea and cast (βάλε) a hook and take the first fish that comes up" (17:27).

- The angel at the empty tomb tells the women, "Then go (πορευθεῖσαι) quickly and tell (εἴπατε) his disciples that he has risen from the dead" (28:7).

Instead of using two coordinate imperatives, it was common to use a participle followed by an imperative. It was understood that the participle mirrored the mood of the imperative, being taken as a command. In each case, it would not make sense to translate the participle as "when/as you go"; instead, the participle clearly functions as an imperative. Therefore, when we come to Matt 28:19 ("Go [πορευθέντες] therefore and make disciples [μαθητεύσατε] of all nations"), it is natural to read the participle as an imperative. In Matthew's Gospel, every instance of the aorist participle of πορεύομαι preceding an aorist main verb is clearly attendant circumstance. This interpretation is represented by most English Bible versions which consistently translate πορευθέντες as an imperative.

18.3 Paradigms

Just as with present participles, we will first present a few representative charts with *possible* translations of the substantival usage. Then we will include comprehensive charts giving all regular aorist participial forms. Note that the particular usage and translation of any participle can only be determined by a careful consideration of the context. Ancient native speakers made these decisions subconsciously and intuitively, but as non-native speakers living thousands of years later, we must be more deliberate and methodical in our approach.

AORIST ACTIVE PARTICIPLE—MASCULINE					
(*possible* substantival translation provided)					
	SINGULAR			PLURAL	
NOM	ὁ	λύσας	the one who loosed	οἱ	λύσαντες	the ones who loosed
GEN	τοῦ	λύσαντος	of the one who loosed	τῶν	λυσάντων	of the ones who loosed
DAT	τῷ	λύσαντι	to/for the one who loosed	τοῖς	λύσασι(ν)	to/for the ones who loosed
ACC	τὸν	λύσαντα	the one who loosed	τοὺς	λύσαντας	the ones who loosed

AORIST MIDDLE PARTICIPLE—MASCULINE					
(*possible* substantival translation provided)					
	SINGULAR			PLURAL	
NOM	ὁ	λυσάμενος	the one who loosed for himself	οἱ	λυσάμενοι	the ones who loosed for themselves
GEN	τοῦ	λυσαμένου	of the one who loosed for himself	τῶν	λυσαμένων	of the ones who loosed for themselves
DAT	τῷ	λυσαμένῳ	to/for the one who loosed for himself	τοῖς	λυσαμένοις	to/for the ones who loosed for themselves
ACC	τὸν	λυσάμενον	the one who loosed for himself	τοὺς	λυσαμένους	the ones that loosed for themselves

FIRST AORIST ACTIVE PARTICIPLE					
	SINGULAR			PLURAL		
	MASC	FEM	NEUT	MASC	FEM	NEUT
NOM	λύσας[4]	λύσασα[5]	λῦσαν[6]	λύσαντες	λύσασαι	λύσαντα
GEN	λύσαντος	λυσάσης	λύσαντος	λυσάντων	λυσασῶν	λυσάντων
DAT	λύσαντι	λυσάσῃ	λύσαντι	λύσασι(ν)[7]	λυσάσαις	λύσασι(ν)
ACC	λύσαντα	λύσασαν	λῦσαν	λύσαντας	λυσάσας	λύσαντα

FIRST AORIST MIDDLE PARTICIPLE					
	SINGULAR			PLURAL		
	MASC	FEM	NEUT	MASC	FEM	NEUT
NOM	λυσάμενος	λυσαμένη	λυσάμενον	λυσάμενοι	λυσάμεναι	λυσάμενα
GEN	λυσαμένου	λυσαμένης	λυσαμένου	λυσαμένων	λυσαμένων	λυσαμένων
DAT	λυσαμένῳ	λυσαμένῃ	λυσαμένῳ	λυσαμένοις	λυσαμέναις	λυσαμένοις
ACC	λυσάμενον	λυσαμένην	λυσάμενον	λυσαμένους	λυσαμένας	λυσάμενα

---

[4] The sigma (ς) case ending caused the –ντ– infix to drop: λυσα + ντ + ς = λυσαντς → λύσας. Regarding morphological comments made concerning this chart, see William D. Mounce, *Basics of Biblical Greek: Grammar*, 4th ed. (Grand Rapids: Zondervan, 2019), 318.

[5] The –ντ– infix is changed to –σα because of a consonantal iota and sigma initially added.

[6] There is no case ending used in the nominative and accusative. Consequently, the tau (τ) drops since it cannot stand as the last letter of the word: λυσα + ντ = λυσαντ → λῦσαν.

[7] The –σι case ending caused the –ντ– infix to drop: λυ + σα + ντ + σι = λυσαντσι → λύσασι.

FIRST AORIST PASSIVE PARTICIPLE					
SINGULAR			PLURAL		
MASC	*FEM*	*NEUT*	*MASC*	*FEM*	*NEUT*
NOM λυθείς	λυθεῖσα	λυθέν	λυθέντες	λυθεῖσαι	λυθέντα
GEN λυθέντος	λυθείσης	λυθέντος	λυθέντων	λυθεισῶν	λυθέντων
DAT λυθέντι	λυθείσῃ	λυθέντι	λυθεῖσι(ν)	λυθείσαις	λυθεῖσι(ν)
ACC λυθέντα	λυθεῖσαν	λυθέν	λυθέντας	λυθείσας	λυθέντα

18.4 Morphology

First Aorist Active

Like the present tense-form, the masculine and neuter aorist active forms follow the third declension endings (masc: –ς/-, –ος, –ι, –α, –ες, –ων, –σιν, –ας; neut: –ς/, –ος, –ι, –ς/-, –α, –ων, –σιν, –α). The feminine forms follow a mixed form of the first declension endings, similar to the adjective πᾶς, using both the alpha (α) and eta (η) patterns (λύσασα, λυσάσης, λυσάσῃ, λύσασαν; compare, πᾶσα, πάσης, πάσῃ, πᾶσαν).

Masculine and neuter active participles have a distinctive –ντ– infix (λύσαντος). This morpheme communicates that the participle is in the active voice. In addition, a sigma (σ) is added to the stem and the connecting vowel changes to an alpha (α): λύσαντος.

Liquid verbs will drop the sigma (σ), similar to the indicative mood:

αἴρω	→	ἄρας
ἀποκτείνω	→	ἀποκτείνας
ἀποστέλλω	→	ἀποστείλας
σπείρω	→	σπείρας

First Aorist Middle

As with aorist indicative verbs, aorist participles (and all other non-indicative moods) have distinct middle (λυσάμενος) and passive (λυθείς) forms.

Like the present tense-form middle/passive participles, aorist middle endings are regular for all genders. In other words, the endings of the participle are the same as the first and second noun declension endings. The only difference with the present forms is that the sigma was added to the stem and the variable vowel is changed to an alpha.

Masculine	λυσάμενος	(cf. λόγος)
Feminine	λυσαμένη	(cf. φωνή)
Neuter	λυσάμενον	(cf. τέκνον)

The –μεν– infix communicates that the voice is middle (λυσά**μεν**ος), with the addition of a sigma added to the stem and an alpha connecting vowel (λυ**σα**μένη).[8]

First Aorist Passive

As stated above, with the aorist tense-form, the middle and passive forms are distinct. The characteristic morpheme of the passive form is a –θε– (λυ**θ**έντος; see the passive indicative ἐλύ**θη**ν). As for the endings, they are the same as the active forms following third declension (masculine and neuter) or first declension mixed (feminine) endings.

Importantly, aorist participles do not have augments. In fact, all non-indicative aorist forms lack the augment. The reason for this is that the augment communicates that the time of the action is in the past, and participles do not convey such information.

Some verbs have passive forms but are really middle in meaning (e.g., Mark 8:39 [ἀποκριθείς]; see also Matt 2:21; 22:15). In the Koine Greek period, passive endings commonly convey a middle idea.

18.5 Second Aorist Forms

If a verb has a second aorist form in the indicative, it will likewise have a second aorist form as a participle. Since second aorist participles use the same endings as present participles, and since there is no augment, the only difference between them is the stem. Below are some second aorist participal forms. If you know the indicative second aorist forms, there is no need to memorize this additional list. You will be able to recognize them.

Present Participle		Aorist Participle
ἄγων	→	ἀγαγών
ἀναβαίνων	→	ἀναβάς[9]
ἀποθνῄσκων	→	ἀποθανών
βάλλων	→	βαλών
βλέπων/ὁρῶν	→	ἰδών
γινόμενος	→	γενόμενος
γινώσκων	→	γνούς[10]
ἐρχόμενος	→	ἐλθών
ἐσθίων	→	φάγων
εὑρίσκων	→	εὑρών

---

[8] Technically, the middle voice morpheme is –μενο/η–.

[9] ἀναβάς follows first aorist participle endings, though without the preceding sigma.

[10] The aorist stem of γινώσκω is γνω–. The added sigma (ς) case ending caused the –ντ– infix to drop, which then caused the vowel to change from omega (ω) to ου: γνω + ντ + ς = γνωντς → γνως → γνούς.

λαμβάνων	→	λαβών
λέγων	→	εἰπών
πίνων	→	πιών
πίπτων	→	πεσών
φέρων	→	ἐνέγκας[11]

A few second aorist passive forms lack the theta (θ): ἀποστέλλω → ἀποσταλέντος.

18.6 Participle Usage

The use of aorist participles is identical to the present tense-form. Because a participle is an adjective, it can be placed into one of the three adjectival positions and thus has three main uses: attributive, substantival, and adverbial. Below is a quick recap of what was presented in the previous chapter with specific reference to the aorist tense-form.

Attributive Use

With the attributive use, the article (when present) occurs *directly in front of* the participle which modifies an expressed noun or pronoun. It is often best to translate an attributive participle with an English relative clause ("who" or "which/that").

ὁ μαθητὴς ὁ ἐλθών	"the disciple who came"
ὁ ἄνθρωπος ὁ εἰπών	"the man who said"

The participle agrees with the noun it modifies in gender, case, and number. Participles can also take direct objects or can be modified by other parts of speech (e.g., adverbs, prepositional phrases, or negative particles).

Substantival Use

A substantive is an adjective (or another part of speech) that functions as a noun. The article (when present) occurs *directly in front of* the participle which modifies an unexpressed noun or pronoun.

ὁ ἐλθών	"the one who came"
ὁ καλέσας	"the one who called"

Adverbial Use

With the adverbial use, the participle is in the predicate position (meaning that the article is *not* directly in front of the participle). Several of the more common uses include temporal, causal, means, and purpose. With an aorist tense-form temporal participle, the action of the participle typically occurs *before* the action of the main

---

[11] ἐνέγκας follows first aorist participle endings, though without the preceding sigma.

verb—whether the main verb is past, present, or future).[12] Most adverbial participles are in the nominative case. In English translation, it is difficult to distinguish whether the underlying Greek adverbial participle is present or aorist. As a general rule, the present participle is selected to present the action as unfolding, while the aorist participle presents the action as a whole (including beginning and ending without attention to its unfolding).

- *Temporal*: communicates the time in which the action was performed in relation to the main verb (add "after" or "when").

  καὶ **ἐλθὼν** ἐκεῖνος ἐλέγξει τὸν κόσμον περὶ ἁμαρτίας καὶ περὶ δικαιοσύνης καὶ περὶ κρίσεως, "**[W]hen he comes**, he will convict the world about sin, righteousness, and judgment" (John 16:8).

- *Causal*: communicates the reason why the verbal idea is performed (add "because" or "since").

  Δημᾶς γάρ με ἐγκατέλιπεν **ἀγαπήσας** τὸν νῦν αἰῶνα, "Demas has deserted me, **since he loved** this present world" (2 Tim 4:10).

- *Means*: communicates how the verbal idea is accomplished (add "by" or "by means of").

  Χριστὸς ἡμᾶς ἐξηγόρασεν ἐκ τῆς κατάρας τοῦ νόμου **γενόμενος** ὑπὲρ ἡμῶν κατάρα, "Christ redeemed us from the curse of the law **by becoming** a curse for us" (Gal 3:13).[13]

- *Attendant Circumstance*: communicates an action that is coordinate or parallel to the main verb, thus taking on the mood of the verb and is translated as a finite verb with "and" inserted between the two verbal ideas.

  καὶ **ἐγερθεὶς** ἀπῆλθεν εἰς τὸν οἶκον αὐτοῦ, "**He got up** and went home" (Matt 9:7).

18.7 Non-Indicative Negation

Just as οὐ (or οὐκ, οὐχ) negates indicative verbs, μή negates non-indicative verbs (such as participles). For example, ὁ πιστεύων εἰς αὐτὸν οὐ κρίνεται· ὁ δὲ **μὴ** πιστεύων ἤδη κέκριται, "Anyone who believes in him is not condemned; and anyone who does **not** believe is already condemned" (John 3:18). Notice that in the first half of the verse, οὐ is used because it negates an indicative verb (κρίνεται). In the second half, however, μή is used because it negates a substantival participle

---

[12] The action could also be virtually simultaneous with the action of the main verb.
[13] Aorist participles almost never convey purpose.

(πιστεύων). It is common for the postpositive δέ and the particle μή to be sand-wiched between the article and the substantival participle (ὁ **δὲ μὴ** πιστεύων).

18.8 Numbers

There are two different types of numbers: cardinals and ordinals. **Cardinal numbers** are used for counting (one, two, three) whereas **ordinal numbers** are used for ordering (first, second, third).

Cardinal Numbers		Ordinal Numbers	
εἷς, μία, ἕν	one	πρῶτος	first
δύο	two	δεύτερος	second
τρεῖς	three	τρίτος	third
τέσσαρες	four	τέταρτος	fourth
πέντε	five	πέμπτος	fifth
ἓξ	six	ἕκτος	sixth
ἑπτά	seven	ἕβδομος	seventh
ὀκτώ	eight	ὄγδοος	eighth
ἐννέα	nine	ἔνατος	ninth
δέκα	ten	δέκατος	tenth
ἕνδεκα	eleven		
δώδεκα	twelve		

Some numbers decline (1–4), whereas others do not (5–12). The paradigms for εἷς (masc) and ἕν (neut) are similar to third declension forms whereas the paradigm for μία (fem) is similar to the first declension alpha pattern.

	MASC	FEM	NEUT	TRANSLATION
NOM	εἷς	μία	ἕν	"one"
GEN	ἑνός	μιᾶς	ἑνός	"of one"
DAT	ἑνί	μιᾷ	ἑνί	"to/for one"
ACC	ἕνα	μίαν	ἕν	"one"

Be sure to distinguish εἷς ("one," masc) from εἰς ("into") and ἕν ("one," neut) from ἐν ("in"). Notice that the numbers are accented and have rough breathing marks.

Whereas εἷς, μία, and ἕν have no plural form, the declinable numbers δύο,[14] τρεῖς, and τέσσαρες have no singular form.

---

[14] The only other orthographically distinct form of δύο is δυσίν (dat pl).

Three (masc/fem)	Three (neut)	Four (masc/fem)	Four (neut)
τρεῖς	τρία	τέσσαρες	τέσσαρα
τριῶν	τριῶν	τεσσάρων	τεσσάρων
τρισί(ν)	τρισί(ν)	τέσσαρσιν	τέσσαρσιν
τρεῖς	τρία	τέσσαρας	τέσσαρα

Numbers are essentially adjectives and therefore can be used attributively, substantively, and predicatively.

> *Attributive*: εἷς κύριος, **μία** πίστις, **ἓν** βάπτισμα, "**one** Lord, **one** faith, **one** baptism" (Eph 4:5).

> *Substantival*: καὶ ἐποίησεν **τοὺς δώδεκα**, "He appointed **the twelve**" (Mark 3:16).

> *Predicate*: εἷς ὁ θεὸς, "God is **one**" (Rom 3:30 ESV).

For counting, ancient Greeks used letters with an oblique stroke above and to the right of the letters (α′ = 1, β′ = 2, γ′ = 3. . . ι′ = 10, κ′ = 20, λ′ = 30 . . . ρ′ = 100, σ′ = 200, τ′ = 300). Several archaic Greek letters were used in this system.[15]

Finally, the word οὐδείς is a combination of οὐ ("no, not") and εἷς ("one"), with a delta (δ) in between for pronunciation purposes.

18.9 Practice

A. Paradigms: Memorize the aorist active, middle, and passive participle paradigms of λύω (masc only) (see section 18.3). Then write out each paradigm ten times from memory.

B. Parsing: Parse the following words.

1. ἐλθόντων

2. ἰδών

3. ἀπολυθέντες

4. ἀποθανών

5. ἀγαπήσαντος

6. λαλήσας

7. εἰσελθόντι

8. λαβόντας

---

[15] See chap. 9, "Numerals," in Evert van Emde Boas, Albert Rijksbaron, Luuk Huitink, and Mathieu de Bakker, *The Cambridge Grammar of Classical Greek* (Cambridge: Cambridge University Press, 2019), 101–4.

9. ἀκούσαντες

10. μαρτυρήσας

C. Participle Usage: Indicate whether the following participles are used Attributively (A), Substantivally (S), or Adverbially (Adv).

1. _____ ἀκούσας δὲ ὁ βασιλεὺς

2. _____ ὁ δὲ ἐγερθεὶς παρέλαβεν τὸ παιδίον

3. _____ ὁ θεὸς ὁ εἰπών

4. _____ ἀπὸ τοῦ καλέσαντος ὑμᾶς ἐν χάριτι Χριστοῦ

5. _____ βαπτισθεὶς δὲ ὁ Ἰησοῦς

6. _____ τοῦ υἱοῦ τοῦ θεοῦ τοῦ ἀγαπήσαντός με

7. _____ ὁ εὑρὼν τὴν ψυχὴν αὐτοῦ

8. _____ εἰς θεὸν τὸν ἐγείραντα αὐτὸν ἐκ νεκρῶν

9. _____ ὁ ἐγείρας Χριστὸν

10. _____ ὃν οὐκ ἰδόντες ἀγαπᾶτε

D. Translation: Translate the following sentences.

1. ἐλθὼν οὖν ὁ Ἰησοῦς εὗρεν αὐτὸν τέσσαρας ἤδη (already) ἡμέρας ἔχοντα ἐν τῷ μνημείῳ (tomb) (John 11:17).

2. καὶ εὐθὺς ἐκ τῆς συναγωγῆς ἐξελθόντες ἦλθον εἰς τὴν οἰκίαν Σίμωνος καὶ Ἀνδρέου μετὰ Ἰακώβου καὶ Ἰωάννου (Mark 1:29).

3. καὶ ἰδὼν ὁ Ἰησοῦς τὴν πίστιν αὐτῶν εἶπεν τῷ παραλυτικῷ (paralytic)... τέκνον, ἀφίενταί (are forgiven) σου αἱ ἁμαρτίαι (Matt 9:2).

4. καὶ ἠγέρθη καὶ εὐθὺς ἄρας τὸν κράβαττον (mat) ἐξῆλθεν ἔμπροσθεν (in front of) πάντων (Mark 2:12).

5. ὁ δὲ ἐγερθεὶς παρέλαβεν (took along) τὸ παιδίον (παιδίον, child) καὶ τὴν μητέρα αὐτοῦ καὶ εἰσῆλθεν εἰς γῆν Ἰσραήλ (Matt 2:21). (Note that the initial article here functions like a personal pronoun: "he." It does not modify the participle ἐγερθείς.)

6. καὶ λαβὼν τοὺς πέντε ἄρτους καὶ τοὺς δύο ἰχθύας (fish) ἀναβλέψας (ἀναβλέπω, I look up) εἰς τὸν οὐρανὸν εὐλόγησεν (he blessed) καὶ κατέκλασεν (he broke) τοὺς ἄρτους καὶ ἐδίδου (he was giving) [them] τοῖς μαθηταῖς αὐτοῦ (Mark 6:41).

7. καὶ ἀποκριθεὶς ὁ Ἰησοῦς ἔλεγεν διδάσκων ἐν τῷ ἱερῷ, Πῶς (How) λέγουσιν οἱ γραμματεῖς ὅτι ὁ Χριστὸς υἱὸς Δαυίδ ἐστιν; (Mark 12:35).

8. καὶ ἀποκριθεῖσα ἡ μήτηρ αὐτοῦ εἶπεν, Οὐχί, ἀλλὰ κληθήσεται Ἰωάννης (Luke 1:60).

9. εὐθὺς κράξας ὁ πατὴρ τοῦ παιδίου (παιδίον, child) ἔλεγεν, Πιστεύω (Mark 9:24).

10. καὶ πάλιν ἀπελθὼν προσηύξατο τὸν αὐτὸν λόγον εἰπών (Mark 14:39).

11. καὶ ὁ θεωρῶν ἐμὲ θεωρεῖ τὸν πέμψαντά με (John 12:45).

12. καὶ ἐλθόντες εἰς τὴν οἰκίαν εἶδον τὸ παιδίον (child) (Matt 2:11).

13. καὶ ἀσπασάμενοι (ἀσπάζομαι, I greet) τοὺς ἀδελφοὺς ἐμείναμεν ἡμέραν μίαν παρ' αὐτοῖς (Acts 21:7).

14. πολλῷ οὖν μᾶλλον (πολλῷ μᾶλλον, much more) δικαιωθέντες (δικαιόω, declare righteous) νῦν ἐν τῷ αἵματι αὐτοῦ σωθησόμεθα δι' αὐτοῦ ἀπὸ τῆς ὀργῆς (wrath) (Rom 5:9).

15. ἀσπάζομαι (I greet) ὑμᾶς ἐγὼ Τέρτιος ὁ γράψας τὴν ἐπιστολὴν (letter) ἐν κυρίῳ (Rom 16:22).

E. Translation: Translate the following sentences into Greek.

1. He went out with his two disciples.

2. After speaking to the crowd, Jesus spoke to the Twelve.

3. The third apostle was released/loosed in his home.

4. The God who sent his Son manifested his glory.

5. The ones who did not believe were departing to the city.

18.10 Vocabulary[16]

προσφέρω	I bring to, offer (*fertile, metaphor* [μετά, "beyond" φέρω, "I carry"])
ἑτοιμάζω	I prepare
δέω	I bind
παιδίον, τό	child (*pedagogy*)
ὄρος, ὄρους, τό	mountain, hill (*orology*)

---

[16] To hear an author of your textbook read through the vocabulary for chapter 18, go to bit.ly/greekvocab18 or beginninggreek.com.

ἐλπίς, ἐλπίδος, ἡ	hope
μόνος, –η, –ον	only, single, alone (*monocle, monograph*)
ὅλος, –η, –ον	whole, entire, complete (*wholistic*)
ἀγαπητός, –ή, –όν	beloved
μέσος, –η, –ον	middle, midst (*Mesopotamia*, land in the midst of two rivers)
λοιπός, –ή, –όν	remaining, rest
δεξιός, –ά, –όν	right (*ambidextrous*—having "both right" hands)
ἄρα	so then
ἤδη	already, now
ὧδε	here

////////////////

CHAPTER 19

PERFECT PARTICIPLES

19.1 Overview[1]

In the previous two chapters, we introduced participles, focusing our attention on present and aorist forms. In this chapter, we will consider perfect participles and will discuss two special uses of participles: genitive absolutes and periphrastic constructions. We will also discuss future participles, although they are uncommon.

Perfect participles are built on the perfect tense-form stem (which includes reduplication) and typically communicate a completed action which has ongoing consequences or results. Whereas present tense-form (imperfective aspect) participles occur more than 3,600 times and aorist tense-form (perfective aspect) participles occur more than 2,200 times, perfect tense-form (stative aspect) participles occur only 673 times in the Greek New Testament. Unlike the other tense-forms, most perfect participles function adjectively and not adverbially.

19.2 Significance

In the letters of 1, 2, and 3 John, there is great emphasis on observable transformation in the life of the Christian. Real Christians will keep God's commands (1 John 3:24) and love other believers (1 John 2:10–11). Yet, it is important to note that John does not say that keeping God's commands and loving other Christians makes one a Christian. Rather, these are the behaviors that characterize people who have experienced a spiritual rebirth in the past. John writes,

> No one who is born of God will continue to sin, because God's seed remains in them;
> they cannot go on sinning, because they have been born of God. (1 John 3:9 NIV)

---

[1] For an overview video lecture of chapter 19, go to bit.ly/greeklecture19 or beginninggreek.com.

"No one who is born of God" is a translation of this Greek phrase: πᾶς ὁ **γεγεννημένος** ἐκ τοῦ θεοῦ. The word in bold is a perfect passive participle, referring to a past completed action that has an ongoing resulting state or relevance. The person of whom John speaks was, in the past, spiritually birthed by the power of God. Now, that individual continues to exist as a Spirit-born child of God. That ongoing state of spiritual sonship makes an observable difference in one's daily ethical decisions and relationships. If there is no reflection of the Savior in one's life (however imperfect and halting), it calls into question whether one really has come to know God at all (1 John 2:4–6).

19.3 Paradigms

Just as we did for the present and aorist participles, we will begin with a few perfect participle paradigms and accompanying *possible* substantive translations. Only by considering literary context can one determine the usage and translation of a participle. After the two sample translation charts below, a comprehensive list of regular perfect participle forms can be found.

PERFECT ACTIVE PARTICIPLE—MASCULINE					
(*possible* substantival translation provided)					
	SINGULAR			PLURAL	
NOM	ὁ	λελυκώς	the one who has loosed	οἱ	λελυκότες	the ones who have loosed
GEN	τοῦ	λελυκότος	of the one who has loosed	τῶν	λελυκότων	of the ones who have loosed
DAT	τῷ	λελυκότι	to/for the one who has loosed	τοῖς	λελυκόσι(ν)	to/for the ones who have loosed
ACC	τὸν	λελυκότα	the one who has loosed	τοὺς	λελυκότας	the ones who have loosed

PERFECT MIDDLE/PASSIVE PARTICIPLE—MASCULINE					
(*possible* passive substantival translation provided)					
	SINGULAR			PLURAL	
NOM	ὁ	λελυμένος	the one who has been loosed	οἱ	λελυμένοι	the ones who have been loosed
GEN	τοῦ	λελυμένου	of the one who has been loosed	τῶν	λελυμένων	of the ones who have been loosed
DAT	τῷ	λελυμένῳ	to/for the one who has been loosed	τοῖς	λελυμένοις	to/for the ones who have been loosed
ACC	τὸν	λελυμένον	the one who has been loosed	τοὺς	λελυμένους	the ones who have been loosed

PERFECT ACTIVE PARTICIPLE					
SINGULAR			PLURAL		
MASC	*FEM*	*NEUT*	*MASC*	*FEM*	*NEUT*
NOM λελυκώς[2]	λελυκυῖα	λελυκός[3]	λελυκότες	λελυκυῖαι	λελυκότα
GEN λελυκότος	λελυκυῖας	λελυκότος	λελυκότων	λελυκυιῶν	λελυκότων
DAT λελυκότι	λελυκυίᾳ	λελυκότι	λελυκόσι(ν)	λελυκυίαις	λελυκόσι(ν)
ACC λελυκότα	λελυκυῖαν	λελυκός	λελυκότας	λελυκυίας	λελυκότα

PERFECT MIDDLE/PASSIVE PARTICIPLE					
SINGULAR			PLURAL		
MASC	*FEM*	*NEUT*	*MASC*	*FEM*	*NEUT*
NOM λελυμένος	λελυμένη	λελυμένον	λελυμένοι	λελυμέναι	λελυμένα
GEN λελυμένου	λελυμένης	λελυμένου	λελυμένων	λελυμένων	λελυμένων
DAT λελυμένῳ	λελυμένη	λελυμένῳ	λελυμένοις	λελυμέναις	λελυμένοις
ACC λελυμένον	λελυμένην	λελυμένον	λελυμένους	λελυμένας	λελυμένα

19.4 Morphology

Perfect Active Participles

Perfect active participles have several component parts: reduplication + perfect tense-form stem + tense formative (κ) + active voice morpheme (οτ, υι)[4] + case ending.

λελυκότες → λε + λυ + κ + οτ + ες

Note that perfect active participles differ from both present and aorist forms (masculine and neuter) which include a nu (ν) as part of the active voice morpheme: present = λύοντος; aorist = λύσαντος. The endings for the active voice follow third declension (masculine and neuter) and first declension (feminine: alpha pattern) endings.

---

[2] The case ending is sigma (ς), which causes the tau (τ) to drop out and omicron (ο) to lengthen to an omega (ω): λελυκοτ + ς = λελυκοτς → λελυκος → λελυκως. Regarding morphological comments made concerning this chart, see William D. Mounce, *Basics of Biblical Greek: Grammar*, 4th ed. (Grand Rapids: Zondervan, 2019), 339.

[3] Like the masculine form, the case ending of the neuter is sigma (ς), which causes the tau (τ) to drop out. This time, however, the omicron (ο) does not lengthen: λελυκοτ + ς = λελυκοτς → λελυκος.

[4] Technically, the feminine active voice morpheme is υια, but for simplification, we are considering the alpha (α) as part of the case ending.

Perfect Middle/Passive Participles

Perfect middle/passive participles have similar component parts as active participles, minus the tense formative and connecting vowel: reduplication + perfect tense-form stem + middle/passive voice morpheme (μεν)[5] + case ending.

λελυμένοι → λε + λυ + μεν + οι

Again, note that the connecting vowel is missing (cf. λυόμενοι and λυσάμενοι). The endings for the middle/passive voice follow first (feminine: eta pattern) and second (masculine and neuter) patterns.

19.5 Second Perfects

Several verbs have somewhat irregular perfect forms. Such verbs lack the tense formative kappa (κ) in the active voice. Below are the most common verbs that fall into this category, including all the various inflected forms used in the New Testament.[6] We recommend students focus on recognizing (not memorizing) these forms.

ἀκούω	→	ἀκηκοότας
ἀνοίγω	→	ἀνεῳγότα
γίνομαι	→	γεγονώς, γεγονότι, γεγονότες, γεγονότας, γεγονός, γεγονυῖα
ἔρχομαι	→	ἐληλυθώς, ἐληλυθότα, ἐληλυθυῖαν
λαμβάνω	→	εἰληφώς
πείθω	→	πεποιθώς, πεποιθότες, πεποιθότας

19.6 Genitive Absolutes

A *genitive absolute* is a subcategory of the adverbial participle used to provide background information. A genitive absolute can be a present, aorist, or perfect participle. It is called "absolute" because it is loosed (Latin: *absolutus*) from syntactical cords and has no grammatical relationship to the rest of the sentence. Both the participle and the subject of the participle are in the genitive case, and they agree in gender and number. Translate the genitive absolute as a normal adverbial participial phrase, most of which will be temporal (though any category of adverbial participle can apply).

Ταῦτα <u>αὐτοῦ</u> **λαλοῦντος** πολλοὶ ἐπίστευσαν εἰς αὐτόν
"**As** <u>he</u> **was saying** these things, many believed in him" (John 8:30).

---

[5] Technically, the masculine and feminine middle/passive voice morphemes are μενο and μενη, but for simplification, we are considering the omicron (ο) or eta (η) as part of the case ending.

[6] Mounce also lists these six verbs as having the most common irregular perfect participles (*Basics of Biblical Greek*, 348).

In the example, both the participle (λαλοῦντος) and the subject of the participle (αὐτοῦ) are in the genitive case. Notice that you do *not* translate a genitive absolute with the typical "of." Also note that the subject of the main verb (πολλοί, "many") is different than the subject of the participle (αὐτοῦ). To differentiate the two subjects, the genitive case is used for the subject of the participle. These constructions are typically found at the beginning of a clause or sentence. By employing the genitive forms, the author visually and phonetically sets these words apart from the rest of the sentence to be translated as a self-contained dependent clause.

19.7 Periphrastic Participles

A *periphrastic participle* is a participle in construction with the verb εἰμί. Unlike English, Greek does not normally use helping verbs (ἐδίδασκεν [impf act ind 3rd sg] = "he was teaching"). Occasionally, however, a participle is used in conjunction with either the present, imperfect, or future form of εἰμί. For example, ἦν διδάσκων could also be translated "he was teaching." Here we have the imperfect indicative of εἰμί (ἦν) followed by a present participle. Because this construction uses two words to convey essentially the same information that could be conveyed with one word, it is called a "periphrastic" (i.e., a "round about" [περί] or less concise way "to say" [φράσις] something). Also note that the verb εἰμί and the participle are not necessarily next to each other but are often separated in the sentence, though the verb εἰμί will precede the participle about 70 percent of the time.

Periphrastic constructions are especially common in the writings of Luke. Grammarians debate why ancient authors chose periphrastic constructions rather than simply indicative verbs (ἦν διδάσκων vs. ἐδίδασκεν). The most likely explanation is that (1) sometimes an author wanted to vary his style and found a periphrastic construction beautiful or helpful in accomplishing that goal, and (2) a periphrastic construction may place greater emphasis on the verbal aspect of the participle than an indicative construction alone. So, for example, in our illustration (ἦν διδάσκων vs. ἐδίδασκεν), the periphrastic construction arguably places more stress on the imperfective (progressive) aspect of teaching.

Here are the possible combinations of Greek periphrastics:

PERIPHRASTIC PARTICIPLES				
εἰμί	+	Participle	=	Tense-Form Equivalent
Present				Present
Imperfect	+	Present	=	Imperfect
Future				Future
Present				Perfect
Imperfect	+	Perfect	=	Pluperfect
Future				Future Perfect

19.8 Future Participles

There are only thirteen future participles in the New Testament, so they don't warrant a separate chapter.[7] They are similar in form to present participles with the addition of a sigma (σ) to the stem for the active (λύσοντος) and middle (λυσομένου) voices and a –θησ– for the passive voice (λυθησομένου). The future participle presents the action as a whole (perfective aspect), like the aorist, and can be divided into two camps: anarthrous and articular usage.

If a future participle occurs anarthrously (without a preceding article) it usually communicates a purpose in relation to the main verb. For example, in Matt 27:49 we read, "But the rest said, 'Let's see if Elijah comes (ἔρχεται) **to save** (σώσων, fut act ptc, masc nom sg) Him!'" Here the future participle expresses purpose in relation to the nearby indicative verb (ἔρχεται) and is future-referring in relation to this verb. Articular future participles (i.e., ones preceded by an article) are simply future-referring and do not express purpose. For example, see Luke 22:49: "When those around him saw **what was going to happen** (τὸ ἐσόμενον), they asked, 'Lord, should we strike with the sword?'" τὸ ἐσόμενον is a future middle participle, neuter accusative singular, from εἰμί, translated here as the substantive, "what was going to happen."[8]

19.9 Practice

A. Paradigms: Memorize the perfect active, middle, and passive participle paradigms of λύω (masc only) (see section 19.3). Then write out each paradigm ten times from memory.

B. Parsing: Parse the following words.

1. πεποιθώς

2. πεποιηκόσιν

3. βεβλημένην

4. γεγεννημένον

5. πεπιστευκότων

6. ἐγνωκότες

7. σώσων

---

[7] The thirteen New Testament forms are ἄξων, ἀποδώσοντες, γενησόμενον, ἐσόμενον, κατακρινῶν, κακώσων, λαληθησομένων, παραδώσων, ποιήσων, προσκυνήσων (2x), συναντήσοντα, and σώσων.

[8] Our understanding of the future participle was significantly shaped by A. T. Robertson's explanation. See *A Grammar of the Greek New Testament in the Light of Historical Research*, 4th ed. (Nashville: Broadman, 1934), 877–78.

8. γεγραμμένα

9. γεγονότας

10. ἠγαπημένῳ

C. **Participle Usage:** Indicate whether the following participles are used Attributively (A), Substantivally (S), Adverbially as a Genitive Absolute (GA), or Periphrastically (P).

1. _____ οἱ ἄνδρες οἱ ἀπεσταλμένοι

2. _____ οἱ ἀπεσταλμένοι εὗρον καθὼς εἶπεν αὐτοῖς

3. _____ καὶ ἦν ἐκβάλλων δαιμόνιον

4. _____ τὸ πῦρ τὸ αἰώνιον τὸ ἡτοιμασμένον τῷ διαβόλῳ

5. _____ ἐν τῷ ἠγαπημένῳ

6. _____ καὶ καταβαινόντων αὐτῶν ἐκ τοῦ ὄρους

7. _____ ἀδελφοί, οἱ ἠγαπημένοι ὑπὸ τοῦ θεοῦ

8. _____ εἰς μαρτύριον τῶν λαληθησομένων

9. _____ τὸ ὕδωρ τὸ γεγενημένον οἶνον

10. _____ καὶ ἐσθιόντων αὐτῶν εἶπεν

D. **Translation:** Translate the following sentences.

1. ἔλεγεν οὖν ὁ Ἰησοῦς πρὸς τοὺς πεπιστευκότας αὐτῷ Ἰουδαίους (John 8:31).

2. ἀκούοντος δὲ παντὸς τοῦ λαοῦ εἶπεν τοῖς μαθηταῖς αὐτοῦ (Luke 20:45).

3. καὶ ἦν κηρύσσων εἰς τὰς συναγωγὰς τῆς Ἰουδαίας (Luke 4:44).

4. ἐγένετο ἄνθρωπος, ἀπεσταλμένος παρὰ θεοῦ, ὄνομα αὐτῷ Ἰωάννης (John 1:6).

5. τὸ γεγεννημένον ἐκ τῆς σαρκὸς σάρξ ἐστιν, καὶ τὸ γεγεννημένον ἐκ τοῦ πνεύματος πνεῦμά ἐστιν (John 3:6).

6. ἔτι λαλοῦντος τοῦ Πέτρου τὰ ῥήματα ταῦτα (these) ἐπέπεσεν (ἐπιπίπτω, I fall upon) τὸ πνεῦμα τὸ ἅγιον ἐπὶ πάντας τοὺς ἀκούοντας τὸν λόγον (Acts 10:44).

7. καλέσω τὸν οὐ λαόν μου λαόν μου καὶ τὴν οὐκ ἠγαπημένην ἠγαπημένην (Rom 9:25).

8. καὶ διὰ παντὸς νυκτὸς (night) καὶ ἡμέρας ἐν τοῖς μνήμασιν (tombs) καὶ ἐν τοῖς ὄρεσιν ἦν κράζων (Mark 5:5).

9. καὶ ἐκπορευομένου αὐτοῦ ἐκ τοῦ ἱεροῦ λέγει αὐτῷ εἷς τῶν μαθητῶν αὐτοῦ, Διδάσκαλε (Mark 13:1).

10. ὁ σπείρων τὸν λόγον σπείρει . . . εὐθὺς ἔρχεται ὁ Σατανᾶς καὶ αἴρει τὸν λόγον τὸν ἐσπαρμένον εἰς αὐτούς (Mark 4:14–15).

11. καὶ ἐξελθόντος αὐτοῦ ἐκ τοῦ πλοίου εὐθὺς ὑπήντησεν (met) αὐτῷ ἐκ τῶν μνημείων (tombs) ἄνθρωπος ἐν πνεύματι ἀκαθάρτῳ (unclean) (Mark 5:2).

12. οὗ (where) γὰρ εἰσιν δύο ἢ τρεῖς συνηγμένοι εἰς τὸ ἐμὸν (my) ὄνομα, ἐκεῖ εἰμι ἐν μέσῳ αὐτῶν (Matt 18:20).

13. [. . .which the Lord will give me on that day . . .] οὐ μόνον δὲ ἐμοὶ ἀλλὰ καὶ πᾶσι τοῖς ἠγαπηκόσι τὴν ἐπιφάνειαν (appearing) αὐτοῦ (2 Tim 4:8).

14. ἔτι γὰρ Χριστὸς ὄντων ἡμῶν ἀσθενῶν (weak) ἔτι κατὰ καιρὸν ὑπὲρ ἀσεβῶν (ungodly) ἀπέθανεν (Rom 5:6).

15. ἦσαν καθήμενοι Φαρισαῖοι καὶ νομοδιδάσκαλοι (law-teachers) οἳ ἦσαν ἐληλυθότες ἐκ πάσης κώμης (village) τῆς Γαλιλαίας καὶ Ἰουδαίας καὶ Ἰερουσαλήμ (Luke 5:17).

E. Translation: Translate the following sentences into Greek.

1. The beloved child, having been bound, was raised by the Lord in their midst.

2. After Jesus healed those remaining, the entire crowd went to the mountain.

3. So then, a place which has been prepared for us is our hope now.

4. The priest comes and offers an animal (ζῷον) here.

5. He was teaching (periphrastic) the women while raising only (μόνον) his right hand.

19.10 Vocabulary[9]

ἀλλήλων	of one another (*alien*)
ἑαυτοῦ, –ῆς, –οῦ	(of) himself, herself, itself
ἐκεῖνος, –η, –ο	that; those (pl)
ἐμαυτοῦ, –ῆς	myself
οὗτος, αὕτη, τοῦτο	this; these (pl)
σεαυτοῦ, –ῆς	(of) yourself
τις, τι	someone, certain
τίς, τί	who? which? what?
ἐμός, –ή, –όν	my, mine
ἔσχατος, –η, –ον	last (*eschatology*)
ἴδιος, –α, –ον	one's own, peculiar (*idiot*)
κακός, –ή, –όν	bad, evil (*cacophony*)
ὅσος, –η, –ον	as much as
τοιοῦτος, –αύτη, οὗτον	of such a kind, such as this
πῶς	how?

[9] To hear an author of your textbook read through the vocabulary for chapter 19, go to bit.ly/greekvocab19 or beginninggreek.com.

/////////////////

CHAPTER 20

OTHER PRONOUNS

20.1 Overview[1]

In chapter 9, we discussed personal pronouns (ἐγώ, σύ, αὐτός) and relative pronouns (ὅς, ἥ, ὅ). In this chapter, we will introduce five other types: (1) demonstrative, (2) reflexive, (3) reciprocal, (4) interrogative, and (5) indefinite pronouns. In addition, we will consider pronominal adjectives (i.e., words that function syntactically like adjectives but have the meaning of a pronoun).

20.2 Significance

One of the things you will learn about in this chapter is demonstrative pronouns. (In English, "this" or "that" are demonstrative pronouns.) An ancient writer could employ demonstrative pronouns for a variety of reasons. The apostle John seems to use them as a matter of idiolect (personal style), with many of his demonstrative pronouns seeming interchangeable with personal pronouns. Such demonstratives are usually translated into modern English Bibles as personal pronouns.[2] Otherwise, a modern English reader would be jarred by the unusual frequency of "this one," "that one," and "those ones" in the translation without apparent contrast or emphasis indicated by the broader context.

Another reason an ancient author employed demonstrative pronouns was for rhetorical emphasis or contrast. We use such pronouns the same way in English: "Don't be like **that** man." The word "that" here has a disparaging function by implicitly contrasting "that" man with other men, who are apparently not as bad as he.

---

[1] For an overview video lecture of chapter 20, go to bit.ly/greeklecture20 or beginninggreek.com.
[2] E.g., John 13:25, ἐκεῖνος, "that one," translated as "he."

In Jas 1:7, James writes, "That person should not expect to receive anything from the Lord" (NIV). Even without further context, we can detect the heightened emphasis and contrast that comes from employing the demonstrative pronoun "that" (ἐκεῖνος in Greek). What exactly is wrong with *that* man such that he should not think he will receive anything from the Lord? James tells us that man has not brought his petitions to God in faith, but rather with doubting (1:6). In the surrounding verses, James describes the doubting petitioner with some colorful images—he is like a blown and tossed sea wave (v. 6), double-minded and unstable in all his ways (v. 8).

James's teaching echoes several places in Jesus's earthly ministry in which the Lord demanded faith of those who came to him. In Matt 9:29, as Jesus touched the blind men's eyes, he said, "According to your faith be it done to you" (ESV). To the father of the demon-possessed child who was wavering in unbelief, Jesus said, "All things are possible for one who believes" (Mark 9:23 ESV). When Jesus was asked by his disciples why they could not cast out an evil spirit, he responded, "Because of your little faith. For truly I tell you, if you have faith the size of a mustard seed, you will tell this mountain, 'Move from here to there,' and it will move. Nothing will be impossible for you" (Matt 17:20). Likewise, the author of Hebrews warns, "Without faith it is impossible to please God, since the one who draws near to him must believe that he exists and that he rewards those who seek him" (Heb 11:6).

When James calls for faith, he is not calling for Christians to work up some sort of invisible faith-o-meter so that they "feel" that the prayer is being answered in an overly-specific way. Rather, Christians are to approach God trustingly—knowing he is powerful, good, and kindly disposed to them because of the relationship secured through Christ's perfect life and atoning death. The opposite of such faith is to think God does not really care, is not good, and does not keep his fatherly promises in Christ.

Sensitive Christians can sometimes fret a great deal over whether they have enough faith. In James's strong words about doubt, he is not addressing such sensitive believers. Rather, James is rebuking the presumptuous and erratic petitioner who seeks to live independent of God at one moment, but offers up a quick, unbelieving plea when desperation or inclination strikes. That person cannot expect to receive anything from God.[3]

20.3 Demonstrative Pronouns

Types of Demonstrative Pronouns

English has two different types of **demonstrative pronouns**: near ("this" [sg], "these" [pl]) and far ("that" [sg], "those" [pl]). For example, if someone says,

[3] A portion of this section was adapted from Robert L. Plummer, "James" in *ESV Expository Commentary: Hebrews–Revelation*, vol. 12 (Wheaton: Crossway, 2018), 230–32.

"**This** pen is mine," the word "this" is the near demonstrative pronoun. It is termed "near" because it refers to something that is physically or conceptually close by. In contrast, if someone says, "This pen is mine; **that** one is yours," the term "that" refers to something farther removed.

Like English, Greek has two different types of demonstrative pronouns: near (οὗτος, αὕτη, τοῦτο) and far (ἐκεῖνος, –η, –ο). The distinction between these two types of pronouns is often not so much spatial (close versus far) but conceptual (e.g., something recently mentioned versus something mentioned earlier in the context). The forms for both near and far demonstrative pronouns should be familiar to you since they closely follow the endings of first and second declension nouns or adjectives.

	SINGULAR			PLURAL		
	MASC	*FEM*	*NEUT*	*MASC*	*FEM*	*NEUT*
NOM	οὗτος	αὕτη	τοῦτο	οὗτοι	αὗται	ταῦτα
GEN	τούτου	ταύτης	τούτου	τούτων	τούτων	τούτων
DAT	τούτῳ	ταύτῃ	τούτῳ	τούτοις	ταύταις	τούτοις
ACC	τοῦτον	ταύτην	τοῦτο	τούτους	ταύτας	ταῦτα

NEAR DEMONSTRATIVE PRONOUNS

There are four features to these forms that should be highlighted.

1. The nominative forms for the masculine (οὗτος, οὗτοι) and feminine (αὕτη, αὗται) genders lack the initial tau (τ) and instead have a rough breathing mark—just like the Greek articles.

2. All feminine forms (excluding the genitive plural: τούτων) and the neuter nominative and accusative plural form (ταῦτα) have the diphthong αυ instead of ου in the first syllable. One easy way to memorize this distinction is that endings with an omicron (ο) or omega (ω) use ου, and endings with an alpha (α) or eta (η) use αυ. Demonstrative pronouns keep all their vowels/diphthongs consistently in the same family—either the "o" vowel family or the "a" vowel family.

3. The neuter nominative and accusative singular forms lack a nu (ν) on the ending (τοῦτο; cf. τέκνον).

4. It is important to distinguish the feminine demonstrative pronouns αὕτη ("this [woman]") and αὗται ("these [women]") from the feminine personal pronouns αὐτή ("she") and αὐταί ("they"). The former have rough breathing marks and accents on the first syllable whereas the latter have smooth breathing marks and accents on the last syllable.

As mentioned above, the far demonstrative pronoun also closely follows first and second declension noun endings (ἐκεῖνος, ἐκείνη, ἐκεῖνο). Again, the only difference is that the neuter nominative and accusative singular forms lack a nu (ν) on the ending (ἐκεῖνο; cf. τέκνον).

Uses of Demonstrative Pronouns

Pronominal Use. Demonstratives can be used pronominally (i.e., as pronouns) or adjectivally. When a demonstrative functions as a pronoun, its gender and number are determined by its antecedent; its case is determined by its function in the sentence. Some pronouns do not modify a noun; thus, in English translation, we frequently need to add a clarifying gender-specific noun: οὗτος = "this one" or "this man"; αὕτη = "this woman"; ἐκεῖνος = "that one" or "that man," etc.

- **οὗτός** ἐστιν ὁ υἱός μου ὁ ἀγαπητός, "**This [one]** is my beloved Son" (Matt 17:5).

- **αὕτη** ἦν πλήρης ἔργων ἀγαθῶν, "**This woman** was full of good works" (Acts 9:36 NKJV).

Sometimes, based on context, a demonstrative pronoun has a weakened force (especially in John's writings) and should be translated as a personal pronoun (οὗτός or ἐκεῖνος = "he"; αὕτη or ἐκείνη = "she").

- **οὗτος** ἦλθεν εἰς μαρτυρίαν, "**He** came as a witness" (John 1:7).

- οὐκ ἦν **ἐκεῖνος** τὸ φῶς, "**He** was not the light" (John 1:8).

Adjectival Use. When used adjectivally, a demonstrative pronoun agrees with the noun it modifies in gender, case, and number. Unlike normal adjectives, however, these pronouns are placed in the predicate position instead of the attributive position. The article is placed in front of the noun but never in front of the demonstrative pronoun.

- **οὗτοι** οἱ λόγοι πιστοὶ καὶ ἀληθινοί εἰσιν, "**these** words are faithful and true" (Rev 21:5).

- εἶπεν δὲ πρὸς αὐτοὺς τὴν παραβολὴν **ταύτην**, "So He spoke **this** parable to them" (Luke 15:3 NKJV).

- πᾶς ὁ πεσὼν ἐπ᾽ **ἐκεῖνον** τὸν λίθον συνθλασθήσεται, "everyone who falls on **that** stone will be broken to pieces" (Luke 20:18).

20.4 Reflexive Pronouns

A ***reflexive pronoun*** is used when the subject of the verb both gives and receives the action. In English, the form is created by taking a personal pronoun and adding "self" or "selves" to the end of the word: "myself," "yourself," "himself/herself/

itself," "ourselves," "yourselves," or "themselves." In the sentence, "I am feeding the child," the subject "I" is different than the object of the sentence (= "child"). But when both the subject and the object refer to the same entity, then a reflexive pronoun is needed (e.g., "I am feeding **myself**").

In Greek, reflexive pronouns function similar to those in English. Such pronouns occur in multiple forms:

- **First Person**: ἐμαυτοῦ ("myself").

- **Second Person**: σεαυτοῦ ("yourself").

- **Third Person**: ἑαυτοῦ ("himself," "itself"), ἑαυτῆς ("herself," "itself"), ἑαυτῶν ("themselves").

The first and second person reflexive pronouns are formed by adding ἐμε or σε to the third person personal pronoun αὐτός. These forms never appear in the nominative case. The first and second person reflexive pronouns have no distinct plural forms in the New Testament, but the third person plural form is sometimes used for the first and second person. In such cases, context must determine the person. For example, in 1 John 5:21 (τεκνία, φυλάξατε **ἑαυτὰ** ἀπὸ τῶν εἰδώλων, "little children, guard **yourselves** from idols"), the third person reflexive pronoun ἑαυτά is functioning as a second person pronoun. Also note that the third person forms have a rough breathing mark (ἑαυτοῦ). The middle voice is also rarely used to communicate a reflexive idea without using a reflexive pronoun (e.g., "So Judas threw the money into the temple and left. Then he went away and **hanged himself** [ἀπήγξατο])" (Matt 27:5 NIV).

The plural forms of the reflexive pronoun are the same for the first, second, and third person. The explicit or implied subject in the sentence will let you know whether to translate the plural reflexive pronoun as "ourselves," "yourselves," or "themselves" in English.

PLURAL REFLEXIVE PRONOUNS		
	MASC	FEM	NEUT
GEN	ἑαυτῶν	ἑαυτῶν	ἑαυτῶν
DAT	ἑαυτοῖς	ἑαυταῖς	ἑαυτοῖς
ACC	ἑαυτούς	ἑαυτάς	ἑαυτά

20.5 Reciprocal Pronouns

The **reciprocal pronoun** represents an interchange of the verbal action among a previously introduced plural subject. For example, if someone says, "We ought to respect **one another**," the words "one another" indicate that those involved should be participating in the action stated. In other words, those who offer love to others should also be receiving love from others. There should be a reciprocating (or give-and-take) participation in the action by the constituent parties of the plural subject.

Likewise, the pronoun ἀλλήλων ("one another") is a reciprocal pronoun because the action stated in the context should be both given and received. For example, John states, ἀγαπητοί, ἀγαπῶμεν **ἀλλήλους**, "Dear friends, let us love **one another**" (1 John 4:7). Believers are thus commanded to love other believers and should not be content with merely being on the receiving end.

Because this pronoun by definition involves two or more parties, it always occurs in the plural. Finally, you will notice that the genitive plural is given in the vocabulary list (ἀλλήλων). This is because the nominative form does not occur. The reciprocal pronoun only has three forms in the New Testament (all masculine): genitive plural (ἀλλήλων = lexical form), dative plural (ἀλλήλοις), and accusative plural (ἀλλήλους).

20.6 Interrogative Pronouns

An ***interrogative pronoun*** is one that introduces a question such as who? which? or what? The interrogative pronoun in Greek is τίς ("who?") or τί ("what?"). The neuter form τί can also be used adverbially to mean "why?" Because these pronouns ask a question, there will be a question mark (;) at the end of a sentence that uses one of them.

- τίς εἶ; "**Who** are you?" (John 1:22).

- τί ἐστιν τοῦτο; "**What** is this?" (Mark 1:27).

- τί με ἐρωτᾷς περὶ τοῦ ἀγαθοῦ; "**Why** do you ask me about what is good?" (Matt 19:17).

The endings for interrogative pronouns follow the same pattern as third declension nouns. The accent is always on the first syllable and is always acute (ί). It is never changed to a grave (ὶ).[4]

	SINGULAR[5]		PLURAL	
	MASC/FEM	*NEUTER*	*MASC/FEM*	*NEUTER*
NOM	τίς	τί	τίνες	τίνα
GEN	τίνος	τίνος	τίνων	τίνων
DAT	τίνι	τίνι	τίσι(ν)	τίσι(ν)
ACC	τίνα	τί	τίνας	τίνα

---

[4] Also, remember that questions negated with οὐ expect a positive answer whereas questions negated with μή expect a negative answer (see section 6.7).

[5] Masc/fem translation (sg or pl): who, whose, to/for whom, whom. Neuter translation (sg or pl): what, of what, to/for what, what.

Below are examples of interrogative pronouns from the New Testament:

Nom τίς ἐστιν οὗτος; "**Who** is this?" (Matt 21:10).

Gen τίνος υἱός ἐστιν; "**Whose** son is he?" (Matt 22:42).

Dat τίνι γὰρ εἶπέν ποτε τῶν ἀγγέλων . . . ; "For **to which** of the angels did he ever say . . .?" (Heb 1:5).[6]

Acc τίνα ζητεῖτε; "**Whom** do you seek?" (John 18:7 ESV).

20.7 Indefinite Pronouns

An *indefinite pronoun* is one that is used when a person or thing is left unspecified ("someone," "anyone," "a certain one," etc.). Like interrogative pronouns, the forms for indefinite pronouns follow the paradigms of third declension nouns and thus look identical. Unlike interrogative pronouns, however, the accent is often absent and *never* on the first syllable. Rather, it appears on the second syllable and is sometimes changed to a grave (ì).

	SINGULAR[7]		PLURAL[8]	
	MASC/FEM	NEUTER	MASC/FEM	NEUTER
NOM	τις	τι	τινές	τινά
GEN	τινός	τινός	τινῶν	τινῶν
DAT	τινί	τινί	τισί(ν)	τισί(ν)
ACC	τινά	τι	τινάς	τινά

The indefinite pronoun can function pronominally without a noun or like an adjective modifying an explicit noun.

- εἴ τις ἔρχεται πρός με, "if **anyone** comes to me" (Luke 14:26).

- ἄνθρωπός τις εἶχεν δύο υἱούς, "a **certain** man had two sons" (Luke 15:11 NKJV).

20.8 Pronominal Adjectives

A *pronominal adjective* is an adjective that has the meaning of a pronoun. As such, it functions as a typical adjective, but its meaning is the same as a pronoun. For example, a more common way to communicate possession is to use a pronoun in the genitive case: ὁ λόγος **μου**, "**my** word." Notice that the noun λόγος is in the nominative case, and the personal pronoun μου is in the genitive ("of me" or "my").

---

[6] In some contexts, it might be best to translate τίνι "to whom."

[7] Masc/fem singular translation: someone, of someone, to/for someone, someone. Neuter singular translation: certain things, of certain things, to/for certain things, certain things.

[8] Masc/fem plural translation: certain ones, of certain ones, to/for certain ones, certain ones. Neuter plural translation: certain things, of certain things, to/for certain things, certain things.

In contrast, a pronominal adjective such as ἐμός ("my") functions as an adjective.⁹ Consequently, it will agree with the noun it modifies in gender, case, and number and will decline like first and second declension adjectives. For instance, ὁ λόγος **ὁ ἐμός** ("my word") has the same meaning as the example above, but this time the term ἐμός agrees with λόγος in gender (masc), case (nom), and number (sg). Pronominal adjectives are perhaps sometimes used for greater emphasis, as when we express possession emphatically in English with the addition of the word "very" or "own": "my very word" or "my own word."

20.9 Practice

A. Parsing: Parse the following words and include the pronoun classification (personal, relative, near demonstrative, far demonstrative, reflexive, reciprocal, interrogative, or indefinite) or note that it is a pronominal adjective.

1. τίνες
2. ταύτῃ
3. αὐτήν
4. ἐκείνου
5. σεαυτόν
6. τινάς
7. μοι
8. οἵ
9. ἐμαυτῷ
10. ὑμεῖς
11. ἐμόν
12. ἡμῶν
13. ἀλλήλους
14. ἥ
15. σε
16. ἑαυτοῖς

---

⁹ Other common pronominal adjectives include σός ("your," sg), ἡμέτερος ("our"), and ὑμέτερος ("your," pl).

B. Matching: Match the Greek phrase with the English translation.

1.	_____ αὕτη ἡ γυνή	A.	these are the sons
2.	_____ εἴ τις ἔρχεται	B.	Do you see anything?
3.	_____ ταῦτα εἶπεν	C.	What do you say about yourself?
4.	_____ ὁ δοῦλος ἐκεῖνος	D.	my command
5.	_____ γυναῖκές τινες	E.	to myself
6.	_____ τίνα ζητεῖς;	F.	with one another
7.	_____ ἡ ἐντολὴ ἡ ἐμή	G.	this woman
8.	_____ τίς ἐστιν οὗτος;	H.	a certain woman
9.	_____ πρὸς ἐμαυτόν	I.	Who is this?
10.	_____ οὗτοί εἰσιν οἱ υἱοί	J.	a certain man
11.	_____ γυνὴ τις	K.	some women
12.	_____ τί λέγεις περὶ σεαυτοῦ;	L.	Whom are you seeking?
13.	_____ ἄνθρωπός τις	M.	that slave
14.	_____ τι βλέπεις;	N.	if anyone comes
15.	_____ σὺν ἀλλήλοις	O.	he said these things

C. Translation: Translate the following sentences.

1. ἀληθῶς (truly) οὗτος ὁ ἄνθρωπος υἱὸς θεοῦ ἦν (Mark 15:39).

2. εἰ δέ τις πνεῦμα Χριστοῦ οὐκ ἔχει, οὗτος οὐκ ἔστιν αὐτοῦ (Rom 8:9).

3. κοινωνίαν (fellowship) ἔχομεν μετ᾽ ἀλλήλων (1 John 1:7).

4. ἐκεῖνος δὲ ἔλεγεν περὶ τοῦ ναοῦ τοῦ σώματος αὐτοῦ (John 2:21).

5. ἀγαπήσεις τὸν πλησίον (neighbor) σου ὡς σεαυτόν (Mark 12:31).

6. οὗτός ἐστιν ἀληθῶς ὁ σωτὴρ (Savior) τοῦ κόσμου (John 4:42).

7. ἀπ᾽ ἐμαυτοῦ οὐκ ἐλήλυθα (John 7:28).

8. ταῦτα πάντα ἐλάλησεν ὁ Ἰησοῦς ἐν παραβολαῖς τοῖς ὄχλοις (Matt 13:34).

9. ὁ δὲ Ἰησοῦς εἶπεν αὐτῷ, Τί με λέγεις ἀγαθόν; οὐδεὶς ἀγαθὸς εἰ μὴ εἷς ὁ θεός (Mark 10:18).

10. αὕτη ἡ ἐντολή ἐστιν, καθὼς ἠκούσατε ἀπ' ἀρχῆς, [that you walk in love] (2 John 6).

11. καὶ οὐκ ἔχουσιν ῥίζαν (root) ἐν ἑαυτοῖς (Mark 4:17).

12. οὐκ οἶδα τὸν ἄνθρωπον τοῦτον ὃν λέγετε (Mark 14:71).

13. σὺ μαθητὴς εἶ ἐκείνου, ἡμεῖς δὲ τοῦ Μωϋσέως ἐσμὲν μαθηταί (John 9:28).

14. τίς με ῥύσεται (will rescue) ἐκ τοῦ σώματος τοῦ θανάτου τούτου; (Rom 7:24).

15. ἡ κρίσις (judgment) ἡ ἐμὴ δικαία ἐστίν, ὅτι οὐ ζητῶ τὸ θέλημα (will) τὸ ἐμὸν ἀλλὰ τὸ θέλημα (will) τοῦ πέμψαντός με (John 5:30).

D. Translation: Translate the following sentences into Greek.

1. How shall we live in these last days?

2. A certain man came to his own father.

3. You (sg) will love one another as much as yourself.

4. I saw myself in my child. [Use a pronominal adjective here.]

5. Whose is that evil son?

20.10 Vocabulary[10]

ἁμαρτάνω	I sin (ἥμαρτον) (*hamartology*)
βούλομαι	I wish, want, desire (*volition*)
δεῖ	It is necessary, one must/should
δοκέω	I seem, suppose, think (*Docetism*)
δύναμαι	I am able, can (*dynamic*)[11]
θέλω	I want, wish, desire (*Monothelitism*)
μέλλω	I am about to, am going to
θέλημα, θελήματος, τό	will, wish, desire
νύξ, νυκτός, ἡ	night

---

[10] To hear an author of your textbook read through the vocabulary for chapter 20, go to bit.ly/greekvocab20 or beginninggreek.com.

[11] Stative verbs, i.e., verbs referring to ongoing states—such as the state of "being able to" or "being powerful enough to"—are frequently middle-only.

μακάριος, –α, –ον	blessed, happy (*macarism*)
μηδείς, μηδεμία, μηδέν	no one, nothing (subst)
τυφλός, –ή, –όν	blind; blind person (subst)
πρό	before, in front of (gen) (prologue)
μηδέ	and not, nor
ὥστε	so that

How Can I See the Structure of a Text?[1]

Introduction to Diagramming

Many students learn Greek, not so they can take vocabulary tests, but so they can read the Greek New Testament, savor its message, and deliver those words of life to others. One essential part of discerning the meaning of any biblical text is understanding how the assertions within that text fit together. What is the author's main point? What appeals does he use to support his point? (e.g., logical? scriptural? emotional?) Also, it is important to consider how any discrete section of text relates to the sections around it and to the author's overarching purposes.

Biblical authors wrote their works to be read aloud to communities (Col 4:16). The original audiences, most of whom spoke Greek as a native language, unconsciously responded to the author's literary clues—discerning the author's purposes, arguments, and emphases. As modern persons who approach the Greek New Testament from a linguistic and chronological distance, we need to think more deliberately about the text's structure.

Greek scholars and teachers have developed several methods to discern and analyze the structure of the Greek text. At best, such methods simply help the reader to see clearly and think carefully about the literary clues that the biblical authors give us. In an intermediate-level Greek class or textbook (such as *Going Deeper with New Testament Greek*),[2] you will learn more about line diagramming, arcing, and discourse analysis. For now, we want to briefly introduce one method of visually representing the structure of the text—phrase diagramming.

Phrase diagrams are also called "sentence-flow," "thought-flow," or "argument" diagrams. They are not as elaborate or detailed as line diagrams or arcs, so they are more likely to be employed by the average student or pastor. Andy Naselli, Associate Professor of New Testament and Theology at Bethlehem College and Seminary, has called phrase diagramming "the

---

[1] Much of the material below is adapted from chap. 13, "Sentences, Diagramming & Discourse Analysis," of our book *Going Deeper with New Testament Greek*. See the next note for more information.

[2] Andreas J. Köstenberger, Benjamin L. Merkle, and Robert L. Plummer, *Going Deeper with New Testament Greek: An Intermediate Study of the Grammar and Syntax of the New Testament*, rev. ed. (Nashville: B&H Academic, 2020).

single most important aspect about knowing New Testament Greek."[3]

In phrase diagramming, the exegete breaks the text down into "phrases"—recognizable related units. Here we are using "phrase" in a non-technical sense, essentially referring to a portion of a sentence. The phrases are then indented and aligned to elucidate the structure. Some phrase diagrammers draw arrows between related grammatical elements to help make those relationships more visually explicit. Others syntactically label the phrase diagram to record the functional relationships of the parts.

Below are some basic principles for phrase diagramming.[4]

- Main or governing propositions should be further to the left on the page.

- Dependent elements are indented under the word(s) they modify.

- Parallel grammatical elements are indented the same distance on the page.

In English, we might represent a simple phrase diagram like this:

> I sent the letter
> > to my mother
> > about my new job
> > with a gift card enclosed

The student should note that no attempt is made to account for every syntactical relationship. Phrases need not be broken up more than is helpful in observing the author's flow of thought.[5] Students always learn much more from attempting a phrase diagram themselves rather than simply relying on someone else's work.

The volumes in the Exegetical Guide to the Greek New Testament (EGGNT) series include phrase diagrams of the biblical text. Suggested homiletical outlines based on the Greek structure are also provided. Below is a Greek diagram of Eph 4:1–3 by Benjamin Merkle from the EGGNT series, followed by an English phrase diagram that mimics the Greek structure.[6] Merkle's suggested homiletical outline from the EGGNT volume appears below the English phrase diagram.[7]

---

[3] Naselli made this written comment while reviewing a pre-publication copy of this manuscript. See also, http://andynaselli.com/languages. Naselli prefers the term "argument diagrams."

[4] These steps (worded slightly differently) are listed by William D. Mounce, *A Graded Reader of Biblical Greek* (Grand Rapids: Zondervan, 1996), xv. For additional instruction in phrase diagramming, see also Mounce, *Graded Reader*, xv–xxiii; Douglas S. Huffman, *The Handy Guide to New Testament Greek: Grammar, Syntax, Diagramming* (Grand Rapids: Kregel, 2012), 84–106; Richard Young, *Intermediate New Testament Greek: A Linguistic and Exegetical Approach* (Nashville: B&H, 1994), 268–73; Gordon D. Fee, *New Testament Exegesis: A Handbook for Students and Pastors*, 3rd ed. (Louisville, KY: Westminster/John Knox, 2002), 41–58; George H. Guthrie and J. Scott Duvall, *Biblical Greek Exegesis: A Graded Approach to Learning Intermediate and Advanced Greek* (Grand Rapids: Zondervan, 1998), 27–37. See also the diagrams in the EGGNT volumes (see the information in note 6 below) and chap. 12 in Andreas J. Köstenberger and Richard D. Patterson, *Invitation to Biblical Interpretation* (Grand Rapids: Kregel, 2011).

[5] Huffman says that students attempting a phrase diagram should remember this freeing question: *"How can I diagram the phrases of this paragraph so its structure is more visible to me?" Handy Guide to New Testament Greek*, 86, emphasis in original.

[6] Benjamin L. Merkle, *Ephesians*, Exegetical Guide to the Greek New Testament (Nashville: B&H, 2016), 112. The English translation is the author's.

[7] Merkle, 119.

Παρακαλῶ οὖν ὑμᾶς
      ἐγὼ ὁ δέσμιος
         ἐν κυρίῳ
ἀξίως περιπατῆσαι τῆς κλήσεως
           ἧς ἐκλήθητε,
      μετὰ πάσης ταπεινοφροσύνης καὶ πραΰτητος,
      μετὰ μακροθυμίας,
ἀνεχόμενοι ἀλλήλων ἐν ἀγάπῃ,
σπουδάζοντες τηρεῖν τὴν ἑνότητα τοῦ πνεύματος
          ἐν τῷ συνδέσμῳ τῆς εἰρήνης·

Therefore, I exhort you,
    I, the prisoner
        in the Lord,
to walk worthy of the calling
         to which you were called,
     with all humility and gentleness,
     with all patience
bearing with one another in love,
being eager to keep the unity of the Spirit
        in the bond of peace.

Walk Worthy of Our Calling (Eph 4:1–3)

1. The manner in which we should walk

   a. With humility
   b. With gentleness
   c. With patience

2. The means by which we should walk

   a. Bearing with one another in love
   b. Being eager to maintain unity of the Spirit in the bond of peace

Optional Assignment: Choose a short paragraph from 1 John. Then, using phrase diagramming, write out the Greek verses with subordinate elements indented underneath the portions they are modifying. If a clear structure emerges, use it to make a teaching/sermon outline. (Note the example provided above.)

CHAPTER 21

/////////////////

INFINITIVES

21.1 Overview[1]

An *infinitive* is a verbal noun. For example, in the sentence, "The dog jumped over the table," the term "jumped" is a verb that describes the action of the dog. But just as a verb can be used as a participle or verbal adjective ("the jumping dog"), it can also be used as an infinitive or verbal noun (**"To jump** is difficult for the dog"). In this last sentence, the phrase "to jump" functions as the subject of the verb "is difficult." Thus, in English, an infinitive is formed by the word "to" plus a verb. This chapter will discuss the forms and usage of Greek infinitives.

21.2 Significance

In Matt 4:17, we read,

> Ἀπὸ τότε ἤρξατο ὁ Ἰησοῦς **κηρύσσειν** καὶ **λέγειν**· μετανοεῖτε· ἤγγικεν γὰρ ἡ βασιλεία τῶν οὐρανῶν.
>
> From then on Jesus began **to preach** and **to say**, "Repent, because the kingdom of the heavens has come near." (authors' translation)

The two Greek words in bold are present active infinitives, translated "to preach" and "to say." They complete the idea of the aorist middle verb ἤρξατο, "began." Without these complementary infinitives to finish the author's verbal assertion, we would be left in suspense: "Jesus began . . ." (Began what?) "Well, he began **to preach** and **to say**." (The two Greek infinitives translated literally sound redundant to us, but the pleonastic style is reflective of an underlying Semitic idiom we often detect in the Gospels.)

---

[1] For an overview video lecture of chapter 21, go to bit.ly/greeklecture21 or beginninggreek.com.

As you will learn in this chapter, there are three possible tense-forms for an infinitive: present, aorist, and perfect. Why do you think Matthew chose present infinitives to complete the idea of ἤρξατο in Matt 4:17? What nuance are we missing in the English translation by simply translating the infinitives as "to" plus the meaning of the verb?

The unpublished work of S. M. Baugh, *Introduction to Greek Tense in the Non-Indicative Moods* (2009) is helpful for us here.[2] Baugh points out that in all eighty-seven instances of the verb ἄρχομαι followed by a complementary infinitive, the infinitive is in the present tense. This is an extremely strong default stylistic pattern, so we should not ask about any special nuance for the present tense. If an aorist or perfect tense infinitive had appeared in this verse, however, that would have been unusual and worthy of consideration. One reason you are learning Greek well (we pray!) is so that you will be guarded against over-interpreting default or expected grammatical constructions.

21.3 Definition and Description

Because an infinitive is a verbal noun, it has some features that are noun-like and other features that are verb-like. Like a verb, an infinitive

- has aspect (perfective, imperfective, or stative) and voice (active, middle, passive).
- can take a direct object or be modified by an adverb.
- is negated by μή (like all other non-indicative mood verbs).

In addition, the subject of the infinitive is in the accusative case rather than the nominative case.[3] In Mark 8:31 we read, δεῖ τὸν υἱὸν τοῦ ἀνθρώπου πολλὰ παθεῖν, "The Son of Man must suffer many things" (NIV). Notice that τὸν υἱόν ("the Son") functions as the subject of the infinitive (παθεῖν, "to suffer") even though it is in the accusative case.

Unlike finite verbs, infinitives do not conjugate. Finite verbs conjugate because each form is limited to a particular subject (first, second, third person singular or plural). For example, βλέπομεν Ἰησοῦν is translated "**we** see Jesus." The ending of the verb (–μεν) limits the subject to first person plural. If the author wanted to state "**he** sees Jesus," he would need to write βλέπει τὸν Ἰησοῦν. Because infinitives have no person and number, there is only one form for each tense-form and voice.[4]

---

[2] A pdf of Baugh's manuscript is available as a free download under the "Resources" tab at www.dailydoseofgreek.com.

[3] Technically, infinitives do not have a subject; rather, the noun in the accusative case acts as a subject (also called an accusative of general reference). This is similar to a genitive absolute where the noun or pronoun in the genitive case functions as the subject of the participle. When certain linking verbs (such as εἰμί or γίνομαι) are used as infinitives, they can take both a subject accusative and a predicate accusative (rather than a predicate nominative, as with the indicative). See, e.g., Rev 2:9 (ἐκ τῶν λεγόντων Ἰουδαίους εἶναι ἑαυτούς, "of those saying themselves to be Jews" [YLT] or "of those calling themselves Jews").

[4] Technically, an infinitive also does not have a mood (similar to a participle) since it is a verbal *noun*. For the sake of simplicity and parsing, however, it is categorized as a mood.

Like a noun, an infinitive can

- take an article (which is always neuter and singular = τό, τοῦ, and τῷ).
- have a variety of different case functions.
- occur after a preposition (infinitives following prepositions are always articular).

Infinitives appear quite frequently in the New Testament (almost 2,300 times). Of these, most are present and aorist. There are, however, forty-nine perfect infinitives and five future infinitives in the New Testament.[5]

21.4 Paradigms

PRESENT AND AORIST INFINITIVES[6]			
TENSE	VOICE	INFINITIVE	TRANSLATION
PRESENT	Active	λύειν	to loose, or to be loosing
	Middle Passive	λύεσθαι	to loose (for) oneself
			to be loosed
AORIST	Active	λῦσαι	to loose
	Middle	λύσασθαι	to loose (for) oneself
	Passive	λυθῆναι	to be loosed

21.5 Morphology

All present and aorist infinitives end in –ειν (λύειν) or –αι (λύεσθαι, λῦσαι, λύσασθαι, λυθῆναι).[7] The chart above only includes present and aorist forms since they are the most common by far. Perfect infinitives will be discussed below, but future infinitives do not warrant further comment.

Present

Present infinitives are based on the present stem of the verb and will either end in –ειν or –αι. The present infinitive of εἰμί is εἶναι. (There is no aorist form).

Contract verbs behave the same way as indicative mood verbs. Remember, only present tense-forms are affected by such changes since the aorist and perfect verbs add a consonant to the verb's stem. To be morphologically precise, the present infinitive

---

[5] The five future infinitives are in Acts 11:28; 23:30; 24:15; 27:10 (all ἔσεσθαι); and Heb 3:18 (εἰσελεύσεσθαι). These are the paradigm forms: active (λύσειν), middle (λύσεσθαι), and passive (λυθήσεσθαι).

[6] To hear a mnemonic song, go to bit.ly/greekinfinsong or beginninggreek.com.

[7] Perfect infinitives also end in –αι.

morpheme (sound unit) is εν, which is preceded by the epsilon connecting vowel (ε) when it is joined to the verb stem. Normally, this results in the infinitive ending ειν (ε + εν = ειν). With contract verbs, however, there is a domino effect of morphological combinations successively from left to right, resulting in a final combined form.

ἀγαπάω   ἀγαπα + ε + εν → ἀγαπᾶν

Starting at the left, alpha and epsilon combine to be alpha. Then, the new alpha combines with the remaining epsilon to be alpha.

ποιέω   ποιε + ε + εν → ποιεῖν

Starting at the left, epsilon combines with epsilon to be ει. Then, the diphthong ει combines with ε to be ει.

πληρόω   πληρο + ε + εν → πληροῦν

Starting at the left, omicron combines with epsilon to be ου. Then, the diphthong ου combines with epsilon to be ου.

Aorist

The aorist active and middle forms have the characteristic –σα and the aorist passive form has –θη (lengthened from –θε). Second aorist infinitives are built on the second aorist stem. Such verbs have present endings but have a spelling change of the stem (and a change in the accent). For example, we read in Matt 17:10, Ἠλίαν δεῖ **ἐλθεῖν** πρῶτον, "Elijah must **come** first" (NIV). Although ἐλθεῖν has a present tense-form ending (–εῖν), it is a second aorist form because the lexical form is ἔρχομαι. Below is a list of common second aorist infinitives. You should be able to recognize these if you know your second aorist indicative forms.

Lexical Form	Second Aorist Infinitive
ἄγω	ἀγαγεῖν
ἀποθνῄσκω	ἀποθανεῖν
βάλλω	βαλεῖν
γίνομαι	γενέσθαι
ἔρχομαι	ἐλθεῖν
ἐσθίω	φαγεῖν
εὑρίσκω	εὑρεῖν
λαμβάνω	λαβεῖν
λέγω	εἰπεῖν
ὁράω	ἰδεῖν
πίνω	πιεῖν
πίπτω	πεσεῖν

Some second aorist verbs end in –αι (καταβαίνω → καταβῆναι, φέρω → ἐνέγκαι, γινώσκω → γνῶναι). Note that aorist infinitives have no augment. (This is similar to all non-indicative aorist forms.)

Perfect

Because there are only forty-nine perfect infinitives in the New Testament, it is unnecessary to memorize their infinitive forms. They are, however, often easily identifiable because of the reduplication and –αι endings: active (**λελυκέναι**) middle/passive (**λελύσθαι**). Also, note that the active form has the additional kappa (λελυ**κ**έναι) and the middle/passive form has no connective vowel (λελύ-σθαι). Both elements are common with perfect verbs.

21.6 Usage

What makes infinitives difficult is not the forms (since they do not conjugate) but the various ways they are used in sentences and the challenge that presents for translation. Perhaps in the majority of cases, an infinitive can simply be translated as "to" + the meaning of the verb. Yet, as we will see from the categories that follow, infinitives are sometimes used in constructions with prepositions. Such uses are idiomatic constructions and cannot usually be translated word-for-word. The following prepositions are used with infinitives in the New Testament: εἰς (72x), ἐν (55x), διά (33x), μετά (15x), πρός (12x), and πρό (9x). When a preposition is used in combination with an infinitive, it will always precede the infinitive.

Below are several categories of uses that should be mastered. We begin with the most common use of the infinitive in the New Testament, the complementary function, which is directly parallel to English and easily translated. Additionally, all but the last category (i.e., substantival) could be classified as adverbial uses of the infinitive because the verbal quality is dominant.

Complementary

Certain (finite) verbs need to be completed by another verb. Sometimes the verb that completes the verbal idea is an infinitive. For example, in English we might say, "I am going **to read** a book tonight." The infinitive "to read" complements or completes the meaning of the verb "going." In Greek, the following verbs require a complementary infinitive: ἄρχομαι ("I am beginning"), δεῖ ("It is necessary"), δύναμαι ("I am able"), and μέλλω ("I am about to"). Additionally, the verbs βούλομαι ("I am wanting"), δοκέω ("I am thinking"), and θέλω ("I am wishing") can also be completed with an infinitive.[8]

- θέλομεν τὸν Ἰησοῦν **ἰδεῖν**, "<u>we want</u> **to see** Jesus" (John 12:21).

---

[8] Other verbs that take complementary infinitives include ἔξεστιν ("it is lawful"), κελεύω ("I order"), and ὀφείλω ("I ought").

- ἤρξατο ὁ Ἰησοῦς **κηρύσσειν**, "Jesus <u>began</u> **to preach**" (Matt 4:17).

- οὐδεὶς <u>δύναται</u> δυσὶ κυρίοις **δουλεύειν**, "none <u>is able</u> **to serve** two lords" (Matt 6:24 YLT).

Purpose

An infinitive can be used to communicate an intended purpose. This can be done using three different constructions: (1) infinitive alone, (2) infinitive with τοῦ, and (3) infinitive with εἰς τό. In most cases, you can still translate the purpose infinitive as "to" + the meaning of the verb.

- πορεύομαι **ἑτοιμάσαι** τόπον ὑμῖν, "I am going **to prepare** a place for you" (John 14:2).

- ἐξῆλθεν ὁ σπείρων <u>τοῦ</u> **σπεῖραι**, "a sower went out **to sow**" (Luke 8:5).

- ἔπεμψα <u>εἰς τὸ</u> **γνῶναι** τὴν πίστιν ὑμῶν, "I sent [him] **to know about** your faith" (1 Thess 3:5).

Result

A result infinitive is one that expresses an actual result and not merely an intended one (i.e., purpose). This usage typically occurs after ὥστε ("so that") and less commonly after εἰς τό (since it usually communicates purpose). Don't forget that any explicit subject of the infinitive will be in the accusative case. In the translations below, you will note that the result infinitive is rendered into more standard English with a finite verb.

- καὶ ἐγένετο ὡσεὶ νεκρός, <u>ὥστε</u> τοὺς πολλοὺς **λέγειν** ὅτι ἀπέθανεν, "And he became as a dead person, <u>so that</u> many **said** that he died" (Mark 9:26).

- ἐπίστευσεν <u>εἰς τὸ</u> **γενέσθαι** αὐτὸν πατέρα πολλῶν ἐθνῶν, "He believed <u>so that</u> he **became** the father of many nations" (Rom 4:18).

Previous Time

Previous (or antecedent) time is communicated by μετὰ τό + infinitive and signals that the action of the infinitive occurs *before* the action of the main verb. The use of the preposition μετά indicates that the action of the main verb occurs *after* the action of the infinitive.

- <u>μετὰ τὸ</u> **ἐγερθῆναί** με προάξω ὑμᾶς εἰς τὴν Γαλιλαίαν, "<u>After</u> I **am raised up**, I will go before you into Galilee" (Mark 14:28 ESV). Note that Jesus is first raised; then he will go to Galilee. Try to translate the opening clause literalistically. "After the to be raised me" does not work. You must transform it into a standard English dependent clause.

Contemporaneous Time

Contemporaneous time is communicated by ἐν τῷ + infinitive and signals that the action of the infinitive occurs *at the same time* as the action of the main verb. The prepositional phrase is usually translated with the English word "while," "as," or "when."

- <u>ἐν τῷ **σπείρειν**</u> αὐτὸν ἃ μὲν ἔπεσεν παρὰ τὴν ὁδόν, "<u>as</u> he **was sowing**, some seeds fell along the path" (Matt 13:4 ISV).

Subsequent Time

Subsequent time is communicated by πρὸ τοῦ or πρίν (ἤ) + infinitive and signals that the action of the infinitive occurs *after* the action of the main verb. The use of the preposition πρό or πρίν indicates that the action of the main verb occurs *before* the action of the infinitive.

- <u>πρὸ τοῦ</u> σε Φίλιππον **φωνῆσαι** . . . εἶδόν σε, "<u>before</u> Philip **called** you . . . I saw you" (John 1:48).
- <u>πρὶν</u> Ἀβραὰμ **γενέσθαι** ἐγὼ εἰμί, "<u>Before</u> Abraham **was**, I am" (John 8:58).

Causal

A causal infinitive is communicated by διὰ τό + infinitive and expresses the reason or ground for the action of the main verb. This use answers the question "Why?" and is usually translated using "because," "since," or "for" plus the meaning of the main verb.

- <u>διὰ τὸ</u> μὴ **ἔχειν** ῥίζαν ἐξηράνθη, "they withered <u>because</u> **they had** no root" (Matt 13:6 NIV).

Substantival Uses

Whereas the categories above could all be seen as adverbial uses of the infinitive, in this category the infinitive will function more like a noun. Such uses can be categorized as *substantival* uses. That is, there are uses where the infinitive functions as either the subject or the object of a sentence.

- ***Subject:*** ἐμοὶ γὰρ τὸ **ζῆν**[9] Χριστὸς καὶ τὸ **ἀποθανεῖν** κέρδος, "For me, **to live** is Christ and **to die** is gain" (Phil 1:21). Here the two infinitives

---

[9] This is the present active infinitive of ζάω.

function as the subject of the understood verb "is." (The verb εἰμί is often implied but not written.)

- ***Object:*** ἐζήτουν αὐτὸν **κρατῆσαι**, "they were seeking **to arrest** him" (Mark 12:12 ESV). Here the phrase "to arrest him" functions as the direct object of the verb "they were seeking."

21.7 Infinitives and Verbal Aspect[10]

Like all non-indicative verbs, infinitives do not convey the time of the action (i.e., tense). The time is not established by tense-form but must be determined by the context (often by prepositions used in infinitive constructions). The various tense-forms convey the author's portrayal of the verb's action (or aspect). Often it is difficult to bring out the aspectual nuance in English, so most of the time there is no difference in translation between a present or aorist infinitive. In addition, the reasons behind an author's choice of a particular tense-form is complex, with multiple factors that limit or influence his choice. Such factors can be categorized as (1) lexical, (2) grammatical, and (3) contextual.

- ***Lexical Factors:*** A verb's semantic meaning often has a significant influence on the tense-form selected by the author. This influence is due to the overlap in function of the verb's aspect and the inherent meaning of the verb. In other words, because the perfective aspect (aorist tense-form) is used by the author to portray the action as a whole, it is more natural to use the perfective aspect with verbs whose actions are normally completed in a relatively short period of time. For example, in the New Testament the infinitive of βάλλω occurs twelve times as an aorist but never as a present. This usage is expected when one considers that the action to "throw" or "put" takes place almost instantaneously. Indeed, it is difficult to conceive of the imperfective aspect being used when there would be virtually no time to portray the action as in progress or incomplete. A specific example can be found in Acts 25:11: οὐ παραιτοῦμαι τὸ **ἀποθανεῖν**, "I do not refuse **to die**" (NIV). The verb ἀποθνῄσκω is found as an infinitive fifteen times in the New Testament, all in the aorist tense-form. Some actions naturally occur quickly without the opportunity for progress to be portrayed.

    Conversely, because the imperfective aspect (present tense-form) is used by the author to portray the action as in progress or ongoing, it is more natural to use the imperfective aspect with verbs whose actions normally are viewed as having no natural endpoint or are stative verbs. For example, in the New Testament, the imperative of ἀγαπάω occurs eight times as a present infinitive but never as an aorist infinitive. Again, this

---

[10] We are indebted to Steven Baugh and his seminal insights on verbal aspect for the ideas expressed in this section.

usage is expected when one considers that the action of "loving" is not normally completed in a short period but is an action that has no natural terminus. Indeed, it is difficult to conceive of the perfective aspect being used when the action is not easily portrayed as a whole. The influence of a verb's lexical meaning can be demonstrated in Phil 1:21: ἐμοὶ γὰρ τὸ ζῆν Χριστὸς καὶ τὸ **ἀποθανεῖν** κέρδος, "For to me, **to live** is Christ and **to die** is gain" (NIV). Note that the first infinitive is present (ζῆν), whereas the second is aorist (ἀποθανεῖν). This example is especially telling since these two infinitives occur in a parallel construction. Why the switch in tense-form? The answer relates to the lexical meaning of each verb. As an infinitive, ζάω occurs as a present infinitive twelve times and never as an aorist. As we saw above, ἀποθνήσκω is just the opposite (fifteen aorists and no presents).

- ***Grammatical Factors:*** Grammatical factors provide the most significant influence on the author's choice of tense form. With infinitives, attention should be given to verb combinations—especially with complementary infinitives (e.g., ἄρχομαι and μέλλω are almost always followed by a present infinitive in the New Testament).

- ***Contextual Factors:*** The most significant contextual factor is the text's literary genre. Certain literary styles are prone to favor certain tense-forms. For example, (in most moods) historical narratives heavily favor the aorist tense-form which is often labeled the "default" form. Letters favor the present tense-form.

So, although every Greek verb conveys a particular aspect, sometimes such choices are influenced by many factors.

21.8 Irregular Verbs

The verbs δύναμαι ("I am able, can") and θέλω ("I want, wish, desire") have slightly irregular forms. In its present indicative form, δύναμαι uses an alpha (α) connecting vowel instead of an omicron (o) or epsilon (ε): δύναμαι, δύνασαι, δύναται, δυνάμεθα, δύνασθε, δύνανται. Additionally, when used as an imperfect indicative, the augment can be either an epsilon (ε–) or an eta (η–): ἐδύνατο or ἠδύνατο. Similarly, the verb θέλω uses an eta for its augment in both the imperfect and aorist forms: ἤθελον and ἠθέλησα. This feature is due to an older spelling of the verb that included an initial epsilon (ἐθέλω).[11]

---

[11] Our explanations in the paragraph above have been influenced by S. M. Baugh's succinct discussion (*A New Testament Greek Primer*, 3rd ed. [Phillipsburg, NJ: P&R, 2012], 126).

21.9 Practice

A. Paradigms: Memorize the present active and middle/passive and aorist active, middle, and passive infinitive forms of λύω (see section 21.4). Then write out the forms ten times from memory.

B. Parsing: Parse the following words.

1. πιστεύειν

2. γνῶναι

3. λαλῆσαι

4. ἀκολουθεῖν

5. πέμψαι

6. φαγεῖν

7. πεποιηκέναι

8. ἀποστέλλειν

9. ἐγεῖραι

10. πεποιθέναι

C. Infinitive Usage: Indicate the specific usage of the following infinitives: Complementary (C), Purpose (P), Previous Time (PT), Contemporaneous Time (CT), Subsequent Time (ST), Causal (CL), or Substantival (S).

1. _____ πρὸ τοῦ δὲ ἐλθεῖν τὴν πίστιν.

2. _____ ἤλθομεν προσκυνῆσαι αὐτῷ.

3. _____ ἀπήγαγον αὐτὸν εἰς τὸ σταυρῶσαι (σταυρόω, I crucify).

4. _____ διὰ τὸ αὐτὸν γινώσκειν πάντας.

5. _____ ἦλθον πληρῶσαι τὸν νόμον.

6. _____ μετὰ τὸ λαβεῖν τὴν ἐπίγνωσιν τῆς ἀληθείας.

7. _____ οὐ δύναται εἶναί μου μαθητής.

8. _____ πρὶν ἐλθεῖν ἡμέραν κυρίου.

9. _____ ἐν τῷ λέγεσθαι.

10. _____ οὐκ ἠδυνήθησαν αὐτὸν θεραπεῦσαι.

D. Translation: Translate the following sentences, indicating the use of the infinitive.

1. καὶ πάλιν ἤρξατο διδάσκειν παρὰ τὴν θάλασσαν (Mark 4:1).

2. οὐκ ἔχετε διὰ τὸ μὴ αἰτεῖσθαι ὑμᾶς (Jas 4:2).

3. μετὰ τὸ γενέσθαι με ἐκεῖ δεῖ με καὶ Ῥώμην ἰδεῖν (Acts 19:21).

4. βούλομαι οὖν προσεύχεσθαι τοὺς ἄνδρας ἐν παντὶ τόπῳ (1 Tim 2:8).

5. ἔδωκεν (He gave) αὐτοῖς ἐξουσίαν πνευμάτων ἀκαθάρτων (unclean) ὥστε ἐκβάλλειν αὐτὰ καὶ θεραπεύειν πᾶσαν νόσον (sickness) (Matt 10:1).

6. οὕτως ὀφείλουσιν (ὀφείλω, I ought) [καὶ] οἱ ἄνδρες ἀγαπᾶν τὰς ἑαυτῶν γυναῖκας ὡς τὰ ἑαυτῶν σώματα (Eph 5:28).

7. ἐν δὲ τῷ πορεύεσθαι αὐτοὺς αὐτὸς εἰσῆλθεν εἰς κώμην (village) τινά (Luke 10:38).

8. οἶδεν γὰρ ὁ πατὴρ ὑμῶν ὧν χρείαν (need) ἔχετε πρὸ τοῦ ὑμᾶς αἰτῆσαι αὐτόν (Matt 6:8).

9. ὅσοι δὲ ἔλαβον αὐτόν, ἔδωκεν (he gave) αὐτοῖς ἐξουσίαν τέκνα θεοῦ γενέσθαι (John 1:12).

10. Κύριε, κατάβηθι (come down) πρὶν ἀποθανεῖν τὸ παιδίον μου (John 4:49).

11. ἤρξατο κηρύσσειν πολλὰ . . . ὥστε μηκέτι αὐτὸν δύνασθαι φανερῶς (openly) εἰς πόλιν εἰσελθεῖν (Mark 1:45).

12. ἦλθεν ἐκ τῶν περάτων (ends) τῆς γῆς ἀκοῦσαι τὴν σοφίαν Σολομῶνος (Luke 11:31).

13. ἐν δὲ τῷ λαλῆσαι ἐρωτᾷ αὐτὸν Φαρισαῖος (Luke 11:37).

14. εἶπεν παραβολὴν διὰ τὸ ἐγγὺς (near) εἶναι Ἰερουσαλὴμ αὐτὸν (Luke 19:11).

15. ἀνέβη δὲ καὶ Ἰωσὴφ . . . εἰς πόλιν Δαυὶδ . . . διὰ τὸ εἶναι αὐτὸν ἐξ οἴκου καὶ πατριᾶς (lineage/line) Δαυίδ (Luke 2:4).

E. Translation: Translate the following sentences into Greek. The expected aspect is given for each infinitive.

1. They are able to sin (imperfective) against the will of God.

2. I want to walk (imperfective) in the light, and he wants to walk (perfective) in the night (use different verbs to translate "want").

3. The blind [man] was about to speak (imperfective) to the servant before he was departing (use infinitive construction for "before he was departing").

4. No one must enter (perfective) nor remain (perfective) in the house.

5. He seems to be (imperfective) blessed so that (as a result) the crowd judges (imperfective) him.

21.10 Vocabulary[12]

δέχομαι	I take, receive, welcome[13]
δικαιόω	I declare righteous, justify
λογίζομαι	I consider, reckon (*theology, apologetics*)[14]
σταυρόω	I crucify
χαίρω	I rejoice; greetings (*charity*)
ἄν	(particle of indefiniteness: untranslated)
ἐάν	if, when
ἐὰν μή	unless
ἵνα	in order that, so that, that
ὅπου	where
ὅπως	in order that, that
ὅστις, ἥτις, ὅ τι	who, whoever, whatever
ὅταν	whenever, when (ὅτε + ἄν)
ὅτε	when
ποῦ	where?

---

[12] To hear an author of your textbook read through the vocabulary for chapter 21, go to bit.ly/greekvocab21 or beginninggreek.com.

[13] As a verb of reciprocity, this action cannot happen without two parties. Verbs of reciprocity are frequently middle-only.

[14] Verbs of cognition are frequently middle-only. Thinking is certainly a highly subject-affected action.

////////////////

CHAPTER 22

SUBJUNCTIVES

22.1 Overview[1]

This chapter will discuss the forms and usage of the subjunctive mood. The mood of a verb indicates the author's attitude toward an event—that is, whether he views the event as factual, possible, desired, commanded, contingent, etc. (see 4.5). Whereas the indicative mood represents the verbal action as certain or asserted ("I broke the window"), the subjunctive mood represents the action as indefinite but possible or probable ("If anyone breaks a window, he must pay for it"). Thus, it is often referred to as the mood of *probability* or *indefiniteness*. Although some describe it as the mood of uncertainty, this description is not always accurate. For example, if someone says, "Whenever I eat tacos, I get indigestion," the use of the subjunctive would not focus on whether or not the person gets indigestion, but rather on the indefiniteness of the timing ("whenever"). In other words, the issue is not whether the person will get indigestion but merely the timing of when it will occur. Also, there are some set grammatical constructions in Greek that simply demand the subjunctive (e.g., to express result following ἵνα); thus, one should not insist on seeing a nuance of indefiniteness in every instance of the subjunctive.

22.2 Significance

As mentioned, the subjunctive mood does not necessarily communicate uncertainty. As a matter of fact, sometimes it communicates something that is emphatically certain (that is, something that certainly will *not* happen). Such is the case with "emphatic negation," which is expressed by the double negative οὐ μή (the indicative and non-indicative negative particles) plus the aorist subjunctive (or

---

[1] For an overview video lecture of chapter 22, go to bit.ly/greeklecture22 or beginninggreek.com.

occasionally the future indicative). As the name suggests, this type of negation is emphatic and strongly denies that something will occur. In fact, it "is the strongest way to negate something in Greek."[2] Interestingly, about 90 percent of the uses are found in the sayings of Jesus and in citations from the Septuagint.

One example of emphatic negation is found in Heb 13:5, which is apparent in the ESV: οὐ μή σε ἀνῶ οὐδ' οὐ μή σε ἐγκαταλίπω ("I will never leave you nor [never] forsake you"). In context, the author claims that the basis of our contentment and freedom from the love of money is that God promises to always be with us and will never forsake us. This verse is a possible composite of Gen 28:15; Deut 31:6–8; and/or Josh 1:8. The message is that the covenant-keeping God promises to continually provide for his people.

But (grammatically speaking) this verse can be considered one of the most powerful verses in the Bible. The reason is that it contains five negative words (two emphatic negations [οὐ μή] plus the conjunction οὐδέ ["nor"]). This idea is well captured in the old hymn, "How Firm a Foundation." The last verse says:

> The soul that on Jesus has leaned for repose,
> I will not, I will not desert to its foes;
> That soul, though all hell should endeavor to shake,
> I'll never, no never, no never forsake.[3]

Charles Spurgeon often referred to this text in his sermons and preached it on more than one occasion. In a sermon titled "Never! Never! Never! Never! Never!" he stated:

> I have no doubt you are aware that our translation does not convey the whole force of the original, and that it would hardly be possible in English to give the full weight of the Greek. We might render it, "He hath said, I will never, never leave thee; I will never, never, never forsake thee;" for, though that would be not a literal, but rather a free rendering, yet, as there are five negatives in the Greek, we do not know how to give their force in any other way. Two negatives nullify each other in our language; but here, in the Greek, they intensify the meaning following one after another.[4]

About ten years later Spurgeon returned to this text:

> In our English language, two negatives would destroy each other, but it is not so in the Greek language—and the heaping up, as it were, of these denials on God's

[2] Daniel B. Wallace, *Greek Grammar Beyond the Basics: An Exegetical Syntax of the New Testament with Scripture, Subject, and Greek Word Indexes* (Grand Rapids: Zondervan, 1997), 468.
[3] The author of this hymn is unknown. It is found in John Rippon's hymnal, *A Selection of Hymns from the Best Authors*. Where the author's name is normally listed, only the initial "K" is referenced. Some think this is a nod to the music director, Robert Keene, who served at Carter's Lane Baptist Church in London, where Rippon was a pastor for over half a century.
[4] "Never! Never! Never! Never! Never!" (no. 477), delivered on Sunday Morning, October 26th, 1862, by Rev. C. H. Spurgeon at the Metropolitan Tabernacle, Newington.

part of all thought of ever forsaking His people ought to be sufficient to satisfy even the most doubtful among us! If God has said, "I will not, not, NOT, no never forsake My people," we must believe Him! And we must chase away all thought of the possibility of the Lord's forsaking His servants, or leaving them to perish.[5]

Though not formally trained in Greek, Spurgeon taught himself the language and knew that studying the Greek text would improve his preaching. What a blessing to follow his example of paying attention to the original text so that we hear (and feel!) the full weight of God's message to us.[6]

22.3 Paradigms

| | PRESENT ACTIVE SUB[7] | | PRESENT MIDDLE/PASSIVE SUB | |
	SINGULAR	PLURAL	SINGULAR	PLURAL
1ST	λύω	λύωμεν	λύωμαι	λυώμεθα
2ND	λύῃς	λύητε	λύῃ	λύησθε
3RD	λύῃ	λύωσι(ν)	λύηται	λύωνται

| | AORIST ACTIVE SUB | | AORIST MIDDLE SUB | | AORIST PASSIVE SUB | |
	SINGULAR	PLURAL	SINGULAR	PLURAL	SINGULAR	PLURAL
1ST	λύσω	λύσωμεν	λύσωμαι	λυσώμεθα	λυθῶ	λυθῶμεν
2ND	λύσῃς	λύσητε	λύσῃ	λύσησθε	λυθῇς	λυθῆτε
3RD	λύσῃ	λύσωσι(ν)	λύσηται	λύσωνται	λυθῇ	λυθῶσι(ν)

22.4 Morphology

The subjunctive mood occurs almost exclusively in the present and the aorist tense-forms. There are no imperfect, future, or pluperfect forms and only ten perfect occurrences (all with the verb οἶδα). In addition, the aorist form occurs about three times more often than the present (1,396 aorist forms and 461 present forms). Therefore, when in doubt, guess that a form is aorist!

---

[5] "Never, No Never, No Never" (no. 3150) delivered on Sunday Evening, March 16, 1873, at the Metropolitan Tabernacle, Newington.

[6] This Significance section is derived directly from Benjamin L. Merkle, *Exegetical Gems from Biblical Greek: A Refreshing Guide to Grammar and Interpretation* (Grand Rapids: Baker, 2019), 82–83.

[7] Note that in the paradigms given there are no English equivalents offered. This is because it is not possible to translate a subjunctive without knowing how it is functioning in a particular context. Though it's an oversimplification, some beginning students find it helpful to think of the subjunctive mood as adding a "may," "might," or "should" into the English translation.

Present

The subjunctive forms are not difficult. The main distinction between indicative and subjunctive forms is that the latter has a lengthened connecting vowel. That is, omicron lengthens to omega (o → ω) and epsilon lengthens to eta (ε → η).

Present Active Indicative				Present Active Subjunctive
λύω	→	ω → ω	→	λύω[8]
λύεις	→	ει → ηι → ῃ[9]	→	λύῃς
λύει	→	ει → ηι → η	→	λύῃ
λύομεν	→	ο → ω	→	λύωμεν
λύετε	→	ε → η	→	λύητε
λύουσιν	→	ου → ω	→	λύωσι(ν)

The present subjunctive forms of εἰμί consist of the endings of the forms above, with a smooth breathing mark and a circumflex: ὦ, ᾖς, ᾖ, ὦμεν, ἦτε, ὦσιν. (There is no aorist form.)

Present Mid/Pass Indicative				Present Mid/Pass Subjunctive
λύομαι	→	ο → ω	→	λύωμαι
λύῃ	→	η → η	→	λύῃ[10]
λύεται	→	ε → η	→	λύηται
λυόμεθα	→	ο → ω	→	λυώμεθα
λύεσθε	→	ε → η	→	λύησθε
λύονται	→	ο → ω	→	λύωνται

Aorist

The aorist active forms are the same as the present active forms, with the tense formative sigma (σ) added to the stem.

λύω	→	λύσω[11]	λύωμεν →	λύσωμεν
λύῃς	→	λύσῃς	λύητε →	λύσητε
λύῃ	→	λύσῃ	λύωσιν →	λύσωσι(ν)

Like in the indicative mood, the aorist has separate forms for the middle and passive. The aorist middle forms add a sigma (σ) to the stem of the present middle/passive forms: λύωμαι → λύσωμαι, λύῃ → λύσῃ, λύηται → λύσηται, etc. The

---

[8] Notice that this form (pres act sub 1st sg) is identical to the first singular active *indicative*.

[9] The iota subscripts once the epsilon (ε) is lengthened to an eta (η).

[10] Notice that this form (pres mid/pass sub 2nd sg) is identical to the *third* singular *active* subjunctive.

[11] Notice that this ending (aor act sub 1st sg) is identical to the first singular *future indicative*.

aorist passive form has a theta (θ) in place of the sigma (σ) in the aorist active from: λύσω → λύθω, λύσῃς → λύθῃς, λύσῃ → λύθῃ, etc.[12]

Remember, all non-indicative aorist verbs, including subjunctives, have no augment since time is not conveyed by the form. Moreover, all subjunctive verbs are negated by μή. Also, first aorist forms look very similar to future *indicative* forms. Recall, however, that there is no future *subjunctive*.

Irregular Forms

Three irregular forms are worth mentioning here: (1) second aorist, (2) contract verbs, and (3) liquid verbs. You will note that if a verb has a second aorist form, its aorist subjunctive will build off the same irregular root. Also, all the rules you learned about contract vowels combining with connecting vowels remain true, as does the pattern of the sigma being rejected immediately after a liquid consonant. The following examples demonstrate these expected patterns:

	Present	Aorist
Second Aorist	λαμβάνῃ	λάβῃ
	γίνηται	γένηται
Contract Verbs	ποιῇ	ποιήσῃ
	ἀγαπᾷ	ἀγαπήσῃ
Liquid Verbs	μένῃ	μείνῃ
	ἀποστέλλῃ	ἀποστείλῃ

22.5 Uses of the Subjunctive

As the mood of probability or indefiniteness, the subjunctive mood is closely related to the future tense.[13] Regardless of tense-form or aspect used, the subjunctive generally refers to an event that may or may not occur in the future. Below are some of the most common uses of the subjunctive mood. Note that in the categories provided, certain words (e.g., ἵνα, ὅπως, ὅς ἄν, ὅταν, ἕως, οὐ μή, ἐάν, ἐάν μή) will almost always be followed by the subjunctive mood.

Purpose/Result (ἵνα, ὅπως + sub)

A purpose clause (usually introduced with ἵνα but sometimes with ὅπως) indicates the intent or purpose of the action of the main verb. Though much less common, both ἵνα and ὅπως can introduce a result clause where the action has already occurred (or certainly will occur). ἵνα and ὅπως will typically be rendered "that" or

---

[12] Technically, –θε has been added but the epsilon (ε) has contracted.
[13] In fact, a historical study of the Greek language demonstrates that the subjunctive mood and future tense are genealogically related.

"in order that." The combination ἵνα μή can be translated "so that . . . not" or with the archaic "lest" (expressing a negative purpose).

- ταῦτα γράφω ὑμῖν <u>ἵνα</u> μὴ **ἁμάρτητε**, "I write these things to you <u>in order that</u> **you might** not **sin**" (1 John 2:1). The term ἵνα introduces the reason why John writes his letter.

- λαμψάτω τὸ φῶς ὑμῶν ἔμπροσθεν τῶν ἀνθρώπων, <u>ὅπως</u> **ἴδωσιν** ὑμῶν τὰ καλὰ ἔργα, "Let your light shine before people, <u>so that</u> **they might see** your good works" (Matt 5:16).

Indefinite Clauses (ὅς ἄν, ὅταν, ἕως ἄν + sub)

There are two types of indefinite clauses that we will highlight here: (1) relative (introduced by ὅς ἄν or ὅς ἐάν, "whoever") and (2) temporal (introduced by ὅταν, "whenever" or ἕως ἄν, "until"). In both uses, the particle ἄν (or ἐάν) causes the pronoun or adverb to become indefinite, thus triggering the subjunctive mood. The older indefinite relative pronoun ὅστις (ὅς + τίς) is normally used in the New Testament interchangeably with the relative pronoun ὅς ("who") and thus no longer has an indefinite meaning.

- <u>ὅς ἄν</u> ἐμὲ **δέξηται**, δέχεται τὸν ἀποστείλαντά με, "<u>Whoever</u> **receives** me receives the one who sent me" (Luke 9:48 NABRE).

- <u>ὅταν</u> **προσεύχησθε**, οὐκ ἔσεσθε ὡς οἱ ὑποκριταί, "<u>Whenever</u> **you pray**, do not be like the hypocrites" (Matt 6:5).

- κἀκεῖ μείνατε <u>ἕως ἄν</u> **ἐξέλθητε**, "Stay there <u>until</u> **you leave**" (Matt 10:11).

Emphatic Negation (οὐ μή + sub)

This construction employs both the indicative negation (οὐ) as well as the non-indicative negation (μή). This double negation functions emphatically to deny that something will occur. The aorist tense-form is always used in this construction. In translation, it is typically best to use something stronger than merely "no" or "not." Instead, we recommend using "never," "certainly not," or "by no means."

- βλέποντες βλέψετε καὶ <u>οὐ μὴ</u> **ἴδητε**, "Seeing you will see and <u>never</u> **perceive**" (Acts 28:26).

Deliberative

This construction of the subjunctive reflects a real or rhetorical question. When the question is rhetorical, the author is not seeking a direct answer but is using the question to call the hearer/reader to think about a deeper issue.

- λέγει αὐτοῖς ὁ Πιλᾶτος, Τί οὖν **ποιήσω** Ἰησοῦν τὸν λεγόμενον Χριστόν; "Pilate asked them, 'What **should I do** then with Jesus, who is called Christ?'" (Matt 27:22).

Conditional (ἐάν, ἐάν μή + sub)

Conditional statements typically have two components: (1) an "if" clause (i.e., the protasis), and (2) a "then" clause (i.e., the apodosis). In Greek, when the "if" clause begins with ἐάν, the verb related to the conditional statement will be in the subjunctive mood. When ἐάν is negated (ἐάν μή), it is usually best translated "unless" rather than "if not."

- ἐὰν ἐγὼ **δοξάσω** ἐμαυτόν, ἡ δόξα μου οὐδέν ἐστιν, "If I **glorify** myself, my glory is nothing" (John 8:54).

- ἐὰν μὴ οὗτοι **μείνωσιν** ἐν τῷ πλοίῳ, ὑμεῖς σωθῆναι οὐ δύνασθε, "Unless these men **remain** in the ship, you yourselves cannot be saved" (Acts 27:31 NASB).

SUBJUNCTIVE USAGE				
MARKER	+	SUBJUNCTIVE	=	USAGE
ἵνα				Purpose
ὅπως				Result
ὅς ἄν	+	Subjunctive Verb	=	Indefinite Relative
ὅταν, ἕως ἄν				Indefinite Temporal
οὐ μή				Emphatic Negation
ἐάν, ἐάν μή				Conditional

22.6 Conditional Sentences

There are four types of conditional sentences. The type above represents only one kind (i.e., third class). Below is a summary of the four types.

First Class (εἰ + indicative)

- The condition is assumed as true for the sake of the argument.
- Consider this example: εἰ πνεύματι ἄγεσθε, οὐκ ἐστὲ ὑπὸ νόμον, "If you are led by the Spirit, you are not under the law" (Gal 5:18; see also Matt 4:6; 18:8). The idea here is that since believers are led by the Spirit, they are not under the law.

Second Class (εἰ + indicative + ἄν)

- The condition is presented by the speaker as contrary-to-fact: "If (and I, the speaker, do not think this is true) . . . ." The particle ἄν is not always present in a contrary-to-fact condition, so pay attention to context.

- εἰ ἦς ὧδε οὐκ ἄν ἀπέθανεν ὁ ἀδελφός μου, "If you had been here, my brother wouldn't have died" (John 11:21; see also Matt 11:23; John 5:46). The meaning is that since Jesus was not present, Lazarus died. It could be paraphrased, "If you were here (but you weren't), my brother would not have died (but he did)."

Third Class (ἐάν + subjunctive)

- The condition is presented more remotely than the first-class conditional—as a hypothetical projection.

- ἐὰν εἴπωμεν ὅτι ἁμαρτίαν οὐκ ἔχομεν, ἑαυτοὺς πλανῶμεν καὶ ἡ ἀλήθεια οὐκ ἔστιν ἐν ἡμῖν (1 John 1:8). In English, the passage reads: "If we say, 'We have no sin,' we are deceiving ourselves, and the truth is not in us." Perhaps the apostle John uses the third-class conditional here because he includes himself and the faithful congregation to which he writes in considering this flawed perspective. We could paraphrase: "Just imagine for a minute, brothers and sisters . . . what if we were to say that we were sinless? What would that say about our spiritual condition? We would be self-deceived and show that the truth is not in us."

Fourth Class (εἰ + optative)

- The condition is presented as an extremely remote possibility.

- ἀλλ᾽ εἰ καὶ πάσχοιτε διὰ δικαιοσύνην, μακάριοι, "But even if you should suffer for righteousness, you are blessed" (1 Pet 3:14).

22.7 Subjunctives and Verbal Aspect

Again, remember that subjunctive verbs do not inherently communicate time. A present subjunctive does not necessarily refer to present time. An aorist subjunctive does not necessarily refer to past time. (Notice there is no augment.) In fact, the indefinite nature of subjunctives usually places the possible action in the future. Instead, the present or aorist tense-forms indicate the author's perspective regarding the nature of the action (imperfective versus perfective). The timing of the action is dependent on the main verb of the sentence.

The precise reason for choosing one tense-form over another (for subjunctives it is limited to present and aorist) is complex since it involves several factors (see 21.7). In most cases, it is neither possible nor necessary to differentiate present subjunctives and aorist subjunctives in English translation.

22.8 Practice

A. Paradigms: Memorize the present active and middle/passive subjunctive forms as well as the aorist active forms of λύω (see section 22.3). Then write out each paradigm ten times from memory.

B. Parsing: Parse the following words.

1. λέγῃ

2. ποιῆς

3. ἐσθίωσιν

4. εἴπω

5. λύσῃ

6. διώξωσιν

7. καλέσητε

8. εὐαγγελίζηται

9. πληρωθῆτε

10. ὦσιν

C. Subjunctive Usage: Indicate the specific use of the following subjunctives: Purpose (P), Indefinite Relative (IR), Indefinite Temporal (IT), Emphatic Negation (EN), Deliberative (D), or Conditional (C).

1. _____ οὐ μὴ εἰσέλθητε εἰς τὴν βασιλείαν τῶν οὐρανῶν

2. _____ ὅταν ἀκούσωσιν

3. _____ ἐὰν εἴπωμεν ὅτι κοινωνίαν ἔχομεν

4. _____ Τί αἰτήσωμαι;

5. _____ ὅπως πληρωθῇ τὸ ῥηθὲν διὰ τῶν προφητῶν

6. _____ ἕως ἂν ἔλθῃ ὁ υἱὸς τοῦ ἀνθρώπου

7. _____ ἵνα πιστεύητε

8. _____ ἐὰν μὴ ἐν ἐμοὶ μένητε

9. _____ ὃς ἂν ἐσθίῃ τὸν ἄρτον

10. _____ οὐ μὴ κριθῆτε

D. Translation: Translate the following sentences, indicating the use of the subjunctive(s).

1. καὶ ἐὰν πορευθῶ καὶ ἑτοιμάσω τόπον ὑμῖν, πάλιν ἔρχομαι (John 14:3).

2. οὐ γὰρ ἀπέστειλεν ὁ θεὸς τὸν υἱὸν εἰς τὸν κόσμον ἵνα κρίνῃ τὸν κόσμον, ἀλλ᾽ ἵνα σωθῇ ὁ κόσμος δι᾽ αὐτοῦ (John 3:17).

3. ἐὰν ὑμεῖς μείνητε ἐν τῷ λόγῳ τῷ ἐμῷ, ἀληθῶς (truly) μαθηταί μού ἐστε (John 8:31).

4. ταῦτα λελάληκα ὑμῖν ἵνα ἡ χαρὰ ἡ ἐμὴ ἐν ὑμῖν ᾖ καὶ ἡ χαρὰ ὑμῶν πληρωθῇ (John 15:11).

5. λέγω γὰρ ὑμῖν, οὐ μή με ἴδητε ἀπ᾽ ἄρτι (now) ἕως ἂν εἴπητε, Εὐλογημένος (Blessed [be]) ὁ ἐρχόμενος ἐν ὀνόματι κυρίου (Matt 23:39).

6. προσηύξαντο περὶ αὐτῶν ὅπως λάβωσιν πνεῦμα ἅγιον (Acts 8:15).

7. ὃς ἂν μὴ δέξηται τὴν βασιλείαν τοῦ θεοῦ ὡς παιδίον, οὐ μὴ εἰσέλθῃ εἰς αὐτήν (Mark 10:15).

8. πῶς δὲ κηρύξωσιν ἐὰν μὴ ἀποσταλῶσιν; (Rom 10:15).

9. ποῦ θέλεις ἑτοιμάσωμέν σοι φαγεῖν τὸ πάσχα (Passover); (Matt 26:17).

10. ἐὰν μή τις γεννηθῇ ἐξ ὕδατος καὶ πνεύματος, οὐ δύναται εἰσελθεῖν εἰς τὴν βασιλείαν τοῦ θεοῦ (John 3:5).

11. καὶ ὃς ἂν θέλῃ ἐν ὑμῖν εἶναι πρῶτος ἔσται ὑμῶν δοῦλος (Matt 20:27).

12. ἐάν τις φάγῃ ἐκ τούτου τοῦ ἄρτου ζήσει εἰς τὸν αἰῶνα (John 6:51).

13. καὶ αὕτη ἐστὶν ἡ ἐντολὴ αὐτοῦ, ἵνα πιστεύσωμεν τῷ ὀνόματι τοῦ υἱοῦ αὐτοῦ Ἰησοῦ Χριστοῦ καὶ ἀγαπῶμεν ἀλλήλους (1 John 3:23).

14. ὅταν ἔλθῃ ἐκεῖνος, ἀναγγελεῖ (will announce) ἡμῖν ἅπαντα (John 4:25).

15. ἀμὴν ἀμὴν λέγω ὑμῖν, ἐάν τις τὸν ἐμὸν λόγον τηρήσῃ, θάνατον οὐ μὴ θεωρήσῃ εἰς τὸν αἰῶνα (John 8:51).

E. Translation: Translate the following sentences into Greek. The expected aspect is given for each subjunctive.

1. Whoever receives (perfective) you (pl) will be called beloved.

2. If/when he is crucified (perfective), he will be raised.

3. Whenever he considers (perfective) the good news, he rejoices.

4. He is declared righteous (imperfective) so that we might live forever [lit. "into the age"].

5. The word of the Lord will be heard until the Son of man comes (perfective).

22.9 Vocabulary[14]

ἀσπάζομαι	I greet[15]
ἐπιγινώσκω	I know, understand (*Gnostic, agnostic, prognosis*)
ἐργάζομαι	I work, do, perform (*ergometer, ergonomics, energy*)[16]
καθίζω	I sit (*cathedral* [seat of bishop])
κατοικέω	I live, dwell (*economy*)
γενεά, –ᾶς, ἡ	generation, family (*generation*)
ἔτος, –ους, τό	year
θηρίον, τό	animal, beast
θλῖψις, –εως, ἡ	tribulation, affliction
χρεία, ἡ	need
κρίσις, –εως, ἡ	judgment, condemnation (*crisis*)
φόβος, ὁ	fear, reverence, respect (*phobia*)
φυλακή, ἡ	watch, guard, prison (*prophylactic*)
ἔμπροσθεν	in front of, before (gen)
ἰδού	behold, look, see

---

[14] To hear an author of your textbook read through the vocabulary for chapter 22, go to bit.ly/greekvocab22 or beginninggreek.com.

[15] As a verb of reciprocity, this action could not happen if one of the two parties involved were removed. Verbs of reciprocity are frequently middle-only.

[16] Verbs in which the subject acts in his own interest are frequently middle-only. Other examples include ἐμπορεύομαι, "buy and sell," and κτάομαι, "get, acquire."

CHAPTER 23

////////////////

IMPERATIVES AND OPTATIVES

23.1 Overview[1]

An **_imperative_** is a verb that expresses a command. Or, more broadly, it is the mood of _intention_ or volition. An imperative can be a command ("Read this chapter!"), a prohibition ("Don't read this chapter!"), or a request ("Please read this chapter."). The optative mood, however, is the mood of _possibility_. It is similar to the subjunctive mood (i.e., the mood of _probability_), but is weaker in tone in regard to certainty ("I wish you would read this entire book tonight."). This chapter will discuss the forms and functions of the imperative mood in some detail, but because of its relatively infrequent usage in the New Testament, the optative mood will be summarized briefly.

23.2 Significance

Imperatives do not always express commands. This is clearly illustrated by the Lord's Prayer. Greek imperative forms are in parentheses below.

> Our Father in heaven,
> **hallowed be** (ἁγιασθήτω) your name.
> Your kingdom **come** (ἐλθέτω),
> your will **be done** (γενηθήτω),
> on earth as it is in heaven.
> **Give** (δός) us this day our daily bread,
> and **forgive** (ἄφες) us our debts,
> as we also have forgiven our debtors.

---

[1] For an overview video lecture of chapter 23, go to bit.ly/greeklecture23 or beginninggreek.com.

And **lead us** (εἰσενέγκῃς)[2] not into temptation,
but **deliver** (ῥῦσαι) us from evil. (Matt 6:9–13 ESV)

The Lord's Prayer demonstrates that imperative forms can function as requests from an inferior to a superior. You have not learned imperative forms yet, but soon you will be able to parse the forms above. You will discover that they are all aorist imperatives. Why aorist? Are we praying for something that has already been determined in the past by God's sovereign counsel? No. Only in the indicative does the aorist tense indicate past time. Even then, 15 percent of aorist indicative forms are not past referring.

Are all these imperatives aorist, then, because this model prayer takes a wholistic view? That is, do the aorist imperatives present the action in perfective aspect—not focusing on the beginning or ending of the action, but presenting any requested activity as a whole, encompassing both beginning and ending? That would be a good guess, but you are missing one key piece of information. As a very strong stylistic pattern in Koine Greek, imperatives in prayers (whether Christian or pagan) are almost always in the aorist tense. So, the literary form essentially dictates the tense used. We would be misguided to inquire further.

23.3 Paradigms

PRESENT ACTIVE IMPERATIVES				
	SINGULAR		PLURAL	
2ND	λῦε	loose (be loosing)	λύετε	loose (be loosing)
3RD	λυέτω	let him/her loose (let him be loosing)	λυέτωσαν	let them loose (let them be loosing)

PRESENT MID/PASS IMPERATIVES[3]				
	SINGULAR		PLURAL	
2ND	λύου	be loosed	λύεσθε	be loosed
3RD	λυέσθω	let him/her be loosed	λυέσθωσαν	let them be loosed

---

[2] An aorist prohibitory subjunctive functioning imperatively.

[3] This paradigm only includes the passive meaning. The middle could be translated as follows: loose (for) yourself, let him/her loose (for) him/herself, loose (for) yourselves, and let them loose (for) themselves.

AORIST ACTIVE IMPERATIVES			
	SINGULAR		PLURAL
2ND	λῦσον	loose	λύσατε	loose
3RD	λυσάτω	let him/her loose	λυσάτωσαν	let them loose

23.4 Morphology

Like the subjunctive mood, the imperative mood occurs almost exclusively in the present and aorist tense-forms. There are no imperfect, future, or pluperfect forms and only two perfect occurrences (Mark 4:39, πεφίμωσο, "be still!"; Acts 15:29, ἔρρωσθε, "Farewell"). But unlike subjunctives, the present and aorist forms occur with similar frequency in the New Testament (just over 900 occurrences for each tense-form). In translation, it is often impossible to distinguish between present and aorist imperatives.

You will notice that the paradigms above are shorter than previous paradigms related to verbs. This distinction is because imperatives have *no first person*. (If you command yourself to do something—perhaps looking in the mirror—you would use the second person singular.) Thus, each paradigm has only four components instead of six.

When it comes to memorizing imperative paradigms, we recommend using a slightly different approach than with other types of verbs. Instead of memorizing the paradigm down the columns (singular then plural), memorize them across (2nd sg, 2nd pl, 3rd sg, 3rd pl). In studying them this way, you will notice that the pattern forms a large "Z" as you go across, then back down and over, and then across again. Because of this Z-motion, we prefer to think of this as the "Zorro method" of memorization.

λῦε	λύετε
λυέτω	λυέτωσαν

The second person singular form is perhaps the most difficult to remember, so it should be given the most attention (present active: λῦε). After memorizing that form, it is best to move to the second person plural form: λύετε. The attentive student will notice that this form is identical to the present active *indicative* second person plural form. (The same is true for the present middle/passive: λύεσθε.) The main way of determining whether the form is an indicative or imperative is context. Also, if it is negated, you will know the mood because indicatives are negated with οὐ and imperatives are negated with μή (οὐ κρίνετε, "you are not judging"; μὴ κρίνετε, "do not judge!"). Because this form is already familiar to you, you will find it helpful to learn the last two forms in relation to the second person plural form. Thus, to learn the third person singular form, simply remove the final epsilon (ε) and replace it with an omega (ω): λύετε → λυέτω. The final step is to add –σαν to the ending of the third person plural form: λυέτω → λυέτωσαν.[4]

Present tense-form contract verbs follow this same pattern with the normal contractions (e.g., ποιεῖ, ποιεῖτε, ποιείτω, ποιείτωσαν).

The same pattern also works for both the present middle/passive forms as well as the aorist active forms. (Note that the aorist forms have no augments.)

Present Middle/Passive: λύου → λύεσθε → λυέσθω → λυέσθωσαν
Aorist Active: λῦσον → λύσατε → λυσάτω → λυσάτωσαν

The paradigms for the aorist middle and passive imperative are given below. Because these forms are not as common, and because they have similarities with other imperative forms, it is not necessary to memorize them.

Aorist Middle Imperative		Aorist Passive Imperatives	
λῦσαι	λύσασθε	λύθητι	λύθητε
λυσάσθω	λυσάσθωσαν	λυθήτω	λυθήτωσαν

Second aorist forms have present endings plus a spelling change of the stem (e.g., λάβε, λάβετε, λαβέτω, λαβέτωσαν).

Summary of Imperative Endings
(without connecting vowels or tense formatives)

Present & Aorist Active		Present Mid/Pass & Aorist Middle	
—	–τε	—	–σθε
–τω	–τωσαν	–σθω	–σθωσαν

23.5 Uses of the Imperative

Like other types of verbs, imperatives have a wide range of uses. In this section, we will discuss three of the most common, providing examples for each.

Command

The imperative is most commonly used to express a command or exhortation. Although we earlier translated the third person imperatives as "let him/her loose" or "let them loose," we should stress that such translations should not be viewed as statements of permission but as commands. Consequently, it is sometimes best to translate them as "he/she must loose" or "they must loose."

- **διώκετε** τὴν ἀγάπην, "**Pursue** love" (1 Cor 14:1).

---

[4] The present forms of εἰμί are ἴσθι, ἔστε, ἔστω, and ἔστωσαν.

- ὃς ἔχει ὦτα ἀκούειν **ἀκουέτω**, "Whoever has ears to hear, **let them hear**" (Mark 4:9 NIV).

Prohibition

A *prohibition* is a *negative* command used to forbid an action. Like all non-indicative verbs, the imperative is negated with μή (and not οὐ). Because prohibitions in the aorist use the subjunctive mood (see 23.6), nearly all imperative prohibitions are found in the present tense-form (imperfective aspect).[5] The present prohibition can sometimes be used to command an action to be stopped though already begun.

- **μὴ ἀγαπᾶτε** τὸν κόσμον, "**Do** not **love** the world" (1 John 2:15).
- **μὴ γίνεσθε** ὡς οἱ ὑποκριταί, "**Do** not **be** as the hypocrites" (Matt 6:16).

Request

A *request* is a weakened form of a command that is given to a superior or someone with a higher social status. In this case, instead of a command, the imperative conveys a mere request since it would be inappropriate for someone of lower rank to give an order ἤ someone of a higher rank. Thus, this category is fitting when a petition is made to God, asking that he hear and answer someone's prayer. In such prayers, the aorist tense-form is almost always used. In translation, it is often appropriate to add the word "please" before the request.

- **ἐλθέτω** ἡ βασιλεία σου· **γενηθήτω** τὸ θέλημά σου, "**Let** your kingdom **come. Let** your will **be done**" (Matt 6:10 GW).
- εἴ τι δύνῃ, **βοήθησον** ἡμῖν, "If you can do anything, **please help** us" (Mark 9:22).

23.6 The Subjunctive as an Imperative

We reserved two important uses of the subjunctive for this chapter since they function as imperatives.

Hortatory Subjunctive

First, the hortatory subjunctive is used when the author includes himself in the command to the audience. That is, he urges his audience to join with him in a particular course of action. Such a command requires a *first person plural* form, and since imperatives have only second and third person forms, the subjunctive is

---

[5] There are only eight aorist prohibitions in the New Testament: Matt 6:3; 24:17–18 [2x]; Mark 13:15–16 [3x]; Luke 17:31 [2x]).

used.[6] These verbs are translated "let us + [verbal meaning]." Unlike most other subjunctives, this type is used without any introductory term (such as ἵνα, ἄν, or ἐάν). This verb is usually located at the beginning of the sentence.

- **ἀγαπῶμεν** ἀλλήλους, "**let us love** one another" (1 John 4:7).

- **κρατῶμεν** τῆς ὁμολογίας, "**let us hold fast** our confession" (Heb 4:14).

Prohibitory Subjunctive

Second, the subjunctive is also used as an imperative when (1) the command is negated *and* (2) the aorist tense-form is employed.

	COMMAND	PROHIBITION
PRESENT	λυέ (loose)	μὴ λυέ (do not loose)
AORIST	λῦσον (loose)	**μὴ λύσῃς** (do not loose)

Notice that the second person aorist prohibition is not μὴ λῦσον (as one might expect) but μὴ λύσῃς. The prohibitory subjunctive should be translated as a prohibition and *not* as a typical subjunctive.

- καὶ <u>μὴ</u> **εἰσενέγκῃς** ἡμᾶς εἰς πειρασμόν, "And **do** <u>not</u> **lead** us **into** temptation" (Matt 6:13 NASB).

- <u>Μὴ</u> **φονεύσῃς**, <u>Μὴ</u> **μοιχεύσῃς**, <u>Μὴ</u> **κλέψῃς**, <u>Μὴ</u> **ψευδομαρτυρήσῃς**, <u>Μὴ</u> **ἀποστερήσῃς**, "**Do** <u>not</u> **murder; do** <u>not</u> **commit adultery; do** <u>not</u> **steal; do** <u>not</u> **bear false witness; do** <u>not</u> **defraud**" (Mark 10:19).

23.7 Imperatives and Verbal Aspect[7]

As mentioned above (see 21.7), the tense-form (present or aorist) of the imperative does not convey the time of the action. In fact, most imperatives are future-oriented since one cannot command something in the past.[8] Instead, the aorist imperative (perfective aspect) portrays the action from an external perspective viewing the action as a whole, without focusing on the unfolding internal details. In contrast, the present imperative (imperfective aspect) portrays the action from an internal perspective, viewing the action as a process without focusing on the end of the

---

[6] There are also five New Testament instances where the hortatory subjunctive is used with the first-person singular (see Matt 7:4; Luke 6:42; Acts 7:34; Rev 17:1; and 21:9).

[7] See Benjamin L. Merkle, "The Abused Aspect: Neglecting the Influence of a Verb's Lexical Meaning on Tense-Form Choice," *Bulletin for Biblical Research* 26.1 (2016): 57–74 and "Verbal Aspect and Imperatives: Ephesians as a Test Case," in *New Testament Philology: Essays in Honor of David Alan Black*, ed. Melton Bennett Winstead (Eugene, OR: Pickwick, 2018), 34–51.

[8] Though perhaps you have had an irrationally demanding supervisor who tried.

action. But other factors, including lexical and contextual ones, also influence the tense-form used.

- *Lexical Factors:* A verbal activity's inherent procedural nature often has a significant influence on the tense-form selected by the author. This influence is due to the overlap in function of the verb's aspect and the inherent meaning of the verb. For example, as an imperative, the verb βάλλω occurs fourteen times as an aorist but never as a present. In Matt 4:6, the devil tells Jesus, **βάλε** σεαυτὸν κάτω, "**throw** yourself down." Here the aorist is used because the lexical meaning of the word fits with the concept of the perfective aspect. That is, it would be difficult to portray the action as ongoing since such a thing is accomplished almost instantly. Conversely, in the New Testament ἀγαπάω occurs nineteen times as a present imperative and only once as an aorist imperative.

- *Contextual Factors:* Two influences are worth noting here: (1) literary context and (2) the specific command/general precept distinction. First, a text's literary genre can influence what tense-form is chosen since certain literary styles are prone to favor certain tense-forms. For example, historical narratives favor the aorist tense-form whereas letters favor the present tense. Thus, in Paul's epistles, he uses the present imperative three times more frequently than the aorist imperative. Additionally, in prayers where imperatives are used to make requests of God, the aorist is the strongly dominant tense-form regardless of the lexical meaning of the verb. Second, the specific command/general precept distinction recognizes the reality that when an author wants to communicate a command that is to be done on a specific occasion as a single occurrence, the aorist tense-form is used. In contrast, when the author wants to communicate a command that is a general precept (multiple occurrence), the present tense-form is used.[9] Although there are plenty of exceptions, this pattern is a helpful guideline. Because the perfective aspect communicates an author's portrayal of an action in its entirety, it is natural for this aspect to be used when communicating a specific command; such an action is to be done in its entirety on that particular occasion. Conversely, because the imperfective aspect communicates an author's portrayal of an action in progress or ongoing, it is natural for this aspect to be used when communicating a general precept; such an action is to be repeated on appropriate occasions.

To summarize, a verbal activity's inherent procedural nature directly influences the aspect because the way an action is *performed* affects the way it can be *portrayed*. The context concerning how the author envisions the readers responding also affects the aspectual choice. If an author envisions the readers only responding

---

[9] Note that this is merely an observed pattern rather than a rule.

once to the command, then it is more natural to use the aorist form; the present form is naturally favored for commands that are to be repeatedly obeyed or carried out as the appropriate situation arises. Thus, the tense-form used with imperatives is influenced by multiple factors.

23.8 Optative Mood

If the subjunctive mood is described as the mood of *probability*, the **optative mood** is the mood of *possibility*, often expressing a wish. Thus, the optative is sometimes viewed as a weaker or less assured subjunctive. During the Koine period, the optative was dying out, getting replaced by the subjunctive. As a result, there are only sixty-eight uses of the optative in the New Testament (forty-five aorists and twenty-three presents), mostly in the writings of Luke and Paul. The two most common forms are γένοιτο, "may it be" (17x), and εἴη, "may it be" (12x). In the present (and second aorist) forms, look for the marker –οι– and for the aorist forms, –σαι–. The optative can be used to express a benediction/prayer, curse, abhorrence, or a possible condition.

- **Benediction/Prayer:** ἔλεος ὑμῖν καὶ εἰρήνη καὶ ἀγάπη **πληθυνθείη**, "**May** mercy, peace, and love **be multiplied** to you" (Jude v. 2).

- **Curse:** μηκέτι εἰς τὸν αἰῶνα ἐκ σοῦ μηδεὶς καρπὸν **φάγοι**, "**May** no one ever **eat** fruit from you again!" (Mark 11:14).

- **Abhorrence:** (μὴ γένοιτο).[10] Paul asks the rhetorical question, "Is the law sin?" His response is emphatic: μὴ **γένοιτο**, "**may it** never **be**" (Rom 7:7). This phrase could also be translated, "by no means" or "never!"

- **Possible Condition:** κρεῖττον γὰρ ἀγαθοποιοῦντας, εἰ **θέλοι** τὸ θέλημα τοῦ θεοῦ, πάσχειν ἢ κακοποιοῦντας, "For it is better to suffer for doing good, if that **should be** God's will, than for doing evil" (1 Pet 3:17 ESV).

23.9 Practice

A. Paradigms: Memorize the present active and middle/passive imperatival forms as well as the aorist active forms (see section 23.3). Then write out each paradigm ten times from memory.

B. Parsing: Parse the following words.

1. λάβε

---

[10] Regarding μὴ γένοιτο, Wallace observes, "[The expression] usually has the force of abhorrence, and may in some contexts be the equivalent of οὐ μή + aorist subjunctive (a very strong negative)" (*Greek Grammar Beyond the Basics*, 481). Fourteen of the fifteen occurrences of μὴ γένοιτο are found in Paul's writings (Luke 20:16; Rom 3:4, 6, 31; 6:2, 15; 7:7, 13; 9:14; 11:1, 11; 1 Cor 6:15; Gal 2:17; 3:21; and 6:14).

2. ποιήσατε

3. πορεύθητι

4. ζητεῖτε

5. ἄρατε

6. ἐλθέτω

7. κάλεσον

8. χαίρετε

9. κρίνατε

10. καταβάτω

C. Imperative Usage: Indicate the specific use of the following imperatives or subjunctives functioning as imperatives: Command (C), Prohibition (P), Hortatory Subjunctive (HS), Prohibitory Subjunctive (PS), or Optative (O).

1. _____ πάντοτε χαίρετε

2. _____ μὴ φοβεῖσθε

3. _____ μὴ ἀδικία παρὰ τῷ θεῷ; μὴ γένοιτο

4. _____ μὴ γνώτω

5. _____ αἰτείτω παρὰ θεοῦ

6. _____ ἀποκτείνωμεν αὐτόν

7. _____ μὴ ἅψῃ

8. _____ εἴ τι ἔχοιεν πρὸς ἐμέ

9. _____ ἀπόλυσον αὐτούς

10. _____ τοῦτο φρονῶμεν

D. Translation: Translate the following sentences, indicating the use of the imperatives.

1. ἀγαπᾶτε τοὺς ἐχθροὺς (enemies) ὑμῶν καὶ προσεύχεσθε ὑπὲρ τῶν διωκόντων ὑμᾶς (Matt 5:44).

2. ἔγειρε ἆρον τὸν κράβαττόν (mat) σου καὶ ὕπαγε εἰς τὸν οἶκόν σου (Mark 2:11).

3. οἱ δὲ λοιποὶ ἔλεγον, . . . ἴδωμεν εἰ ἔρχεται Ἠλίας σώσων αὐτόν (Matt 27:49).

4. προσκυνησάτωσαν αὐτῷ πάντες ἄγγελοι θεοῦ (Heb 1:6).

5. Ἀγαπητοί, μὴ παντὶ πνεύματι πιστεύετε ἀλλὰ δοκιμάζετε (test!) τὰ πνεύματα (1 John 4:1).

6. ἄλλους ἔσωσεν, σωσάτω ἑαυτόν (Luke 23:35).

7. βαπτισθήτω ἕκαστος ὑμῶν ἐπὶ τῷ ὀνόματι Ἰησοῦ Χριστοῦ (Acts 2:38)

8. μὴ εἴπῃς ἐν τῇ καρδίᾳ σου, Τίς ἀναβήσεται εἰς τὸν οὐρανόν; (Rom 10:6).

9. ὑμεῖς λογίζεσθε ἑαυτοὺς εἶναι νεκροὺς τῇ ἁμαρτίᾳ (Rom 6:11).

10. πάτερ ἅγιε, τήρησον αὐτοὺς ἐν τῷ ὀνόματί σου (John 17:11).

11. πᾶς λόγος σαπρὸς (rotten) ἐκ τοῦ στόματος ὑμῶν μὴ ἐκπορευέσθω (Eph 4:29).

12. εἶπεν δὲ Μαριάμ, Ἰδοὺ ἡ δούλη κυρίου· γένοιτό μοι κατὰ τὸ ῥῆμά σου (Luke 1:38).

13. εἰ νεκροὶ οὐκ ἐγείρονται, φάγωμεν καὶ πίωμεν αὔριον (tomorrow) γὰρ ἀποθνήσκομεν (1 Cor 15:32).

14. ἢ οὐκ οἴδατε ὅτι ἄδικοι (unrighteous) θεοῦ βασιλείαν οὐ κληρονομήσουσιν (inherit); μὴ πλανᾶσθε (deceive)· (1 Cor 6:9).

15. αὐτὸς δὲ ὁ κύριος ἡμῶν Ἰησοῦς Χριστὸς καὶ [ὁ] θεὸς ὁ πατὴρ ἡμῶν . . . παρακαλέσαι ὑμῶν τὰς καρδίας καὶ στηρίξαι (establish, optative mood) ἐν παντὶ ἔργῳ καὶ λόγῳ ἀγαθῷ (2 Thess 2:16–17).

E. Translation: Translate the following sentences into Greek. The expected aspect is given for each imperative.

1. Behold, sit (imperfective aspect, middle, sg) before the Lord in fear.

2. Greet (perfective aspect, pl) those in prison and those having need.

3. All generations, dwell (imperfective aspect, pl) in peace.

4. Work (imperfective aspect, pl) as for the Lord.

5. Know (imperfective aspect, pl) me in the year of tribulation and judgment.

23.10 Vocabulary[11]

ἀνίστημι	I stand up, arise (*Anastasia*)
ἀποδίδωμι	I give back, pay
ἀπόλλυμι	I destroy, am lost (mid) (*Apollyon*)
ἀφίημι	I forgive, let go, divorce
δίδωμι	I give (*donation*)
ἵστημι	I stand, set (*stand*)
παραδίδωμι	I hand over, betray, entrust
τίθημι	I put, place, appoint
φημί	I say, affirm (*prophet*)
ἁμαρτωλός, –όν	sinful, sinner (subst)
ἔρημος, –όν	desolate; desert, wilderness (subst)[12]
μικρός, –ά, –όν	small (*microphone, micrometer*)
ὅμοιος, –α, –ον	same nature, similar
ἄχρι	until
οὐαί	woe

---

[11] To hear an author of your textbook read through the vocabulary for chapter 23, go to bit.ly/greekvocab23 or beginninggreek.com.

[12] The substantive form of ἔρημος is a masculine noun of the first declension, ἡ ἔρημος.

CHAPTER 24

///////////////

Mι VERBS

24.1 Overview[1]

Up to this point, we have studied verbs that have similar conjugations (i.e., omega verbs whose lexical forms end in –ω or middle-only –ομαι verbs that follow middle and passive omega verb endings). The only exception has been the verb εἰμί. Like εἰμί, verbs in this chapter are known as *μι verbs* because their lexical form ends with –μι. This type of verb represents an older conjugation in the history of the Greek verbal system. Although there are few μι verbs in the New Testament, those that are used are very common.[2] In this chapter, then, we will highlight unique features of μι verbs, using three key verbs as examples: δίδωμι ("I give"), τίθημι ("I put"), and ἵστημι ("I stand").

24.2 Significance

Have you ever heard someone declare that a faithful Bible translation always renders a Greek or Hebrew word with the same English word? Is that true? Consider applying that principle to the verses below. Each bold word in English is a rendering of the same underlying Greek word, ἀφίημι (a –μι verb):

- Jesus answered him, "**Allow** it for now, because this is the way for us to fulfill all righteousness." Then John **allowed** him to be baptized (Matt 3:15).

---

[1] For an overview video lecture of chapter 24, go to bit.ly/greeklecture24 or beginninggreek.com.
[2] The three key μι verbs in this chapter, along with their various compound forms, occur nearly 1,300 times in the New Testament.

- Then the devil **left** him, and angels came and began to serve him (Matt 4:11).

- And **forgive** us our debts, as we also have forgiven our debtors (Matt 6:12).

- To the rest I say (I, not the Lord) that if any brother has a wife who is an unbeliever, and she consents to live with him, he should not **divorce** her (1 Cor 7:12 ESV).

The truth is that all words have a semantic range (range of meaning), and it is essential to consider the surrounding context to land on the correct one. Always rendering a Greek word with the same English word would produce a strange translation and actually distort the inspired author's meaning.

24.3 Indicative Forms

μι verbs differ from omega verbs only in the present, imperfect, and second aorist tense-forms. (The meaning or translation approach to all tenses, voices, and moods of μι verbs is exactly the same as in the case of omega verbs.) Below is a chart of the tense-forms for the indicative mood. Pay special attention to those forms that differ from omega verbs.

ACTIVE INDICATIVE FORMS OF δίδωμι				
	PRESENT	IMPERFECT	FUTURE	AORIST	PERFECT
1S	δίδωμι	ἐδίδουν	δώσω	ἔδωκα	δέδωκα
2S	δίδως	ἐδίδους	δώσεις	ἔδωκας	δέδωκας
3S	δίδωσι(ν)	ἐδίδου	δώσει	ἔδωκε(ν)	δέδωκε(ν)
1P	δίδομεν	ἐδίδομεν	δώσομεν	ἐδώκαμεν	δεδώκαμεν
2P	δίδοτε	ἐδίδοτε	δώσετε	ἐδώκατε	δεδώκατε
3P	διδόασι(ν)	ἐδίδοσαν	δώσουσι(ν)	ἔδωκαν	δέδωκαν

As seen in the chart below, the aorist indicative is the most common tense-form.

INDICATIVE FORM FREQUENCY

	δίδωμι	τίθημι	ἵστημι	Total
Present	24	12	1	37
Imperfect	12	4	0	16
Future	66	5	8	79
Aorist	**120**	**41**	**30**	**191**
Perfect	35	4	20	59

Based on these numbers, the aorist occurs with the same frequency as all the other tense-forms combined.[3] Thus, it seems odd that most textbooks focus on the present tense-forms, often forcing students to memorize lists of forms that occur rarely.

Verbal Roots

It is crucial to know the roots of μι verbs since the lexical forms include a prefix (reduplication) that is not included on most forms. That is, the various tense-forms are not formed from the present stem but from the verbal root. Here are the roots for our three key verbs:

δίδωμι	δο–
τίθημι	θε–
ἵστημι	στα–

Present Tense

The initial reduplication (e.g., δίδωμι, τίθημι, and ἵστημι) is the sign for the present (and imperfect) μι verbs. Notice that this reduplication differs from that which we find with perfect verbs because an iota (ι) is added between the consonants, not an epsilon (ε). In the present *active* forms, the final vowel is long in the singular forms (e.g., δίδωμι, δίδως, δίδωσιν) and short in the plural forms (δίδομεν, δίδοτε, διδόασιν). The present *middle/passive* forms have short forms in both the singular and plural. Because the stem ends with a vowel, a connecting vowel is not needed.[4]

Aorist Tense Form

First aorist forms are regular except that they use a kappa (κ) tense formative instead of a sigma (σ): e.g., ἔδωκα (not ἔδωσα). This can easily be differentiated from the perfect form which has the normal reduplication (δέδωκα). Like omega verbs, these forms will include an augment (indicative mood only). Passive forms will be marked with the characteristic –θη/θε. Some μι verbs, such as ἵστημι, use both first aorist (ἔστησεν) and second aorist (ἔστη) forms.

24.4 Principal Parts

The key to mastering μι verbs is to know well the six *principal parts* for each verb.[5] This is far more beneficial than memorizing any one paradigm.

---

[3] We have not included pluperfect forms which amount to seventeen occurrences.

[4] Because connecting vowels are not used, μι verbs are often referred to as *athematic*, whereas omega verbs are called *thematic*. Connecting vowels are used with imperfect singular and future forms.

[5] There are six principal parts to a verb, and these are always listed in the same order. These forms help you learn the various ways a verb changes in various tense-forms and voices in the indicative mood.

Present Active	Future Active	Aorist Active	Perfect Active	Perfect Mid/Pass	Aorist Passive
δίδωμι	δώσω	ἔδωκα	δέδωκα	δέδομαι	ἐδόθην
τίθημι[6]	θήσω	ἔθηκα	τέθεικα[7]	τέθειμαι	ἐτέθην[8]
ἵστημι[9]	στήσω	ἔστησα[10]	ἔστηκα	ἔσταμαι	ἐστάθην

24.5 Non-Indicative Forms

ACTIVE NON-INDICATIVE FORMS OF δίδωμι			
PRESENT ACTIVE SUBJUNCTIVE	**2ND AORIST ACTIVE SUBJUNCTIVE**	**PPRESENT ACTIVE IMPERATIVE**	**AORIST ACTIVE IMPERATIVE**
1S διδῶ	δῶ	—	—
2S διδῷς	δῷς	δίδου	δός
3S διδῷ	δῷ	διδότω	δότω
1P διδῶμεν	δῶμεν	—	—
2P διδῶτε	δῶτε	δίδοτε	δότε
3P διδῶσι(ν)	δῶσι(ν)	διδότωσαν	δότωσαν

	Pres Act	Pres M/P	Aor Act	Aor Mid	Aor Pass
Infinitives	διδόναι	δίδοσθαι	δοῦναι	δόσθαι	δοθῆναι
Participles[11]	διδούς	διδόμενος	δούς	δόμενος	δοθείς

Like the indicative mood, all non-indicative moods favor the aorist over the present and perfect. (Remember, there is no imperfect for non-indicative verbs and no future forms occur with the three verbs selected.)

With non-indicative forms, the aorist is even more dominant than with indicative forms. As seen in the following chart, aorists occur more than twice as frequently as all the present and perfect forms combined.

---

[6] The reduplication uses the non-aspirated form (τίθημι not θίθημι).
[7] The final stem vowel of the perfect active and middle/passive forms lengthens from θε– to θει– (instead of θη–).
[8] The final stem vowel is not lengthened (ἐτέθην), and the stem is changed from θε– to the non-aspirated form (τε–) in order to avoid having two thetas in successive syllables (ἐθέθην).
[9] With ἵστημι, the first letter (σ) is not reduplicated but is replaced with a rough breathing mark (ἵστημι).
[10] This form uses a sigma (σ) tense formative (ἔστησα) instead of the normal kappa (κ). This helps distinguish it from the perfect active form (ἔστηκα), which does not fully reduplicate.
[11] Masculine nominative singular forms are listed.

FREQUENCY OF NON-INDICATIVE FORMS

	δίδωμι	τίθημι	ἵστημι	Total
Present	25	5	0	30
Aorist	**127**	**26**	**37**	**190**
Perfect	2	1	41[12]	44

24.6 Other Forms

The verb ἵστημι has both a first aorist form (ἔστησα) and a second aorist form (ἔστην). The first aorist form is transitive. It takes a direct object meaning "I stood [something] up," whereas the second aorist is intransitive. It takes no direct object, but means "I stood up."

The verb ἀφίημι is a compound verb composed of the preposition ἀπό and the verb ἵημι ("I throw, hurl").[13] This verb conjugates like a typical μι verb in the singular but like an omega verb in the plural.

24.7 Practice

A. Principal Parts: Memorize the principle parts of δίδωμι, τίθημι, and ἵστημι (see section 24.4). Then write out each form ten times from memory.

B. Indicative μι Verbs: Identify the correct tense-form of the μι verbs given below: Present (P), Imperfect (I), Future (F), Aorist (A), or Perfect (Pf).

1. _____ δώσει

2. _____ δίδοται

3. _____ ἔδωκαν

4. _____ δοθήσεται

5. _____ δέδωκας

6. _____ διδόασιν

7. _____ δώσουσιν

8. _____ ἐδόθη

9. _____ δέδοται

---

[12] The perfect form of ἵστημι occurs more than the aorist. "Standing" is an activity that fits well with a stative presentation of the action. Of the 41 perfect occurrences, 38 are participles.

[13] ἵημι does not occur in the New Testament without a prepositional prefix. As odd as it sounds, the root of this verb is σε–, but when the beginning of the root reduplicates, the intervocalic sigma drops. The initial sigma becomes a rough breathing mark. The original epsilon of the root lengthens to an eta (William D. Mounce, *The Morphology of Biblical Greek* [Grand Rapids: Zondervan, 1994], 314).

10. _____ ἐδίδου

11. _____ ἔθηκα

12. _____ ἐτίθουν

13. _____ θήσεις

14. _____ ἔθετο

15. _____ τέθειται

16. _____ ἔστησεν

17. _____ ἔστηκας

18. _____ σταθήσεται

19. _____ ἀφίομεν

20. _____ ἔφη

C. Non-Indicative μι Verbs: Identify the correct mood of the μι verbs given: subjunctive (sub), imperative (imp), infinitive (inf), or participle (ptc).

1. _____ δοθῆναι

2. _____ δόντος

3. _____ δοθῇ

4. _____ δοῦναι

5. _____ δότε

6. _____ δώσωμεν

7. _____ δούς

8. _____ δίδοτε

9. _____ θῇ

10. _____ θεῖναι

11. _____ τιθέτω

12. _____ θέντος

13. _____ σταθῆναι

14. _____ σταθῆτε

15. _____ σταθείς

16. _____ ἀφιέτω

17. _____ ἀφιέναι

18. _____ ἀφέντες

19. _____ ἀφῆτε

20. _____ ἀπολλυμένοις

D. Translation: Translate the following sentences.

1. καὶ ἐδίδου [ἄρτους] τοῖς μαθηταῖς, οἱ δὲ μαθηταὶ τοῖς ὄχλοις (Matt 15:36).

2. ὁ Χριστὸς ἠγάπησεν ἡμᾶς καὶ παρέδωκεν ἑαυτὸν ὑπὲρ ἡμῶν (Eph 5:2).

3. ἦλθεν ὁ Ἰησοῦς καὶ ἔστη εἰς τὸ μέσον καὶ λέγει αὐτοῖς, Εἰρήνη ὑμῖν (John 20:19).

4. θήσω τὸ πνεῦμά μου ἐπ᾽ αὐτόν, καὶ κρίσιν τοῖς ἔθνεσιν ἀπαγγελεῖ (Matt 12:18).

5. ὁ νόμος διὰ Μωϋσέως ἐδόθη, ἡ χάρις καὶ ἡ ἀλήθεια διὰ Ἰησοῦ Χριστοῦ ἐγένετο (John 1:17).

6. ... ἵνα ὁ θεὸς τοῦ κυρίου ἡμῶν Ἰησοῦ Χριστοῦ, ὁ πατὴρ τῆς δόξης, δώῃ ὑμῖν πνεῦμα σοφίας (Eph 1:17).

7. φοβήθητε τὸν θεὸν καὶ δότε αὐτῷ δόξαν (Rev 14:7).

8. μείζονα ταύτης ἀγάπην οὐδεὶς ἔχει, ἵνα τις τὴν ψυχὴν αὐτοῦ θῇ ὑπὲρ τῶν φίλων (friends) αὐτοῦ (John 15:15).

9. εἰ οὖν ὑμεῖς πονηροὶ ὄντες οἴδατε δόματα (gifts) ἀγαθὰ διδόναι τοῖς τέκνοις ὑμῶν, πόσῳ (how much) μᾶλλον ὁ πατὴρ ὑμῶν ὁ ἐν τοῖς οὐρανοῖς δώσει ἀγαθὰ τοῖς αἰτοῦσιν αὐτόν (Matt 7:11).

10. εἰ δέ τις ὑμῶν λείπεται (lacks, takes gen obj) σοφίας, αἰτείτω παρὰ τοῦ διδόντος θεοῦ πᾶσιν ... καὶ δοθήσεται αὐτῷ (Jas 1:5).

11. οὐδεὶς αἴρει [τὴν ψυχήν μου] ἀπ᾽ ἐμοῦ, ἀλλ᾽ ἐγὼ τίθημι αὐτὴν ἀπ᾽ ἐμαυτοῦ. ἐξουσίαν ἔχω θεῖναι αὐτήν, καὶ ἐξουσίαν ἔχω πάλιν λαβεῖν αὐτήν (John 10:18).

12. . . . ὥστε ὁ δοκῶν ἑστάναι βλεπέτω μὴ πέσῃ (1 Cor 10:12).

13. ἀμὴν ἀμὴν λέγω ὑμῖν, οὐ Μωϋσῆς δέδωκεν ὑμῖν τὸν ἄρτον ἐκ τοῦ
     οὐρανοῦ, ἀλλ᾿ ὁ πατήρ μου δίδωσιν ὑμῖν τὸν ἄρτον ἐκ τοῦ οὐρανοῦ τὸν
     ἀληθινόν (true) (John 6:32).

14. καὶ ὁ ἄγγελος, ὃν εἶδον ἑστῶτα ἐπὶ τῆς θαλάσσης καὶ ἐπὶ τῆς γῆς, ἦρεν
     τὴν χεῖρα αὐτοῦ τὴν δεξιὰν εἰς τὸν οὐρανόν (Rev 10:5).

15. ἐὰν δὲ μὴ ἀφῆτε τοῖς ἀνθρώποις, οὐδὲ ὁ πατὴρ ὑμῶν ἀφήσει τὰ
     παραπτώματα (trespasses) ὑμῶν (Matt 6:15).

E. Translation: Translate the following sentences into Greek.

1. The small and the great stood and gave glory to God.

2. Up to this day, he raised up disciples like his master.

3. Woe to the one who betrays me, because God will pay him back accord-
    ing to his deeds.

4. Sinners are forgiven and are not destroyed.

5. He said to him, "I will place my Spirit on him in the desert."

How Can I Study the Greek New Testament on my Smartphone, Tablet, or Computer?

Introducing Digital Resources

Not long ago, no one had ever heard of an app, an iPad, or a Kindle. If you are reading these words a decade or more after we write them, perhaps you don't know what they are either! The point is that nowadays technology changes quickly. Nevertheless, one thing that will remain constant going forward is this: the ability to read the Greek New Testament and access Greek resources digitally. The majority of students who continue faithfully reading their Greek New Testaments, in fact, do so in digital format because of (1) ease of access and (2) linking of resources.

Let's consider these benefits in turn. First, while it is inconvenient to carry a printed edition of the Greek New Testament, one can easily access a digital text on one's smartphone, tablet, or computer. In our current culture, the smartphone has become the ubiquitous digital assistant—replacing cameras, books, wallets, and even printed Greek New Testaments! Second, many digital texts have search features that mirror concordance capabilities and are linked with lexicons, parsing

information, and even grammatical diagrams so that students can quickly gain assistance with the text.

We realize that any digital recommendations might quickly become outdated, but we tentatively offer below our best-of-the-best suggestions.

Free Resources

There are many high-quality free digital resources to help you learn, retain, and use Greek. On the top of our list is this website: www.dailydoseofgreek.com (overseen by Rob Plummer, an author of this book). Subscribers are provided with a free daily screencast overviewing one verse from the Greek New Testament; each is only two to three minutes in length. We also recommend the website www.biblearc.com, which gives access to Greek texts (New Testament and Septuagint), lexicons, and search capabilities. Both the Daily Dose of Greek and Biblearc also have free smartphone apps. Additionally, the website www. mastergreek.com can help you hone your parsing. And numerous digital tools exist to fortify your Greek vocabulary. (Just search for Greek vocabulary sets on Quizlet, Memrise, or Anki). Also, see links to several free vocabulary flash card sets keyed to the intermediate Greek grammar *Going Deeper with New Testament Greek* at www.deepergreek.com.

Resources for Purchasing

While the free resources above will suffice for many, there are also premium tools available for purchase. If you are planning to be a vocational minister, you will likely want to buy a top-tier Bible software program for original language work in the Greek and Hebrew texts. There are two clear frontrunners—Logos and Accordance. But before making the significant financial investment in a program, we recommend that you talk to your Greek professor and explore the Logos and Accordance products via their websites. B&H Academic (the publisher of this textbook) also has a Bible software, Wordsearch. Though Wordsearch has fewer Greek capabilities than Logos or Accordance, it has proven invaluable to thousands of pastors around the world. (Visit wordsearch-bible.com/bntg to purchase a digital version of this book at a discounted rate.) Logos, Accordance, and Wordsearch all have smartphone apps that sync with one's purchased library. For a purely app-based approach to the Greek text (on a smartphone or iPad), we recommend the Olive Tree Bible Study app, which provides intuitive access to biblical texts and resources. For a premium vocabulary-learning experience, we recommend these for-purchase apps: Bible Vocab, Flash Greek, and Parse Greek.

RECOMMENDED FREE DIGITAL TOOLS	
DEVICE/FORMAT	RECOMMENDATION
Websites	www.dailydoseofgreek.com www.biblearc.com www.mastergreek.com
Smartphone apps	Daily Dose of Greek app Biblearc app

RECOMMENDED DIGITAL TOOLS FOR PURCHASE	
DEVICE/FORMAT	RECOMMENDATION
Computer software	Logos or Accordance
Smartphone apps	Olive Tree "Bible Study" app or Logos app Bible Vocab app FlashGreek and ParseGreek app *(Note: Olive Tree and Logos apps are free, but Greek resources must be purchased within apps.)*

Optional Assignment: Spend fifteen minutes exploring the Biblearc app and website. (1) Place the Greek New Testament and an English translation side by side. (2) Click on Greek words to access parsing and lexical information. (3) Click on a verse number of the Greek New Testament. What happens? Be prepared to orally and visually show someone the basic functions of the Biblearc app/website.

Appendix

PARADIGMS

	SINGULAR			PLURAL		
	FIRST DECLENSION NOUN—ETA PATTERN					
NOM	ἡ	φωνή	the voice	αἱ	φωναί	the voices
GEN	τῆς	φωνῆς	of the voice	τῶν	φωνῶν	of the voices
DAT	τῇ	φωνῇ	to/for the voice	ταῖς	φωναῖς	to/for the voices
ACC	τὴν	φωνήν	the voice	τὰς	φωνάς	the voices

	SINGULAR			PLURAL		
	FIRST DECLENSION NOUN—ALPHA PATTERN					
NOM	ἡ	καρδία	the heart	αἱ	καρδίαι	the hearts
GEN	τῆς	καρδίας	of the heart	τῶν	καρδιῶν	of the hearts
DAT	τῇ	καρδίᾳ	to/for the heart	ταῖς	καρδίαις	to/for the hearts
ACC	τὴν	καρδίαν	the heart	τὰς	καρδίας	the hearts

	SINGULAR			PLURAL		
	SECOND DECLENSION NOUN—MASCULINE					
NOM	ὁ	λόγος	the word	οἱ	λόγοι	the words
GEN	τοῦ	λόγου	of the word	τῶν	λόγων	of the words
DAT	τῷ	λόγῳ	to/for the word	τοῖς	λόγοις	to/for the words
ACC	τὸν	λόγον	the word	τοὺς	λόγους	the words

	SINGULAR			PLURAL		
	SECOND DECLENSION NOUN—NEUTER					
NOM	τὸ	τέκνον	the child	τὰ	τέκνα	the children
GEN	τοῦ	τέκνου	of the child	τῶν	τέκνων	of the children
DAT	τῷ	τέκνῳ	to/for the child	τοῖς	τέκνοις	to/for the children
ACC	τὸ	τέκνον	the child	τὰ	τέκνα	the children

THIRD DECLENSION NOUN—FEMININE					
	SINGULAR			PLURAL	
NOM	ἡ	σάρξ	the flesh	αἱ	σάρκες	the flesh(es)
GEN	τῆς	σαρκός	of the flesh	τῶν	σαρκῶν	of the flesh(es)
DAT	τῇ	σαρκί	to/for the flesh	ταῖς	σαρξί(ν)	to/for the flesh(es)
ACC	τὴν	σάρκα	the flesh	τὰς	σάρκας	the flesh(es)

THIRD DECLENSION NOUN—NEUTER					
	SINGULAR			PLURAL	
NOM	τὸ	πνεῦμα	the spirit	τὰ	πνεύματα	the spirits
GEN	τοῦ	πνεύματος	of the spirit	τῶν	πνευμάτων	of the spirits
DAT	τῷ	πνεύματι	to/for the spirit	τοῖς	πνεύμασι(ν)	to/for the spirits
ACC	τὸ	πνεῦμα	the spirit	τὰ	πνεύματα	the spirits

FIRST AND SECOND DECLENSION ADJECTIVE					
	SINGULAR			PLURAL		
	MASC	FEM	NEUT	MASC	FEM	NEUT
NOM	ἀγαθός	ἀγαθή	ἀγαθόν	ἀγαθοί	ἀγαθαί	ἀγαθά
GEN	ἀγαθοῦ	ἀγαθῆς	ἀγαθοῦ	ἀγαθῶν	ἀγαθῶν	ἀγαθῶν
DAT	ἀγαθῷ	ἀγαθῇ	ἀγαθῷ	ἀγαθοῖς	ἀγαθαῖς	ἀγαθοῖς
ACC	ἀγαθόν	ἀγαθήν	ἀγαθόν	ἀγαθούς	ἀγαθάς	ἀγαθά

THIRD DECLENSION ADJECTIVE					
	SINGULAR			PLURAL		
	MASC	FEM	NEUT	MASC	FEM	NEUT
NOM	πᾶς	πᾶσα	πᾶν	πάντες	πᾶσαι	πάντα
GEN	παντός	πάσης	παντός	πάντων	πασῶν	πάντων
DAT	παντί	πάσῃ	παντί	πᾶσι(ν)	πάσαις	πᾶσι(ν)
ACC	πάντα	πᾶσαν	πᾶν	πάντας	πάσας	πάντα

FIRST PERSON PERSONAL PRONOUN				
	SINGULAR		PLURAL	
NOM	ἐγώ	I	ἡμεῖς	we
GEN	μου	of me, my	ἡμῶν	of us, our
DAT	μοι	to/for me	ἡμῖν	to/for us
ACC	με	me	ἡμᾶς	us

SECOND PERSON PERSONAL PRONOUN				
	SINGULAR		PLURAL	
NOM	σύ	you	ὑμεῖς	you
GEN	σου	of you, your	ὑμῶν	of you, your
DAT	σοι	to/for you	ὑμῖν	to/for you
ACC	σε	you	ὑμᾶς	you

THIRD PERSON PERSONAL PRONOUN					
	SINGULAR			PLURAL		
	MASC	FEM	NEUT	MASC	FEM	NEUT
NOM	αὐτός	αὐτή	αὐτό	αὐτοί	αὐταί	αὐτά
GEN	αὐτοῦ	αὐτῆς	αὐτοῦ	αὐτῶν	αὐτῶν	αὐτῶν
DAT	αὐτῷ	αὐτῇ	αὐτῷ	αὐτοῖς	αὐταῖς	αὐτοῖς
ACC	αὐτόν	αὐτήν	αὐτό	αὐτούς	αὐτάς	αὐτά

RELATIVE PRONOUN					
	SINGULAR			PLURAL		
	MASC	FEM	NEUT	MASC	FEM	NEUT
NOM	ὅς	ἥ	ὅ	οἵ	αἵ	ἅ
GEN	οὗ	ἧς	οὗ	ὧν	ὧν	ὧν
DAT	ᾧ	ᾗ	ᾧ	οἷς	αἷς	οἷς
ACC	ὅν	ἥν	ὅ	οὕς	ἅς	ἅ

NEAR DEMONSTRATIVE PRONOUN					
	SINGULAR			PLURAL		
	MASC	*FEM*	*NEUT*	*MASC*	*FEM*	*NEUT*
NOM	οὗτος	αὕτη	τοῦτο	οὗτοι	αὗται	ταῦτα
GEN	τούτου	ταύτης	τούτου	τούτων	τούτων	τούτων
DAT	τούτῳ	ταύτῃ	τούτῳ	τούτοις	ταύταις	τούτοις
ACC	τοῦτον	ταύτην	τοῦτο	τούτους	ταύτας	ταῦτα

INTERROGATIVE / INDEFINITE PRONOUNS			
	SINGULAR		PLURAL	
	MASC/FEM	*NEUT*	*MASC/FEM*	*NEUT*
NOM	τίς / τις	τί / τι	τίνες / τινές	τίνα / τινά
GEN	τίνος / τινός	τίνος / τινός	τίνων / τινῶν	τίνων / τινῶν
DAT	τίνι / τινί	τίνι / τινί	τίσι(ν) / τισί(ν)	τίσι(ν) / τισί(ν)
ACC	τίνα / τινα	τί / τι	τίνας / τινάς	τίνα / τινά

PRESENT ACTIVE INDICATIVE			
	SINGULAR		PLURAL	
1ST	λύω	I am loosing	λύομεν	we are loosing
2ND	λύεις	you are loosing	λύετε	you are loosing
3RD	λύει	he/she/it is loosing	λύουσι(ν)	they are loosing

PRESENT MIDDLE/PASSIVE INDICATIVE			
	SINGULAR		PLURAL	
1ST	λύομαι	I am being loosed	λυόμεθα	we are being loosed
2ND	λύῃ	you are being loosed	λύεσθε	you are being loosed
3RD	λύεται	he/she/it is being loosed	λύονται	they are being loosed

PRESENT INDICATIVE—εἰμί			
	SINGULAR		PLURAL	
1ST	εἰμί	I am	ἐσμέν	we are
2ND	εἶ	you are	ἐστέ	you are
3RD	ἐστίν	he/she/it is	εἰσίν	they are

IMPERFECT ACTIVE INDICATIVE				
	SINGULAR		PLURAL	
1ST	ἔλυον	I was loosing	ἐλύομεν	we were loosing
2ND	ἔλυες	you were loosing	ἐλύετε	you were loosing
3RD	ἔλυε(ν)	he/she/it was loosing	ἔλυον	they were loosing

IMPERFECT MIDDLE/PASSIVE INDICATIVE				
	SINGULAR		PLURAL	
1ST	ἐλυόμην	I was being loosed	ἐλυόμεθα	we were being loosed
2ND	ἐλύου	you were being loosed	ἐλύεσθε	you were being loosed
3RD	ἐλύετο	he/she/it was being loosed	ἐλύοντο	they were being loosed

IMPERFECT INDICATIVE—εἰμί				
	SINGULAR		PLURAL	
1ST	ἤμην	I was	ἦμεν	we were
2ND	ἦς	you were	ἦτε	you were
3RD	ἦν	he/she/it was	ἦσαν	they were

FUTURE ACTIVE INDICATIVE				
	SINGULAR		PLURAL	
1ST	λύσω	I will loose	λύσομεν	we will loose
2ND	λύσεις	you will loose	λύσετε	you will loose
3RD	λύσει	he/she/it will loose	λύσουσι(ν)	they will loose

FUTURE MIDDLE INDICATIVE				
	SINGULAR		PLURAL	
1ST	λύσομαι	I will loose (for) myself	λυσόμεθα	we will loose (for) ourselves
2ND	λύσῃ	you will loose (for) yourself	λύσεσθε	you will loose (for) yourselves
3RD	λύσεται	he/she/it will loose (for) him-/her-/itself	λύσονται	they will loose (for) themselves

FUTURE PASSIVE INDICATIVE			
	SINGULAR		PLURAL
1ST	λυθήσομαι	I will be loosed	λυθησόμεθα	we will be loosed
2ND	λυθήσῃ	you will be loosed	λυθήσεσθε	you will be loosed
3RD	λυθήσεται	he/she/it will be loosed	λυθήσονται	they will be loosed

AORIST ACTIVE INDICATIVE			
	SINGULAR		PLURAL
1ST	ἔλυσα	I loosed	ἐλύσαμεν	we loosed
2ND	ἔλυσας	you loosed	ἐλύσατε	you loosed
3RD	ἔλυσε(ν)	he/she/it loosed	ἔλυσαν	they loosed

AORIST MIDDLE INDICATIVE			
	SINGULAR		PLURAL
1ST	ἐλυσάμην	I loosed (for) myself	ἐλυσάμεθα	we loosed (for) ourselves
2ND	ἐλύσω	you loosed (for) yourself	ἐλύσασθε	you loosed (for) yourselves
3RD	ἐλύσατο	he/she/it loosed (for) him-/her-/itself	ἐλύσαντο	they loosed (for) themselves

AORIST PASSIVE INDICATIVE			
	SINGULAR		PLURAL
1ST	ἐλύθην	I was loosed	ἐλύθημεν	we were loosed
2ND	ἐλύθης	you were loosed	ἐλύθητε	you were loosed
3RD	ἐλύθη	he/she/it was loosed	ἐλύθησαν	they were loosed

SECOND AORIST ACTIVE INDICATIVE—λαμβάνω			
	SINGULAR		PLURAL
1ST	ἔλαβον	I took	ἐλάβομεν	we took
2ND	ἔλαβες	you took	ἐλάβετε	you took
3RD	ἔλαβεν	he/she/it took	ἔλαβον	they took

SECOND AORIST MIDDLE INDICATIVE—γίνομαι

	SINGULAR		PLURAL	
1ST	ἐγενόμην	I became	ἐγενόμεθα	we became
2ND	ἐγένου	you became	ἐγένεσθε	you became
3RD	ἐγένετο	he/she/it became	ἐγένοντο	they became

PERFECT ACTIVE INDICATIVE

	SINGULAR		PLURAL	
1ST	λέλυκα	I have loosed	λελύκαμεν	we have loosed
2ND	λέλυκας	you have loosed	λελύκατε	you have loosed
3RD	λέλυκε(ν)	he/she/it has loosed	λελύκασι(ν) λελύκαν	they have loosed

PERFECT MIDDLE/PASSIVE INDICATIVE

	SINGULAR		PLURAL	
1ST	λέλυμαι	I have been loosed	λελύμεθα	we have been loosed
2ND	λέλυσαι	you have been loosed	λέλυσθε	you have been loosed
3RD	λέλυται	he/she/it has been loosed	λέλυνται	they have been loosed

ACTIVE INDICATIVE FORMS OF δίδωμι

	PRESENT	IMPERFECT	FUTURE	AORIST	PERFECT
1S	δίδωμι	ἐδίδουν	δώσω	ἔδωκα	δέδωκα
2S	δίδως	ἐδίδους	δώσεις	ἔδωκας	δέδωκας
3S	δίδωσι(ν)	ἐδίδου	δώσει	ἔδωκε(ν)	δέδωκε(ν)
1P	δίδομεν	ἐδίδομεν	δώσομεν	ἐδώκαμεν	δεδώκαμεν
2P	δίδοτε	ἐδίδοτε	δώσετε	ἐδώκατε	δεδώκατε
3P	διδόασι(ν)	ἐδίδοσαν	δώσουσι(ν)	ἔδωκαν	δέδωκαν

PRESENT ACTIVE PARTICIPLE

	SINGULAR			PLURAL		
	MASC	FEM	NEUT	MASC	FEM	NEUT
NOM	λύων	λύουσα	λῦον	λύοντες	λύουσαι	λύοντα
GEN	λύοντος	λυούσης	λύοντος	λυόντων	λυουσῶν	λυόντων
DAT	λύοντι	λυούσῃ	λύοντι	λύουσι(ν)	λυούσαις	λύουσι(ν)
ACC	λύοντα	λύουσαν	λῦον	λύοντας	λυούσας	λύοντα

PRESENT MIDDLE/PASSIVE PARTICIPLE

	SINGULAR			PLURAL		
	MASC	*FEM*	*NEUT*	*MASC*	*FEM*	*NEUT*
NOM	λυόμενος	λυομένη	λυόμενον	λυόμενοι	λυόμεναι	λυόμενα
GEN	λυομένου	λυομένης	λυομένου	λυομένων	λυομένων	λυομένων
DAT	λυομένῳ	λυομένῃ	λυομένῳ	λυομένοις	λυομέναις	λυομένοις
ACC	λυόμενον	λυομένην	λυόμενον	λυομένους	λυομένας	λυόμενα

FIRST AORIST ACTIVE PARTICIPLE

	SINGULAR			PLURAL		
	MASC	*FEM*	*NEUT*	*MASC*	*FEM*	*NEUT*
NOM	λύσας	λύσασα	λῦσαν	λύσαντες	λύσασαι	λύσαντα
GEN	λύσαντος	λυσάσης	λύσαντος	λυσάντων	λυσασῶν	λυσάντων
DAT	λύσαντι	λυσάσῃ	λύσαντι	λύσασι(ν)	λυσάσαις	λύσασι(ν)
ACC	λύσαντα	λύσασαν	λῦσαν	λύσαντας	λυσάσας	λύσαντα

FIRST AORIST MIDDLE PARTICIPLE

	SINGULAR			PLURAL		
	MASC	*FEM*	*NEUT*	*MASC*	*FEM*	*NEUT*
NOM	λυσάμενος	λυσαμένη	λυσάμενον	λυσάμενοι	λυσάμεναι	λυσάμενα
GEN	λυσαμένου	λυσαμένης	λυσαμένου	λυσαμένων	λυσαμένων	λυσαμένων
DAT	λυσαμένῳ	λυσαμένῃ	λυσαμένῳ	λυσαμένοις	λυσαμέναις	λυσαμένοις
ACC	λυσάμενον	λυσαμένην	λυσάμενον	λυσαμένους	λυσαμένας	λυσάμενα

FIRST AORIST PASSIVE PARTICIPLE

	SINGULAR			PLURAL		
	MASC	*FEM*	*NEUT*	*MASC*	*FEM*	*NEUT*
NOM	λυθείς	λυθεῖσα	λυθέν	λυθέντες	λυθεῖσαι	λυθέντα
GEN	λυθέντος	λυθείσης	λυθέντος	λυθέντων	λυθεισῶν	λυθέντων
DAT	λυθέντι	λυθείσῃ	λυθέντι	λυθεῖσι(ν)	λυθείσαις	λυθεῖσι(ν)
ACC	λυθέντα	λυθεῖσαν	λυθέν	λυθέντας	λυθείσας	λυθέντα

PERFECT ACTIVE PARTICIPLE					
	SINGULAR			PLURAL		
	MASC	*FEM*	*NEUT*	*MASC*	*FEM*	*NEUT*
NOM	λελυκώς	λελυκυῖα	λελυκός	λελυκότες	λελυκυῖαι	λελυκότα
GEN	λελυκότος	λελυκυῖας	λελυκότος	λελυκότων	λελυκυιῶν	λελυκότων
DAT	λελυκότι	λελυκυῖα	λελυκότι	λελυκόσι(ν)	λελυκυῖαις	λελυκόσι(ν)
ACC	λελυκότα	λελυκυῖαν	λελυκός	λελυκότας	λελυκυῖας	λελυκότα

PERFECT MIDDLE/PASSIVE PARTICIPLE					
	SINGULAR			PLURAL		
	MASC	*FEM*	*NEUT*	*MASC*	*FEM*	*NEUT*
NOM	λελυμένος	λελυμένη	λελυμένον	λελυμένοι	λελυμέναι	λελυμένα
GEN	λελυμένου	λελυμένης	λελυμένου	λελυμένων	λελυμένων	λελυμένων
DAT	λελυμένῳ	λελυμένῃ	λελυμένῳ	λελυμένοις	λελυμέναις	λελυμένοις
ACC	λελυμένον	λελυμένην	λελυμένον	λελυμένους	λελυμένας	λελυμένα

PRESENT AND AORIST INFINITIVES			
TENSE	VOICE	INFINITIVE	TRANSLATION
PRESENT	Active	λύειν	to loose, or to be loosing
	Middle Passive	λύεσθαι	to loose (for) oneself to be loosed
AORIST	Active	λῦσαι	to loose
	Middle	λύσασθαι	to loose (for) oneself
	Passive	λυθῆναι	to be loosed

	PRESENT ACTIVE SUB		PRESENT MIDDLE/PASSIVE SUB	
	SINGULAR	PLURAL	SINGULAR	PLURAL
1ST	λύω	λύωμεν	λύωμαι	λυώμεθα
2ND	λύῃς	λύητε	λύῃ	λύησθε
3RD	λύῃ	λύωσι(ν)	λύηται	λύωνται

	AORIST ACTIVE SUB		AORIST MIDDLE SUB		AORIST PASSIVE SUB	
	SINGULAR	PLURAL	SINGULAR	PLURAL	SINGULAR	PLURAL
1ST	λύσω	λύσωμεν	λύσωμαι	λυσώμεθα	λύθω	λύθωμεν
2ND	λύσῃς	λύσητε	λύσῃ	λύσησθε	λύθῃς	λύθητε
3RD	λύσῃ	λύσωσι(ν)	λύσηται	λύσωνται	λύθῃ	λύθωσι(ν)

PRESENT ACTIVE IMPERATIVE				
	SINGULAR		PLURAL	
2ND	λῦε	loose (be loosing)	λύετε	loose (be loosing)
3RD	λυέτω	let him/her loose (let him be loosing)	λυέτωσαν	let them loose (let them be loosing)

PRESENT MIDDLE/PASSIVE IMPERATIVE				
	SINGULAR		PLURAL	
2ND	λύου	be loosed	λύεσθε	be loosed
3RD	λυέσθω	let him/her be loosed	λυέσθωσαν	let them be loosed

AORIST ACTIVE IMPERATIVE				
	SINGULAR		PLURAL	
2ND	λῦσον	loose	λύσατε	loose
3RD	λυσάτω	let him/her loose	λυσάτωσαν	let them loose

ACTIVE NON-INDICATIVE FORMS OF δίδωμι				
	P A SUB	2A A SUB	P A IMP	A A IMP
1S	διδῶ	δῶ	—	—
2S	διδῶς	δῷς	δίδου	δός
3S	διδῷ	δῷ	διδότω	δότω
1P	διδῶμεν	δῶμεν	—	—
2P	διδῶτε	δῶτε	δίδοτε	δότε
3P	διδῶσι(ν)	δῶσι(ν)	διδότωσαν	δότωσαν

MASTER VERB CHART (INDICATIVE)				
PRESENT	**FUTURE**	**IMPERFECT (SECOND AORIST)**	**FIRST AORIST**	**PERFECT**
ACTIVE —ω —εις —ει —ομεν —ετε —ουσι(ν) I am loosing	—σω —σεις —σει —σομεν —σετε —σουσι(ν) I will loose	χ—ον χ—ες χ—ε(ν) χ—ομεν χ—ετε χ—ον I was loosing	χ—σα χ—σας χ—σε(ν) χ—σαμεν χ—σατε χ—σαν I loosed	χχ—κα χχ—κας χχ—κε(ν) χχ—καμεν χχ—κατε χχ—κασι(ν) I have loosed
MIDDLE —ομαι —ῃ —εται —ομεθα —εσθε —ονται I am loosing (for) myself	—σομαι —σῃ —σεται —σομεθα —σεσθε —σονται I will loose (for) myself	χ—ομην χ—ου χ—ετο χ—ομεθα χ—εσθε χ—οντο I was loosing (for) myself	χ—σαμην χ—σω χ—σατο χ—σαμεθα χ—σασθε χ—σαντο I loosed (for) myself	χχ—μαι χχ—σαι χχ—ται χχ—μεθα χχ—σθε χχ—νται I have loosed (for) myself
PASSIVE I am being loosed	—θησομαι —θησῃ| —θησεται —θησομεθα —θησεσθε —θησονται I will be loosed	I was being loosed	χ—θην χ—θης χ—θη χ—θημεν χ—θητε χ—θησαν I was loosed	I have been loosed

In this chart, χ stands for an augment and χχ stands for reduplication. This chart was created by one of Dr. Plummer's former students for free distribution to other Greek students.

ADJECTIVE FLOWCHART

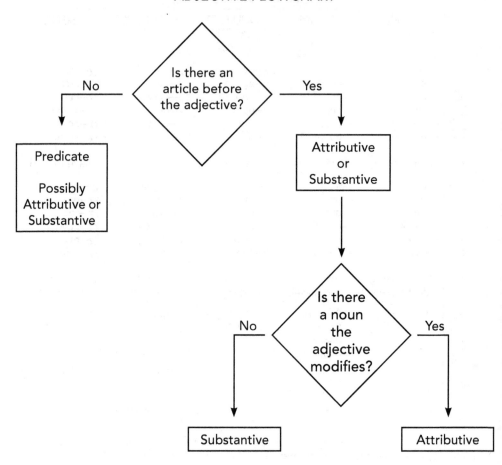

INDICATIVE VERB FLOWCHART

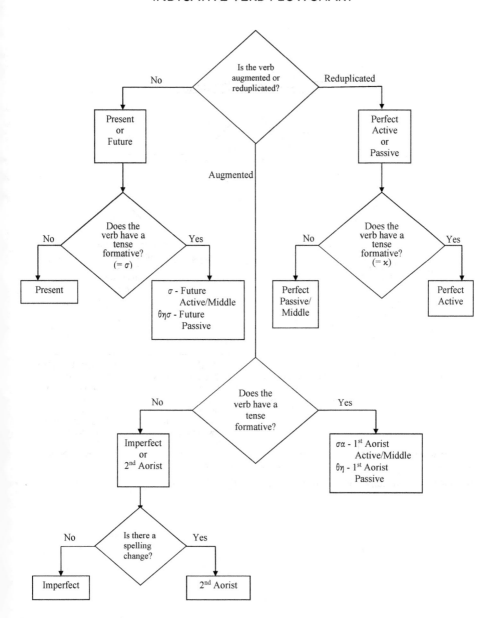

PARTICIPLE FLOWCHART

Translating the Participle

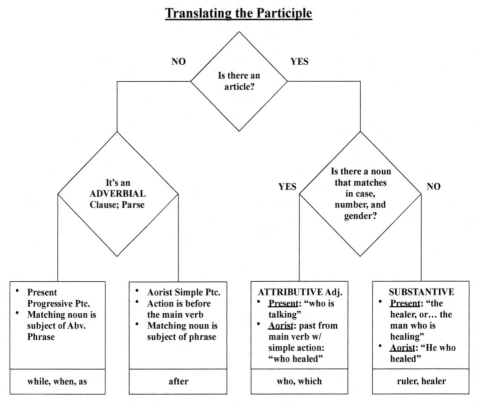

Translating the Participle flowchart was created by Ryan Fullerton.

THE NINE VERBS THAT USE MORE THAN ONE ROOT[1]

As .in English, the vast majority of verbs in the New Testament use only one root. An exception in English is the verb "go," which uses a different root in the past tense: "went." In the New Testament, there are six verbs that use two roots, and three verbs that use three! These nine verbs are listed below, together with the roots they use.

As is the case for the English verb "go," these nine Greek verbs convey actions that are quite common. This commonness played a role in the forms of these verbs becoming what they are. It also means that it is important for you to learn them (especially the four that are the most common)! Please use the learning activity below to do so.

FREQ[2]	PRESENT			AORIST[3]			FUTURE[4]		
2,353	λέγω	λεγ	I say	εἶπον	ϝεπ[5]	I said	ἐρῶ[6]	ϝερ	I will say
632	ἔρχομαι	ερχ	I come	ἦλθον[7]	ελευθ	I came	ἐλεύσομαι[8]	ελευθ	I will come
454	ὁράω	ϝορα	I see	εἶδον	ϝιδ[9]	I saw	ὄψομαι[10]	οπ	I will see
318	οἶδα[11]	οιδ	I know	ᾔδειν[12]	ϝιδ	I knew	εἰδήσω[13]	ϝιδ	I will know
158	ἐσθίω[14]	εδ	I eat	ἔφαγον	φαγ	I ate	φάγομαι[15]	φαγ	I will eat
66	φέρω	φερ	I carry	ἤνεγκα[16]	ενεκ	I carried	οἴσω	οι	I will carry
42	πάσχω[17]	παθ	I suffer	ἔπαθον	παθ[18]	I suffered	—[19]		
20	τρέχω[20]	θρεχ	I run	ἔδραμον	δραμ	I ran	—		
3	αἱρέομαι	αιρε	I prefer	εἱλόμην	ϝελ	I preferred	αἱρήσομαι	αιρε	I will prefer

---

[1] This content is a simplified version of page 319 in *MBG* (*The Morphology of Biblical Greek* by William D. Mounce [Grand Rapids: Zondervan, 1994]). Chart created by Richard Osborn and used with permission.

[2] These frequencies of occurrence in the New Testament do not include the many compound verbs that include these verbs.

[3] Note that except for οἶδα and φέρω, these aorist forms follow the second aorist paradigm. Note that for ἔρχομαι, the aorist is in the active voice even though the present and future are in the middle voice.

[4] Note that for ὁράω and ἐσθίω, the future is in the middle voice even though the present and aorist are in the active voice.

[5] Although the letter digamma (ϝ, pronounced "v") had dropped out of the Greek language by the Koine period, it plays a part in how certain vowels appear.

[6] Since ρ is a liquid consonant, ρσω becomes ρῶ.

[7] The dipthong ευ drops out: ελευθ > ελθ.

[8] When θ (a dental) precedes σ, it assimilates to σ; the resulting σσ simplifies to σ: θσ > σσ > σ.

[9] Note that εἶδον (I saw) and ᾔδειν (I knew) use the same root (ϝιδ). This makes sense when one realizes that in this regard Greek is similar to English: He saw/knew what she meant.

[10] When π (a labial) precedes σ, the combination πσ becomes the labial double consonant ψ.

[11] "οἶδα is really a second perfect that through time became used as a present" (*MBG*, 263, n.9).

[12] ᾔδειν "actually is an augmented pluperfect that functions as an aorist" (*MBG*, 263, n.11).

[13] εἰδήσω was "reduplicated to form the future (since it probably is an old future perfect), ϝ dropped out, the vowels contracted, and η was inserted" (*MBG*, 263, n.10).

[14] "To the root was added θι, which was an old way of forming the present tense stem" (*MBG*, 263, n.3). When δ (a dental) immediately precedes θ (another dental), δ dissimilates to σ. The result is εδ + θι > εσθι.

[15] Note that the future form φάγομαι does not contain a σ (the future tense formative).

[16] See *MBG*, 265, n.8.

[17] To the root παθ was added σκ. Then, θσ > σ (see n.8): παθ + σκ > πασκ. Although θ is not seen, it's aspiration causes κ (a velar) to aspirate to χ (the aspirate velar): πασκ > πασχ (see *MBG*, 313, n.11).

[18] The perfect (πέπονθα) uses the root πενθ.

[19] Forms that do not occur in the New Testament are not included.

[20] When a stem has two aspirates, the first deaspirates: θρεχ > τρεχ (see *MBG*, 29).

CONSONANTAL MORPHOLOGY[1]

Some consonants change when they encounter other consonants. The simple reason for consonant changes is that they make words easier to pronounce. Changes
occur when a consonant is immediately before δ, before θ, before μ, after ν, before
σ, and before τ.

BEFORE δ:	BEFORE θ:	BEFORE μ:
δδ > σδ[2]	βθ > φθ[5]	βμ > μμ[8]
ζδ > σδ[2]	γθ > χθ[6]	δμ > σμ[9]
θδ > σδ[2]	δθ > σθ[7]	ζμ > σμ[9]
κδ > γδ[3]	ζθ > σθ[7]	θμ > σμ[9]
πδ > βδ[4]	θθ > σθ[7]	κμ > γμ[10]
τδ > σδ[2]	κθ > χθ[6]	νμ > μμ[11]
φδ > βδ[4]	ξθ > χθ[6]	πμ > μμ[8]
χδ > γδ[3]	πθ > φθ[5]	τμ > σμ[9]
	τθ > σθ[7]	φμ > μμ[8]
	ψθ > φθ[5]	χμ > γμ[10]

---

[1] This content is a simplified version of sections 20–25 (on pages 33–43) of *MBG* (*The Morphology of
Biblical Greek* by Mounce). Chart created by Richard Osborn and used with permission.

[2] When one dental (δ, ζ, θ, or τ) precedes δ (another dental), the first dental dissimilates to σ. [ζ can be
considered to be a dental since it includes the δ sound. "Precedes" here and throughout these footnotes is
shorthand for "*immediately* precedes."]

[3] When velars κ and χ precede δ (voiced), they become γ (the voiced velar).

[4] When labials π and φ precede δ (voiced), they become β (the voiced labial).

[5] When labials β, π, and ψ precede θ (an aspirate), they aspirate to φ (the labial aspirate). πτθ becomes
φθ or β.

[6] When velars γ, κ, and ξ precede θ (an aspirate), they aspirate to χ (the velar aspirate). γθ can also
become γ.

[7] When dentals δ, ζ, θ, and τ precede θ (another dental), they dissimilate to σ. σκθ becomes σθ.

[8] When labials β, π, and φ precede μ (labial nasal), they totally assimilate to μ. πτμ and ψμ (= πσμ) also
become μμ.

[9] When dentals δ, ζ, θ, and τ precede μ (labial nasal), they assimilate to σ.

[10] When velars κ and χ precede μ (labial nasal), they assimilate to γ (the voiced velar).

[11] When ν (a liquid) precedes another liquid (λ, μ, or ρ), ν may totally assimilate to the other liquid.

AFTER ν:	BEFORE σ:	BEFORE τ:
νβ > μβ[12]	βσ > ψ[15]	βτ > πτ[20]
νγ > γγ[13]	γσ > ξ[16]	γτ > κτ[21]
νκ > γκ[13]	δσ > σ[17]	δτ > στ[22]
νλ > λλ[11]	ζσ > σ[17]	ζτ > στ[22]
νμ > μμ[11]	θσ > σ[17]	θτ > στ[22]
νξ > γξ[13]	κσ > ξ[16]	ττ > στ[22]
νπ > μπ[12]	λσ > λ[18]	φτ > πτ[20]
νρ > ρρ[11]	μσ > μ[18]	χτ > κτ[21]
νσ > σ[14]	νσ > ν[18]	
νφ > μφ[12]	πσ > ψ[15]	
νχ > γχ[13]	ρσ > ρ[18]	
νψ > μψ[12]	σσ > σ[19]	
	τσ > σ[17]	
	φσ > ψ[15]	
	χσ > ξ[16]	

---

[12] When ν precedes labials β, π, φ, and ψ, it assimilates to μ (labial nasal).

[13] When ν precedes velars γ, κ, ξ, and χ, it assimilates to γ-nasal; the resulting γ is pronounced as if it were a ν.

[14] When ν precedes σ, ν usually drops out. The ν in συν + σ may totally assimilate to σ: συσσ. νσπ becomes σπ; νστ becomes στ.

[15] When labials β, π, and φ precede σ, the combination becomes the labial double consonant ψ.

[16] When velars γ, κ, and χ precede σ, the combination becomes the velar double consonant ξ. σκσ becomes σ.

[17] When dentals δ, ζ, θ, and τ precede σ, the dental assimilates to σ. The resulting σσ then simplifies to σ. ζσ can also become ξ.

[18] When a liquid (λ, μ, ν, or ρ) precedes σ, the σ may drop out. When this happens, the preceding vowel lengthens.

[19] When σσ is the result of an inflection or a phonetic change, σσ usually reduces to σ. When not the result of such a change, σσ conceals a velar (γ, κ, ξ, or χ). Thus, σσ + σ > ξ (the velar double consonant). When a σ is intervocalic (occurs between two vowels), it usually drops out. When a σ is interconsonantal (occurs between two consonants), it often drops out.

[20] When labials β and φ precede τ (voiceless), they assimilate to π (the voiceless labial).

[21] When velars γ and χ precede τ (voiceless), they assimilate to κ (the voiceless velar).

[22] When dentals δ, ζ, θ, and τ precede τ (another dental), the first dental dissimilates to σ.

MASCULINE FIRST DECLENSION NOUNS[1]

Most *masculine* nouns follow the *second* declension; most *feminine* nouns follow the *first* declension. But there is a group of *masculine* nouns in the New Testament that follow the *first* declension! The fact that these nouns have masculine articles makes it clear that they are actually masculine nouns.

Do these *masculine* nouns have *feminine* endings? No. Rather, for this exceptional group of nouns (which tend to be categories of people), the use of the first declension marks identity or status. These categories may be people who have a particular occupation, or a particular position in society, or who are part of some other group of people with the same characteristics.[2]

The nouns in this group that occur ten times or more in the New Testament are listed here:

FREQUENCY	ENGLISH GLOSS(ES)	NOMINATIVE SINGULAR	GENITIVE SINGULAR
261	disciple	ὁ μαθητής	τοῦ μαθητοῦ
144	prophet	ὁ προφήτης	τοῦ προφήτου
26	soldier	ὁ στρατιώτης	τοῦ στρατιώτου
21	tax collector	ὁ τελώνης	τοῦ τελώνου
20	servant, assistant	ὁ ὑπηρέτης	τοῦ ὑπηρέτου
19	judge	ὁ κριτής	τοῦ κριτοῦ
17	hypocrite	ὁ ὑποκριτής	τοῦ ὑποκριτοῦ
16	worker	ὁ ἐργάτης	τοῦ ἐργάτου
16	thief	ὁ κλέπτης	τοῦ κλέπτου
15	robber, revolutionary	ὁ λῃστής	τοῦ λῃστοῦ
12	baptizer, immerser	ὁ βαπτιστής	τοῦ βαπτιστοῦ
11	false prophet	ὁ ψευδοπροφήτης	τοῦ ψευδοπροφήτου
10	master, lord	ὁ δεσπότης	τοῦ δεσπότου
10	liar	ὁ ψεύστης	τοῦ ψεύστου

---

[1] See *MBG* (*The Morphology of Biblical Greek* by Mounce), 177–78. Chart created by Richard Osborn and used with permission.

[2] This group of 139 nouns includes 21 proper nouns; the most common of which are ὁ Ἰωάννης (John, 135), ὁ Ἡρῴδης (Herod, 43), ὁ Ἰορδάνης (the Jordan River, 15), and ὁ ᾅδης (Hades, 10).

Typically, when a noun ends in –ης, we identify it as a first declension noun that is genitive singular. But for this special group of nouns, –ης is the *nominative* singular ending. When a noun ends in –ου, that noun is usually a second declension noun, and the form is genitive singular. But for this group of nouns, –ου is the genitive singular ending of a *first* declension noun![3] Other than these two exceptions, the endings of this group of nouns are typical first declension endings:

	SINGULAR		PLURAL	
NOM	ὁ	προφήτης	οἱ	προφῆται
GEN	τοῦ	προφήτου	τῶν	προφητῶν
DAT	τῷ	προφήτῃ	τοῖς	προφήταις
ACC	τόν	προφήτην	τούς	προφήτας

---

[3] Since –ης has already been used for the nominative case, it can't be used for the genitive case.

NEUTER THIRD DECLENSION NOUNS
WITH STEMS ENDING IN εϛ[1]

There is a group of 62 nouns in the New Testament that (1) are third declension, (2) are neuter, and (3) have stems that end in εϛ. The most common of these is τὰ ἔθνη ("the nations," or "the Gentiles"), the accusative plural of τὸ ἔθνος, which occurs in the New Testament 162 times!

The stem of ἔθνος is εθνεσ. When the standard neuter third declension endings are attached to this stem, the resulting forms are as follows:

	STEM	ENDING	CHANGES	FORM
NOM SG	εθνεσ	-	εσ > οσ[2]	τὸ ἔθνος
GEN SG	εθνεσ	ος	εσο > εο[3] > ου[4]	τοῦ ἔθνους
DAT SG	εθνεσ	ι	εσι > ει[3]	τῷ ἔθνει
ACC SG	εθνεσ	-	εσ > οσ[2]	τὸ ἔθνος
NOM PL	εθνεσ	α	εσα > εα[3] > η[5]	τὰ ἔθνη
GEN PL	εθνεσ	ων	εσω > εω[3] > ῶ[6]	τῶν ἐθνῶν
DAT PL	εθνεσ	σι(ν)	εσσι > εσι[7]	τοῖς ἔθνεσιν
ACC PL	εθνεσ	α	εσα > εα[3] > η[5]	τὰ ἔθνη

The nouns in this group that occur ten times or more in the New Testament are listed here:

FREQUENCY	ENGLISH GLOSS(ES)	NOMINATIVE SINGULAR	GENITIVE SINGULAR
162	nation, Gentile	τὸ ἔθνος	τοῦ ἔθνους
63	mountain, hill	τὸ ὄρος	τοῦ ὄρους
49	year	τὸ ἔτος	τοῦ ἔτους
42	part	τό μέρος	τοῦ μέρους
40	end, outcome	τό τέλος	τοῦ τέλους
34	member, part	τό μέλος	τοῦ μέλους

---

[1] See *MBG* (*The Morphology of Biblical Greek* by Mounce), 200–1. Chart created by Richard Osborn and used with permission.

[2] The final stem vowel changes from ε to ο.

[3] The intervocalic σ drops out.

[4] εο > ου. Energy often oozes.

[5] εα > η. Energy of awful people is anger.

[6] εω > ῶ. ω "eats" everything before it!

[7] σσ > σ. The σ of the stem and the σ of the case ending simplify to a single σ.

Appendix /////////////// 303

FREQUENCY	ENGLISH GLOSS(ES)	NOMINATIVE SINGULAR	GENITIVE SINGULAR
31	multitude	τό πλῆθος	τοῦ πλήθους
31	darkness	τό σκότος	τοῦ σκότους
23	vessel, instrument (pl) goods, things	τό σκεῦος	τοῦ σκεύους
20	descendent, kind	τό γένος	τοῦ γένους
12	custom, habit	τὸ ἔθος	τοῦ ἔθους

PRINCIPAL PARTS OF IRREGULAR VERBS

Present Act	Future Act	Aorist Act	Perfect Act	Perfect M/P	Aorist Pass
ἄγω	ἄξω	ἤγαγον	—[1]	—	ἤχθην
αἴρω	ἀρῶ	ἦρα	ἦρκα	ἦρμαι	ἤρθην
αἰτέω	αἰτήσω	ᾔτησα	ᾔτηκα	—	—
ἀκούω	ἀκούσω	ἤκουσα	ἀκηκόα	—	ἠκούσθην
ἁμαρτάνω	ἁμαρτήσω	ἥμαρτον	ἡμάρτηκα	—	—
ἀναβαίνω	ἀναβήσομαι	ἀνέβην	ἀναβέβηκα		
ἀνοίγω	ἀνοίξω	ἤνοιξα	ἀνέῳγα	ἀνέῳγμαι	ἀνεῴχθην
ἀπαγγέλλω	ἀπαγγελῶ	ἀπήγγειλα	—	—	ἀπηγγέλην
ἀποθνήσκω	ἀποθανοῦμαι	ἀπέθανον	—		
ἀποκρίνομαι	—	ἀπεκρινάμην	—	—	ἀπεκρίθην
ἀποκτείνω	ἀποκτενῶ	ἀπέκτεινα	—	—	ἀπεκτάνθην
ἀποστέλλω	ἀποστελῶ	ἀπέστειλα	ἀπέσταλκα	ἀπέσταλμαι	ἀπεστάλην
ἀφίημι	ἀφήσω	ἀφῆκα	—	ἀφέωμαι	ἀφέθην
βάλλω	βαλῶ	ἔβαλον	βέβληκα	βέβλημαι	ἐβλήθην
βλέπω	βλέψετε	εἶδον	ἑόρακα	—	ὤφθην
γίνομαι	γενήσομαι	ἐγενόμην	γέγονα	γεγένημαι	ἐγενήθην
γινώσκω	γνώσομαι	ἔγνων	ἔγνωκα	ἔγνωσμαι	ἐγνώσθην
γράφω	γράψω	ἔγραψα	γέγραφα	γέγραμμαι	ἐγράφην
δέχομαι	—	ἐδεξάμην	—	δέδεγμαι	—
δίδωμι	δώσω	ἔδωκα	δέδωκα	δέδομαι	ἐδόθην
ἐγγίζω	ἐγγιῶ	ἤγγισα	ἤγγικα	—	—
ἐγείρω	ἐγερῶ	ἤγειρα	—	ἐγήγερμαι	ἠγέρθην
ἔρχομαι	ἐλεύσομαι	ἦλθον	ἐλήλυθα	—	—
ἐσθίω	φάγομαι	ἔφαγον	—	—	—
εὑρίσκω	εὑρήσω	εὗρον	εὕρηκα	—	εὑρέθην
ἔχω	ἕξω	ἔσχον	ἔσχηκα	—	—
ἵστημι	στήσω	ἔστησα	ἕστηκα	—	ἐστάθην
καλέω	καλέσω	ἐκάλεσα	κέκληκα	κέκλημαι	ἐκλήθην
κράζω	κράξω	ἔκραξα	κέκραγα	—	—
κρίνω	κρινῶ	ἔκρινα	κέκρικα	κέκριμαι	ἐκρίθην

---

[1] The em dash (—) signifies that the form does not occur in the New Testament.

Present Act	Future Act	Aorist Act	Perfect Act	Perfect M/P	Aorist Pass
λαμβάνω	λήμψομαι	ἔλαβον	εἴληφα	—	—
λέγω	ἐρῶ	εἶπον	εἴρηκα	εἴρημαι	ἐρρέθην
πείθω	πείσω	ἔπεισα	πέποιθα	πέπεισμαι	ἐπείσθην
πίνω	πίομαι	ἔπιον	πέπωκα	—	—
πίπτω	πεσοῦμαι	ἔπεσον	πέπτωκα	—	—
σπείρω	—	ἔσπειρα	—	ἔσπαρμαι	ἐσπάρην
τίθημι	θήσω	ἔθηκα	τέθεικα	τέθειμαι	ἐτέθην
φέρω	οἴσω	ἤνεγκα	—	—	ἠνέχθην

KEY TO THE PRACTICE EXERCISES

ANSWER KEY TO CHAPTER 1

A. Alphabet: Write out the lowercase script of the alphabet in the correct order and form.

α β γ δ ε ζ η θ ι κ λ μ ν ξ ο π ρ σ/ς τ υ φ χ ψ ω

B. Vowels: Circle the words that have a diphthong (Eph 1:3–6).
(Words in bold font have diphthongs, with the diphthong(s) being underlined.)

Εὐλογητὸς ὁ θεὸς **καὶ** πατὴρ **τοῦ κυρίου** ἡμῶν **Ἰησοῦ Χριστοῦ**, ὁ **εὐλογήσας** ἡμᾶς ἐν πάσῃ **εὐλογίᾳ πνευματικῇ** ἐν **τοῖς ἐπουρανίοις** ἐν Χριστῷ, καθὼς ἐξελέξατο ἡμᾶς ἐν **αὐτῷ** πρὸ καταβολῆς **κόσμου εἶναι** ἡμᾶς **ἁγίους καὶ ἀμώμους** κατενώπιον **αὐτοῦ** ἐν ἀγάπῃ, προορίσας ἡμᾶς **εἰς υἱοθεσίαν** διὰ **Ἰησοῦ Χριστοῦ εἰς αὐτόν**, κατὰ τὴν **εὐδοκίαν τοῦ** θελήματος **αὐτοῦ, εἰς ἔπαινον** δόξης τῆς χάριτος **αὐτοῦ** ἧς ἐχαρίτωσεν ἡμᾶς ἐν τῷ ἠγαπημένῳ.

C. Accents: Identify the accent marks (A = acute; G = grave; C = circumflex) and the breathing marks (S = smooth; R = rough), if any, in the following words.

Key Word	Accent	Breathing Mark
1. Εὐλογητὸς	G	S
2. Ἰησοῦ	C	S
3. ἡμᾶς	C	R
4. καθὼς	G	—
5. αὐτῷ	C	S
6. πρὸ	G	—

7. εἶναι   C   S

8. ἁγίους   A   R

9. ἀγάπη   A   S

10. ἧς   C   R

ANSWER KEY TO CHAPTER 2

A. Paradigms: Memorize the paradigms for φωνή and καρδία (see section 2.6).

B. Eta and Alpha Nouns: Circle the forms that are incorrect. (Incorrect forms are listed below.)

1.	—	—	ζῷα	—
2.	ἁμαρτίη	—	ἀγάπα	—
3.	—	—	—	φωνᾷ
4.	—	ἐκκλησιῆς	—	—
5.	—	—	—	ἀληθείην

C. The Article: Parse the following nouns, circling examples in which the article does not match the noun (in gender, case, and number). Then supply the correct article. (Articles in bold below are incorrect.)

1. τὴν ἀλήθειαν   fem, acc, sg

2. τῆς ζωῆς   fem, gen, sg

3. **αἱ** ἡμέρα   fem, nom, sg (correct article: ἡ)

4. **τὴν** ἁμαρτιῶν   fem, gen, pl (correct article: τῶν)

5. ταῖς ἐκκλησίαις   fem, dat, pl

6. **τὰς** ἀγάπης   fem, gen, sg (correct article: τῆς)

7. **ἡ** γῇ   fem, dat, sg (correct article: τῇ)

8. τῇ βασιλείᾳ   fem, dat, sg

9. **ταῖς** καρδίας   fem, gen, sg *or* fem, acc, pl (correct article: τῆς or τάς)

10. τὴν δόξαν   fem, acc, sg

D. Case: Circle the Greek word that best translates the English phrase. (Answers are listed rather than circled below.)

1.	to the churches	—	—	ταῖς ἐκκλησίαις
2.	of the heart	—	τῆς καρδίας	—

3. the days (subject)　　αἱ ἡμέραι　　　　—　　　　　　—

4. for the truth　　　　　　—　　　　τῇ ἀληθείᾳ　　　　—

5. of the love　　　　　　　—　　　　　　—　　　　τῆς ἀγάπης

E. Translation: Locate the first declension nouns learned for this chapter. Then parse and translate each one. (The nouns in bold font below are first declension nouns.)

1. **ἡ φωνὴ τὴν γῆν** ἐσάλευσεν (Heb 12:26).

   ἡ φωνή—fem, nom, sg, from φωνή, meaning "the voice" [acting as subject]

   τὴν γῆν—fem, acc, sg, from γῆ, meaning "the earth" [acting as the direct object]

   Literal translation: "The voice shook the earth."[1]

2. λέγει αὐτῷ [ὁ] Ἰησοῦς, Ἐγώ εἰμι ἡ ὁδὸς καὶ **ἡ ἀλήθεια** καὶ **ἡ ζωή** (John 14:6).

   ἡ ἀλήθεια—fem, nom, sg, from ἀλήθεια, meaning "the truth" [acting as part of a compound predicate nominative]

   ἡ ζωή—fem, nom, sg, from ζωή, meaning "the life" [acting as part of a compound predicate nominative]

   Literal translation: "Jesus says to him, 'I am the way and the truth and the life.'"

3. τὸ δὲ τέλος τῆς παραγγελίας ἐστὶν **ἀγάπη** ἐκ καθαρᾶς **καρδίας** καὶ συνειδήσεως ἀγαθῆς καὶ πίστεως ἀνυποκρίτου (1 Tim 1:5).

   ἀγάπη—fem, nom, sg, from ἀγάπη, meaning "love" [acting as a predicate nominative]

   καρδίας—fem, gen, sg from καρδία, meaning "heart" [acting as object of the preposition ἐκ][2]

   Literal translation: "But the goal of this instruction is love from a pure heart and a good conscience and a sincere faith."

---

[1] You, as a beginning student, are *not* expected to translate the entire selection at this point in the semester. Nor are you expected to know detailed grammatical functioning.

[2] Given your limited knowledge as a first-year Greek student, you may have guessed that this form was fem, acc, pl. Based on what you have learned thus far, you were not wrong. You will soon learn that the preposition ἐκ is always followed by a genitive. (See ἐκ two words prior to καρδίας in the verse above).

4. Ἐγένετο δὲ ἐν ἐκείνη **τῇ ἡμέρα** διωγμὸς μέγας ἐπὶ **τὴν ἐκκλησίαν** τὴν ἐν Ἱεροσολύμοις (Acts 8:1).

τῇ ἡμέρα—fem, dat, sg, from ἡμέρα, meaning "to/for/on the day" [acting as dative of time—something you will learn in the future]

τὴν ἐκκλησίαν—fem, acc, sg, from ἐκκλησία, meaning "the church" [acting as object of preposition ἐπί—something you have not been taught yet]

Literal translation: "And on that day, a great persecution came upon the church in Jerusalem."

ANSWER KEY TO CHAPTER 3

A. Paradigms: Memorize the paradigms for λόγος and τέκνον (see section 3.6).

B. Masculine Nouns: Circle the words that are masculine, including articles. (Masculine forms are listed rather than circled below.)

1. ἀδελφοῦ   θεόν   —   —

2. τούς   —   νόμου   υἱῶν

3. —   ὁ   —   λόγους

4. ἀνθρώποις   —   —   κόσμῳ

5. —   τοῖς¹   —   Χριστοῦ

C. The Article: Parse the following nouns, circling examples in which the article does not match the noun (in gender, case, and number). Then supply the correct article. (In answers below, incorrect articles are in bold rather than circled.)

1. τῷ θεῷ   masc, dat, sg

2. **τόν** εὐαγγέλιον   neut, nom/acc, sg (correct article: τό)

3. **αἱ** ἄνθρωποι   masc, nom, pl (correct article: οἱ)

4. τοῦ κυρίου   masc, gen, sg

5. τῶν σημείων   neut, gen, pl

6. **τὴν** νόμον   masc, acc, sg (correct article: τόν)

7. ὁ υἱός   masc, nom, sg

8. **ταῖς** οὐρανοῖς   masc, dat, pl (correct article: τοῖς)

9. τῷ Ἰησοῦ   masc, dat, sg (note that endings for this noun are irregular.)

10. τά ἔργα   neut, nom/acc, pl

D. Case: Circle the Greek word that best translates the English phrase. (Answers provided below rather than circled.)

1. for the Lord   —   τῷ κυρίῳ   —

---

¹ The article τοῖς in number 5 could be masculine or neuter.

2. of heaven   τοῦ οὐρανοῦ   —   —

3. to the sons   —   —   τοῖς υἱοῖς

4. the brothers (subject) —   —   οἱ ἀδελφοί

5. of the temple   —   τοῦ ἱεροῦ   —

E. Translation: Locate the second declension nouns you have learned. Then parse and translate each one. (Bold font below marks second declension nouns.)

1. ὥστε **κύριός** ἐστιν **ὁ υἱὸς τοῦ ἀνθρώπου** καὶ τοῦ σαββάτου (Mark 2:28).

κύριός—masc, nom, sg, from κύριος, "Lord" [functioning as predicate nominative]

ὁ υἱός—masc, nom, sg, from υἱός, "the Son" [functioning as subject]

τοῦ ἀνθρώπου—masc, gen, sg, from ἄνθρωπος, "of (the) Man" [Because "Son of Man" is a title alluding to Dan 7, "the" is not used in a final translation.]

Literal translation: ". . . so that the Son of Man is Lord of the Sabbath."

2. ἣν προηκούσατε ἐν **τῷ λόγῳ** τῆς ἀληθείας **τοῦ εὐαγγελίου** (Col 1:5).

τῷ λόγῳ—masc, dat, sg, from λόγος, "to/for the word" [In the final English translation, "to/for" is not used. λόγος is in the dative because it is the object of a preposition requiring a dative form. You have not been taught this yet.]

τοῦ εὐαγγελίου—neut, gen, sg, from εὐαγγέλιον, "of the Gospel" [In the final English translation, "of" is not used because τοῦ εὐαγγελίου is functioning as an epexegetical genitive, further explaining a previous noun. You have not been taught this yet.]

Literal translation: "which you all heard about beforehand in the word of the truth, the Gospel."

3. Καὶ ἐξελθὼν **ὁ Ἰησοῦς** ἀπὸ **τοῦ ἱεροῦ** ἐπορεύετο, καὶ προσῆλθον οἱ μαθηταὶ αὐτοῦ ἐπιδεῖξαι αὐτῷ τὰς οἰκοδομὰς **τοῦ ἱεροῦ** (Matt 24:1).

ὁ Ἰησοῦς—masc, nom, sg, from Ἰησοῦς, "[the] Jesus" [Note: Greek frequently has articles with proper names, but we do not use the definite article with proper names in English.]

τοῦ ἱεροῦ—neut, gen, sg, from ἱερόν, "of the temple" [Note: In a final English translation, the word "of" is not used because ἱερόν is following a preposition that requires a genitive object. You have not been taught this yet.]

τοῦ ἱεροῦ—neut, gen, sg, from ἱερόν, "of the temple"

Literal translation: "And departing, Jesus left from the temple, and his disciples came to him to show him the buildings of the temple."

4. ἐν τούτῳ φανερά ἐστιν **τὰ τέκνα** τοῦ θεοῦ καὶ **τὰ τέκνα** τοῦ διαβόλου· πᾶς ὁ μὴ ποιῶν δικαιοσύνην οὐκ ἔστιν ἐκ **τοῦ θεοῦ**, καὶ ὁ μὴ ἀγαπῶν **τὸν ἀδελφὸν** αὐτοῦ (1 John 3:10).

τὰ τέκνα—neut, nom, pl, from τέκνον, "the children" [Note: If you parsed the noun as accusative, that's fine. The context of the sentence indicates that it is nominative, but you, as a first-year Greek student, are not expected to read the rest of the sentence yet. This noun functions as a subject nominative, the first of two nominatives in a compound subject.]

τὰ τέκνα—neut, nom, pl, from τέκνον, "the children"

τοῦ θεοῦ—masc, gen, sg, from θεός, "of [the] God." [Note: In English, we do not use the article "the" with God, but New Testament Greek frequently does. Greek has a tendency to use the article in front of monadic nouns. A monadic noun is an entity which the speaker thinks is only represented by one—for example, God, the sun, or the moon.]

τὸν ἀδελφόν—masc, acc, sg, from ἀδελφός, "[the] brother" [This accusative noun functions as a direct object.]

Literal translation: "By this, the children of God and the children of the devil are obvious/clear; everyone who does not do righteousness is not from God, and the one not loving his brother."

ANSWER KEY TO CHAPTER 4

A. Paradigms: Memorize the present active paradigm of εἰμί (see section 4.8).

B. Person and Number: Choose the correct pronoun that would correspond to the description of the person and number.

1.	E	second person plural	A.	I	
2.	A	first person singular	B.	you (sg)	
3.	F	third person plural	C.	he/she/it	
4.	D	first person plural	D.	we	
5.	B	second person singular	E.	you (pl)	
6.	C	third person singular	F.	they	

C. Voice: Identify the highlighted verbs in the following sentences as active (A), middle (M), or passive (P). Middle voice will be nearly impossible to detect in English translation alone, so verbal forms that are middle in Greek have an asterisk (*). For those sentences, think about how the action described fits in one of the categories of the middle voice outlined above.

1. A "Jesus **took** bread, **blessed** and **broke** it, **gave** it to the disciples" (Matt 26:26).

2. M "For He **chose*** us [for himself] in Him" (Eph 1:4).

3. P "Now the Son of Man **is glorified**, and God **is glorified** in Him" (John 13:31).

4. M "For they don't **wash*** their hands when they eat!" (Matt 15:2).

5. A "John came **baptizing** in the wilderness and **preaching** a baptism of repentance for the forgiveness of sins" (Mark 1:4).

6. M "So I **ask*** you not to lose heart" (Eph 3:13).

7. A "Long ago God **spoke** to our ancestors by the prophets at different times and in different ways" (Heb 1:1).

8. M "knowing that whatever good each one does . . . he will **receive*** this **back** from the Lord" (Eph 6:8).

9. P "In those days Jesus came from Nazareth in Galilee and **was baptized** in the Jordan by John" (Mark 1:9).

D. Aspect: Indicate whether the descriptions below best describe the Imperfective (I), Perfective (P), or Stative (S) aspect.

1. P The author depicts the action as complete or as a whole.

2. S The author depicts a state of affairs resulting from a previous action or state.

3. I The author depicts the action as in process.

4. I Is represented by the present or imperfect tense-forms.

5. P Is represented by the aorist tense-form.

6. S Is represented by the perfect or pluperfect tense-forms.

E. Translation: Translate the following sentences.

1. "I am the bread of life."

2. "He is king of Israel." [Note: The word Ἰσραήλ is indeclinable (all case forms look alike), so only the context can tell you that it is genitive here.]

3. "We are [the] temple of God."

4. "I am [the] Son of God."

5. "I am the way and the truth and the life."

6. "God is love."

7. "I am the Alpha and the Omega."

8. "He is [the] Son of Man."

9. "We are children of God."

10. "He is the Christ?" or "Is he the Christ?" [Note: A question mark in Greek looks like a semicolon!]

F. Translation: Translate the following sentences into Greek. Include breathing marks, but not accents.

1. ἡ ἐκκλησια ἐστιν το ἱερον του θεου.

2. οἱ λογοι (της) ἀληθειας εἰσιν του κυριου.

3. ἡ καρδια (του) ἀνθρωπου ἐστιν ἁμαρτια.

4. (ὁ) οὐρανος και (ἡ) γη εἰσιν ἡ δοξα (του) Ἰησου.

5. το σημειον της βασιλειας (του) θεου ἐστιν το εὐαγγελιον. [Note: At this point, don't worry about having the article—in Greek or in your English translations. The Greek article follows many patterns that you will learn about later.]

ANSWER KEY TO CHAPTER 5

A. Paradigms: Memorize the present active and middle/passive paradigms of λύω (see section 5.6).

B. Parsing: Parse the following verbs.

1. **ἀκούεις**—ἀκούω pres act ind 2nd sg, "You (sg) are hearing" or "You (sg) hear"

2. **πιστεύουσιν**—πιστεύω pres act ind 3rd pl, "They are believing" or "They believe"

3. **ἔρχονται**—ἔρχομαι pres mid ind 3rd pl, "They are coming/going" or "They go/come"

4. **βλέπετε**—βλέπω pres, act, ind 2nd pl, "You (pl) are seeing" or "You (pl) see"

5. **ἐγείρεται**—ἐγείρω pres mid/pass ind 3rd sg, "He/She/It is being raised," "He/she/it is raised," "He/she/it is raising for him/her/itself," or "He/she/it raises for him/her/itself"

6. **λέγει**—λέγω pres act ind 3rd sg, "He is saying" or "He says"

7. **ἀποκρίνῃ**—ἀποκρίνομαι pres mid ind 2nd sg, "You (sg) answer" or "You (sg) are answering"

8. **μένομεν**—μένω pres act ind 1st pl, "We are remaining" or "we remain"

9. **κρίνομαι**—κρίνω pres mid/pass ind 1st sg, "I am being judged," "I am judged," "I am judging for myself," or "I judge for myself"

10. **ἄγεσθε**—ἄγω pres mid/pass ind 2nd pl, "You (pl) are being led, "You (pl) are led," "You (pl) are leading for yourself," or "You (pl) lead for yourself"

C. Translation: Translate the following sentences. Be sure to start with the verb. Then find the subject and then the object (if there is one).

1. "I am seeing the men." Or "I see the men."

2. "They are leading/bringing Jesus." Or "They lead/bring Jesus."

3. "I am going into Jerusalem." Or "I go into Jerusalem."

4. "But Jesus answers them" Or "But Jesus is answering them" [Note: The Greek particle δέ is postpositive. It always comes second in a clause, frequently dividing a noun and its article. In English, we put adversative particles (e.g., "but") at the beginning of clauses. ἀποκρίνεται is employed as a historical present; thus, in a final translation, it would be rendered in English as a past tense verb. Only context can indicate such usage.]

5. "You (pl) know the grace of our Lord, Jesus Christ." [Ἰησοῦ Χριστοῦ is in the genitive case because it restates the earlier genitive noun, τοῦ κυρίου.]

6. "The Son of Man has authority on the earth." Or "The Son of Man is having authority on the earth." [Why did we not translate τῆς γῆς as "of the earth"? For one thing, it would sound weird. For another, the noun γῆ is in the genitive because the preposition ἐπί requires its object to be in the genitive. In such case, we do not translate the genitive with the word "of."]

7. "I am not receiving glory from men." Or "I receive not glory from men." [ἀνθρώπων is in the genitive because of the preposition παρά. Thus, no "of" in translation.]

8. "The Son of Man is departing, just as it is written." Or "The Son of Man departs, just as it is written."

9. "Why are you (sg) judging your brother?" "Why do you judge your brother?" Or "Why are you judging the brother of you?"

10. "You believe that God is one." Or "You are believing that God is one."

11. "But an hour is coming and now is." Or "But an hour comes and now is."

12. "How is the love of God remaining in him?" Or "How does the love of God abide/remain in him?"

D. Translation: Translate the following sentences into Greek. Include breathing marks, but not accents.

1. ὁ κυριος του κοσμου ἀκουει την φωνην.

2. ὁ νομος κρινει τας καρδιας των ἀνθρωπων.

3. αἱ ψυχαι των ἀνθρωπων γινωσκουσιν την ἀληθειαν.

4. ὁ δουλος ἀγεται τῳ κυριῳ.

5. διδασκομεν τα τεκνα.

ANSWER KEY TO CHAPTER 6

A. Paradigms: Memorize the imperfect active and middle/passive paradigms of λύω (see section 6.5).

B. Parsing: Parse the following verbs.

1. **ἐθεραπεύοντο**—θεραπεύω impf mid/pass ind 3rd pl, "They were healing for themselves," or "They were being healed."

2. **ἔβλεπον**—βλέπω impf act ind 1st sg or 3rd pl, "I was seeing," or "They were seeing."

3. **ἐκρινόμεθα**—κρίνω impf mid/pass ind 1st pl, "We were judging for ourselves," or "We were being judged."

4. **ἐπορευόμην**—πορεύομαι impf mid ind 1st sg, "I was going."

5. **ἤγεσθε**—ἄγω impf mid/pass ind 2nd pl, "You all were being led/brought" or "You all were leading/bringing for yourselves."

6. **ἤρχου**—ἔρχομαι impf mid ind 2nd sg, "You were coming."

7. **ἐγίνετο**—γίνομαι impf mid ind 3rd sg, "He/she was arriving" or "It was happening."

8. **ἐπιστεύετε**—πιστεύω impf act ind 2nd pl, "You all were believing."

9. **ἤκουεν**—ἀκούω impf act ind 3rd sg, "He/she/it was hearing."

10. **εἶχες**—ἔχω impf act ind 2nd sg, "You were having."

C. Translation: Translate the following sentences.

1. "Jesus himself was not baptizing."

2. "They were crying out, saying that 'You are the Son of God.'" [Of course, ἔκραζον could be translated "I was crying out" in a different context.]

3. "A man was having two children."

4. "And he was teaching and was saying to them"

5. "Many were going away (of the Jews), and they were believing in Jesus." [Normally, we would expect τῶν Ἰουδαίων to immediately follow πολλοί: πολλοὶ τῶν Ἰουδαίων.]

6. "And Jesus was going/coming with them."

7. "He was writing on the ground/earth."

8. "And they were receiving [the] Holy Spirit."

9. "And they were being baptized in the Jordan."

10. "For not even his brothers were believing in him."

11. "You (sg) were not having authority"

12. "The crowd was going/coming to him, and he was teaching them."

D. Translation: Translate the English sentences into Greek.

1. ἐδιδασκομεθα τον νομον.

2. ὁ ὀχλος ἐκραζεν τῳ προφητῃ.

3. οὐ γινωσκω την ἡμεραν και την ὡραν.

4. ὁ μαθητης του κυριου ἐθεραπευετο.

5. ὁ ἀγγελος της δοξας ἐγειρει το τεκνον.

ANSWER KEY TO CHAPTER 7

A. Paradigms: Memorize the imperfect active paradigm of εἰμί (see section 7.5).

B. Parsing: Parse the following verbs.

1. **γεννῶσιν**—γεννάω pres act ind 3rd pl, "They are begetting/giving birth."

2. **ἦμεν**—εἰμί impf ind 1st pl, "We were." [Note: εἰμί is not active in voice because it refers to a state. If you parsed it as active, because it follows active endings, that's fine.]

3. **ἠρώτων**—ἐρωτάω impf act ind 1st sg or 3rd pl, "I was asking," or "they were asking."

4. **ἠκολούθουν**—ἀκολουθέω impf act ind 1st sg or 3rd pl, "I was following," or "They were following."

5. **ἐζήτει**—ζητέω impf act ind 3rd sg, "He was seeking."

6. **φοβούμεθα**—φοβέομαι pres mid ind 1st pl, "We are fearing" or "We are afraid." [Verbs of emotion are often middle-only in voice.]

7. **ἐμαρτυρεῖτο**—μαρτυρέω impf mid/pass ind 3rd sg, "He was testifying [for himself]," or "He was being testified to"

8. **παρακαλοῦμεν**—παρακαλέω pres act ind 1st pl, "We are urging/comforting."

9. **ἐποιοῦντο**—ποιέω impf mid/pass ind 3rd pl, "They were doing [for themselves]," or "They were being done/made."

10. **φοβῇ**—φοβέομαι pres mid ind 2nd sg, "You are fearing," or "You are afraid." [Verbs of emotion are often middle-only in voice.]

C. Translation: Translate the following sentences.

1. "You (pl) were doing the works of Abraham."

2. "For they were fearing the people."

3. "And Jesus was walking in the temple."

4. "We know that we love the children of God."

5. "You (pl) are asking and you (pl) are not receiving" or "You (pl) ask and you (pl) do not receive."

6. "But we are speaking a wisdom from/of God."

7. "You (pl) were slaves of sin." [Note: The verb εἰμί takes a predicate nominative (δοῦλοι) in the nominative case. εἰμί does not take a direct object.]

8. "Brothers, we are asking you and we are urging [you] in the Lord Jesus" [Note: The second [you] in brackets here is simply implied.]

9. "They were asking [for themselves] peace." [Note: Verbs for asking are not infrequently found in the middle voice.]

10. "And his disciples are following him." [Note: αὐτῷ (him) is in the dative case because the verb ἀκολουθέω takes its direct object in the dative. There are some other verbs that take their objects in cases other than the expected accusative.]

11. "And they are seeking my life/soul."

12. "And/but the rock was [the] Christ." [Note: In this sentence with a copulative verb [εἰμί], you have two nominatives—both a subject nominative and a predicate nominative. The broader context of 1 Cor 10 makes clear that the subject is ἡ πέτρα. In sentences that parallel this construction—where both nominatives are preceded by an article—if the context does not make clear the subject, the first nominative is likely the subject.]

13. "And the disciples were filled of/with joy." [The genitive singular χαρᾶς expresses what they were filled *with*, and in context, the preposition "with" works better in English.]

14. "But why are you calling me 'Lord, Lord,' and you are not doing what I say?"

D. Translation: Translate the following sentences into Greek.

1. ἐκαλειτε τους υἱους [των] ἀνθρωπων.

2. ζητεις τον κυριον;

3. ἐλαλουν τους λογους [της] ἀληθειας.

4. ὁ δουλος ἀγαπα την ἐκκλησιαν.

5. ὁ προφητης περιπατει τοις μαθηταις.

ANSWER KEY TO CHAPTER 8

A. Cases and Meaning: Identify the case(s) that can be used in construction with the following prepositions. Then provide a possible gloss for the preposition for each case.

1. ὑπέρ—gen (for, on behalf of), acc (above)
2. ὑπό—gen (by), acc (under)
3. ἐκ—gen (from, out of)
4. περί—gen (concerning, about), acc (around)
5. σύν—dat (with)
6. κατά—gen (against), acc (according to)
7. ἐν—dat (in)
8. ἀπό—gen (from)
9. πρός—acc (to, toward)
10. εἰς—acc (into)
11. διά—gen (through), acc (because of)
12. ἐπί—gen (on), dat (upon), acc (against)
13. μετά—gen (with), acc (after)
14. παρά—gen (from), dat (with), acc (beside)

B. Form Variations: Identify the lexical form of the following forms:

1. ἐφ'—ἐπί
2. παρ'—παρά
3. καθ'—κατά
4. ἐξ—ἐκ
5. ὑφ'—ὑπό
6. μετ'—μετά
7. δι'—διά
8. ἀφ'—ἀπό
9. κατ'—κατά
10. ἐπ'—ἐπί

C. Translation: Translate the following sentences.

1. "And he is coming/going into a house."

2. "And he was beside the lake."

3. "Not concerning/about the world I am asking." Or "I am not asking about/ concerning the world."

4. "After three days, I am being raised." [Note: In context, the verb has a future reference, even though it is a present tense verb; thus, it can rightly be translated, "After three days, I will be raised."]

5. "They were seeking against Jesus testimony." Or "They were seeking testimony against Jesus."

6. "You are believing/believe in the Son of Man?" Or "Do you believe in the Son of Man?" Or "Are you believing in the Son of Man?"

7. "And they were being baptized by him in the Jordan River." Or "They were baptized by him in the Jordan River."

8. "We have peace to/toward God through our Lord Jesus Christ."

9. "A disciple is not above the teacher nor a slave above his master/lord." [Note: The possessive idea is implied, so one could translate this as "[his] teacher."]

10. "Jesus went out with his disciples."

11. "To persons/those/men under the law, I became as under the law." [Note: The article τοῖς turns the prepositional phrase ὑπὸ νόμον into a substantive—that is, a noun-type thing. Because it is masculine plural, we add to our English translation the words "persons/those/men."]

12. "Glory in the highest to God and upon earth, peace to/in men."

13. "Grace to you and peace from God, our Father, and [the] Lord Jesus Christ."

14. "The love of the Father is not in him."

D. Translation: Translate the following sentences into Greek.

1. γινωσκουσιν το εὐαγγελιον κατα τους μαθητας.

2. λαμβανομεθα [ὑπο] [του] θεου δια [τον] χριστον. [Note: The words in brackets are not necessary. There are often several ways to say the same thing in Greek.]

3. τα τεκνα ἐρχονται προς τον ὀχλον.

4. ὁ ἀγγελος ἐλεγε(ν) ἐπι της γης. [Note: Actually, ἐπι can mean "upon" followed by the genitive, dative, or accusative, but the biblical usage with this phrase is always genitive.]

5. οἱ ἀνθρωποι της εἰρηνης πιστευουσιν ἐν τῃ ἀληθειᾳ ἀπο της καρδιας.

ANSWER KEY TO CHAPTER 9

A. Paradigms: Memorize the paradigms for ἐγώ and σύ (see section 9.4).

B. Personal Pronouns: Match the correct personal pronouns.

1.	C	1st person dative plural	A. αὐτά
2.	H	3rd person feminine accusative singular	B. σύ
3.	E	2nd person genitive plural	C. ἡμῖν
4.	A	3rd person neuter nominative plural	D. αὐταῖς
5.	G	1st person accusative singular	E. ὑμῶν
6.	F	2nd person dative singular	F. σοι
7.	J	3rd person masculine accusative plural	G. με
8.	B	2nd person nominative singular	H. αὐτήν
9.	D	3rd person feminine dative plural	I. μου
10.	I	1st person genitive singular	J. αὐτούς

C. Relative Pronouns: Circle the relative pronouns. (In the answers below, relative pronouns are listed rather than circled.)

1.	ᾗ	—	οὕς	—
2.	ᾧ	—	—	ὅ
3.	ὅστις	—	ἥ	ὅς
4.	ὧν	αἵ	—	ἥτις
5.	—	ἧς	—	ἅς

D. Translation: Translate the following sentences.

1. "Your brother has something against you." Or "The brother of you has something against you." Or "Your brother is having something against you."

2. "And they believed the Scripture and the word which Jesus said." [Note: The verb πιστεύω takes a dative direct object, thus τῇ γραφῇ and τῷ λόγῳ are in the dative. Also note how the antecedent of the relative pronoun ὅν is the masculine word τῷ λόγῳ, thus the relative pronoun must be mascu-

line to match its antecedent in gender. In English, however, we would use "which" or "that" to refer back to the noun, "word."]

3. "For you are doing the same things." [Note: αὐτά is neuter plural—thus the addition of "things" in the translation.]

4. "But Jesus himself was not entrusting him[self] to them." [Note: αὐτὸν would normally be translated as "him," but here it seems to be functioning like a reflexive pronoun, thus the "himself" translation in most modern versions. Be sure to see chap. 9, n. 12 on translating the verb πιστεύω as "entrust" here.]

5. "That which I do, you do not know." Or "What I am doing, you know not." Or, rearranging the order: "You do not know what I am doing."

6. "I myself also am a man" Or "And I myself am a man."

7. "And he who is not taking up his cross and is following after me, is not worthy of me." Or "And he who does not take up the cross of him and follow after me, is not worthy of me." [Note: The preposition ὀπίσω is always followed by the genitive. Also, it would be more common for μου to occur after ἄξιος, but here μου is drawn forward for emphasis.]

8. "Therefore, everyone who is hearing my words . . . and doing them" Or "Therefore, everyone who hears my words and does them." [Note: μου would normally occur after τοὺς λόγους, but is drawn forward for emphasis.]

9. "The works which I am doing in the name of my father . . . are testifying about me." Or "The works which I do in the name of my father . . . testify concerning me." [Note: The less common personal pronoun form ἐμοῦ (as opposed to μου) is more likely to occur as an object of a preposition.]

10. "I am going up to my Father and your [pl] Father and my God and your [pl] God." [Theological point: Jesus can refer to the Father as "God," just as Jesus himself is called "God" in John 20:28. It is significant that Jesus never includes himself along with the disciples in referring to God as "our Father" or "our God." Jesus's relationship with the Father is unique and eternal.]

11. "And he also was saying to his disciples, 'A certain man was rich, who was having a steward.'" Or "And he also was saying to his disciples, 'A certain man was rich, who had a steward.'"

12. "But Christ as a son over (upon) his house, whose house we are." [Note: Prepositions like ἐπί have a wide range of meaning.]

E. Translation: Translate the following sentences into Greek.

1. ὁ οἶκος μου ἐστιν ἡ οἰκια σου or ὁ οἶκος μου ἐστιν ὁ οἶκος σου or ὁ οἶκος μου ἐστιν οἰκος ὑμων. (etc.)

2. (αὐτος) λεγει (την) εἰρηνην αὐτῃ.

3. ὁ ἀνθρωπος, ὅς ἀκουει την φωνην σου or . . . ὁ ἀνθρωπος, ὅς ἀκουει την φωνην ὑμων or . . . ὁ ἀνθρωπος, ὅς ἀκουει της φωνης σου [Note: The verb ἀκούω takes its direct object in both the accusative and genitive.]

4. το τεκνον αὐτο περιπατεῖ παρα την θαλασσαν αὐτων or αὐτο το τεκνον περιπατεῖ παρα την θαλασσαν αὐτων.

5. ὁ λαος ἐχει ἀρτον ὅς ἐρχεται ἀπ᾽ οὐρανου.

ANSWER KEY TO CHAPTER 10

A. Paradigms: Memorize the future active, middle, and passive paradigms of λύω (see section 10.5).

B. Parsing: Parse the following verbs.

1. **βαπτίσει**—βαπτίζω fut act ind 3rd sg, "He/She/It will baptize."

2. **κράξουσιν**—κράζω fut act ind 3rd pl, "They will cry out."

3. **σωθήσομαι**—σῴζω fut pass ind 1st sg, "I will be saved."

4. **διωχθήσονται**—διώκω fut pass ind 3rd pl, "They will be persecuted."

5. **τηρήσω**—τηρέω fut act ind 1st sg, "I will keep."

6. **ἔσῃ**—εἰμί fut mid ind 2nd sg, "You will be."

7. **πράξετε**—πράσσω fut act ind, 2nd pl, "You (pl) will do/practice."

8. **ἕξουσιν**—ἔχω fut act ind 3rd pl, "They will have."

9. **βλέψετε**—βλέπω fut act ind 2nd pl, "You (pl) will see."

10. **φοβηθήσομαι**—φοβέομαι fut pass ind 1st sg, "I will fear/be afraid." [Note: φοβεομαι is a middle-preference verb, and in the Koine Greek period both the passive and middle endings sometimes functioned to convey a middle idea.]

C. Translation: Translate the following sentences.

1. "I will send my son." Or "I will send the son of me."

2. "He will have the light of life."

3. "I will ask the Father."

4. "And they will walk with me"

5. "They will be called sons of God." [Note: If you see a verb with κλ in it, it's almost certainly from καλέω. Also note that κληθήσονται functions here almost like the copulative verb εἰμι—thus the sentence has a subject nominative (αὐτοί) and a predicate nominative (υἱοὶ θεοῦ).]

6. "I am departing and you (pl) will seek me." Or "I am going away and you (pl) will seek me."

7. "He will save his soul/life from death."

8. "But my God will fulfill your (pl) every need." Or, "But my God will provide every need of you (pl)."

9. "You (sg) shall love [the] Lord your God with [or "in"] all your heart." Or, "You (sg) will love [the] Lord your God with all your heart." [Note: κύριον lacks an article because it reflects the same anarthrous construction in Deut 6:5 (from the Septuagint). κύριον is there used to translate the divine name (Yahweh) from Hebrew.]

10. "And God will glorify him in him [or "in himself"], and immediately he will glorify him." Or "God also will glorify him in him [or "in himself"], and immediately he will glorify him."

11. "Believe upon the Lord Jesus and you (sg) will be saved . . . and your house!" [Note: Outside of the present tense, imperfect tense, and perfect middle/passive forms, σῴζω does not have an iota subscript under the initial vowel.]

12. "And they will be his people, and God himself will be with them."

13. "The Lord will deliver me from every evil deed and will save [implied: "me"] into his kingdom."

14. "And you [pl] will know (for yourselves) the truth, and the truth will liberate you [pl]." [Note: The verb γινώσκω prefers a middle voice paradigm in the future. There are several verbs that prefer middle voice futures.]

D. Translation: Translate the following sentences from English to Greek.

1. ὁ ἀποστολος δοξασει τον κυριον [της] ἀληθειας.

2. [ἡμεις] οὐ διωξομεν τα τεκνα.

3. ὁ θεος σωσει τους ἀνθρωπους οἵ ἀκολουθοῦσιν αὐτῳ. [Note: The verb ἀκολουθέω is followed by a dative object/complement rather than the usual accusative.]

4. [αὐτοι] τηρησουσιν και πραξουσιν τας ἐντολας του θεου.

5. [ὑμεις] βαπτισετε την κεφαλην του οικου/της οικιας.

ANSWER KEY FOR CHAPTER 11

A. Paradigms: Memorize the aorist active, middle, and passive paradigms of λύω (see section 11.5).

B. Parsing: Parse the following verbs.

1. **ἐπέμψατε**—πέμπω aor act ind 2nd pl, "You (all) sent."

2. **ἐπράξαμεν**—πράσσω aor act ind 1st pl, "We did/practiced."

3. **ἐδίωξα**—διώκω aor act ind 1st sg, "I pursued/persecuted."

4. **ἐπιστεύσατε**—πιστεύω aor act ind 2nd pl, "You (all) believed."

5. **προσεκύνησεν**—προσκυνέω aor act ind 3rd sg, "He/She/It worshipped." [Note: The augment comes after the prepositional prefix.]

6. **ἐτήρησας**—τηρέω aor act ind 2nd sg, "You kept." [Note: The contract vowel (ε) lengthens to an η before the tense formative (σα).]

7. **ἀπελύθησαν**—ἀπολύω aor pass ind 3rd pl, "They were released." [Note: The augment (ε) knocked out the last letter of the prepositional prefix (ἀπο).]

8. **προσηύξατο**—προσεύχομαι aor mid ind 3rd sg, "He prayed." [Note: προσεύχομαι is a middle preference verb. Verbs of reciprocity (where two parties are involved, and if one is removed, the action cannot happen) are frequently middle preference verbs.]

9. **ἤνοιξεν**—ἀνοίγω aor act ind 3rd sg, "He/She/It opened." [Note: The verb ἀνοίγω sometimes double augments after the prepositional prefix (ἀνέῳξεν, John 9:14). It can even triple augment (ἠνεῴχθησαν, Acts 16:26).]

10. **ἐσώθη**—σώζω aor pass ind 3rd sg, "He/She/It was saved." [Note: The iota subscript in the present, imperfect, and perfect passive forms of σώζω are absent in the other tenses.]

C. Translation: Translate the following sentences.

1. "I wrote to you (all) in the letter." [Note: Many English translations have "my letter," because the context makes clear it is Paul's letter and a possessive idea (usually made explicit in English) is not infrequently implied in Greek.]

2. "Therefore, Jesus cried out in the temple."

3. "John taught his disciples." Or "John taught the disciples of him."

4. "For in this way, God loved the world." [Note: οὕτως can be intensive ("so much") but more frequently expresses an instrumental idea ("in this way"). The Christian Standard Bible (CSB) is one of the few translations to render οὕτως "in this way."]

5. "And he was baptized in the Jordan by John."

6. "And they glorified the God of Israel."

7. "We pray always about you (all)." Or "We always are praying concerning/ for you (pl)."

8. "The Lord of the slave . . . released him."

9. "He began to teach beside the sea/lake."

10. "Satan filled your heart."

11. "And he asked for/requested the body of Jesus."

12. "And their eyes were opened."

D. Translation: Translate the following sentences into Greek.

1. (αὐτος) προσηυξατο ἐν τη συναγωγη.

2. ὁ διδασκαλος συνηγεν τους μαθητας και ἐδιδαξεν αὐτους.

3. ὁ ἀγγελος ἐδοξασεν (τον) θεον ἐνωπιον του θρονου αὐτου. [Note: When a noun has a genitive personal pronoun after it, that noun is also almost always preceded by an article.]

4. οὐκ ἐπιστευσαμεν το δαιμονιον [Or τῳ δαιμονιῳ, because the verb πιστευω can take both a dative or accusative object.]

5. ἡ χαρα του κυριου ἐτηρησε(ν) ἡμας ἐν τῳ πλοιῳ.

ANSWER KEY TO CHAPTER 12

A. Second Aorist Stem: Match the lexical form of the verb with its second aorist form.

1.	E καταβαίνω	A. ἐγενόμην
2.	G λαμβάνω	B. εἶδον
3.	H ἀποθνήσκω	C. ἔσχον
4.	B βλέπω	D. ἦλθον
5.	P ἐσθίω	E. κατέβην
6.	N γινώσκω	F. εἶπον
7.	O εὑρίσκω	G. ἔλαβον
8.	D ἔρχομαι	H. ἀπέθανον
9.	K ἄγω	I. ἔβαλον
10.	M πίπτω	J. ἤνεγκον
11.	A γίνομαι	K. ἤγαγον
12.	F λέγω	L. ἔπιον
13.	J φέρω	M. ἔπεσον
14.	C ἔχω	N. ἔγνων
15.	I βάλλω	O. εὗρον
16.	L πίνω	P. ἔφαγον

B. Parsing: Parse the following verbs.

1. **ἀπέθανον**—ἀποθνήσκω aor act ind 1st sg or 3rd pl, "I died" or "They died."

2. **ἐφάγομεν**—ἐσθίω aor act ind 1st pl, "We ate."

3. **ἀνέβην**—ἀναβαίνω aor act ind 1st sg, "I went up."

4. **εὑρέθημεν**—εὑρίσκω aor pass ind 1st pl, "We were found."

5. **κατέβησαν**—καταβαίνω aor act ind 3rd pl, "They went down."

6. ἠνέχθη—φέρω aor pass ind 3rd sg, "He/she/it was carried."

7. ἠγάγετε—ἄγω aor act ind 2nd pl, "You (all) led/brought."

8. ἐγένετο—γίνομαι aor mid ind 3rd sg, "He/she/it became."

9. ἔσχες—ἔχω aor act ind 2nd sg, "You had."

10. συνήχθησαν—συνάγω aor pass ind 3rd pl, "The were gathered/assembled."

C. Translation: Translate the following sentences.

1. "We received a commandment from the Father."

2. "For, I, through law, died to law." Or "For, I, through [the] law, died to [the] law."

3. "I carried/brought my son to you."

4. "Jesus went up into the temple and was teaching."

5. "And they departed in the boat to a deserted place."

6. "Christ died on behalf of our sins according to the Scriptures." Or "Christ died for our sins according to the Scriptures."

7. "(The) sin entered into the world and through (the) sin . . . death."

8. "An angel went out of the temple which was in the heaven." [Note: The prepositional phrase ἐν τῷ οὐρανῷ functions as an adjective modifying τοῦ ναοῦ.]

9. "His disciples went down to the lake/sea."

10. "I fell at/toward his feet as [if] dead."

11. "In that hour, the disciples went to Jesus."

12. "He saw his glory and he spoke about him."

13. "For they knew that to/toward/against them, he spoke the parable."

14. "He was in the world, and the world through him became/came about, and the world did not know him."

15. "He entered into the house of God and they ate the bread/loaves of the presence."

D. Translation: Translate the following sentences into Greek.

1. το τεκνον ἐπεσεν ἐπι της ὁδου.

2. εὑρετε τον κυριον της ζωης.

3. κατεβη τῃ συναγωγῃ.

4. εἰσηλθομεν εἰς τον οἰκον του θεου και ἠκουσαμεν τον λογον.

5. εἰπον την ἐπαγγελιαν τῳ ὀχλῳ.

ANSWER KEY TO CHAPTER 13

A. Stem Recognition: Indicate whether the form is Present (P), Future (F), or Aorist (A).

1. P   ἐγείρομαι

2. A   ἤρατε

3. F   ἀπαγγελεῖ

4. A   ἐμείναμεν

5. P   σπείρεται

6. F   ἀποκριθήσονται

7. F   ἀποκτενοῦσιν

8. P   ἀποστέλλει

9. A   ἐκρίθησαν

10. P   ἀποκρίνῃ

B. Parsing: Parse the following verbs.

1. **ἀροῦσιν**—αἴρω fut act ind 3rd pl, "They will take up/away."

2. **ἀπήγγειλαν**—ἀπαγγέλλω aor act ind 3rd pl, "They announced/reported."

3. **ἀποκριθήσονται**—ἀποκρίνομαι fut pass ind 3rd pl, "They will answer." [Note: The passive ending here conveys a middle idea. The verb ἀποκρίνομαι is middle-preference.]

4. **ἀπεκτείνατε**—ἀποκτείνω aor act ind 2nd pl, "You (all) killed."

5. **ἀποστελῶ**—ἀποστέλλω fut act ind 1st sg, "I will send."

6. **ἠγέρθη**—ἐγείρω aor pass ind 3rd sg, "He/she/it was raised."

7. **ἔκρινας**—κρίνω aor act ind 2nd sg, "You judged."

8. **μενεῖ**—μένω fut act ind 3rd sg, "He/She/It will remain."

9. **ἐσπείραμεν**—σπείρω aor act ind 1st pl, "We sowed."

10. **κρινοῦμεν**—κρίνω fut act ind 1st pl, "We will judge."

C. Translation: Translate the following sentences.

1. "I will announce your name to my brothers."

2. "The slave announced/reported these things to his lord/master."

3. "I say to you that the kingdom of God will be taken away from you." Or "I am saying to you that the kingdom of God will be taken away from you."

4. "His disciples took up/took away the corpse."

5. "Jesus answered and said to him, 'Truly truly, I say to you'"

6. "And they will kill him, and on the third day, he will be raised."

7. "Lord, they killed your prophets."

8. "The Son of man will send out his angels."

9. "Just as you sent me into the world, I also sent them into the world."

10. "The God of our fathers raised Jesus."

11. "(The) Lord will judge his people." [Note: κύριος lacks an article because this is a direct quotation of Deut 32:36 in the LXX, where the anarthrous ("without an article") κύριος translates the divine Hebrew name ("Yahweh").]

12. "And each (person) was judged according to their works." [Note: Here we see a singular subject used with a plural verb. The singular subject has a distributive sense in context.]

13. "And you (all) will remain in the Son and in the Father." Or "And you (all) will remain both in the Son and in the Father."

14. "After this, he went down to/into Capernaum—he, and his mother, and his brothers, and his disciples and there they remained not many days."

15. "A man sowed/planted in his field." Or "A man scattered seed in his field."

D. Translation: Translate the following sentences into Greek.

1. ὁ λιθος ἤρθη.

2. ἀπαγγελοῦσιν την σοφιαν των γραφων/της γραφης. [Note: The singular form of γραφη can refer to the Scriptures collectively, and thus be translated "Scriptures."]

3. (ἐγω) οὖν μενῶ ἐν τῳ ἱερῳ. [Note: The particle οὖν normally occurs second (or later) in a sentence—never in the first position.]

4. ὁ ἀνθρωπος ἐκρινεν τον καιρον της σωτηριας.

5. ὁ κυριος ἀποστελεῖ το εὐαγγελιον τῳ διδασκαλῳ.

ANSWER KEY TO CHAPTER 14

A. Paradigms: Memorize the paradigms for σάρξ and πνεῦμά (see section 14.4).

B. Declensions: Circle the third declension nouns and then parse them. (Third declension nouns listed rather than circled below.)

1. —   ἀρχιερεῦσιν   σάρξ   —
                 masc, dat, pl   fem, nom, sg

2. αἰῶνι   —   —   πατέρα
   masc, dat, sg   masc, acc, sg

3. γυναιξίν   —   πόλεως   ἔθνη
   fem, dat, pl   fem, gen, sg   neut, nom/acc pl

4. —   —   μητρί   βασιλεῖ
                              fem, dat, sg   masc, dat, sg

5. πίστει   ἄνδρες   —   —
   fem, dat, sg   masc, nom, pl

6. —   χάριν   —   ὀνομάτων
                  fem, acc, sg   neut, gen, pl

7. πνεύματα   —   σωμάτων   —
   neut nom/acc pl   neut, gen, pl

C. Translation: Translate the following sentences.

1. "And to our God and Father (be) [the] glory into the ages of the ages, Amen!" [Note: "Into the ages" is a Greek idiom meaning "forever." The verb "be" is implied.]

2. "The woman answered and said to him, 'I do not have a husband/man.'"

3. "We have a high priest, who sat down at the right hand of the throne of the Most High in the heavens."

4. "Are you the king of the Jews?"

5. "For a man is not of/out of/from a woman, but a woman (is) from/of/out of a man."

6. "Honor your father and mother, which is (the) first commandment with/in a promise."

7. "What/That which (is) not from/of/out of faith is sin."

8. "The woman departed into the city and says to the men/people" [Note: The present tense is sometimes used in historical narrative, especially for verbs of speech and motion, and these verbs are rightly translated into an English past tense in a final translation.]

9. "But you (pl) are not in (the) flesh, but in (the) Spirit, if (the) Spirit of God dwells in you (pl)."

10. "But if by grace, no longer of/out of works, since grace would no longer be grace."

11. "He will announce/proclaim judgment to the nations."

12. "They believed Phillip . . . about/concerning the kingdom of God and the name of Jesus Christ, they were being baptized—both men and women."

13. "But we did not receive the spirit of the world, but the Spirit from God." [Note: The final article τό turns the following prepositional phrase into an adjective to modify πνεῦμα.]

14. "And he is the head of the body of the church." Or "And he is the head of the body—the church." [Note: The second translation reflects a use of the genitive you will learn in intermediate Greek—the epexegetical genitive.]

D. Translation: Translate the following sentences into Greek.

1. ἡ μητηρ του ἀρχιερεως ἐπιστευσεν ἐν τῳ ὀνοματι του κυριου.

2. ὁ ἀνηρ/ὁ ἀνθρωπος της πιστεως γινωσκει το πνευμα του θεου.

3. ὁ βασιλευς της πολεως κρινεῖ τα ἐθνη.

4. ἡ γυνη ἠλθεν τῳ πατρι και προσηυξατο ἐπι το σωμα του τεκνου.

5. ἡ χαρις του χριστου ἀποκτεινεῖ την σαρκα εἰς αἰωνας αἰωνων.

ANSWER KEY TO CHAPTER 15

A. Paradigms: Memorize the perfect active and middle/passive paradigms of λύω (see section 15.4).

B. Tenses: Identify the tense of the following verbs as Present (P), Imperfect (I), Future (F), Aorist (A), or Perfect (Pf).

1.	A	ἔζησεν	11.	I	ἠκολούθουν
2.	Pf	οἶδεν (perfect [form] or present [meaning])	12.	Pf	κέκληται
3.	I	ἐδίδασκεν	13.	A	περιεπατήσαμεν
4.	Pf	κέκρικα	14.	P	ποιεῖς
5.	F	μενεῖτε (liquid verb)	15.	Pf	σέσωται
6.	A	ἐβαπτίσθητε	16.	F	πράξετε
7.	P	γίνεται	17.	A	ἔσπειρας
8.	Pf	κέκραγεν	18.	Pf	ἀπολέλυσαι
9.	Pf	γεγέννηκα	19.	I	ἐδίωκον
10.	F	ἐρωτήσετε	20.	Pf	δεδόξασμαι

C. Parsing: Parse the following words.

1. **τετήρηκας**—τηρέω per act ind 2nd sg, "You have kept."

2. **ᾐτήκαμεν**—αἰτέω per act ind 1st pl, "We have asked/requested."

3. **βέβληται**—βάλλω per mid/pass ind 3rd sg, "He/she/it has been thrown," or "He/she/it threw for himself/herself/itself."

4. **πέποιθα**—πείθω per act ind 1st sg, "I have persuaded" or "I am persuaded" [stative idea].

5. **ἠγαπήκαμεν**—ἀγαπάω per act ind 1st pl, "We have loved."

6. **ἀκηκόατε**—ἀκούω per act ind 2nd pl, "You (all) have heard."

7. **γεγόνασιν**—γίνομαι per act ind 3rd pl, "They have become."

8. **εἴληφας**—λαμβάνω per act ind 2nd sg, "You have received."

9. **εὕρηκα**—εὑρίσκω per act ind 1st sg, "I have found."

10. **εἰρήκατε**—λέγω per act ind 2nd pl, "You (all) have said."

D. Translation: Translate the following sentence.

1. "The time has been fulfilled, and the kingdom of God has drawn near/ approached."

2. "It has been written, 'Not upon bread only will live (a) man,' or 'Not upon bread only will a man live.'" [Note: In generic or proverbial statements, Greek will use the article with the person or category being discussed (ὁ ἄνθρωπος). In English, proverbial or generic statements will use nouns with an indefinite article ("a man") or a plural noun ("men").]

3. "Rabbi, we know that from God you have come—a teacher."

4. "You (all) worship what/that which you do not know. We worship what we know, because [the] salvation is from the Jews."

5. "I know from where I came and where I am going/departing. But you (all) do not know from where I come or where I go/depart."

6. "And I have seen and I have testified that this one is the Son of God."

7. "But I said to you (all) that you (all) also have seen me and you (all) are not believing."

8. "But we have been persuaded in [the] Lord upon/about you (all)."

9. "I have come in the name of my Father, and you (all) are not receiving me."

10. "For I have not yet gone up/ascended to the Father."

11. "And we have known and we have believed [or: have relied upon] the love which God has in/for us."

12. "But he said to her, 'Daughter, your faith has saved/healed you.'" [Note: The Greek article can sometimes function like a personal pronoun, as it does in this verse.]

13. "And we have believed, and we have known that you are the holy one of God."

14. "And this is the message which we have heard from him and we proclaim to you (all), that God is light." Or "And [it] is this message which we have heard" Or "And this message is that which we have heard"

E. Translation: Translate the following sentences into Greek.

1. οἱ γραμματεις ἠγγικαν/ασιν τῳ πυρι. [Note: The verb ἐγγίζω is frequently followed by a dative of the person or thing approached. You were not taught this before reading this note, so don't be hard on yourself if you tried another construction. In fact, a few constructions are grammatically possible.]

2. πεποιθα ἐν τῃ δυναμει του θεου. [Note: The perfect tense conveys an ongoing state of being persuaded.]

3. ἑωρακαν/ασιν το αἱμα ἐπι των χειρων αὐτου και (των) ποδων (αὐτου).

4. ἡ γυνη οἰδεν/γινωσκει τον λογον/το ῥημα (του) φωτος.

5. ζῶμεν εἰς το στομα του ὑδατος. [Note: Greek prepositions (and the dative case itself) are quite flexible, and several possible constructions could convey the idea of "at the mouth."]

ANSWER KEY TO CHAPTER 16

A. Adjective Case: Circle the words of the designated cases. Here and in C. below, answers are listed rather than circled.

1. **Nominative**	σοφοί	—	μείζονες	—
2. **Genitive**	πονηρᾶς	νεκρῶν	—	παντός
3. **Dative**	παντί	—	ἁγίοις	—
4. **Accusative**	—	—	ἄλλους	ἀγαθά

B. Adjective Use: Indicate whether the following adjectives are used Attributively (A), Substantivally (S), or Predicatively (P).

1. P ὁ θεὸς φῶς ἐστιν

2. A φωνῇ μεγάλῃ

3. S τὸ ἀγαθόν

4. P ἅγιον τὸ ὄνομα αὐτοῦ

5. S οἱ ἅγιοι τὸν κόσμον κρινοῦσιν

6. A καρποὺς καλούς

7. A πᾶν ἔθνος

8. P πιστὸς ὁ θεός

9. S ἐγείρει τοὺς νεκρούς

10. P ὁ υἱός μου νεκρὸς ἦν

C. Adjective Degrees: Circle the words of the designated degrees.

1. **Positive**	—	ἀγαθός	—	ἄλλος
2. **Comparative**	—	μείζων	πονηρότερος	—
3. **Superlative**	μέγιστος	τιμιώτατος	—	—

D. Translation: Translate the following sentences.

1. "The good man out of the good treasure brings out/throws out good things, and the evil man out of the evil treasure brings out/throws out evil things."

2. "The Holy Spirit, whom the Father will send in my name, that one will teach you (pl) all things."

3. "For the sanctuary/temple of God is holy, which you (pl) are."

4. "But Simon Peter was following Jesus—and another disciple" [Note: The verb ἀκολουθέω is followed by a dative object or dative complement—thus, τῷ ᾿Ιησοῦ is in the dative case.]

5. "Or you (pl) receive a different spirit which you (pl) did not receive, or [implied: you receive] another gospel which you (pl) did not receive"

6. "You will be a good servant of Christ Jesus." [Note: The placement of the attributive adjective καλός is unusual. It could be drawn forward for emphasis and/or as a method of setting apart a unit of thought through splitting syntactical items that are usually found in close proximity—an ancient Greek structural method named "hyperbaton."]

7. "He will be great and will be called Son of [the] Most High."

8. "Truly, truly I say to you (pl) that an hour is coming and now is when the dead (people/men) will hear the voice of the Son of God." [Note: The verb ἀκούω frequently takes a genitive direct object, thus τῆς φωνῆς is genitive.]

9. "For if [the] dead [people/men] are not raised, neither has Christ been raised."

10. "And I saw/looked, and I heard [the] sound of many angels."

11. "[The] law is holy, and the commandment is holy and just and good."

12. "Truly truly, I say to you (pl), a slave is not greater than his master/lord."

13. "The foolishness of God is wiser than men, and the weakness of God is stronger than men."

14. "But the smallest/least (μικρότερος is a comparative used as a superlative) in the kingdom of the heavens is greater than he."

15. "For I am the least/smallest of the apostles."

E. Translation: Translate the following sentences into Greek.

1. παλιν λεγω, ὁ κυριος ἐστιν ἁγιος, δικαιος, και ἀγαθος/καλος.

2. ὁ πονηρος οὐκ ἐστιν μειζων του πιστου or οὐδεις εστιν μειζων ἡ ὁ πιστος.

3. ὁ πλειστος ὀχλος ἠκουσεν παντα λογον/παν ῥημα.

4. νῦν οἱ νεκροι ἐν Χριστῷ ἐγερθησονται.

5. ἑτερος/ἀλλος δουλος κηρυξει/ἀπαγγελεῖ ἑτερον/ἀλλον τοπον.

ANSWER KEY TO CHAPTER 17

A. Paradigms: Memorize the present active and middle/passive paradigms of λύω—masculine only (see section 17.4).

B. Parsing: Parse the following words.

1. **θεωροῦντας**—θεωρέω pres act ptc masc acc pl

2. **καθημένῳ**—κάθημαι pres mid ptc masc/neut dat sg

3. **μένουσαν**—μένω pres act ptc fem acc sg

4. **λαμβάνοντες**—λαμβάνω pres act ptc masc nom pl

5. **κρίνοντα**—κρίνω pres act ptc masc acc sg or neut nom/acc pl

6. **ὑπάρχοντος**—ὑπάρχω pres act ptc masc/neut gen sg

7. **γραφόμενα**—γράφω pres mid/pass ptc neut nom/acc pl

8. **ἔχοντι**—ἔχω pres act ptc masc/neut dat sg

9. **καλούμενον**—καλέω pres mid/pass ptc masc acc sg or neut nom/acc sg

10. **οὔσῃ**—εἰμί pres ptc fem dat sg

C. Participle Usage: Indicate whether the following participles are used Attributively (A), Substantivally (S), or Adverbially (Adv).

1. A   τὴν ἀλήθειαν τὴν μένουσαν ἐν ἡμῖν

2. S   ὁ μένων ἐν τῇ διδαχῇ

3. Adv   πορευόμενοι δὲ κηρύσσετε λέγοντες ὅτι ἤγγικεν ἡ βασιλεία τῶν οὐρανῶν

4. A   ὁ πατήρ σου ὁ βλέπων

5. S   ἔστιν ὁ ζητῶν καὶ κρίνων

6. A   ὁ ἄρτος ὁ ἐκ τοῦ οὐρανοῦ καταβαίνων

7. Adv   βλέπει τὸν Ἰησοῦν ἐρχόμενον πρὸς αὐτὸν

8. S   ὁ καταβαίνων ἐκ τοῦ οὐρανοῦ

9. A   τῷ θεῷ τῷ ἐγείροντι τοὺς νεκρούς

10. Adv   ἦλθεν ὁ υἱὸς τοῦ ἀνθρώπου ἐσθίων καὶ πίνων

D. Translation: Translate the following sentences.

1. "The one who believes in the Son has eternal life."

2. "He sees Jesus (while) coming to him and says, 'Behold the lamb of God who is taking away the sin of the world.'" [Note: βλέπει and λέγει are historical presents and would be rendered as English past tenses in a final translation.]

3. "And he went (while) preaching in their synagogues in all of Galilee and (while) casting out demons."

4. "The one who receives you receives me, and the one who receives me receives the one who sent me."

5. "[The] righteousness of God has been revealed, being testified to by the law and the prophets."

6. "He comes to them, (while) walking upon the sea." [Note: ἔρχεται is a historical present and would be rendered as a past tense verb in a final English translation.]

7. "And the Pharisees came/went out . . . seeking from him a sign from heaven, testing him" (or: "in order to test him.").

8. "Simon Peter said, 'You are the Christ, the Son of the Living God.'"

9. "And immediately, (as he was) coming out of the water, he saw . . . the Spirit as a dove coming down upon him."

10. "And I saw another strong angel (as he was) coming down out of heaven."

11. "The people who are sitting (living) in darkness saw a great light."

12. "But when they believed Philip (as he was) preaching concerning the kingdom of God and the name of Jesus Christ." [Note: The verb πιστεύω frequently takes a dative object. Also, the verb εὐαγγελίζω frequently occurs in the middle voice.]

13. "But the one coming after me is stronger than I."

14. "And you (all), while being dead in your trespasses and sins"

15. "And he was teaching in their synagogues, (while) being glorified by all (people)."

E. Translation: Translate the following sentences into Greek.

1. ἦλθεν ἔξω αὐτοις κηρυσσων τον αἰωνιον λογον (or τον λογον τον αἰωνιον).

2. ἀμην ἀμην λεγω σοι, αὐτοι οὐκ/οὐδε γινωσκουσιν την ἡμεραν οὐδε ὡραν.

3. οἱ πρεσβυτεροι ἠγαγον ἑκαστον τεκνον θεωρουν τα σημεια.

4. τοτε ὁ Ἰησους εἰπεν, ἐγω εἰμι ὁ καθημενος ἐπι τῳ θρονῳ.

5. οὐδεις εἰδεν τον κηρυσσοντα το εὐαγγελιον.

ANSWER KEY TO CHAPTER 18

A. Paradigms: Memorize the aorist active, middle, and passive paradigms of λύω—masculine only (see section 18.3).

B. Parsing: Parse the following words.

1. **ἐλθόντων**—ἔρχομαι aor act ptc masc/neut gen pl

2. **ἰδών**—βλέπω aor act ptc masc nom sg

3. **ἀπολυθέντες**—ἀπολύω aor pass ptc masc nom pl

4. **ἀποθανών**—ἀποθνήσκω aor act ptc masc nom sg

5. **ἀγαπήσαντος**—ἀγαπάω aor act ptc masc/neut gen sg

6. **λαλήσας**—λαλέω aor act ptc masc nom sg

7. **εἰσελθόντι**—εἰσέρχομαι aor act ptc masc/neut dat sg

8. **λαβόντας**—λαμβάνω aor act ptc masc acc pl

9. **ἀκούσαντες**—ἀκούω aor act ptc masc nom pl

10. **μαρτυρήσας**—μαρτυρέω aor act ptc masc nom sg

C. Participle Usage: Indicate whether the following participles are used Attributively (A), Substantivally (S), or Adverbially (Adv).

1. Adv   ἀκούσας δὲ ὁ βασιλεὺς

2. S   ὁ δὲ ἐγερθεὶς παρέλαβεν τὸ παιδίον

3. A   ὁ θεὸς ὁ εἰπών

4. S   ἀπὸ τοῦ καλέσαντος ὑμᾶς ἐν χάριτι Χριστοῦ

5. Adv   βαπτισθεὶς δὲ ὁ Ἰησοῦς

6. A   τοῦ υἱοῦ τοῦ θεοῦ τοῦ ἀγαπήσαντός με

7. S   ὁ εὑρὼν τὴν ψυχὴν αὐτοῦ

8. A/S   εἰς θεὸν τὸν ἐγείραντα αὐτὸν ἐκ νεκρῶν

9. S   ὁ ἐγείρας Χριστὸν

10. Adv   ὃν οὐκ ἰδόντες ἀγαπᾶτε

D. Translation: Translate the following sentences.

1. "Therefore, after Jesus came, he found him [Lazarus] having already been four days in the tomb."

2. "And immediately, after they went out of the synagogue, they came into the house of Simon and Andrew, with James and John."

3. "And after Jesus saw their faith, he said to the paralytic, 'Child, your sins are forgiven.'"

4. "And he was raised (or "he got up") and immediately, after taking up (his) mat, he went out in front of all." [Note: The passive form ἠγέρθη likely is intended to convey a middle idea: "He got up" rather than "He was raised."]

5. "But he, after being raised (better: "after having gotten up," with the passive form conveying a middle idea), took along the child and his mother and entered into the land of Israel."

6. "And after he took the five loaves and two fish, after looking up into the heaven, he blessed and broke the loaves and he was giving [them] to his disciples."

7. "And after he answered, Jesus was saying, (while) teaching in the temple, 'How do the scribes say that the Christ is (the) son of David?'"

8. "And after she answered, his mother said, 'No! But he will be called John.'"

9. "Immediately, after the father of the child cried out, he was saying, 'I believe.'"

10. "And again, after he went away, he prayed the same word, saying"

11. "And the one who sees/beholds me, sees/beholds the one who sent me."

12. "And entering into the house, they saw the child."

13. "And after we greeted the brothers, we remained one day with them."

14. "Therefore, having been declared righteous now by his blood, how much more will we be saved through him from the wrath."

15. "I greet you (pl), I, Tertius, the one who wrote the letter, in [the] Lord."

E. Translation: Translate the following sentences into Greek.

1. ἐξῆλθεν μετα των δυο μαθητων αὐτου.

2. λαλησας τῳ ὀχλῳ, Ἰησους ἐλαλησεν τοις δωδεκα.

3. ὁ τριτος ἀποστολος ἐλυθη ἐν τῳ οἰκῳ αὐτου.

4. ὁ θεος ὁ ἀποστειλας τον υἱον αὐτου ἐφανέρωσεν τὴν δόξαν αὐτοῦ.

5. οἱ μη πιστευσαντες ὑπηγον εἰς τὴν πόλιν.

ANSWER KEY TO CHAPTER 19

A. Paradigms: Memorize the perfect active, middle, and passive paradigms of λύω—masculine only (see section 19.3).

B. Parsing: Parse the following words.

1. **πεποιθώς**—πείθω per act ptc masc nom sg

2. **πεποιηκόσιν**—ποιέω per act ptc masc/neut dat pl

3. **βεβλημένην**—βάλλω per mid/pass ptc fem acc sg

4. **γεγεννημένον**—γεννάω per mid/pass ptc masc acc sg or neut nom/acc sg

5. **πεπιστευκότων**—πιστεύω per act ptc masc/neut gen pl

6. **ἐγνωκότες**—γινώσκω per act ptc masc nom pl

7. **σώσων**—σῴζω fut act ptc masc nom sg

8. **γεγραμμένα**—γράφω per mid/pass ptc neut nom/acc pl

9. **γεγονότας**—γίνομαι per act ptc masc acc pl

10. **ἠγαπημένῳ**—ἀγαπάω per mid/pass ptc masc/neut dat sg

C. Participle Usage: Indicate whether the following participles are used Attributively (A), Substantivally (S), Adverbially as a Genitive Absolute (GA), or Periphrastically (P).

1.	A	οἱ ἄνδρες οἱ ἀπεσταλμένοι
2.	S	οἱ ἀπεσταλμένοι εὗρον καθὼς εἶπεν αὐτοῖς
3.	P	καὶ ἦν ἐκβάλλων δαιμόνιον
4.	A	τὸ πῦρ τὸ αἰώνιον τὸ ἡτοιμασμένον τῷ διαβόλῳ
5.	S	ἐν τῷ ἠγαπημένῳ
6.	GA	καὶ καταβαινόντων αὐτῶν ἐκ τοῦ ὄρους
7.	S	ἀδελφοί, οἱ ἠγαπημένοι ὑπὸ τοῦ θεοῦ
8.	S	εἰς μαρτύριον τῶν λαληθησομένων
9.	A	τὸ ὕδωρ τὸ γεγενημένον οἶνον
10.	GA	καὶ ἐσθιόντων αὐτῶν εἶπεν

D. Translation: Translate the following sentences.

1. "Therefore, Jesus was speaking to the Jews who had believed in him."

2. "And, as all the people were listening, he said to his disciples"

3. "And he was preaching in the synagogues of Judea."

4. "There was a man, having been sent from God, name [belonging] to him—John."

5. "The thing which is born of flesh is flesh, and the thing which is born of spirit is spirit."

6. "While Peter was still speaking these words, the Holy Spirit fell upon all those hearing the word/message."

7. "I will call 'the not my people' [as] 'my people' and 'her not having been loved one' [as] 'having been loved."

8. "And through every night and day, in the tombs and in the mountains, he was crying out."

9. "And as he was going out of the temple, one of his disciples says [historical present, "said"] to him, 'Teacher'"

10. "The one who sows plants the word . . . immediately Satan comes and takes away the word which was having been sown in them."

11. "And after he got out of the boat, immediately, a man with an unclean spirit from the tombs met him."

12. "For where two or three are having been gathered in my name, there I am in their midst."

13. "Not only to me but to everyone who has loved his appearing"

14. "For while we were yet weak, at the (right) season/time, Christ died for the ungodly."

15. "Pharisees and law-teachers were seated, the ones who were having come from every village of Galilee and Judea and Jerusalem."

E. Translation: Translate the following sentences into Greek.

1. το ἀγαπητον τεκνον, δεδεμενον, ἠγερθη ὑπο του κυριου ἐν (τῳ) μεσῳ αὐτων.

2. θεραπευσαντος Ἰησους τους λοιπους, ὁ ὁλος ὀχλος ἠλθεν τῳ ὀρει.

3. ἀρα [οὐν], τοπος ἡτοιμασμενος ἡμιν ἐστιν την ἐλπιδα ἡμων νυν [or ἤδη].

4. ὁ ἱερευς ἐρχεται και προσφερει ζῳον ὡδε.

5. ἠν διδασκων τας γυναικας ἐγειρων μονον την δεξιαν (χειρα) αὐτου.

ANSWER KEY TO CHAPTER 20

A. Parsing: Parse the following words and include the pronoun classification (personal, relative, near demonstrative, far demonstrative, reflexive, reciprocal, interrogative, or indefinite, or note as a pronominal adjective).

1. **τίνες**—Interrogative, masc/fem nom pl, "who (pl)?"

2. **ταύτῃ**—Near Demonstrative, fem dat sg, "to/for this woman"

3. **αὐτήν**—Personal, fem acc sg, "her"

4. **ἐκείνου**—Far Demonstrative, masc/neut gen sg, "of that one"

5. **σεαυτόν**—Reflexive (2nd person sg), masc/neut acc sg, "yourself"

6. **τινάς**—Indefinite, masc/fem acc pl, "certain ones"

7. **μοι**—Personal (1st person), masc/fem dat sg, "to/for me"

8. **οἵ**—Relative, masc nom pl, "who/which"

9. **ἐμαυτῷ**—Reflexive (1st person), masc dat sg, "to/for myself"

10. **ὑμεῖς**—Personal (2nd person), masc/fem nom pl, "you (pl)"

11. **ἐμόν**—Pronominal Adj (1st person), masc acc sg or neut nom/acc sg, "my/mine"

12. **ἡμῶν**—Personal (1st person), masc/fem gen pl, "our"

13. **ἀλλήλους**—Reciprocal, masc acc pl, "one another"

14. **ἥτις**—Relative fem nom sg, "who, which"

15. **σε**—Personal (2nd person), masc/fem acc sg, "you"

16. **ἑαυτοῖς**—Reflexive (3rd person), masc/neut dat pl, "to/for themselves." [Note: *Plural* forms of the reflexive pronoun are all the same for the 1st, 2nd, and 3rd person; therefore, only context will let the reader know whether this is "themselves"(3rd), "yourselves" (2nd), or "ourselves" (1st).]

B. Matching: Match each Greek phrase with its English translation.

1. G αὕτη ἡ γυνή   A. these are the sons

2. N εἴ τις ἔρχεται   B. Do you see anything?

3. O ταῦτα εἶπεν   C. What do you say about yourself?

4. M ὁ δοῦλος ἐκεῖνος   D. my command

5. K γυναῖκές τινες   E. to myself

6. L τίνα ζητεῖς;   F. with one another

7. D ἡ ἐντολὴ ἡ ἐμή   G. this woman

8. I τίς ἐστιν οὗτος;   H. a certain woman

9. E πρὸς ἐμαυτόν   I. Who is this?

10. A οὗτοί εἰσιν οἱ υἱοί. J. a certain man

11. H γυνή τις   K. some women

12. C τί λέγεις περὶ σεαυτοῦ; L. Whom are you seeking?

13. J ἄνθρωπός τις   M. that slave

14. B τι βλέπεις;   N. if anyone comes

15. F σὺν ἀλλήλοις   O. he said these things

C. Translation: Translate the following sentences.

1. "Truly, this man was [the] son of God."

2. "But if anyone does not have [the] spirit of Christ, this person is not his."

3. "We have fellowship with one another."

4. "But that one was speaking concerning/about the temple of his body."

5. "You will/shall love your neighbor as yourself." (an imperatival future)

6. "This (man) is truly the Savior of the world."

7. "From myself, I have not come."

8. "Jesus spoke all these things in parables to the crowds."

9. "But Jesus said to him, 'Why do you call me good? No one is good, except one—God.'"

10. "This commandment is, just as you (all) heard from [the] beginning, [that you walk in love]."

11. "And they do not have root in themselves."

12. "I do not know this man whom you are speaking [about]."

13. "You are a disciple of that man, but we are disciples of Moses."

14. "Who will rescue me from this body of death?"

15. "My judgment is just/righteous, because I am not seeking my will but the will of the one who sent me."

D. Translation: Translate the following sentences into Greek.

1. πῶς ζήσομεν ἐν ταῖς ἐσχάταις ἡμέραις ταύταις;

2. ἄνθρωπός τις ἦλθεν πρὸς τὸν πατέρα ἑαυτοῦ or ἄνθρωπός τις ἦλθεν πρὸς τὸν πατέρα τὸν ἴδιον.

3. ἀγαπήσεις ἀλλήλους ὅσον σεαυτόν.

4. εἶδον ἐμαυτόν ἐν τῳ ἐμῳ παιδιῳ or εἶδον ἐμαυτόν ἐν τῳ παιδιῳ τῳ ἐμῳ.

5. τίνος ἐστιν ὁ υἱος ὁ πονηρος ἐκεινος; or τίνος ἐστιν ὁ πονηρος υἱος ἐκεινος;

ANSWER KEY TO CHAPTER 21

A. Paradigms: Memorize the present active and middle/passive and aorist active, middle, and passive infinitive forms of λύω (see section 21.4).

B. Parsing: Parse the following words.

1. **πιστεύειν**—πιστεύω pres act inf, "to be believing" or "to believe."

2. **γνῶναι**—γινώσκω aor act inf, "to know."

3. **λαλῆσαι**—λαλέω aor act inf, "to speak."

4. **ἀκολουθεῖν**—ἀκολουθέω pres act inf, "to be following" or "to follow."

5. **πέμψαι**—πέμπω aor act inf, "to send."

6. **φαγεῖν**—ἐσθίω aor act inf, "to eat."

7. **πεποιηκέναι**—ποιέω perf act inf, "to have done."

8. **ἀποστέλλειν**—ἀποστέλλω pres act inf, "to be sending," or "to send."

9. **ἐγεῖραι**—ἐγείρω aor act inf, "to raise up."

10. **πεποιθέναι**—πείθω perf act inf, "to have persuaded."

C. Infinitive Usage: Indicate the specific usage of the following infinitives: Complementary (C), Purpose (P), Previous Time (PT), Contemporaneous Time (CT), Subsequent Time (ST), Causal (CL), or Substantival (S).

1. ST   πρὸ τοῦ δὲ **ἐλθεῖν** τὴν πίστιν.

2. P   ἤλθομεν **προσκυνῆσαι** αὐτῷ.

3. P   ἀπήγαγον αὐτὸν εἰς τὸ **σταυρῶσαι** (σταυρόω, I crucify).

4. CL   διὰ τὸ αὐτὸν **γινώσκειν** πάντας.

5. P   ἦλθον **πληρῶσαι** τὸν νόμον.

6. PT   μετὰ τὸ **λαβεῖν** τὴν ἐπίγνωσιν τῆς ἀληθείας.

7. C   οὐ δύναται **εἶναί** μου μαθητής.

8. ST   πρὶν **ἐλθεῖν** ἡμέραν κυρίου.

9. CT   ἐν τῷ **λέγεσθαι**.

10. C   οὐκ ἠδυνήθησαν αὐτὸν **θεραπεῦσαι**.

D. Translation: Translate the following sentences and also indicate the use of the infinitive.

(Note: The infinitive use is indicated in parentheses.)

1. "And again he began to teach beside the sea." (complementary inf).

2. "You (pl) do not have because you (pl) are not asking [for yourselves]." (causal) [Note: Verbs of asking/requesting are often in middle voice.]

3. "After I am there (or, "After I have been there"), it is necessary that I also see Rome." (previous time, complementary)

4. "Therefore, I wish (for) men to pray in every place." (complementary)

5. "He gave to them authority (over) unclean spirits so that [they] were casting them out and were healing every sickness." (result, 2x)

6. "So men ought to love their own wives like [they love] their own bodies." (complementary)

7. "While they were going, he went into a certain village." (contemporaneous time)

8. "For your (pl) Father knows of what need you have before you (pl) ask him." (subsequent time)

9. "But as many as received him, he gave to them authority to become/be children of God." [Note: This is technically an epexegetical infinitive, a type which you have not yet been taught. It's similar to a complementary infinitive, but it completes the idea of a noun or adjective.]

10. "Lord, come down before my child dies." (subsequent time)

11. "He began to preach/announce many things . . . so that he was no longer able to enter openly into a city." (complementary, result, complementary)

12. "She came from the ends of the earth to hear the wisdom of Solomon." (purpose)

13. "But while he [was] speaking, a Pharisee asks him" (contemporaneous time) [Note: ἐρωτᾷ is a historical or narrative present and would be translated as a past tense verb in a final English translation. The time frame of the infinitive is purely determined from context.]

14. "He spoke a parable because he was near Jerusalem." (causal)

15. "So Joseph went up . . . to the city of David . . . because he was from the house and lineage of David." (causal)

E. Translation: Translate the following sentences into Greek. Note that the expected aspect is given for each infinitive.

1. δύνανται ἁμαρτάνειν κατὰ θελήματος θεοῦ.

2. θέλω περιπατεῖν ἐν τῷ φωτί καί βούλεται περιπατῆσαι ἐν τῷ νυκτί.

3. ὁ τυφλὸς ἤμελλεν λαλεῖν πρὸς τὸν δοῦλον πρὸ τοῦ ὑπάγειν αὐτόν.

4. δεῖ μηδείς εἰσελθεῖν μηδέ μεῖναι ἐν τῇ οἰκίᾳ.

5. δοκεῖ μακάριος εἶναι ὥστε τὸν ὄχλον κρίνειν αὐτόν.

ANSWER KEY TO CHAPTER 22

A. Paradigms: Memorize the present active and middle/passive subjunctive forms as well as the aorist active forms of λύω (see section 22.3).

B. Parsing: Parse the following words.

1. λέγῃ—λέγω pres act sub 3rd sg, "He may say" or "He may be saying."

2. ποιῇς—ποιέω pres act sub 2nd sg, "you may do" or "you may be doing."

3. ἐσθίωσιν—ἐσθίω pres act sub 3rd pl, "They may eat" or "They may be eating."

4. εἴπω—λέγω aor act sub 1st sg, "I may say."

5. λύσῃ—λύω aor act sub 3rd sg, "He/she/it may loose." (Also can be aor mid sub 2nd sg)

6. διώξωσιν—διώκω aor act sub 3rd pl, "They may persecute/pursue."

7. καλέσητε—καλέω aor act sub 2nd pl, "You (pl) may call."

8. εὐαγγελίζηται—εὐαγγελίζω pres mid/pass sub 3rd sg, "He may be evangelized" or "He may preach the good news to himself."

9. πληρωθῆτε—πληρόω aor pass sub 2nd pl, "You (pl) may be fulfilled" or "You (pl) may be being fulfilled."

10. ὦσιν—εἰμί pres sub 3rd pl, "They may be."

C. Subjunctive Usage: Indicate the specific usage of the following subjunctives: Purpose (P), Indefinite Relative (IR), Indefinite Temporal (IT), Emphatic Negation (EN), Deliberative (D), or Conditional (C).

1. EN   οὐ μὴ εἰσέλθητε εἰς τὴν βασιλείαν τῶν οὐρανῶν

2. IT   ὅταν ἀκούσωσιν

3. C   ἐὰν εἴπωμεν ὅτι κοινωνίαν ἔχομεν

4. D   Τί αἰτήσωμαι;

5. P   ὅπως πληρωθῇ τὸ ῥηθὲν διὰ τῶν προφητῶν

6. IT   ἕως ἂν ἔλθῃ ὁ υἱὸς τοῦ ἀνθρώπου

7. P   ἵνα πιστεύητε

8. C   ἐὰν μὴ ἐν ἐμοὶ μένητε

9. IR   ὃς ἂν ἐσθίῃ τὸν ἄρτον

10. EN οὐ μὴ κριθῆτε

D. Translation: Translate the following sentences and also indicate the use of the subjunctive(s).

(Note: Subjunctive use appears in parentheses below.)

1. "And if I go and prepare a place for you (pl), again I will come." (conditional)

2. "For God did not send the son into the world in order that he judge the world, but in order that the world might be saved through him." (purpose)

3. "If you (all) remain in my word, truly you (pl) are my disciples." (conditional)

4. "These things I spoke to you (all) so that my joy may be in you (all) and your joy may be fulfilled." (purpose)

5. "For I say to you (all), you will certainly not see me from now on until you say, 'Blessed be the one who comes in the name of the Lord.'" (emphatic negation, indef. temp.)

6. "They prayed concerning them so that they would receive [the] Holy Spirit." (purpose)

7. "Whoever does not receive the kingdom of God as a child, certainly will not enter into it." (indef. rel., emphatic negation)

8. "But how will they preach unless they are sent?" (delib., conditional)

9. "Where do you wish that we prepare for you to eat the Passover?" (delib.)

10. "Unless someone is born out of 'water and Spirit,' he is not able to enter into the kingdom of God." (conditional)

11. "And whoever wishes to be first in/among you (pl) shall be your (pl) slave." (indef. rel.)

12. "If anyone eats from this bread, he will live forever (lit.: "into the age")." (conditional)

13. "And this is his commandment, that we believe in the name of his Son, Jesus Christ, and that we love one another." [Note: ἵνα normally introduces

a purpose statement, but here it conveys the content of the commandment. ἵνα can introduce a "content clause."]

14. "Whenever that one comes, he will announce to us all things." (indef. temporal)

15. "Truly, truly I say to you (all), if anyone keeps my word, he will certainly not see death into the age (forever)." (conditional, emphatic negation)

E. Translation: Translate the following sentences into Greek. Note that the expected aspect is given for each subjunctive.

1. ὃς ἂν [not ὅστις] δέξηται ὑμᾶς κληθήσεται ἀγαπητός.

2. ἐὰν σταυρωθῇ [or ὅτε σταυροῦται] ἐγερθήσεται.

3. ὅταν λογίσηται τὸ εὐαγγέλιον, χαίρει.

4. δικαιοῦται ἵνα [or ὅπως] ζῶμεν εἰς τὸν αἰῶνα.

5. ὁ λόγος τοῦ κυρίου ἀκουσθήσεται ἕως [ἂν] ἔλθῃ ὁ υἱὸς τοῦ ἀνθρώπου.

ANSWER KEY TO CHAPTER 23

A. Paradigms: Memorize the present active and middle/passive imperatival forms as well as the aorist active forms of λύω (see section 23.3).

B. Parsing: Parse the following words.

1. **λάβε**—λαμβάνω aor act imp 2nd sg, "take."

2. **ποιήσατε**—ποιέω aor act imp 2nd pl, "do."

3. **πορεύθητι**—πορεύομαι aor pass imp 2nd sg, "go."

4. **ζητεῖτε**—ζητέω pres act imp 2nd pl, "seek" or "be seeking." (could also be indicative)

5. **ἄρατε**—αἴρω aor act imp 2nd pl, "take up."

6. **ἐλθέτω**—ἔρχομαι aor act imp 3rd sg, "let [it] come."

7. **κάλεσον**—καλέω aor act imp 2nd sg, "call."

8. **χαίρετε**—χαίρω pres act imp 2nd pl, "rejoice." (could also be indicative)

9. **κρίνατε**—κρίνω aor act imp 2nd pl, "judge."

10. **καταβάτω**—καταβαίνω aor act imp 3rd sg, "let [him] come down."

C. Imperative Usage: Indicate the specific usage of the following imperatives or subjunctives functioning as imperatives: Command (C), Prohibition (P), Hortatory Subjunctive (HS), Prohibitory Subjunctive (PS), or Optative (O).

1. C   πάντοτε (always) χαίρετε

2. P   μὴ φοβεῖσθε

3. O   μὴ ἀδικία (unrighteousness) παρὰ τῷ θεῷ; μὴ γένοιτο

4. P   μὴ γνώτω

5. C   αἰτείτω παρὰ θεοῦ

6. HS   ἀποκτείνωμεν αὐτόν

7. PS   μὴ ἄψῃ

8. O   εἴ τι ἔχοιεν πρὸς ἐμέ

9. C   ἀπόλυσον αὐτούς

10. HS   τοῦτο φρονῶμεν

D. Translation: Translate the following sentences and also indicate the use of the imperatives.

(Note: Imperative use appears in parentheses below.)

1. "Love your enemies and pray for those persecuting you." (commands)

2. "Arise, take up your mat and go to your house." (commands) [Note how the present imperative is often preferred for verbs of motion.]

3. "But the remaining ones were saying, 'Let us see if Elijah comes to save [saving—participle used to express purpose here] him.'" (hortatory subjunctive)

4. "Let all God's angels worship him." Or "All God's angels must worship him." (command) [Note: The verb προσκυνέω takes a dative object (αὐτῷ).]

5. "Beloved ones, do not believe every spirit, but test the spirits." (prohibition, command)

6. "He saved others, let him save himself." Or "He saved others, he should save himself." (command)

7. "Let each one of you be baptized in the name of Jesus Christ." (command)

8. "Do not say in your heart, 'Who will ascend into heaven?'" (prohibitory subjunctive)

9. "You reckon/consider yourselves to be dead to sin." (command)

10. "Holy Father, [please] keep them in your name." (request)

11. "Do not let any rotten word come out of your mouth." (prohibition)

12. "And Mary said, 'Behold—the (female) servant of the Lord—may it be to me according to your word.'" (optative)

13. "If the dead [people] are not raised, let us eat and let us drink for tomorrow we die." (hortatory subjunctives)

14. "Or, do you not know that unrighteous [people] will not inherit the kingdom of God? Do not be deceived!" (prohibition)

15. "Now may our Lord Jesus Christ himself and God our Father comfort your hearts and establish (you) in every good word and work." (optatives)

E. Translation: Translate the following sentences into Greek. Note that the expected aspect is given for each imperative.

1. Ἰδού, κάθου ἔμπροσθεν τοῦ κυρίου ἐν φόβῳ.

2. ἀσπάσασθε τοὺς ἐν φυλακῇ καὶ τοὺς χρείαν ἔχοντα.

3. πᾶσαι αἱ γενεαί, κατοικεῖτε ἐν εἰρήνῃ.

4. ἐργάζεσθε ὡς τῷ κυρίῳ.

5. ἐπιγινώσκετε με ἐν ἔτει τῆς θλίψεως καὶ κρίσεως.

ANSWER KEY TO CHAPTER 24

A. Principal Parts: Memorize the principle parts of δίδωμι, τίθημι, and ἵστημι (see section 24.4).

B. Indicative μι Verbs: Choose the correct *tense-form* of the μι verbs given below: Present (P), Imperfect (I), Future (F), Aorist (A), or Perfect (Pf).

1.	F	δώσει	11.	A	ἔθηκα
2.	P	δίδοται	12.	I	ἐτίθουν
3.	A	ἔδωκαν	13.	F	θήσεις
4.	F	δοθήσεται	14.	A	ἔθετο
5.	Pf	δέδωκας	15.	Pf	τέθειται
6.	P	διδόασιν	16.	A	ἔστησεν
7.	F	δώσουσιν	17.	Pf	ἔστηκας
8.	A	ἐδόθη	18.	F	σταθήσεται
9.	Pf	δέδοται	19.	P	ἀφίομεν
10.	I	ἐδίδου	20.	A	ἔφη

C. Non-Indicative μι Verbs: Choose the correct *mood* of the μι verbs given below: Subjunctive (Sub), Imperative (Imp), Infinitive (Inf), or Participle (Ptc).

1.	Inf	δοθῆναι	11.	Imp	τιθέτω
2.	Ptc	δόντος	12.	Ptc	θέντος
3.	Sub	δοθῇ	13.	Inf	σταθῆναι
4.	Inf	δοῦναι	14.	Sub	σταθῆτε
5.	Imp	δότε	15.	Ptc	σταθείς
6.	Sub	δώσωμεν	16.	Imp	ἀφιέτω
7.	Ptc	δούς	17.	Inf	ἀφιέναι
8.	Imp	δίδοτε	18.	Ptc	ἀφέντες
9.	Sub	θῇ	19.	Sub	ἀφῆτε
10.	Inf	θεῖναι	20.	Ptc	ἀπολλυμένοις

D. Translation: Translate the following sentences.

1. "And he was giving bread [loaves] to the disciples, and the disciples [were giving them] to the crowds."

2. "Christ loved us and gave himself up for us."

3. "Jesus came and stood in the midst and said to them, 'Peace to you (pl).'" [Note: λέγει is a historical present, so within context, it is translated in the past time frame.]

4. "I will place my Spirit upon him, and he will announce judgment to the nations."

5. "The law was given through Moses. Grace and truth came through Jesus Christ."

6. ". . . so that the God of our Lord Jesus Christ, the Father of glory, may give to you a spirit of wisdom"

7. "Fear (pl) God and give (pl) to him glory."

8. "No one has greater love than this, that someone put/place [lay down] his life on behalf of his friends."

9. "Therefore, if you, being evil, know [how] to give good gifts to your children, how much more your Father who is in the heavens will give good things to those who ask him."

10. "But if any one of you lacks wisdom, let him ask from the God who gives to all . . . and it will be given to him."

11. "No one takes up/away my soul from me, but I put/place it [lay it down] from myself. I have authority to place/put [lay down], and I have authority again to take it."

12. "So that the one thinking/seeming to stand, let him watch/look, lest he fall."

13. "Truly, truly, I say to you, Moses has not given to you bread from heaven, but my Father is giving to you the true bread from heaven."

14. "And the angel, whom I saw standing upon the sea and upon the earth, raised up his right hand to the heaven."

15. "But if you do not forgive men, neither will your Father forgive your trespasses."

E. Translation: Translate the following sentences into Greek.

1. οἱ μικροὶ καὶ οἱ μεγάλοι ἔστησαν καὶ ἔδωκαν δόξαν τῷ θεῷ.

2. ἄχρι τῆς ἡμέρας ταύτης, ἀνέστη μαθητὰς ὁμοίους τὸν κύριον αὐτοῦ.

3. οὐαὶ τῷ παραδιδόντι με ὅτι ὁ θεὸς ἀποδώσει αὐτῷ κατὰ τὰ ἔργα αὐτοῦ.

4. ἁμαρτωλοὶ ἀφίενται καὶ οὐκ ἀπόλλυνται.

5. ἔφη αὐτῷ, θήσω τὸ πνεῦμά μου ἐπ᾽ αὐτόν ἐν τῇ ἐρήμῳ.

VOCABULARY

//////////////

The number in brackets [ ] indicates the chapter in which the word is introduced as vocabulary.

A

ἀγαθός, –ή, –όν	good [15]
ἀγαπάω	I love [6]
ἀγάπη, ἡ	love [1]
ἀγαπητός, –ή, –όν	beloved [18]
ἄγγελος, ὁ	angel, messenger [5]
ἅγιος, –α, –ον	holy; saints (pl subst) [15]
ἄγω	I lead, bring [4]
ἀδελφός, ὁ	brother (and sister) [2]
αἷμα, –ατος, τό	blood [14]
αἴρω	I take up/away [12]
αἰτέω	I ask, demand [6]
αἰών, –ῶνος, ὁ	eternity, age, world [13]
αἰώνιος, –α, –ον	eternal [16]
ἀκολουθέω	I follow [6]
ἀκούω	I hear, listen to, obey [3]
ἀλήθεια, ἡ	truth [1]
ἀλλά	but, yet, nevertheless [3]
ἀλλήλων	of one another [19]
ἄλλος, –η, –ο	other, another, different [15]
ἁμαρτάνω	I sin (ἥμαρτον) [20]
ἁμαρτία, ἡ	sin [1]
ἁμαρτωλός, –όν	sinful, sinner (subst) [23]
ἀμήν	amen, truly, so be it [16]
ἄν	(particle of indefiniteness: untranslated) [21]
ἀναβαίνω	I go up, ascend [11]
ἀνήρ, ἀνδρός, ὁ	man, husband [13]
ἄνθρωπος, ὁ	man, human being, husband [2]
ἀνίστημι	I stand up, arise [23]

ἀνοίγω	I open [10]
ἀπαγγέλλω	I announce, report [12]
ἀπέρχομαι	I go away, depart [11]
ἀπό	from, away from (gen) [7]
ἀποδίδωμι	I give back, pay [23]
ἀποθνήσκω	I die [11]
ἀποκρίνομαι	I answer, reply [3]
ἀποκτείνω	I kill, put to death [12]
ἀπόλλυμι	I destroy, am lost (mid) [23]
ἀπολύω	I set free, dismiss, divorce [10]
ἀποστέλλω	I send out [12]
ἀπόστολος, ὁ	apostle, messenger [9]
ἄρα	so then [18]
ἄρτος, ὁ	bread, food [8]
ἀρχή, ἡ	beginning [10]
ἀρχιερεύς, –έως, ὁ	high priest [13]
ἄρχω	I rule, begin (mid) [10]
ἀσπάζομαι	I greet [22]
αὐτός, –ή, –ό	he, she, it; self, same [8]
ἀφίημι	I forgive, let go, divorce [23]
ἄχρι	until [23]

B

βάλλω	I throw, cast out [11]
βαπτίζω	I baptize, immerse, dip [5]
βασιλεία, ἡ	kingdom, reign [1]
βασιλεύς, –έως, ὁ	king [13]
βλέπω	I see, look at [4]
βούλομαι	I wish, want, desire [20]

Γ

γάρ	for, because [5]
γενεά, –ᾶς, ἡ	generation, family [22]
γεννάω	I give birth to, bear, beget [6]
γῆ, ἡ	earth, land, ground [1]
γίνομαι	I become, come, exist, am born [3]
γινώσκω	I know, understand, acknowledge [3]
γλῶσσα, ἡ	language, tongue [12]
γραμματεύς, –εως, ὁ	scribe [14]
γραφή, ἡ	writing, Scripture [12]
γράφω	I write [3]
γυνή, γυναικός, ἡ	woman, wife [13]

Δ

δαιμόνιον, τό	demon [10]
δέ	and, but, now [1]
δεῖ	It is necessary, one must/should [20]
δέκα	ten [17]
δεξιός, -ά, -όν	right [18]
δεύτερος, -α, -ον	second [17]
δέχομαι	I take, receive, welcome [21]
δέω	I bind [18]
διά	through (gen); because of (acc) [7]
διδάσκαλος, ὁ	teacher [10]
διδάσκω	I teach [4]
δίδωμι	I give [23]
δίκαιος, -α, -ον	righteous, just [15]
δικαιοσύνη, ἡ	righteousness, justice [8]
δικαιόω	I declare righteous, justify [21]
διό	therefore, for this reason [12]
διώκω	I pursue, persecute [9]
δοκέω	I seem, suppose, think [20]
δόξα, ἡ	glory, majesty [1]
δοξάζω	I glorify, praise [9]
δοῦλος, ὁ	slave [4]
δύναμαι	I am able, can [20]
δύναμις, -εως, ἡ	power, miracle [14]
δύο	two [17]
δώδεκα	twelve [17]

Ε

ἐὰν μή	unless [21]
ἐάν	if, when [21]
ἑαυτοῦ, -ῆς, -οῦ	(of) himself, herself, itself [19]
ἐγγίζω	I approach, draw near [14]
ἐγείρω	I raise up [4]
ἐγώ, ἡμεῖς	I; we [8]
ἔθνος, -ους, τό	nation, people; Gentiles (pl) [13]
εἰ	if, whether [4]
εἰμί	I am, exist [3]
εἰρήνη, ἡ	peace [8]
εἰς	into, among, for (acc) [7]
εἷς, μία, ἕν	one [17]
εἰσέρχομαι	I go in, enter [11]
εἴτε	if, whether [4]

ἐκ	from, out of (gen) [7]
ἕκαστος, –η, –ον	each [16]
ἐκβάλλω	I drive/send out [11]
ἐκεῖ	there, in that place [5]
ἐκεῖνος, –η, –ο	that; those (pl) [19]
ἐκκλησία, ἡ	congregation, assembly, church [1]
ἐλπίς, –ίδος, ἡ	hope [18]
ἐμαυτοῦ, –ῆς	myself [19]
ἐμός, –ή, –όν	my, mine [19]
ἔμπροσθεν	in front of, before [22]
ἐν	in, on, at, by, with (dat) [7]
ἐντολή, ἡ	command [9]
ἐνώπιον	before, in the presence of [7]
ἐξέρχομαι	I go out, depart, leave [11]
ἐξουσία, ἡ	authority, right, power [8]
ἔξω	outside [16]
ἐπαγγελία, ἡ	promise [11]
ἐπερωτάω	I ask [6]
ἐπί	on, upon, over (gen); on, upon, at, in (dat); on, upon, to, for (acc) [7]
ἐπιγινώσκω	I know, understand [22]
ἑπτά	seven [17]
ἐργάζομαι	I work, do, perform [22]
ἔργον, τό	work, deed [2]
ἔρημος, –όν	desolate; desert, wilderness (subst) [23]
ἔρχομαι	I come, go [3]
ἐρωτάω	I ask, question, request [6]
ἐσθίω	I eat [11]
ἔσχατος, –η, –ον	last [19]
ἕτερος, –α, –ον	other, another, different [15]
ἔτι	still, yet, more [9]
ἑτοιμάζω	I prepare [18]
ἔτος, –ους, τό	year [22]
εὐαγγελίζω	I announce good news, preach [16]
εὐαγγέλιον, τό	good news, gospel [2]
εὐθύς	immediately, straightaway [12]
εὑρίσκω	I find, discover [11]
ἔχω	I have, hold [3]
ἕως	until, while [16]

Z

ζάω	I live [14]
ζητέω	I seek, look for [6]

ζωή, ἡ   life [1]

Η

ἤ   or, than [15]
ἤδη   already, now [18]
ἡμέρα, ἡ   day [1]

Θ

θάλασσα, ἡ   lake, sea [8]
θάνατος, ὁ   death [4]
θέλημα, –ατος, τό   will, wish, desire [20]
θέλω   I want, wish, desire [20]
θεός, ὁ   God [2]
θεραπεύω   I heal [5]
θεωρέω   I gaze, behold, look at [16]
θηρίον, τό   animal, beast [22]
θλῖψις, –εως, ἡ   tribulation, affliction [22]
θρόνος, ὁ   throne [10]

Ι

ἴδιος, –α, –ον   one's own, peculiar [19]
ἰδού   behold, look, see [22]
ἱερόν, τό   temple, sanctuary [2]
ἱμάτιον, τό   clothing, garment [10]
ἵνα   in order that, so that, that [21]
ἵστημι   I stand, set [23]

Κ

κἀγώ   and I (καί + ἐγώ) [5]
κάθημαι   I sit [16]
καθίζω   I sit [22]
καθώς   as, just as, even as [4]
καί   and, even, also [1]
καιρός, ὁ   time, season [9]
κακός, –ή, –όν   bad, evil [19]
καλέω   I call, invite, name [6]
καλός, –ή, –όν   good, beautiful [15]
καρδία, ἡ   heart [1]
καρπός, ὁ   fruit, crop [10]
κατά   down, against (gen); according to (acc) [7]
καταβαίνω   I go down, descend [11]
κατοικέω   I live, dwell [22]

κεφαλή, ἡ	head [9]
κηρύσσω	I herald, proclaim, preach [16]
κόσμος, ὁ	world, universe; adornment [2]
κράζω	I cry out [5]
κρατέω	I grasp, seize, arrest [17]
κρίνω	I judge, condemn [4]
κρίσις, –εως, ἡ	judgment, condemnation [22]
κύριος, ὁ	Lord, master, sir [2]

Λ

λαλέω	I speak, say [6]
λαμβάνω	I take, receive [3]
λαός, ὁ	people, crowd [8]
λέγω	I say, speak [3]
λίθος, ὁ	stone [12]
λογίζομαι	consider, reckon [21]
λόγος, ὁ	word, message, account [2]
λοιπός, –ή, –όν	remaining, rest [18]
λύω	I loose, destroy [3]

Μ

μαθητής, ὁ	disciple, follower [5]
μακάριος, –α, –ον	blessed, happy [20]
μᾶλλον	more, rather [9]
μαρτυρέω	I testify, bear witness [6]
μέγας, μεγάλη, μέγα	large, great [15]
μέλλω	I am about to, am going to [20]
μέν	on the one hand, indeed [1]
μένω	I remain, abide, dwell [4]
μέσος, –η, –ον	middle, midst [18]
μετά	with, among (gen); after (acc) [7]
μή	no, not (employed with non-indicative verbs) [17]
μηδέ	and not, nor [20]
μηδείς, μηδεία, μηδέν	no one, nothing (subst) [20]
μήτηρ, –τρός, ἡ	mother [13]
μικρός, –ά, –όν	small [23]
μόνος, –η, –ον	only, single, alone [18]

Ν

ναός, ὁ	temple, sanctuary [12]
νεκρός, –ά, –όν	dead [15]
νόμος, ὁ	law, principle [2]

νῦν	now, at present [15]
νύξ, νυκτός, ἡ	night [20]

Ο

ὁ, ἡ, τό	the [1]
ὁδός, ἡ	way, road [8]
οἶδα	I know, understand [14]
οἰκία, ἡ	home, dwelling, family [8]
οἶκος, ὁ	house, household, family [8]
ὅλος, –η, –ον	whole, entire, complete [18]
ὅμοιος, –α, –ον	same nature, similar [23]
ὄνομα, –ατος, τό	name [13]
ὅπου	where [21]
ὅπως	in order that, that [21]
ὁράω	I see, perceive [14]
ὄρος, –ους, τό	mountain, hill [18]
ὅς, ἥ, ὅ	who, which, that [8]
ὅσος, –η, –ον	as much as [19]
ὅστις, ἥτις, ὅ τι	whoever, whatever, who [21]
ὅταν	whenever, when (ὅτε + ἄν) [21]
ὅτε	when [21]
ὅτι	that, because [3]
οὐ, οὐκ, οὐχ	no, not [5]
οὐαί	woe [23]
οὐδέ	and not, neither, nor [16]
οὐδείς, οὐδεμία, οὐδέν	no one, nothing (subst) [16]
οὐκέτι	no longer [9]
οὖν	then, so, therefore [5]
οὐρανός, ὁ	heaven, sky [2]
οὔτε	and not, neither, nor [16]
οὗτος, αὕτη, τοῦτο	this; these (pl) [19]
οὕτως	in this manner, thus, so [5]
οὐχί	no! (emphatic) [5]
ὀφθαλμός, ὁ	eye [8]
ὄχλος, ὁ	crowd [5]

Π

παιδίον, τό	child [18]
πάλιν	again [15]
παρά	from (gen); with (dat); beside, on, at (acc) [7]
παραβολή, ἡ	parable [12]
παραδίδωμι	I hand over, betray, entrust [23]

παρακαλέω	I call, urge, comfort [6]
πᾶς, πᾶσα, πᾶν	every, all [15]
πατήρ, πατρός, ὁ	father, ancestor [13]
πείθω	I persuade, convince [14]
πέμπω	I send [9]
πέντε	five [17]
περί	about, concerning (gen); around (acc) [7]
περιπατέω	I walk, live [6]
πίνω	I drink [11]
πίπτω	I fall [11]
πιστεύω	I believe, have faith/trust in [3]
πίστις, –εως, ἡ	faith, trust [13]
πιστός, –ή, –όν	faithful, believing [15]
πλοῖον, τό	ship, boat [10]
πληρόω	I fill, fulfill, complete [6]
πνεῦμα, –ατος, τό	Spirit, spirit, wind [13]
ποιέω	I do, make [6]
πόλις, –εως, ἡ	city, town [13]
πολύς, πολλή, πολύ	much, many, large, great [15]
πονηρός, –ά, –όν	evil, wicked [15]
πορεύομαι	I go, travel [3]
ποῦ	where? [21]
πούς, ποδός, ὁ	foot [14]
πράσσω	I do, practice [9]
πρεσβύτερος, –α, –ον	elder, older [16]
πρό	before, in front of (gen) [20]
πρός	to, toward (acc) [7]
προσέρχομαι	I go to, approach [11]
προσεύχομαι	I pray [10]
προσκυνέω	I worship [10]
προσφέρω	I bring to, offer [18]
πρόσωπον, τό	face, appearance [9]
προφήτης, ὁ	prophet [5]
πρῶτος, –η, –ον	first [17]
πῦρ, –ός, τό	fire [14]
πῶς	how? [19]

Ρ

ῥῆμα, –ατος, τό	word, saying [14]

Σ

σάββατον, τό	Sabbath, week [9]

σάρξ, σαρκός, ἡ	flesh, body, mortal nature [13]
σεαυτοῦ, –ῆς	(of) yourself [19]
σημεῖον, τό	sign [2]
σοφία, ἡ	wisdom [12]
σπείρω	I sow, plant [12]
σταυρόω	I crucify [21]
στόμα, –ατος, ἡ	mouth [14]
σύ, ὑμεῖς	you (sg); you (pl) [8]
σύν	with (dat) [7]
συνάγω	I gather, bring together [10]
συναγωγή, ἡ	synagogue, assembly [10]
σῴζω	I save, rescue, heal [9]
σῶμα, –ατος, τό	body [13]
σωτηρία, ἡ	salvation, deliverance [12]

T

τέ	and, but [5]
τέκνον, τό	child, son, descendant [2]
τέσσαρες	four [17]
τέταρτος, –η, –ον	fourth [17]
τηρέω	I keep, guard, obey [9]
τίθημι	I put, place, appoint [23]
τις, τι	someone, certain [19]
τίς, τί	who? which? what? [19]
τοιοῦτος, –αύτη, οῦτον	of such a kind, such as this [19]
τόπος, ὁ	place [8]
τότε	then [16]
τρεῖς	three [17]
τρίτος, –η, –ον	third [17]
τυφλός, –ή, –όν	blind; blind person (subst) [20]

Υ

ὕδωρ, –ατος, τό	water [14]
υἱός, ὁ	son, descendant [2]
ὑπάγω	I go away, depart [4]
ὑπάρχω	I exist, am [16]
ὑπέρ	for, on behalf of (gen); above, beyond (acc) [7]
ὑπό	by (gen); under, below (acc) [7]

Φ

φανερόω	I reveal, make known, manifest [17]
φέρω	I bear, carry [11]

φημί	I say, affirm [23]
φοβέομαι	I am afraid, fear, respect [6]
φόβος, ὁ	fear, reverence, respect [22]
φυλακή, ἡ	watch, guard, prison [22]
φωνή, ἡ	voice, sound [1]
φῶς, φωτός, τό	light [14]

X

χαίρω	I rejoice; greetings [21]
χαρά, ἡ	joy [10]
χάρις, –ιτος, ἡ	grace, thanks [13]
χείρ, χειρός, ἡ	hand [14]
χρεία, ἡ	need [22]
Χριστός, ὁ	Christ, Messiah, Anointed One [2]
χρόνος, ὁ	time [12]

Ψ

ψυχή, ἡ	soul, life, living being [4]

Ω

ὧδε	here [18]
ὥρα, ἡ	hour [4]
ὡς	as, like [4]
ὥστε	so that [20]

GLOSSARY OF TERMS

///////////////

The number in brackets [ ] at the end of each entry indicates the chapter in which the term is first (or primarily) discussed.

ablaut. A technical term for vowels that change their length (short → long or long → short). [1]

accent marks. Marks added to most New Testament Greek words to aid in correct pronunciation for non-native speakers. There are three accents: (1) acute: ά; (2) grave: ὰ; and (3) circumflex: ᾶ. [1]

accusative case. The case form of a noun (or other substantive) that often functions as the direct object of the verb, answering the question "what" (ἀγαπῶμεν τοὺς ἀδελφούς; "We love <u>the brothers</u>"). [2]

action verb. A verb that requires an act of will to perform the action ("I run"). [4]

active voice. See *Voice.* [4]

adjective. A word that describes or qualifies a noun (e.g., the *tall* man). [16]

adverb. A word that modifies a verb (e.g., The tall man *quickly* ate his meal). [16]

affix. A sound unit added to a word to change its meaning or function. See *Prefixes*, *Infixes*, and *Suffixes*. [4]

agent. The one performing the action of a verb when the verb is in the passive voice, which can be either implied or stated. [4]

anarthrous. Adjective meaning "having no article," as in "anarthrous noun." [2]

antecedent. A noun that is replaced by a pronoun. In the example, "You shall call His name Jesus, for He will save His people from their sins" (Matt 1:21 NKJV), "Jesus" is the antecedent for the pronoun "he." [9]

aorist tense. The Greek tense-form that communicates the perfective aspect (in which the author depicts the action as complete or as a whole). For indicative aorist verbs, the time of the action is typically in the past. [11]

arthrous. (synonym: *Articular. See below.*). [2]

articular. Adjective meaning "having an article," as in "articular noun" (synonym: *arthrous*). [2]

aspect. See *Verbal Aspect*. [4]

aspirant. A Greek consonant that allows air to escape from the speaker's mouth throughout its pronunciation (θ = th, φ = ph, χ = ch). [15]

attraction. When a part of speech (esp. a relative pronoun) is attracted to (and thus takes on) the case of its antecedent (esp. the genitive case), even though its function would normally require a different case. [9]

attributive position. When an adjective (or participle) functions adjectivally (i.e., modifies a noun or other substantive), the article (when present) occurs directly in front of the adjective. [16]

augment. An epsilon prefix (ε–), normally used with imperfect and aorist indicative forms, which indicates that the verb's time of action occurs in the past. [6]

breathing mark. A mark placed above the first letter or diphthong of every Greek word that begins with a vowel. With a smooth breathing mark (') there is no change in pronunciation, but with a rough breathing mark ('), an "h" sound is added to the beginning of the word (which is also added when a Greek word begins with the consonant rho: ῥήτωρ, "speaker"). [1]

cardinal numbers. Numbers used for counting or adjectives (one, two, three; two boats). [18]

case. The function of a noun (or other substantive) which is identified by its ending. There are five cases in Greek: nominative, genitive, dative, accusative, and vocative. [2]

comparative adjective. An adjective that compares two things. (e.g.,"The lion is *stronger* than the zebra.") [16]

compensatory lengthening. When a vowel is lengthened to compensate for losing another letter. When forming the aorist with some liquid verbs, the sigma tense formative is dropped and the main vowel in the verb stem lengthens to compensate for its loss (μένω → ἔμεινα). [13]

compound verb. A verb that has a prepositional prefix (e.g., ἐκβάλλω). [8]

concord. Grammatical agreement such as when a verb agrees with the subject of the sentence in both person and number. [4]

conjugation. A standard arrangement of the forms of a verb in relation to person and number. [5]

conjunction. An indeclinable word used to link words, phrases, clauses, and larger discourse (communication) units, designating the relationship between various parts of a discourse (e.g., δέ, καί, and μέν). [1]

connecting vowel. Sometimes called a variable or theme vowel, it is one that connects the stem to the suffix (i.e., an infix). [4]

consonantal iota. The letter iota that appears in archaic forms and was pronounced as a consonant. Compare to the English letter "y," which can be a vowel or consonant (e.g., Mary, yes). In the Koine period, iota is only a vowel, but the former presence of a consonantal iota sometimes influences the spelling of a word. The symbol for the consonantal iota is: ι [14]

contract verb. A verb whose stem ends with the short vowels alpha (α), epsilon (ε), or omicron (o) (e.g., γεννάω, ποιέω, or πληρόω). In the present and imperfect forms, these vowels contract with the connecting vowel or personal ending. [7]

contract vowels. The vowels alpha (α), epsilon (ε), or omicron (o) at the end of the stem of contract verbs. [7]

copulative verb. Also called an equative verb (e.g., εἰμί, γίνομαι, and ὑπάρχω), it joins together two words in a predicate statement—not taking a direct object (which would typically be in the accusative case) but a predicate nominative. [4]

crasis. The merger of two words into one (e.g., καί + ἐγώ = κἀγώ). [5]

dative case. The case form of a noun (or other substantive) that often functions as the indirect object of the verb (δὸς δόξαν τῷ θεῷ; "Give glory to God"). The word "to" or "for" is added to convey this function in English, which answers the question "to/for whom?" [2]

declension. A pattern used with nouns, adjectives, pronouns, and participles. This book follows the standard order: nominative, genitive, dative, and accusative (sg and pl). [2]

definite article. The word "the" in English is very similar to the Greek article, ὁ (masc), ἡ (fem), and τό (neut). [2]

degree. The character of an adjective that expresses whether it is positive ("strong"), comparative ("stronger"), or superlative ("strongest"). [16]

demonstrative pronouns. Pronouns that can be used alone or as modifiers to "point out" (Latin: *demonstrō*) something. There are two types of demonstrative pronouns: near (οὗτος, αὕτη, τοῦτο; "this" [sg], "these" [pl]) and far (ἐκεῖνος, –η, –ο; "that" [sg], "those" [pl]). [20]

dental. A Greek consonant pronounced by the speaker's tongue touching the back of his upper teeth (τ, δ, and θ). [10]

deponent. Term referring to verbs that have no active form. They are better viewed as middle-only verbs. [4]

diaeresis mark. Two raised dots above the vowel that indicate that two consecutive vowels are not a diphthong and should be pronounced separately (Κάϊν = Kah-een). [1]

digamma. An archaic letter (ϝ) that was not used in Koine Greek but whose former presence influences the spelling of certain words. [14]

diphthong. Two vowels together that are pronounced as one sound: αι, αυ, ει, ευ, οι, ου, υι. [1]

direct object. A noun (or other substantive) that receives the action of a transitive verb. [2]

discord. Grammatical disagreement such as when the subject and the verb do not formally agree in person and number. [4]

double consonant. A Greek consonant that requires two letters when transliterated into English: θ (th), ξ (xs), φ (ph), χ (ch), and ψ (ps). [1]

elative adjective. A superlative (or sometimes a comparative) adjective used to convey the idea of "very" or "exceedingly." [16]

elision. The omission of a letter (usually a vowel), which is sometimes marked with an apostrophe and often caused when the next word begins with a vowel (e.g., διά → δι'). [8]

enclitic. A word that lacks an accent and is pronounced with the previous word (ὁ πατήρ μου → ὁ πατήρμου). [9]

equative verb. See *Copulative Verb*. [4]

euphony. To sound pleasing to the ear. Koine Greek speakers sometimes slightly altered the pronunciation of words for euphonic reasons (e.g., σύν → συμ). [8]

finite verb. A verb limited to a particular subject by its person and number. [21]

genitive absolute. A subcategory of the adverbial participle used to provide background information which is grammatically unrelated to the rest of the sentence. Both the participle and the subject of the participle are in the genitive case. [19]

genitive case. The case form of a noun (or other substantive) that often expresses possession or family relationship indicated by adding "of," answering "whose?" (εἰσῆλθεν τὸν ναὸν <u>τοῦ κυρίου</u>, "He entered the temple <u>of the Lord</u>"). [2]

gloss. A brief English equivalent of a term from another language. [1]

head noun. The noun (or pronoun) that begins or governs a syntactical relationship with another noun—often a noun to which a genitive noun is appended. [2]

headless relative clause. When a relative pronoun has no explicit antecedent. [9]

imperative mood. Verbal mood communicating a request or command (e.g., "Go fishing!" "Please, go fishing."). [4, 23]

imperfect tense. The Greek tense-form that communicates the imperfective aspect (where the author depicts the action as ongoing or in process, without attention to the action's beginning or ending). In the indicative mood, the time of the action is typically in the past. [6]

improper preposition. A preposition that is never prefixed to a verb (e.g., ἐνώπιον). [8]

indeclinable. A word that does not "decline" or add case endings; rather, its spelling remains unchanged. [2]

indefinite article. The word "a/an" in English. Koine Greek has no indefinite article, though a few words are beginning to function that way (e.g., εἷς, "one" or τις, "any"). [2]

indefinite pronoun. A pronoun used when a person or thing is left unspecified (τις or τι = "someone," "anyone," "a certain one," etc.). [20]

indefinite relative pronoun. A combination of a relative pronoun and the indefinite pronoun (ὅς + τις → ὅστις). During the New Testament era, these forms typically functioned synonymously with the regular relative pronoun (ὅς). [9]

indicative mood. Mood of the verb that represents something as certain or asserted. (e.g., "He went fishing." or "Will he go fishing?"). [4]

infinitive. A verbal noun (e.g., <u>τὸ ζῆν</u> Χριστὸς καὶ <u>τὸ ἀποθανεῖν</u> κέρδος, "<u>to live</u> is Christ and <u>to die</u> is gain"). Unlike finite verbs, infinitives do not conjugate and thus are not limited by person or number. Its subject, if expressed, will be in the accusative case. [21]

infix. A morpheme (sound unit conveying meaning) that is added between the stem and the suffix. [4]

inflection. A change or addition made to a word that alters its meaning or function in a sentence. [2]

interrogative pronoun. A pronoun that introduces a question such as who? which? or what? (τίς = "who?"; τί = "what?"; or "why?"). [20]

intervocalic sigma. A sigma (σ) in between two vowels, usually causing the sigma to drop and the vowels to contract. [6]

intransitive. Verbs that do not take direct objects to complete their meaning (e.g., "I am walking"). [4]

iota subscript. The letter iota (ι) written underneath a (long) vowel: καρδίᾳ, ἀγάπῃ, λόγῳ. [1]

labial. A consonant pronounced by the speaker's lips meeting together (π, β, and φ). [10]

lexical form. The dictionary (lexicon) form of a word which is the nominative singular for nouns and first-person singular for verbs. [1]

lexicon. Another word for a dictionary. [p. 134]

liquid consonant. Lambda (λ), mu (μ), nu (ν), or rho (ρ). [13]

liquid verbs. A verb whose stems end in lambda (λ), mu (μ), nu (ν), or rho (ρ), which typically will reject the sigma (σ) in the future and aorist forms. [13]

μι verb. A verb whose lexical form ends with –μι (e.g., δίδωμι, "I give"; τίθημι, "I put"; and ἵστημι, "I stand"). [24]

middle-only verb. Traditionally called a deponent verb, this category of verbs has no active voice form and is often found in verbs of reciprocity, movement, self-involvement, and passivity. [4]

middle voice. See *Voice.* [4]

mood. Indicates an author's understanding of the verbal action's relation to reality, i.e., whether the author views the event as factual, possible, desired, commanded, or contingent. The four moods in Greek are indicative, subjunctive, optative, and imperative. [4]

morpheme. The smallest meaning-unit of a word. [2]

morphology. The study of the formation of a word's form, often with an emphasis in historical development within a language. [2]

movable nu. In Koine Greek, the nu (ν) sometimes dropped from the end of a word (e.g., ἐστίν → ἐστί) or was added to a word (ἔλυσε → ἔλυσεν). [4]

nominative case. The case form of a noun (or other substantive) that often functions as the subject of the verb, answering "who?" (ὁ θεὸς ἠγάπησεν ἡμᾶς, "God loved us"). [2]

noun. A word that refers to a person, place, thing, or idea. [2]

number. Refers to whether only one person is related to the action of the verb ("I," "you" sg, or "he/she/it") or more than one person ("we," "you" pl, or "they"). [2]

optative mood. Rare mood of the verb signaling that something is possible or hoped for (e.g., "I wish he would go fishing"). [4, 24]

ordinal numbers. Numbers used for ordering (first, second, third). [18]

palatal. A consonant pronounced by the speaker touching the back of the roof of his mouth (soft palate) with the top, back part of his tongue (κ, γ, and χ). [10]

paradigm. A representative pattern or example chart, such as a noun, pronoun, or adjective declension or a verb conjugation. [2]

parse. To describe all the grammatical elements of a word to determine its meaning. [2]

participle. A verbal adjective, it is built on a verb stem but is declined like an adjective (e.g., "The *running* girl fell on the path"). As a verb, it has tense, voice, and mood. As an adjective, it has gender, case, and number. [17]

particle. A small indeclinable word that communicates a grammatical relationship (e.g., οὐ). [2]

passive voice. See *Voice.* [4]

perfect tense. The Greek tense-form that usually conveys, in the indicative mood, an action completed in the past that has continuing results. The action itself is no longer being performed, but the consequences of that action still exist in the present (in relation to the time of the author). [15]

periphrastic participle. A participle that is in construction with the verb εἰμί (e.g., ἦν διδάσκων, "he was teaching"). It is called a "periphrastic" because it is a "round about" (περί) or less concise way "to say" (φράσις) something. [19]

person. Refers to the subject of the verbal idea and includes first person ("I" or "we"), second person ("you" [sg or pl]), or third person ("he/she/it" or "they"). [2]

personal ending. A suffix that identifies the built-in subject of the verb, specifying both the person and number (e.g., –μεν = "we"). [4]

personal pronoun. A pronoun that designates a person. There are three "persons" (1st, 2nd, 3rd) in Greek grammar: first person = ἐγώ ("I") and ἡμεῖς ("we"); second person = σύ ("you") and ὑμεῖς ("you" or "you all"); third person = αὐτός, –ή, –ό ("he/she/it") and αὐτοί, –αί, –ά ("they"). [9]

pluperfect tense. The Greek tense-form that primarily describes, in the indicative mood, a past state brought about by an action even further in the past. This tense is uncommon, occurring only eighty-six times in the New Testament. [15]

positive adjective. An adjective that is merely stating something and is not comparing two or more things (e.g., "The *strong* lion has no fears"). [16]

postpositive. A conjunction (e.g., γάρ, δέ, καί, οὖν) that will never occur as the first word in a clause but is usually found as the second word (though when translated into English, it will usually appear first in a clause). [2]

predicate nominative. A nominative form that predicates (asserts or claims) something about the subject of a copulative verb (e.g., Ἰησοῦς ἐστιν ὁ Χριστός, "Jesus is the Christ"). [4]

predicate position. Placement of the adjective that communicates that it is functioning as a predicate adjective, asserting (i.e., "predicating") something about another noun (usually in the nominative) with a "to be" verb present or implied in the sentence. When an adjective functions as a predicate adjective, there is no article directly in front of it. [16]

prefix. A morpheme (sound unit conveying meaning) that is added in front of the stem. [4]

preposition. A word used with a noun or pronoun to clarify that noun or pronoun's relationship to another word or words in a sentence. [8]

prepositional prefix. A preposition that is attached to the beginning of a verb, forming a compound verb (e.g., ἐκ + βάλλω = ἐκβάλλω). [8]

principal parts. Following long-standing grammatical terminology, the "principal parts" of a verb are the six essential indicative forms of a verb, from which all other verbal forms can be deduced: (1) present active, (2) future active, (3) aorist active, (4) perfect active, (5) perfect middle/passive, and (6) aorist passive. [24]

proclitic. A word that has no accent (such as some articles or prepositions) and is linked with the following word (e.g., ἐκ πίστεως → ἐκπίστεως). [9]

pronominal adjective. An adjective that has the meaning of a pronoun but functions as an adjective (e.g., ὁ λόγος ὁ ἐμός, "my word"). [20]

pronoun. A word that takes the place of a noun or other substantive which is called an antecedent (see *Antecedent*). [9]

proper noun. A noun that identifies a person, place, or thing and is capitalized in Greek. [3]

proper preposition. A preposition that can be prefixed to a verb (e.g., εἰσέρχομαι). [8]

reciprocal pronoun. A pronoun that represents a reciprocating (or give-and-take) participation in the action by the constituent parties of the plural subject (e.g., ἀλλήλων, "one another"). [20]

reduplication. When the perfect tense-form duplicates the initial letter of the stem. The first letter of the stem is added to the beginning of the verb with an epsilon (ε) in between the two consonants to aid in pronunciation (λε + λυ = λελυ–). [15]

reflexive middle. A rare use of the middle voice in which the subject does something *to* himself/herself/itself. [4]

reflexive pronoun. A pronoun that refers back to the subject of the verbs as its antecedent: first person = ἐμαυτοῦ ("myself"); second person = σεαυτοῦ ("yourself"); third person = ἑαυτοῦ ("himself," "itself"), ἑαυτῆς ("herself," "itself"), ἑαυτῶν ("themselves"). [20]

relative pronoun. A pronoun that introduces a dependent clause which further expands upon its antecedent (e.g., "They were bringing a man *who* (ὅς) was a paralytic"). The relative pronoun will agree with the antecedent in gender and number but not necessarily case. [9]

second aorist. An irregular form of the aorist tense-form. There is no difference in meaning (function) with first aorist verbs, only in spelling (form). [12]

special interest middle. The use of the middle voice in which the subject does something *for* himself/herself/itself. [4]

stative verb. A verb that describes a state or condition (e.g., "I am thirsty"). [4]

stem. A word's uninflected part to which affixes may be added; it carries its basic (lexical) meaning. [4]

subjunctive mood. Verbal mood that represents something as probable, contingent, or indefinite (e.g., "He might go fishing" or "whenever he goes fishing"). [4, 22]

substantive. Any part of speech that functions as a noun. [2]

suffix. A morpheme (sound unit conveying meaning) that is added at the end of the word. [4]

superlative adjective. An adjective that compares three or more things (e.g., "Between the lion, the zebra, and the giraffe, the lion is the *strongest*"). [16]

tense. A grammatical category usually related to the time an action occurs. In Greek, the tense (or *tense-form*) relates to time only in the indicative mood. New Testament Greek has six main tenses: present, future, imperfect, aorist, perfect, and pluperfect. [4]

tense-form. The present, imperfect, future, aorist, perfect, and pluperfect forms for a Greek verb. These communicate primarily aspect and secondarily time (only in the indicative mood). This book uses the terms "tense" and "tense-form" interchangeably. The term "tense-form" is sometimes preferred as a reminder that, in Greek, time is not the primary element of Greek indicative verbs. Outside of the indicative mood, Greek tenses have no inherent time. [4]

tense formative. The addition of a sigma (σ) to the stem of a verb for future or aorist forms, or a kappa (κ) for perfect forms (λύσω, ἔλυσα, λέλυκα). [10]

textual criticism. The study of differing ancient manuscripts with the goal of determining the original wording from which they were derived. [pp. 89–95]

transitive. Verbs that can take a direct object. [4]

transliteration. The writing of one language phonetically (that is, writing out the sounds) with another language's letters or characters. [1]

velar. See *Palatal.*

verb. A word that conveys an action or state. [4]

verbal aspect. The subjective perspective or viewpoint from which an author communicates the action of a verb. In Greek, the three main aspects are perfective (a wholistic depiction of the action), imperfective (a progressive presentation of the action), or stative (presenting an abiding state that has resulted from a prior action). [4]

vocative case. The case form of a noun used for direct address, i.e., when an author or speaker addresses someone (or a group) directly (Κύριε, δός μοι τοῦτο τὸ ὕδωρ, "Sir, give me this water"). [3]

voice. Verbal characteristic that indicates the way in which the subject relates to the action or state expressed by the verb. There are three voices in Greek: (1) active voice: the subject performs the action ("I see a tree"); (2) middle voice: the subject both performs and is affected by the action ("I cut down a tree [for myself]"); and (3) passive voice: the subject receives the action ("I was seen [by someone else]"). [4]

NAME INDEX

///////////////

SUBJECT INDEX

////////////////

A

ablaut *7, 127, 129, 381*
abstract noun. *See* noun, abstract
accent marks *9–10, 381*
  acute *10*
  circumflex *10*
  grave *10*
accusative case *381. See also* cases, accusative
  adverbial *175*
  (direct) object (or object complement) *98, 104*
  general reference *236*
  predicate *236*
  subject *236, 240*
action verb. *See* verb, action
active voice. *See* voice, active
adjective *167, 294, 381*
  attributive *170, 204, 345*
  elative *174*
  predicate *171, 204*
  pronominal *225–26*
  substantival *171, 204*
adverb *167, 175, 187, 201, 381*
affix *41, 381*
agent *39, 381*
alphabet *3–13*
anarthrous *21, 101, 170, 172, 214, 330, 337, 381*
antecedent *97–98, 102, 104, 222, 326, 381*
aorist adverbial participle
  attendant circumstance *196–97, 202*
  causal *201–02*
  means *201–02*
  purpose *201*
  temporal *196, 201–02*
aorist participle. *See* participle, aorist
aorist tense *53, 117–23, 382*
  constative *118*
  epistolary *118*

inceptive *118*
  second *125–32*
apodosis *253*
arthrous. *See* articular
article *3, 31*
  definite *12, 21, 313*
  indefinite *12, 21, 342*
  previous reference *3–4*
articular *21, 27, 101, 214, 237, 382*
aspect *40, 54, 251, 382*
  contextual factors *243, 265*
  grammatical factors *243*
  imperfective *41, 62, 189, 209, 213, 236, 242, 254, 260, 263–65*
  lexical factors *242, 265*
  perfective *41, 118, 126, 157, 189, 209, 214, 236, 242, 254, 264–65*
  stative *41, 156, 189, 209, 236*
aspirant/aspirated form *82, 113, 151, 161, 274, 382*
attraction *104, 382*
attributive position *172, 222, 382*
augment *64, 83, 120–21, 129, 144, 158, 163, 200, 239, 243, 251, 254, 262, 273, 293, 297, 331, 382*
autographs *91*

B

breathing mark *382*
  rough *8–9, 66*
  smooth *8, 64, 66*
Byzantine text *90, 91*

C

capitalization *11*
cardinal numbers *203, 382*
cases *17–18, 382*

accusative *16, 18, 29, 148. See also* accusative case
dative *18, 29, 148. See also* dative case
genitive *16, 18, 29, 148. See also* genitive case
nominative *18, 29, 148. See also* nominative case
vocative *31. See also* vocative case
cognate *13, 134*
comparative adjective. *See* degree, comparative
compensatory lengthening *143, 382*
compound verb. *See* verb, compound
concord *37, 383*
conditional sentences. *See also* subjunctive mood, conditional
  first class *253*
  fourth class *254*
  second class *254*
  third class *254*
conjugation *42, 58, 71, 143, 271, 383*
conjunction *12, 383*
  coordinating *22*
  subordinating *22*
connecting vowel *42, 120, 129–30, 142, 158–59, 163, 185, 200, 212, 239, 243, 250, 262, 273, 383*
consonantal iota *150–51, 198, 383*
construction *ad sensum* *37*
contract verb. *See* verb, contract
contract vowels *72–73, 113, 121, 251, 331, 383*
copulative verb. *See* verb, copulative
crasis *383*

SCRIPTURE INDEX

//////////////////